Emile de Antonio

VISIBLE EVIDENCE

Edited by Michael Renov, Faye Ginsburg, and Jane Gaines

Public confidence in the "real" is everywhere in decline. The Visible Evidence series offers a forum for the in-depth consideration of the representation of the real, with books that engage issues bearing upon questions of cultural and historical representation, and that forward the work of challenging prevailing notions of the "documentary tradition" and of nonfiction culture more generally.

Volume 8 :: Douglas Kellner and Dan Streible, editors
Emile de Antonio:
A Reader

Volume 7 :: Patricia R. Zimmermann
States of Emergency:
Documentaries, Wars, Democracies

Volume 6 :: Jane M. Gaines and Michael Renov, editors
Collecting Visible Evidence

Volume 5 :: Diane Waldman and Janet Walker, editors
Feminism and Documentary

Volume 4 :: Michelle Citron
Home Movies and Other Necessary Fictions

Volume 3 :: Andrea Liss
Trespassing through Shadows:
Memory, Photography, and the Holocaust

Volume 2 :: Toby Miller
Technologies of Truth:
Cultural Citizenship and the Popular Media

Volume 1 :: Chris Holmlund and Cynthia Fuchs, editors
Between the Sheets, In the Streets:
Queer, Lesbian, Gay Documentary

VISIBLE EVIDENCE, VOLUME 8

Emile de Antonio

A Reader

Douglas Kellner and Dan Streible, editors

Foreword by Haskell Wexler

University of Minnesota Press
Minneapolis
London

Copyright 2000 by the Regents of the University of Minnesota

"Smoke Signals Blown" (1975) copyright Emile de Antonio.

All rights reserved. No part of this publication may be reproduced, stored in a retrieval system, or transmitted, in any form or by any means, electronic, mechanical, photocopying, recording, or otherwise, without the prior written permission of the publisher.

Published by the University of Minnesota Press
111 Third Avenue South, Suite 290
Minneapolis, MN 55401-2520
http://www.upress.umn.edu

Library of Congress Cataloging-in-Publication Data

Emile de Antonio ; a reader / Douglas Kellner and Dan Streible, editors.
    p.   cm.
   (Visible evidence ; v. 8)
   Includes bibliographical references and index.
   ISBN 0-8166-3363-0 (alk. paper) — ISBN 0-8166-3364-9 (pbk. : alk. paper)
   1. De Antonio, Emile.   I. De Antonio, Emile.   II. Kellner, Douglas, 1943–
III. Streible, Dan.   IV. Title.   V. Series.
PN1998.3.D3846 E65 2000
791.43′0233′092—dc21   99-050923

Printed in the United States of America on acid-free paper

The University of Minnesota is an equal-opportunity educator and employer.

11 10 09 08 07 06 05 04 03 02 01 00   10 9 8 7 6 5 4 3 2 1

Contents

Foreword   HASKELL WEXLER   xi

Introduction
Emile de Antonio: Documenting the Life of a Radical Filmmaker
DOUGLAS KELLNER AND DAN STREIBLE   1

PART I. DE ON DE: OVERVIEWS AND INTERVIEWS

An In-Depth Interview with Emile de Antonio (1972)
TERRY DE ANTONIO   87

Movies and Me (1974)   EMILE DE ANTONIO   97

An Interview with Emile de Antonio (1973)
TANYA NEUFELD   102

Irrepressible Emile de Antonio Speaks (1982)
SUSAN LINFIELD   113

Red Bass Interview: Emile de Antonio (1983)
JAY MURPHY   124

Emile de Antonio with Jean-Michel Basquiat (1984)
JEAN-MICHEL BASQUIAT   129

Emile de Antonio (1986)   JEAN W. ROSS   136

Why I Make Films (1987)   EMILE DE ANTONIO   143

PART II. THE FILMS

POINT OF ORDER — 147

The Point of View in *Point of Order* (1964)
EMILE DE ANTONIO — 149

Re-creating the Incredible McCarthy Days (1964)
JUDITH CRIST — 152

McCarthy's Last Stand (1964) *TIME* MAGAZINE — 154

Letter to Hubert Bals and Wendy Lidell (197?)
EMILE DE ANTONIO — 156

THAT'S WHERE THE ACTION IS — 163

Running to Win, Outline and Letter to BBC (1965)
EMILE DE ANTONIO — 165

That's Where The Action Is (1976) THOMAS WAUGH — 169

RUSH TO JUDGMENT — 173

Rush to Judgment: A Conversation with
Mark Lane and Emile de Antonio (1967) — 175

Homo Americanus (1967) LOUIS MARCORELLES — 190

Liner Notes for *Rush to Judgment* LP (1967)
EMILE DE ANTONIO — 192

Letter to Jean Hill (1966) EMILE DE ANTONIO — 194

Journal Entry on *Rush to Judgment* (1980)
EMILE DE ANTONIO — 196

IN THE YEAR OF THE PIG — 199

Blood and Snow (1969) PAULINE KAEL — 201

De Antonio in Hell (1968) ALAN ASNEN — 205

Inter/view with Emile de Antonio (1969) LIL PICARD — 211

Movie Journal (1969) JONAS MEKAS — 220

"De Antonio: *Year of the Pig* Marxist Film" and
"Nichols Replies" (1978) EMILE DE ANTONIO and
BILL NICHOLS — 224

AMERICA IS HARD TO SEE — 227

From Joe to Eugene: To Hell and Back (1970)
DEAC ROSSELL — 229

America Is Hard to See (1971) JOAN MELLEN — 232

MILLHOUSE: A WHITE COMEDY — 235

Interview with Emile de Antonio: Director of *Millhouse* (1972) GLENN O'BRIEN — 237

Minor Surgery (1971) JAY COCKS — 243

Leave Your Wits at the Entrance (1971)
WILLIAM F. BUCKLEY JR. — 245

Millhouse (1971) DAVID THORSTAD — 249

"The Real History of Our Times Is on Film": Filmmaker Emile de Antonio Talks about Nixon, the '50s, and Now (1972) CINDA FIRESTONE — 252

PAINTERS PAINTING — 259

The Agony of the Revolutionary Artist (1971)
EMILE DE ANTONIO — 261

Films: *Painters Painting* (1973) LAWRENCE ALLOWAY — 265

Films: *Painters Painting* (1973) STANLEY KAUFFMANN — 268

My Brush with Painting (1984) EMILE DE ANTONIO — 270

UNDERGROUND — 277

How It Began (1976) EMILE DE ANTONIO — 279

Mallards and Trombones by Lake Mendota: An Interview with Emile de Antonio and Mary Lampson (1976) GAGE, JIM, and REBECCA — 281

Rendezvous with the Weather Underground (1976)
LUCINDA FRANKS — 286

Pro-Terrorist Propaganda in the Movies (1975)
LARRY McDONALD — 289

Interview with Emile de Antonio and Mary Lampson (1976)
DAN GEORGAKAS and PAUL McISAAC — 291

IN THE KING OF PRUSSIA — 299

In the King of Prussia: Emile de Antonio
Interviews Himself (1982)   EMILE DE ANTONIO — 301

On the Making of *In the King of Prussia*: An Interview
with Emile de Antonio (1983)   SHARON GALLAGHER — 309

De Antonio and the Plowshares Eight (1982)   DAVID SEGAL — 315

Swords into Plowshares (1983)   MICHAEL H. SEITZ — 319

Antinuclear Narcissism (1983)   DAVID S. MACHLOWITZ — 323

MR. HOOVER AND I — 327

Mr. Hoover and I (1989)   EMILE DE ANTONIO — 329

Emile de Antonio's Thoughts on Himself and the FBI:
A Leftist's Sympathies (1990)   VINCENT CANBY — 333

The Life and File of an Anarchist Filmmaker (1990)
JONATHAN ROSENBAUM — 335

PART III. INDISCREET INTERVENTIONS ON LIFE, ART, AND POLITICS

Salt of the Earth (1966)   EMILE DE ANTONIO — 345

Chasing Checkers by Richard M. Nixon (1968)
EMILE DE ANTONIO and ALBERT MAHER — 348

Some Discrete Interruptions on Film, Structure, and
Resonance (1971)   EMILE DE ANTONIO — 350

Pontus Hultén and Some '60s Memories in
New York (1973)   EMILE DE ANTONIO — 354

Visions of Vietnam (1974)   EMILE DE ANTONIO — 357

Emile de Antonio's *CIA Diary* (1975)   MICHAEL FELLNER — 361

Smoke Signals Blown (1975)   EMILE DE ANTONIO — 365

Celluloid Reportage (1976)   EMILE DE ANTONIO — 368

Letter to *The Militant* (1977)   EMILE DE ANTONIO — 371

Point of Order (Hic) (1980)   EMILE DE ANTONIO — 373

Different Drummers (1985)   EMILE DE ANTONIO   377

American History: A Fiction (1988)   EMILE DE ANTONIO   381

PART IV. ENVOI

Quotations from Chairman De:
Decodifying de Antonio (1984)   PETER WINTONICK   387

De Wore Khakis   RON MANN   394

Poker and Good Advice   CINDA (FIRESTONE) FOX   396

Making *Painters Painting*, or My Brush with Art History
MARC N. WEISS   398

Low Overhead and Independence:
Working with Emile de Antonio   MARY LAMPSON   401

A Keen Political Conscience   PHILIP BERRIGAN   403

A Man of Extremes   ALLAN SIEGEL   405

Filmography   407

Bibliography   415

Permissions   427

Index   431

HASKELL WEXLER

Foreword

Emile de Antonio could swim under water longer than anyone I ever met. I remember "de" lapping the pool without coming up for air, staying submerged long after everyone else had surfaced. Although this may have been the least of his many amazing traits, it could be a metaphor for his life. De spent most of his remarkable career beneath the surface, an underwater and underground man, subverting enemies of the people.

The legacy of Emile de Antonio as a filmmaker, political activist, and passionate human being will not be found in the archives of the mainstream media. A person's legacy is limited by what the establishment chooses to print or broadcast. If we were to assess de Antonio's career based on what the *New York Times* or the television networks revealed, there would be little to go on. Fortunately, a legacy is also created by how someone is remembered by those who knew him. I remember de as a fiercely independent person, a person who expressed his extremely strong views about people and about the world in which he lived. He could not be defined by any of the words typically used to characterize him—"leftist," "radical," or other such labels.

If I had to choose a single term to describe Emile de Antonio, the best might be "ex-Catholic" (although de would shoot me for suggesting it). His family roots in Catholicism gave him a worldview that—though it was certainly not the pope's—reflected the best aspects of Christianity: compassion, social conscience, devotion to justice, concern for others. In talking to him and recognizing the depth of his commitment, I realize he had what I can only call a religious zeal.

I'm not sure when we first met. De and I were often in the same places and knew many of the same people in the documentary film "brotherhood" (even if de, always on his own path, wasn't exactly a brotherhood type). We knew his first film, *Point of Order,* very well. Most documentary people in those days were anti-establishment, but de was a courageous maverick. He not only questioned authority, he challenged it. When he contacted me in 1975 about shooting a film with the Weather Underground, I thought I had some idea of what working on a de Antonio film would mean. But with *Underground* the shit really hit the fan.

Although I (like de) had been under surveillance by the federal government for over thirty years, I was still shocked by the harassment that followed us when de, Mary Lampson, and I began making the film. I was doing cinematography on *One Flew over the Cuckoo's Nest* at the time. Shortly before principal photography was complete, director Milos Forman told me I would not be allowed to finish the picture. He gave no explanation, but I later learned that the FBI had been investigating, questioning maids at my hotel and accountants at the production company.

De persuaded the Weatherpeople that I should handle camera duties for the interviews. After passing their elaborate security precautions, I shot two days of conversations with five young fugitives in a safe house outside of Los Angeles. I became aware of FBI surveillance shortly after. A helicopter followed me whenever I left my house in the Hollywood hills. Two men in suits pretended to change a flat tire for several days as they kept watch outside my home. My house was burglarized. The files in the office were disturbed and the Oscar I had won for *Who's Afraid of Virginia Woolf?* was missing. Agents delivered a subpoena. They wanted all of the footage I had shot.

The American Civil Liberties Union recognized our case as a First Amendment issue. Demanding our unedited film was like taking a journalist's notebook. De refused to turn over the film. Hollywood producer Bert Schneider marshaled big names in the movie industry to back us—Warren Beatty, Jack Nicholson, Greg Peck, and many others. I was encouraged by the strong show of support by Hollywood, the community that had been so cowed by the blacklist of the 1940s and 50s.

De won his legal victory and went on to finish *Underground* with Mary. I distanced myself from the Weather project. I am against violence and believed the Weatherpeople's terrorist bombings were counterproductive. But now, ten years after de Antonio's passing and twenty-five years since that secretive filming in Los Angeles, I still find myself screening de's *Underground* with receptive audiences.

What's missing is de. He was a colorful and indefinable radical. In his own time, few things scared people more than to hear that someone was a communist, but de was just completely attractive and interesting. He knew a lot about a lot of things. He knew about art, about history. And he could connect with people. That ability to reach audiences is crucial. Tight control of the media has made it very difficult to hear and see the work of new de Antonios. But there is much hope in a new generation armed with camcorders. They are finding ways to reach their audiences. These principled working artists will challenge the status quo in the best of an American documentary tradition, a de Antonio tradition. De showed us that filmmakers can communicate ideas dedicated to progressive change.

That is the true de Antonio legacy.

DOUGLAS KELLNER
DAN STREIBLE

Introduction
Emile de Antonio: Documenting
the Life of a Radical Filmmaker

Emile de Antonio (1919–89) was one of the world's great documentary filmmakers. His collected works constitute a political history that critically dissects the crucial events and issues of Cold War America. The films de Antonio created in the 1960s and 70s made a significant impact on both the form of documentary cinema and the political practice of filmmaking. He was a leading advocate and practitioner of a politically committed, independent cinema, as well as one of the most articulate radical critics of the establishment. Cumulatively, de Antonio's films present an overview of the most important political events of the postwar epoch and a valuable cinematic legacy of innovative documentaries.

Until now, however, no major studies have been written about de Antonio or his film career.[1] This is surprising given the attention afforded his work in both the political arena and the film world during his lifetime. This reader is designed to correct this gap by documenting the life, art, and politics of this major figure in modern cinema.

Emile de Antonio's films begin with *Point of Order* (1963), a brilliantly edited compilation of the 1954 Army-McCarthy hearings that pioneered the use of television images in documentary cinema and did so without conventional narration. This widely seen feature helped cement the image of Joseph McCarthy as a rogue demagogue. It also established de Antonio's reputation as an auteur whom film historian Richard Barsam characterizes as a "unique master of a compilation genre that he created and can call his own."[2] Politically, *Point of Order* has been called "the first indication that a radical film revival might be imminent in the United States" in the 1960s.[3] De Antonio followed his auspicious film debut with *Rush to Judgment* (1966), a politically explosive documentary on the Kennedy assassination that combines 1963 news footage of events in Dallas with original interviews of witnesses who undermined the Warren Commission Report. These low-budget, independent radical films established de Antonio as one of the most provocative documentary auteurs of his time, a role he pursued with relish over the following two decades.

His subsequent films—particularly *In the Year of the Pig* (1968), *Millhouse* (1971), and *Painters Painting* (1972)—deploy collage, compilation techniques, and imaginative sound tracks to create a distinctive documentary corpus. *In the Year of the Pig* continues de Antonio's analysis of major political events of the time with an innovative documentary on the Vietnam War, a film still regarded as a paragon of its genre. *Millhouse* dissects the director's longtime nemesis Richard Nixon. This "White Comedy" intermixes archival newsreels and interview material to reveal both Nixon's ability as a political creature and the phoniness of his public facade. Such films made de Antonio a nemesis of the conservative establishment and earned him intensified FBI scrutiny and government harassment. However, he next turned his creative energy on a seemingly apolitical subject: postwar American painting. By interviewing his friends (Andy Warhol, Jasper Johns, Robert Rauschenberg, Frank Stella, and others) and adopting their collage techniques, he created in *Painters Painting* a definitive record of the New York art scene.

Indeed, de Antonio's legacy is that of a political modernist, providing models of creative film form that exploit the archives of history in a way that speaks truth to the ideology of dominant powers. His films provide historical montages of his era and history lessons for subsequent generations, reminding us of the abuses of power in postwar America, the forces that threatened U.S. democracy, and the movements that opposed them. De Antonio emerges as a great documentary historian of his time who captures the political theater and struggles of the turbulent postwar period. His work shows how documentaries can generate historical knowledge as well as preserve images of the past, providing insight into the events of the period.

For de Antonio, continual rejuvenation of film form was crucial to producing a cinema of quality as well as a cinema of opposition. To be a subversive meant undoing the stultifying conventions of commercial film. He experimented with technique and form throughout his career. The last two films de Antonio completed depart from his trademark synthetic compilation style, developing new strategies. *In the King of Prussia* (1982) combines documentary film footage with a videotaped reenactment of the trial of eight antinuclear protesters. Designed as an organizing tool for the nuclear freeze movement and radical peace activists, de Antonio's unconventional film is an attempt both to condemn the production of atomic weapons and to heighten awareness of the justice system's mistreatment of political dissidents. His final contribution, *Mr. Hoover and I* (1989), weaves together documents about his nemesis, FBI director J. Edgar Hoover, with intimate, self-reflective footage drawn from his own life. Together, de Antonio's works constitute one of cinema's most challenging documentary oeuvres, produced by a man whose life was as interesting and tumultuous as his films.

Indeed, "de," as he was known to friends, was a fascinating and complex personality. A bon vivant and aesthete, de Antonio was also a political romantic and self-styled revolutionary. He traveled widely, participated passionately in the events of his times, and knew many important artists, intellectuals, and political figures. "De Antonio is an enormous, powerfully built man with a Rabelaisian taste for life and its varied pleasures," wrote Hendrik Hertzberg after a dinner in 1964. Interacting with diverse groups of people, de Antonio aptly described himself as a "radical scavenger" who took what he could from his life and times to assemble his cinematic documents. De was a complicated man, whose contradictions between his politics, aesthetics, and lifestyle were often striking. He wrestled with these conflicts in his work, producing a legacy of challenging documentary film.[4]

A Turbulent Life: From Desuetude to Defiance

Emile Francisco de Antonio was born on May 14, 1919, in Scranton, Pennsylvania. His father, Emilio, was a prominent doctor who late in life married Anna Connapinch, a Lithuanian immigrant of working-class background, nearly thirty years younger than her husband. Emile was the oldest of seven children, including two sets of twins. His father, an Italian immigrant, exercised immense intellectual influence on his son, fostering a lifelong love of philosophy, classical literature, history, and the arts.

After attending the Wyoming Seminary prep school in Scranton, de Antonio entered Harvard University in 1936, becoming a member of the class that included John F. Kennedy. There he joined the Young Communist League, the John Reed Club, and other radical organizations, although he was admittedly more dedicated to partying than party building. Concerning his political radicalization, he later claimed that at the age of ten he discerned the vast class inequalities and differences in the lives of the rich and the poor through living in a wealthy part of a town with a large community of poor coal miners and the unemployed. These experiences created his lifelong anger against an unjust economic system.[5]

Although his later FBI records claimed that he was "dismissed from Harvard University for Communistic activity," in fact de Antonio was

Figure 1. Dr. Emilio de Antonio, ca. 1920, the father who imbued his son with a devotion to classical literature and history. The filmmaker called his production company Turin Film, after his father's birthplace in the Italian Piedmont.

suspended for disciplinary reasons, including excessive drunkenness and starting a fire in a dormitory. Returning to Scranton, de Antonio graduated from the University of Scranton (then called St. Thomas's College) and secretly joined the Communist Party. After graduation, he went to Baltimore, where he worked as a laborer on the docks, waiting to get drafted in World War II.[6] De Antonio married the first of six wives, Ruth Baumann, in 1939 and they had a son, Emile, in 1940. He served in the Marine Corps from May until August 1942, when he was dismissed for drunkenness and going

Figure 2. This sketch of the ten-year-old Emile and his brother Carlo was done by a family friend in 1929.

AWOL to visit his wife. He soon joined the Army Air Force and served from October 1942 to January 1946.

Wartime service became a rite of passage for many men of his generation, but de Antonio seldom discussed his military experiences. After flight training in Texas, he spent most of the duration on Tinian, the Pacific island where an enormous Allied airfield was built and the Enola Gay departed with the Hiroshima bomb. Although a veteran of numerous B-29 bombing missions, airman de Antonio chafed under the boredom of regimented life.

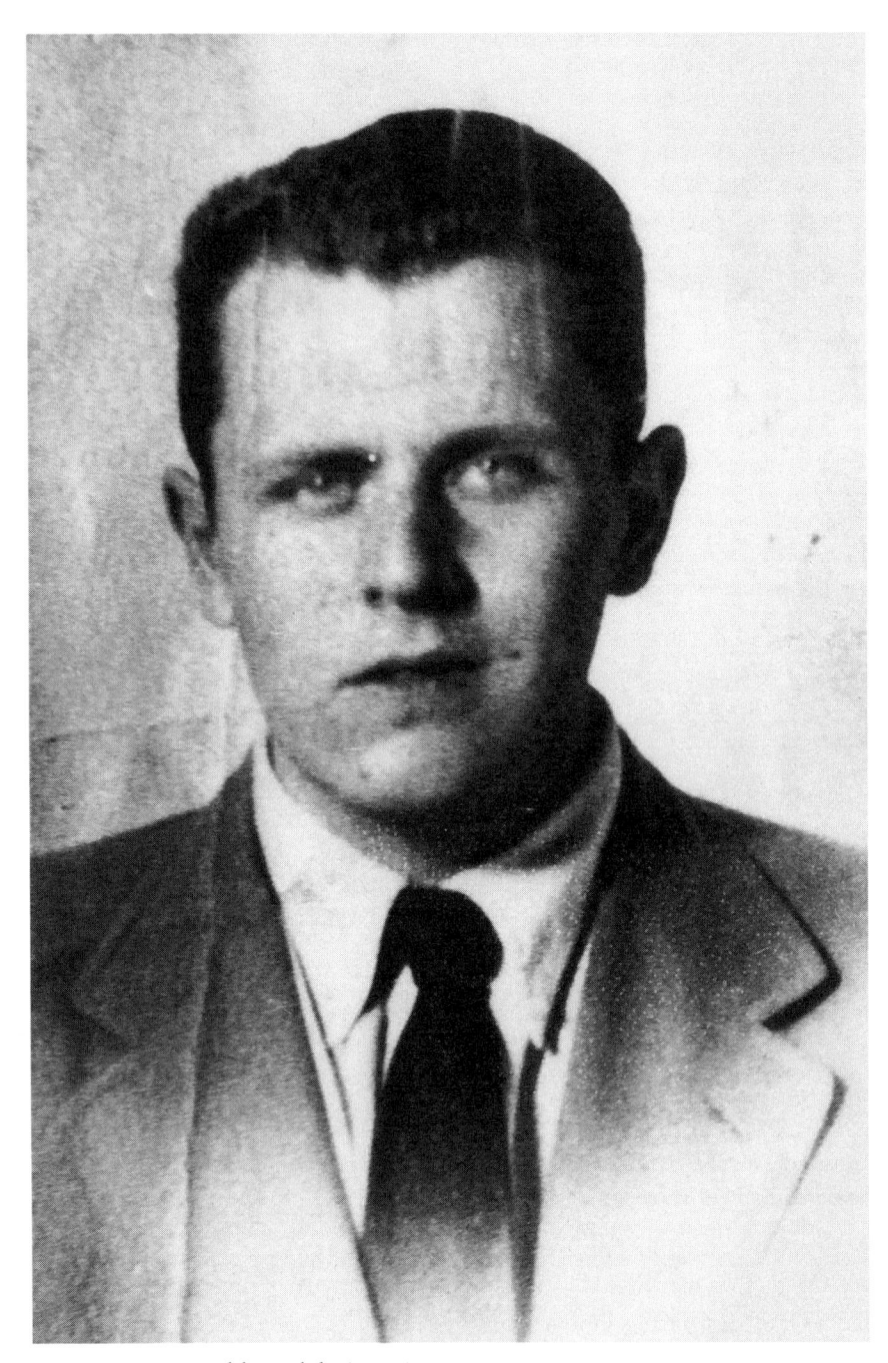

Figure 3. A Harvard-bound de Antonio, ca. 1936.

He recalled it as yet another socially alienating institution that would later lead him to make such angry, antiestablishment films.

> Did I hate that army world more than anyone else? I hated shitting with others. I was frightened. I didn't like anyone at all except my bombardier. All the rest were drones, in spite of class, schooling or lack. They were equal in their mediocrity and indifference. The perfect corporation men. More frightened by a general than by planes blowing up on takeoff. The madmen took possession on an island with the highest security and got off from the entire world. We got drunk. We sat on ammo crates and watched movies. I walked out even then. Even on Tinian I walked out on Hollywood and its puerile bullshit, particularly films to soothe the troops.[7]

Upon his demobilization, de Antonio was divorced from his wife Ruth. He began studying philosophy and literature at Columbia University, and obtained his M.A. in 1947. He married his second wife, Adrienne "Mimi" Vanderbilt, and they had a daughter, Adrienne, nicknamed Wren. During this time he worked on a river barge, as the occupation supplemented his GI Bill stipend and provided plenty of time to read. During the 1947–48 academic year, de Antonio taught at William and Mary College. "I found [it] boring and dispiriting," he later said. "Faculty rank and maneuvering seemed bitchier and slimier than the army. Too many sherry parties, too many posteriors to be kissed." He returned to New York to obtain a doctorate in philosophy at Columbia, but he "finally quit," he wrote, "when I realized that the whole Ph.D. program was part of an unnecessary production process. Thesis was the last straw—to produce an unwanted book written by a man who didn't want to write it for a non-existent public."[8] He also went through his second divorce at this time.

During the late 1940s and early 1950s, de Antonio lived a bohemian life in Greenwich Village, immersing himself in the New York art and intellectual scene. He never lacked for money, but worked at an odd variety of jobs, a freelance editor one year, an economist for the Bureau of Labor Statistics the next. He later wrote about how he formed a company "which was a satire on American business":

> It was called Conservative Enterprises and I made up a list of names of officers. Elton Marsh III, etc. The company made a lot of money with me thinking up ideas and lying in bed reading. As soon as it made money, I rented a house near the ocean and read, swam, drank until it was gone. Owned a surplus company. Translated operas. Lived as an intellectual does when he wants to stay out of the system.[9]

De Antonio married his third wife, Lois Long, a successful designer, and moved with her to Rockland County, New York. There he met his

Figure 4. De in uniform, 1944. Initially kicked out of the U.S. Marine Corps, he spent the duration of World War II in the Army Air Corps, serving in the Pacific theater.

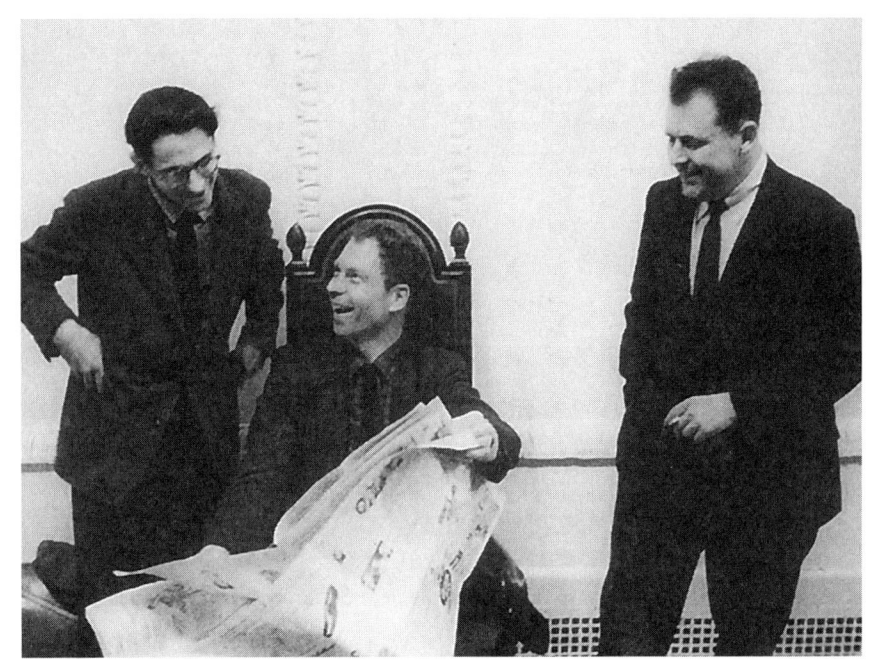

Figure 5a. Pianist David Tudor, dancer Merce Cunningham (seated), and de Antonio, backstage at the landmark John Cage twenty-fifth anniversary concert held at Town Hall in New York, May 15, 1958. Photograph by Aram Avakian; courtesy of Alexandra Avakian.

neighbor, avant-garde composer John Cage, and became further involved with the New York modernist art scene. Becoming an entrepreneur for the avant-garde, in October 1955 he organized a concert for Cage at Clarkstown High School in Rockland County. Despite a passing hurricane, busloads of New York artists and patrons filled the auditorium, reacting to Cage's recital with a mixture of delight and consternation.[10]

The day before the concert, while inspecting the school theater, de Antonio met two men, nails in mouth and hammers in hand, working on the set. They were Robert Rauschenberg and Jasper Johns, who became his close friends. Soon after, he became their advocate, helping Bob and "Jap" get some of their first jobs as commercial artists and promoting them with galleries. Living in cheap lofts, the two often went to de Antonio's home to bathe and to cash checks.

Calling themselves Impresarios, Inc., de Antonio, Johns, and Rauschenberg each put up $1,000 to produce a major musical event showcasing the experimental work of their mutual friend John Cage. On May 15, 1958, "The 25-Year Retrospective Concert of the Music of John Cage" was an upscale version of their high-school production three years earlier. De Antonio staged the avant-garde spectacle at Town Hall

Figure 5b. Impresarios, Inc. Jasper Johns, Robert Rauschenberg, record producer George Avakian, and others assemble in Town Hall before the John Cage twenty-fifth anniversary concert. De Antonio stands back, far right. Photograph by Aram Avakian; courtesy of Alexandra Avakian.

in Manhattan. "The New York art world, in a last reassertion of its old tribal solidarity," wrote critic Calvin Tompkins, "turned out *en masse*" for the event. Dancer Merce Cunningham conducted the program of eclectic, modernist pieces that featured electronic instruments, tape-recorded soundscapes, lyrics from *Finnegans Wake,* and previously unperformed instrumental works. George Avakian's recording of the concert came to be regarded as a milestone in the history of twentieth-century music.[11]

Another important moment came in the spring of 1957, when Stephen Greene, artist in residence at Princeton, told de Antonio about Frank Stella, his most brilliant student. De Antonio went to see Stella's paintings and later said "it was the greatest exhibit of a young artist I had ever seen. The paintings were premonitions of the great black series which was to come later." In 1958, Stella moved to New York. De Antonio became friends with the painter and helped him find a gallery. That same year, de Antonio met Andy Warhol through his friend Tina Fredericks, art director of *Glamour, Vogue,* and other fashion magazines, who had given Warhol work. Warhol's studio was close to de Antonio's Manhattan apartment and after they met, de Antonio frequently visited the young commercial artist, profoundly influencing Warhol's transformation into the prince of pop art.[12] "De was the first person I know of to see commercial art as real art and real art as commercial art, and he made the whole New York art world see it that way, too," Warhol said in *POPism*. According to both men, it was de who told Andy to abandon his attempts to paint in the manner of the abstract expressionists and to focus instead on the mechanical renderings of Coca-Cola bottles and other objects of mass culture.

De Antonio's aesthetic vision was in turn shaped by his friends in the artistic avant-garde. Although he is best known as a political documentary filmmaker, he was also a rigorous cinematic artist who believed that formal innovation was the key to quality films. Thus, de Antonio himself is part of the cohort of New York-based modernist artists who were seeking new forms for painting, music, and writing, as he sought new forms for film.

▶

A Maverick among Independents:
De Antonio and the New American Cinema Group

However, it was not painters who drew de Antonio to film. New York in the late fifties was producing a thriving, avant-garde, self-proclaimed "New American Cinema." De Antonio became a force in this movement, helping to establish an infrastructure for the distribution, exhibition, and promotion of new forms of moviemaking. He often said that his viewing of the 1959 underground film *Pull My Daisy* was a revelation of the possibilities of cinema as a mode of artistic expression. Made by photographer Robert Frank and artist Alfred Leslie, the film featured the antics of Beat generation personalities such as poet Allen Ginsberg and painter Larry Rivers, with narration written and performed by Jack Kerouac. *Daisy* was made for $12,000 and, de Antonio said, it "revealed to me that a film could be as interesting as hell and be made for nothing"—and both financially and philosophically independent of the Hollywood system that he despised.[13]

Using his entrepreneurial skills, de Antonio became a film distributor for *Pull My Daisy*. The Beat cult film became (alongside John Cassavettes' *Shadows*, 1959) the sine qua non of alternative cinema, often cited by proponents as a paradigm for what film might be.[14] In September 1960, two dozen filmmakers—including de Antonio, Frank, and Leslie—formed "The Group," a collective of iconoclastic cineastes. They publicly denounced the "official cinema" of Hollywood as "morally corrupt, aesthetically obsolete." Rather than prescribing a set of aesthetic principles, they sought to form alternative institutions for financing and disseminating personal films. The Group elected de Antonio to its executive board. "De Antonio called,"

Figure 6. The New American Cinema Group, ca. 1961, outside the New Yorker Theater. De Antonio (far right) was a prominent player in the group, which included (from left) writer Eugene Archer, filmmakers Adolphus Mekas, Sheldon Rochlin, and Jonas Mekas. Photograph courtesy of Jonas Mekas.

Jonas Mekas wrote in his journal a week later. "Said he found somebody with money. Always, those people with money!"[15] At a time when Mekas and his compatriots were literally starving artists, de Antonio's ability to tap patrons was crucial.

Some of the money went to help Mekas publish the journal *Film Culture*. There, in 1961, the New American Cinema Group's manifesto announced: "We plan to establish our own cooperative distribution center. This task has been entrusted to Emile de Antonio, our charter member."[16] He proved too much a maverick to function in an organization, however, and abandoned his position within a year. Thanks in part to his groundwork, by 1962 the Film-Makers' Cooperative was up and running, a clearinghouse for the rental of low-budget films. (Under Mekas's long-time leadership, the Cooperative and its Anthology Film Archive are still in operation and continue to serve the purpose for which they were created.)

After leaving the collective, de Antonio distributed films on an ad hoc basis. He forged a working relationship with another Group signatory, Daniel Talbot, who ran the New Yorker Theater, a West Side art house that became a locus for independent films. Using some of the artful deal-making skills that had become his modus operandi, de Antonio helped Talbot obtain prints of the Josef von Sternberg classic *The Blue Angel* (1930). Its copyright had expired, so the two profited from its theatrical distribution. In the years that followed, Talbot's New Yorker Films became the leading distributor of art films in the United States.[17]

In 1961, de Antonio graduated from distributor to producer. His first venture was with the short film *Sunday* (1961), directed by Dan Drasin. The teenage filmmaker edited together 16mm footage he and friends shot of the Washington Square police riot that followed a protested ban on folk singing (!) in the park. The freewheelin', vérité images and wild sound captured the spirit of the early sixties' Greenwich Village folk-music scene and the violent intrusion of the police. One of the protesters captured on film was writer Harold "Doc" Humes, yet another cofounder of the New American Cinema Group. Humes invited de Antonio to a screening of a rough cut of *Sunday*. "On the spot," Drasin recalled, "De offered to be my main distributor/agent. For domestic distribution he placed it with Contemporary Films. . . . De also entered the film in various festivals and brokered its distribution overseas."[18]

De Antonio's promotional efforts helped land Drasin critical attention in the premier issue of *Vision: A Journal of Film Comment* (Spring 1962). Soon known by its now-familiar name, *Film Comment* announced its advocacy for "the rise of the New American Cinema" by publishing a cover photo of Drasin. Standing alone under the Washington Square Arch with his unholstered Arriflex and a Bogarted cigarette, the "Young American filmmaker" was offered up as a signifier of the new spirit of the cinematic age.

No longer officially part of The Group, de Antonio was nonetheless accomplishing its mission: getting new artists access to cameras, screens, and a viewing public. It was a mentoring process he would engage in for the rest of his life. In Drasin's case, the producer did something he otherwise shunned. De Antonio invested $4,000 of his own money to fund Drasin's second film. The experimental short *X* (aka *The Transist-ites*, 1964) starred the noted underground director Stan Vanderbeek as a mad scientist who uses subliminal radio broadcasts to take over the White House and destroy the world. De Antonio entered *X* in festival competition, while Drasin's career took off in other directions.[19]

By this time, Emile de Antonio was putting his own name before the public, becoming a filmmaker himself. He pursued an overtly political cinema, rather than the films of personal expression that characterized postwar American underground cinema. Before the decade was over, he would create a series of documentaries that made him one of cinema's best-known practitioners of the politically committed nonfiction film.

Figure 7. "The Young American Filmmaker, 1961." This publicity shot of nineteen-year-old Dan Drasin showed the de Antonio protégé beneath the Washington Square Arch, Greenwich Village, where he shot *Sunday* on April 9, 1961. With de Antonio's promotion, the photo made the cover of the first issue of *Vision: A Journal of Film Comment* (Spring 1962). Photograph courtesy of Dan Drasin.

Figure 8. Dan Drasin directs Stan Vanderbeek (seated in de Antonio's Volkswagen Beetle) during the production of the short film *X* (aka *The Transist-ites*, 1964). Photograph courtesy of Dan Drasin.

The Point of View in *Point of Order*

De Antonio's film career grew directly out of his work as a promoter of the New American Cinema. Searching for a way to supply the New Yorker Theater with novel and profitable programming, he and Dan Talbot considered exhibiting television footage.[20] Both agreed that the eventful 1954 Army-McCarthy hearings had been the most exciting television they had witnessed. Like millions of others, they had watched the live broadcasts of Senator Joseph McCarthy alleging subversion in the U.S. military while his investigative subcommittee investigated his own machinations. The partners resolved to make a film out of these images. *Variety* magazine kept the industry apprised of plans to make *Point of Order,* identifying de Antonio as an "artie film distributor" as early as 1961.[21]

Discovering that CBS owned kinescopes of the hearings, de Antonio negotiated the purchase of prints with money supplied by Elliot Pratt and Henry Rosenberg (co-owner of the New Yorker). Over the next two years, *Point of Order* was pieced together as a "handmade" film. Talbot and de Antonio spent months screening reels in their living rooms. With no production experience, they put the project in the hands of Paul Falkenberg, a veteran editor who had worked on films such as Fritz Lang's *M* (1931) and G. W. Pabst's *Diary of a Lost Girl* (1929). The film was done to professional conventions. Falkenberg transferred the 16mm kinescopes to 35mm, added stock footage, and laid on music. De Antonio hired his friend Mike Wallace to record narration written to Falkenberg's cut. (Wallace was becoming a well-known television interviewer and doing narration for David Wolper TV documentaries.) This first version of *Point of Order* took a heavy-handed and didactic approach. Joseph McCarthy was painted in villainous terms, his opponents as righteous. Talbot, de Antonio, and others who saw it at a private screening at the New Yorker considered it artless overkill. Falkenberg may have shared de Antonio's leftist politics, but he could not produce the sort of raw presentation of the hearings that Talbot and de Antonio had in mind.

Their money depleted, the two started over. They agreed something dramatically simple was needed. A like-minded aspiring filmmaker, Robert Duncan, attended the dispiriting screening and began talking with the producers. Duncan met de Antonio through his roommate Dan Drasin. Although he had done only a few stints as an assistant editor, Duncan signed on as the new editor in charge, bringing a budding cineaste's enthusiasm. According to Duncan, he and de Antonio took several weeks to edit transcripts of the Senate hearings into a dramatic structure. With a cut-and-pasted script, Duncan spent a year and half doing the physical cutting in his East Village apartment. De Antonio screened sequences as they were completed, critiquing the work as it progressed.

The result was a major documentary constructed entirely out of these "found" materials—much as Rauschenberg incorporated found objects in his artworks and Cage used environmental sounds in his music. *Point of Order* was groundbreaking in its rejection of conventional narration, using only selectively edited excerpts from the hearings. Nearly 200 hours of material were digested into a taut 97-minute drama of political theater.

De Antonio labeled his documentary technique "the theater of fact,"[22] using actual footage to demonstrate the hubris of Joseph McCarthy. *Point of Order* shows McCarthy attacking the Army, the CIA, and the attorney general, as well as the Democratic Party, fellow senators (particularly Stuart Symington), and even President Eisenhower. McCarthy emerges from de Antonio's construction as an American monster who epitomizes the arrogance of power, with his demagogic bullying and hypocritical behavior on display. But the stark presentation of McCarthy's performance also shows his raw charisma and his ability to deploy populist rhetoric against the establishment. Although most reviewers saw Army counsel Joseph Welch

Figure 9. Roy Cohn and Senator Joseph McCarthy as seen in the 1954 Army-McCarthy hearings and *Point of Order* (1963). Photograph courtesy of New Yorker Films.

as the hero of the affair, de Antonio believed that the hearings revealed the corruption of the entire political system. He also believed that Welch himself used McCarthyite tactics, that the military appeared spineless and incompetent, and that McCarthy himself was not a sincere anticommunist, merely a political opportunist.[23] As he often said, he saw no heroes in the episode, except perhaps the TV cameras that put the crude spectacle on display.

By the end of 1964, *Point of Order* had received mostly admiring reviews in the mainstream press and gained a wide audience in both Europe and North America thanks to a lucrative theatrical distribution deal— a rare feat for a documentary. It was, however, a project instigated by the New American Cinema Group that helped the film get attention. In its 1961 declaration the Group argued, "It's about time that the East Coast had its own film festival." The New York International Film Festival debuted in September 1963. The event sparked new interest in non-Hollywood cinema, exciting critics and moviegoers.[24] Critic Stanley Kauffmann reported that "the audience was extraordinary. They generated the keenest sense of intrinsic interest that I have felt since the proletarian plays of the thirties, the feeling that they were there because nothing could have kept them away."[25] Demand for screenings exceeded the space at Lincoln Center, so the Museum of Modern Art exhibited an additional eleven features. There *Point of Order* premiered to three sold-out shows. Critic Dwight MacDonald lauded it in *Esquire* magazine: "*Point of Order* is good cinema and better history."[26] Although he misidentified its creator as "Emile de Antonia," MacDonald chided the movie business for not distributing quality documentaries such as this.

On January 14, Talbot opened the film at the Beekman Theater, a luxurious first-run venue, rather than his own repertory house. *Point of Order!* (an exclamation mark added for promotional punch) became a surprise hit. During its Manhattan run, articles on the breakthrough documentary appeared in the mainstream press. Talbot was given space in the *New York Times* to describe the film's genesis. *Time, Newsweek,* the *New Yorker,* and others published reviews. Critics of influence—Judith Crist, Stanley Kauffmann, Bosley Crowther—applauded the creative ingenuity of its makers. "The only successful spectacle shown this winter dealing with public issues," wrote Susan Sontag," was a work which was both a pure documentary *and* a comedy." *Point of Order,* not *Dr. Strangelove,* "was the real *comédie noire* of the season, as well as the best political drama."[27] Film periodicals paid particular attention, with *Film Comment* offering three essays, one penned by de Antonio himself. In December 1963, a special screening for members of Congress piqued interest among the political establishment. The publicity bonanza quickly led to a distribution coup. Within a week, a prominent distributor paid the producers a $100,000 guarantee, plus an escalating percentage of the movie's gross—a deal rarely matched by low-budget independent productions. Critical praise escalated. "For 97 minutes, I was held in a stranglehold," said San Francisco reviewer Stanley Eichelbaum, by what "may well be the most powerful documentary ever made." In May, *Point of Order* played the Cannes Film Festival, where it was the surprise hit of Critics' Week. "Applause broke out in a dozen spots and turned into a massive ovation at the end for its producer, Emile de Antonio, who had come to Cannes," one Paris journalist recorded.[28]

Point of Order not only enjoyed an extensive theatrical run, it had a particularly long afterlife. For years, de Antonio capitalized on interest in the film's subject matter by producing reedited versions and spin-off projects. With the national release of the film, W. W. Norton published a book version, and Columbia Masterworks issued a record album narrated by CBS News commentator Eric Sevareid.

In 1968, a new round of media interest followed, spurred by the release of Roy Cohn's book *McCarthy* and his February cover story in *Esquire*. In January, William F. Buckley's *Firing Line* televised a two-episode discussion of the Army-McCarthy hearings that featured excerpts from de Antonio's film. Buckley began both episodes by inviting de Antonio to introduce a clip from "his controversial documentary 'A Point of Order.'" The conservative host slighted his Marxist guest, saying "Mr. de Antonio has very kindly brought along some of his home movies," which had "tendentiously depicted" McCarthy "last year." The director began by correcting Buckley on the film's release date, pricking an antagonism that remained throughout the two-hour encounter. The other voices on the roundtable, all anticommunist, dominated the discussion (Roy Cohn, Leo Cherne, and Joseph Welch's law partner James St. Clair), ridiculing de Antonio's contention that the McCarthy committee "never discovered a Communist." Buckley was entirely dismissive of his views, but de Antonio stood his ground. "I am very happy, Mr. Buckley, to be an absolute minority here." When he suggested that "the correct view" on China was to support Mao Zedong over "that bankrupt clown, Chiang Kai-Shek," the host derided de Antonio as "Ohhhh—[groan] one of *those*." "Let's face it," Buckley said, cutting him off, "this is Bolshevik rhetoric."

Although largely shut out of the *Firing Line* exchanges, the director did find his film still being taken seriously. Roy Cohn went so far as to say that he had no intention of publishing his book until he saw *Point of Order* and felt compelled to defend himself. "*Point of Order* is about the greatest example of cropped photography you're ever going to find," he told de Antonio in the televised confrontation. Cohn read from negative reviews, including Senator Karl Mundt's statement that "the film does not conform with the facts."[29]

A larger audience and a more accommodating showcase came in April, when ABC-TV condensed *Point of Order* into a one-hour, primetime news special titled *The Confrontation*.[30] De Antonio's name appeared in TV listings as the producer and director, but a conventional prologue and voice-over narration by reporter Bob Young were added. De Antonio then issued his own abridged edition for the educational market, retitled *Charge and Countercharge* (1968). He proved willing to compromise his prized narration-less technique, providing a voice-over himself for a new introductory sequence showing McCarthy outside of the Army hearings. Still later, friend and political ally Paul Newman contributed an additional on-camera introduction to the film, which de Antonio shot at an ABC television studio in Los Angeles and included on some versions of both *Point of Order* and *Charge and Countercharge*.[31] Foreign television aired the film with a sound track read by columnist Anthony Lewis. In addition, de Antonio reworked his McCarthy text and audio into a second record album, *Senator Joseph R. McCarthy: A Documentary of the McCarthy Hearings* (Folkways, 1968). Performing the extensively revised narration himself, de Antonio replaced much of the Army hearings material with archival sounds of the anticommunist inquisitor chairing investigations in earlier years. The voices of McCarthy detractors Adlai Stevenson and Harry Truman were also woven into the LP documentary.

The fact that the established mass media helped promulgate *Point of Order* undercuts the notion that de Antonio burst upon the scene with a radical film. Although the director always discussed it from a leftist firebrand's perspective, the film was most often read as an orthodox, liberal interpretation of Joe McCarthy's downfall. The episodes that de Antonio highlights in his editorial restructuring of the political spectacle are not substantially different from accounts that appeared, for example, in *Life* magazine during the 1954 hearings or from Michael Straight's book *Trial by Television* (1954).[32] After de Antonio's voice introduces the film, he establishes the cast of characters, drawing the lines between the U.S. Army (defended by trial lawyer Joseph Welch) and McCarthy (assisted by attorney Roy Cohn). The Army had charged that McCarthy and Cohn pressured officials to give their staffer David Schine preferential treatment when he was drafted. McCarthy countercharged that they were trying to sabotage his investigation into communist subversion. De Antonio selects well-known interchanges to develop the conflict: Welch charges that a photograph of Schine has been doctored and that a letter from J. Edgar Hoover was a "phony." McCarthy and Welch exchange innuendos about "pixies" and "fairies" (while a closeted Roy Cohn looks on uneasily).

Point of Order climaxes with the moment from the original broadcasts that had lodged in public memory. When the combative McCarthy tries to smear Welch's young Republican law partner Fred Fischer as a red sympathizer, the counselor delivers an eloquent, melodramatic denunciation of the senator's "cruelty" and "recklessness." The film concludes with an artfully constructed denouement, showing images of Senator Symington storming out of the chamber while McCarthy rants about his enemies. De Antonio shows the hearing room emptying out while the Wisconsin senator raves on. When McCarthy says he wants the stenographer to get everything down, we see an insert shot of a stenographer—actually a piece of stock footage, the only element of the film not taken from the original kinescopes. The ending is completely and deliberately constructed, combining sounds and images recorded weeks apart.[33]

The critical point is not that de Antonio manipulated documentary material to represent his subject in a particular way. It is that, although the narration-less form and revival of compilation technique may have been bold in 1963, the film's representation of McCarthy was quite conventional. With CBS getting half of *Point of Order*'s profits and commercial theaters playing it to good box office, its subversive intentions were mitigated. Even while firmly advocating strong leftist views in public, de Antonio concluded his audio documentary on the subject with an extraordinarily conventional line: "My own view of McCarthyism is to be found in Webster's Dictionary...."

De Antonio said he "was disappointed by the inanity of the reviews,"[34] which did little more than say his film showed that McCarthy was bad. It was the price he realized he paid for refusing to rely on the "fascist" technique of "voice-of-God" narration to explain events to his audience. "That's what this film is really about," he later said, "Technique"—the demagogic technique of McCarthyism and of mainstream filmmaking. By letting viewers draw their own conclusions from the raw materials of history, however, de Antonio found that reviewers and audiences might miss the point of *Point of Order*.

Nevertheless the commercial and critical success of his first film put de Antonio in a position to deliver far more oppositional critiques of the American social order in the documentaries that followed over the next eventful decade. He might have traded in his commercial success for a certain amount of fame, but took a relatively uncompromising stand with his political beliefs.

In Search of a Method: Cinematic Adventures of 1965

In 1962, while working on *Point of Order,* he married his fourth wife, model Marilyn Ambrose, but the next year they too were divorced.[35] During the succeeding decade, de Antonio had many affairs, but in 1965 married Terry Brook, a poet and professor of literature. They remained together until her death from cancer in January 1975. He often credited her with encouraging his best creative impulses and indeed the years of their marriage were those of de Antonio's most productive filmmaking.

The second half of the sixties was as dynamic and invigorating for de Antonio's cinematic career as it was for the culture at large. Between 1965 and 1971, he made his mark on the film world, creating five notable political documentaries. Operating as an ad hoc independent film company himself, he cobbled together film stock and finances that yielded three of his key works: a 1966 rebuttal of the Warren Report, *Rush to Judgment*; the first major antiwar documentary on Vietnam, *In the Year of the Pig*; and his 1971 satire on the sitting president, *Millhouse: A White Comedy.*

However, before hitting his stride with these three major works, de Antonio spent 1965 searching for a mode of production and a form appropriate to his interests. His brushes with hyperrealist experimentation, journalistic vérité, and television documentary production all ended disappointingly. But the year's events allowed him to gain a greater working knowledge of film production and further immersed him in politics and celebrity.

Before de Antonio released another of his own films, he found himself the subject of someone else's. On January 19, 1965, Andy Warhol made one of his famed long-take films with de Antonio as its star. In *Drunk* (aka *Drink*), the director recorded de downing a quart of J & B scotch in one sitting, a death-defying act suggested by the infamous drinker himself. Warhol let the camera roll for more than an hour, showing the binge and its staggering aftereffects. Curator Callie Angell, one of the few people to have seen the film, describes the work as one of Warhol's most interesting. While consuming the bottle of whiskey (with soda, on the rocks), de Antonio begins to talk. He sings snatches of opera and speaks in tongues (English, Latin, French, Italian, a little Yiddish).

> Very self-conscious. *Déclassé enfant.* . . . A well-known learned asshole getting tanked in front of the lens. Very self-conscious. Andy's walking away. . . . Very good, I think, Andy. $400 an hour as an actor . . .
> I will not tell you about the history of modern art. Henry Geldzahler invented it. He was at Johns Hopkins. And Rauschenberg was stealing from Andy Warhol. . . . Nobody knows who Andy is, but *I* know who Andy is.

Then he adds, "Very few people would say this to the camera—how do I say this?" Pointing threateningly, he says, "Camera: I like people better." After smashing his glass, swigging from the bottle and lighting a cigarette, de Antonio declaims "I want ice. I want soda. I want reality, Andy. Is there any reality left, Andy?" He shouts repeatedly, "This movie is not a commercial!" then addresses the handful of onlookers behind the camera. "It looks like someone's taking a picture of us. It makes me extraordinarily nervous, and I am already quite nervous. Click, click! CLICK!" The still photographer was Factory resident Billy Name ("star" of Warhol's 1963 film *Haircut*), who later published a photograph of the drunken de Antonio lying on his back.

The "action" resumes some minutes later, after a gap caused by Warhol's inexperience in reloading his new sync-sound movie camera. De Antonio soon lies semiconscious on the staircase of the Factory studio. He never passes out, but is reduced to a helpless state, pitifully mumbling, "What's wrong with me?" The final reel, with its disturbing image of the near-death of de Antonio, maintains the first reel's static, merciless framing. Angell likens the image to a beautiful abstract painting, revealing only a wall and the barely visible hulk of the degraded de Antonio at the bottom of the frame.

At his friend's request, Warhol never released the film. Had *Drunk* been exhibited, the maker of *Point of Order* might have gained that vaunted fifteen-minutes of fame at the expense of his public credibility.[36] With the success of *Point of Order,* de Antonio made his midlife transition into a full-fledged identity as a documentary filmmaker.

As a classmate of John F. Kennedy at Harvard, de Antonio followed the Kennedy family's involvement in U.S. politics. As early as December 1963, Mark Lane, a self-promoting attorney and tangential member of the Kennedy political machine, began publishing articles questioning the assumption that Lee Harvey Oswald acted alone in the assassination of JFK. He interviewed eyewitnesses in Dallas and twice testified before the Warren Commission. In February 1964, Marguerite Oswald retained him to defend her son's name. That same month de Antonio and Lane met. Although the Warren Report was still seven months from publication, the two agreed to produce a film "for the defense." It would be nearly three years before the release of *Rush to Judgment*. While they researched the film, Lane saw to the publication of his best-selling book and de Antonio arranged financing for two other—largely forgotten—documentaries in England: *That's Where the Action Is* (1965), a BBC television record of New York's mayoral campaign, and an aborted "film obituary" profiling philosopher Bertrand Russell.

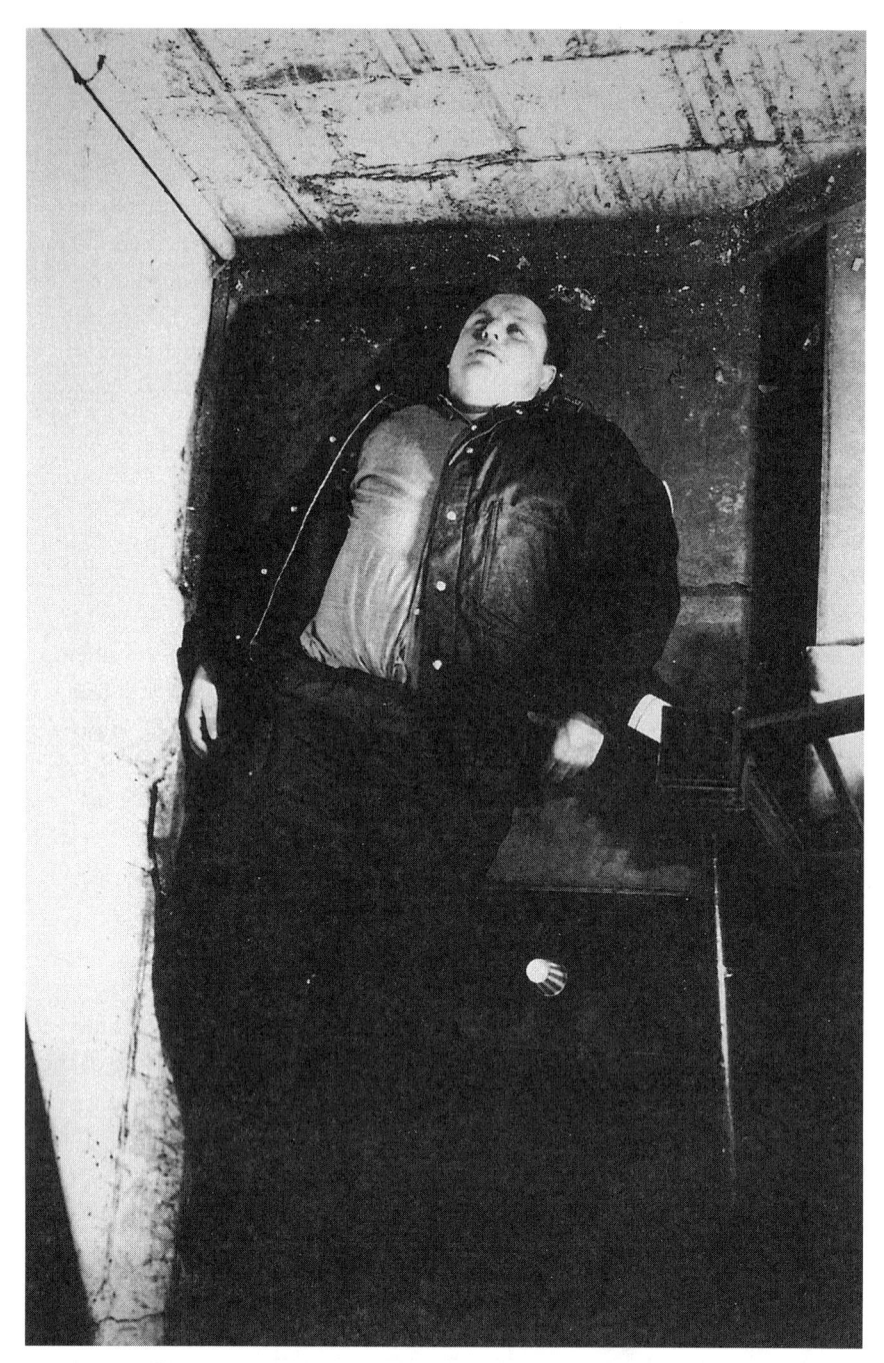

Figure 10. Billy Name, resident photographer at the Warhol Factory, recorded this infamous moment in de Antonio's career during the shooting of Warhol's *Drunk*, January 19, 1965. Photograph courtesy of Billy Name.

In these British-financed projects, de Antonio worked for the first time with movie crews, and the results were mixed at best. In retrospect, the prosaic nature of these two vérité-styled efforts serve to point up de Antonio's gift for documentary collage and montage. When he returned to structuring found footage in *Rush to Judgment, In the Year of the Pig,* and *Millhouse,* the results were often more forceful than they had been in *Point of Order.* In addition, the vérité documentaries disappointed de Antonio because he found himself beholden to greater institutional powers who prevented him from conveying radical political messages as well as radical form. He had first pitched the idea for a freewheeling documentary about New York urban politics to Jacob and Marian Javits early in 1965. The wife of the liberal Republican senator connected de Antonio with BBC producer David Webster, who set him up with a professional film crew. De Antonio enjoyed collaborating with the camera and sound technicians but was ambivalent about the outcome. "I learned what a bureaucracy can do in the arts," he wrote in his journals. "The three man crew was very good, very professional. . . . They never missed one point and they were totally without imagination."[37]

In the summer of 1965, de Antonio and the British crew shot campaign scenes and interviews all around New York. De Antonio "wanted to catch the mood in the streets . . . to acquaint a then staid British audience with the hype and jazz of an American mayoral campaign." He captured many of the city's most fascinating political figures on film, including Abraham Beame, William F. Buckley, Robert Kennedy, Patrick Moynihan, Jesse Gray (a Harlem rent-strike leader, and later assemblyman), and the victor, John Lindsay. In the conventional political vérité manner of the early sixties they were filmed on the run and on location—on bandstands and street corners, at Coney Island, the Brooklyn Bridge, and Gracie Mansion.

He got the footage he sought of these historic actors in the political fray, but de Antonio was not optimistic about what the BBC would do to the finished product. "The idiot BBC would turn all that lively footage, collage material over to an editor and that would be it." His fears proved justified. His July 14, 1965, outline of an editing strategy indicates his plan to make a film in the style of his later *In the Year of the Pig.* Calling the film *Running to Win,* the director begins with the emphatic instruction: "*No narration.* Voices will be voices of the real people." When the finished 50-minute film aired on BBC 2 in October, however, a conventional voice-over commentary was used and a rather stock treatment of the subject emerged under producer David Webster's bureaucracy. The trendy "mod" release title—taken from a song by pop group Paul Revere and the Raiders—was chosen without the director's approval as well.

However, de Antonio was not totally uninvolved in the postproduction of *That's Where the Action Is*. At summer's end, he traveled to England to supervise editing, accepting the BBC's largesse as well. But the main reason he flew to Britain was to reunite with Mark Lane, who was trying to raise money for the *Rush to Judgment* book/film. Mark was "urging me to come to London," de Antonio wrote, "to meet a pigeon, Richard Stark, who would put $10,000 into a new film on the assassination . . . and also to meet Ralph Schoenman who seemed to head the Bertrand Russell Peace Foundation and had free access to money."

Stark (a rich heir) and Schoenman (a Princeton classmate of Frank Stella) were both young Americans moving in Europe's left-wing circles. Eventually de Antonio came to regard both Lane and Schoenman as shameless con men, albeit ones who shared his political leanings. Stark and Schoenman delivered on their promise to help fund *Rush to Judgment*. But before embarking on the Kennedy assassination film, they enabled de Antonio to begin a documentary on Bertrand Russell. Past ninety and quite frail, the philosopher had taken the ambitious Schoenman on as his caretaker and attaché. Using the influence of Lord Russell's name, Schoenman established the Peace Foundation and other activist ventures (such as an International War Crimes Tribunal to publicize U.S. atrocities in Vietnam). After meeting Lane and de Antonio, he added their names to the Foundation's board of directors.

In October, Schoenman arranged for de Antonio to meet Russell. True to form, de, the sophisticate, hit it off with his famous dinner companion. Russell, he wrote, "was keen and bright and I made my proposal of making a film with him. I enchanted him by saying, 'Lord Russell, you are the only man I know of to whom I could make this suggestion. I would like to film your obituary.'" The great philosopher agreed. Shortly thereafter, de Antonio and a small film crew began shooting.

> My idea for the film was to take a train ride with Russell to Wales and to attempt a portrait of the intellectual, of the nonconformist, of the peer who sought social change in the context of freedom. Who had done great things, who had changed philosophy, who knew everyone of his time. Filmmakers are generally numskulls. I had hoped to bring to it some knowledge of English and world history and to make a radical document.

The several hours of footage shot in Wales never became a finished film. De Antonio blamed his bankrollers. Stark had insisted on hiring an inexperienced crew, who failed to get suitable sound or pictures. Schoenman and Lane both, according to de Antonio, insisted on putting themselves on camera and becoming part of the interviews. After much contention, the demoralized director sold all he had recorded back to Schoenman and returned to the United States. "I talked to the BBC but it was wiser than I. With Schoenman there could be no film. Only trouble.... It was the most profound failure I knew."[38]

▶ A Shooting in Dallas: Making *Rush to Judgment*

Despite the Russell fiasco, de Antonio and Lane were able to formally begin production of *Rush to Judgment* with the assistance they found in England. In October 1965, Stark gave them the seed money to form an outfit de Antonio dubbed "Current Events Documentary Films, Ltd." When de returned to New York in December, he had already purchased several hours of news library footage about the Kennedy assassination. More important for their financial interests, Lane secured a book contract for *Rush to Judgment.* The Bodley Head Press had ghostwriter Ben Sonnenberg Jr. turn Lane's messy manuscript into a readable one. It became the best-selling nonfiction book in America when Holt, Rinehart and Winston published it in August 1966.[39]

The filming Lane and de Antonio did in Dallas actually preceded completion of the book. The stonewalling and intimidation they encountered during the shoot added to the ammunition of the print version. As with *Point of Order* and *Millhouse,* the acquisition of the TV networks' film footage would prove crucial to making a documentary about the Kennedy assassination. De Antonio's dealings with CBS in this regard proved instructive.

Virginia Dillard, the CBS film librarian who helped procure the Army-McCarthy reels, alerted de Antonio to the existence of some crucial Oswald footage in the archives. When the Warren Commission delivered its report in September 1964, CBS News aired a four-part TV special called *26 Witnesses.* Although it was, as de Antonio put it, a "Walter Cronkite whitewash," CBS had archived dozens of hours of filmed interviews with the most crucial eyewitnesses to the events in Dealey Plaza—including many who contradicted the official indictment of Oswald (some of whom had since died). After watching six hours of this amazing collection, de Antonio immediately filled out papers to purchase all of it. Suspiciously, the network withdrew its offer to sell, apparently having it destroyed instead. *Variety* magazine carried an item about the incident, which led, he said, to Dillard's being fired.

Frustrated but emboldened, de Antonio searched for more filmic evidence throughout 1966. He and Lane formed Judgment Films. More money (about $60,000) was raised from the usual de Antonio sources: rich liberals and celebrities. Among the contributors were British film director Tony Richardson, his producer Oscar Lewenstein, playwrights John Osborne and John Arden, and socialite Madeleine Goddard. Although no network would open its vaults of stock footage, de Antonio got some ABC film secondhand from the Sherman Grinberg library and additional scenes from a local Dallas TV station, WFAA.

However, most of the finished film came from interviews that Lane and de Antonio recorded in and around Dallas. They traveled to Texas several times in the spring, working with a commercial film crew from California. A hostile atmosphere greeted them. "It was a very hard film to make," de Antonio told a 1971 interviewer. It was my first contact with physical fear of a sustained order in the making of a film. I went down to Dallas alone and spent two weeks looking at their television footage, and by this time the FBI was after us . . . and there were people following me around."[40] Lane had become a recognizable public figure from his lectures and television appearances. Both the press and the FBI were trailing him. His name scared off many initial contacts, so he began using a pseudonym when approaching potential interviewees.

No one represented the dissenting-witness-under-intimidation better than Jean Hill, now one of the best-known people to offer testimony about a second gunman. Millions had heard her live telephone interview on NBC television minutes after the assassination, where she told of a man firing the fatal shot from the "grassy knoll." She and her friend Mary Moorman stood only a few feet to the left of the president's limousine at the moment of the gunfire. De Antonio saw her on film at the WFAA archive and sought a new, on-camera interview. Like others, she initially agreed, but reneged. Hill explained that after Lane had visited her she had been beset by FBI agents.

De Antonio's letter to Jean Hill, dated April 14, 1966, turned up in his FBI files. It shows the filmmaker trying to persuade her to come to New York to see a rough cut of *Rush to Judgment* and sit for a final interview, adding that "of all the people I talked to in Dallas you are the only one whose views could be construed as even closely related to my own." We also see de Antonio representing himself as an award-winning filmmaker and classmate of John F. Kennedy. But Hill never appeared for Judgment Films. Her displeasure with lawyer Arlen Specter's treatment of her during the Warren investigation, the threat of losing her job, and FBI harassment kept her away from de Antonio's camera.[41]

Eventually, the filmmakers persuaded a number of compelling witnesses to talk to them on camera. Some had talked to Commission investigators, others had not; but all offered testimony contradicting official conclusions. Lane and de Antonio also traveled to New Orleans, where District Attorney Jim Garrison was beginning a more widely publicized investigation into a conspiracy to kill Kennedy. Little useful filming was done there, but they returned to New York with nearly thirty hours of negative to edit.

Awaiting the August publication of the book, de Antonio and Lane spent most of the summer working together in Manhattan. Although strapped for money, de Antonio did not shy from his usual indulgences. He blithely used the film company's expense account for food, drink, and rooms at the Chelsea Hotel, always looking for more socialite investors. With the success of *Rush to Judgment* the book, de Antonio spent the fall cutting down his footage to a two-hour feature. Dan Drasin and others helped in the cutting, though the sparse collage style was de Antonio's conception. In November, three years after the assassination itself, the film was done. Lionel Rogosin's Impact Films signed on as distributor a month later.

As was so often the case with de Antonio's avant-garde work, *Rush to Judgment* opened strong in Europe, but only gradually received exhibition in the United States. The BBC telecast the premiere (January 29, 1967), making the film a centerpiece for a four-hour special investigation. In *A Citizen's Dissent* (1968), Mark Lane wrote about the manner in which the producers of "The Death of Kennedy" broadcast allowed Arlen Specter and other Warren Commission apologists to attack the film at length while forcing him to sit in the studio with virtually no chance to reply. The British press and viewing public found the film's case compelling and criticized the blatant attempts to muzzle the makers of *Rush to Judgment*.[42] But it was good publicity. Theatrical screenings followed in Paris and elsewhere. The American media were more reluctant to play up the film. After all, for the networks to lend credence to its thesis would be to admit that their television news divisions had missed the biggest story in the history of their medium.

Of the myriad documents and films generated by the Kennedy assassination and its presumed cover-up, *Rush to Judgment* was the seminal entry in a burgeoning field of exploration that became a virtual cottage industry. Its rebuttal of the Warren Commission Report fueled public skepticism about the official account of the facts. The film remains the benchmark against which all subsequent investigations must be judged. In fact, what is remarkable about de Antonio's treatment of the subject is the understatement of its case, its lack of tabloidish paranoia or hysterical speculation. *Rush to Judgment* remains precisely what its makers intended: a detached, rational, coolheaded case for the defense. Cinematically, it is not calculated to excite or mystify viewers. The usually fiery and loud Mark Lane appears as the on-screen attorney: soft-spoken, deliberate (and even pipe-smoking), he narrates the points of his argument one by one and interviews multiple witnesses who corroborate them. The film offers no speculation about who killed JFK, but simply punches holes in the Warren Report.

In a 1967 cover story for *Film Comment,* de Antonio spoke about the different creative decisions he weighed before completing the final version of the film. Late into postproduction he was considering several unusual documentary strategies. "I will speak the narration offering the Warren point of view. We were going to get an actor, but on second thought it seems that an actor—in a completely documentary situation—detracts from the atmosphere of facts that we create." Given de Antonio's oft-repeated disavowal of voice-over narration in documentary practice, his discussion of constructing himself as an offscreen voice of Warren is an interesting digression. Ultimately, this plan was abandoned (as were overly expensive reenactments and animation of events in Dallas).

However, early in the film, de Antonio violates his own rule against voice-over, presumably for the sake of narrative economy. We hear de Antonio (unidentified) describe the Warren Commission as still photos of its members are shown. Later, he also explains the layout of Dealey Plaza as an aerial photo is displayed. Ironically, as a performer the director possessed a rich, dramatic baritone voice, precisely the type conventional

Figure 11. Mark Lane, de Antonio, and Dan Drasin in the Movielab building during the editing of *Rush to Judgment,* 1966. The multivolume Warren Report lines the wall. Photograph courtesy of Dan Drasin.

documentaries used for their omniscient narrators. For the remainder of the film, however, de Antonio withdraws, allowing defense attorney Lane and his witnesses to present evidence to the camera.[43]

After an opening montage of familiar stock footage (police arresting Oswald, Oswald proclaiming innocence, Ruby shooting him), Lane appears with law books and a copy of the report, reading passages he sets up for rebuttal. As cinema, the presentation is simple, bare-boned, nearly amateurish with its grainy 16mm film stock and flatly lit, frontally framed black-and-white images. Awkward jump cuts from medium to medium-close-up shots of Lane appear frequently. When he is joined by witnesses on camera, no pretense is made to make the sessions appear smooth or well rehearsed. Sometimes stiff, the witnesses speak carefully and formally, often nervously glancing at the camera. The cumulative effect of the scenes is one of genuineness and credibility.

Was this radical form? Or was it merely an inexpensive way to record a radical thesis about government misconduct? In a press kit for the movie's first run, the director appended "A Very Brief Note on the Style of *Rush to Judgment*":

> In documentary film content is all. Further, documentary is anti-camp. Susan Sontag, *pace*.
>
> *Rush to Judgment* is like "art brut" [Dubuffet's term for the raw work of amateurs, psychotics, and graffiti artists]. The camera simply records what's there. Angles, tricks, staging, effects would have been self-defeating as well as unneeded. Content carries itself: it is quite simply a brief for the defense which becomes an attack on tin gods and power structures.
>
> The editing makes it clear that the film is edited, that it is not a series of long takes. Any optical house can do that.
>
> The repetitions are intentional and reveal the character of the witnesses. The audience is a kind of jury; the credibility of witnesses can be judged only in depth.

Although de Antonio may not have had resources to make a more polished film, clearly he was applying a deliberate theory of artistic representation to his practice. "It's a kind of Brechtian cinema," he told *Film Comment*. The film breaks sharply with the cinema verité and standard journalistic treatments of documentaries like *That's Where the Action Is*. De Antonio's collage editing juxtaposes official statements with testimony and images to put in question the account of the assassination by political officials and the Warren Commission. Using low-budget black-and-white footage and TV outtakes, this consort of the rich was making poverty a virtue—but doing so out of political choice. By making *Rush to Judgment* intentionally "spare, unsparing, didactic," de Antonio was expanding on the conceptions he had begun in *Point of Order* and would significantly develop with *In the Year of the Pig*.[44]

In fact, the links between *Rush* and *Pig* are stronger than might be apparent at first. However, the connection has little to do with the fact that one is a film about the death of President Kennedy and the other examines Kennedy–Johnson policies in Vietnam. Rather, they are both films that document and critique American power structures from a leftist, class-conscious perspective. *Rush to Judgment* offers no Marxist analysis per se, but it reveals a populist, collective portrait of ordinary citizens speaking truth to power. Against the official version of history, the "heroes of the film" emerge as a group of unassuming "working-class Texans who testify about what they saw the day Kennedy was assassinated."[45] Although few of these individuals shared the filmmaker's political views, de Antonio clearly saw class as an oppositional, antielite force. He reached out across racial and ethnic lines as few investigators had. Black and Hispanic witnesses appear in the film as peers of great credibility, including Acquilla Clemons—whose existence the Warren Commission denied—Nelson Delgado, Napoleon Daniels, and Harold Williams.

Finally, de Antonio made explicit the connection between this film and his next when he pointed out that he had not made a film to lionize the slain JFK or to prove who planned his murder. As he told *Artforum* in 1973: "The film I made was out of outrage at the police and judicial conspiracy. . . . *In the Year of the Pig* is a cry of outrage against our war in Vietnam."[46] With the latter project, de Antonio would venture further into the experimental, modernist collage style that would help revolutionize documentary film. But even by making *Rush to Judgment* he was being hailed by cineastes such as Louis Marcorelles, who wrote that de Antonio "represents in the cinema one of the last authentic adventurers, a man always ready to take all the risks."[47]

▶
──

In the Years of Vietnam

After two years of extensive research, de Antonio released perhaps his best and most influential film. Paradoxically, however, his provocatively titled documentary was as much a cool, intellectual work of cinematic art as it was a hot "cry of outrage" or piece of agitprop. The movie's title signaled its sympathies for an Asian perspective on historical time, while it also emphatically scorned Western power for its greedy, ravenous maw. He later wrote that *In the Year of the Pig* was an attempt to "make a movie that was not a lecture, not a scream."[48] It was in fact both. In making a film that communicated the historical background of the war in Vietnam while also compelling people to turn against American involvement in it, de Antonio brought together massive filmic documentation and daring, modernist cinematic form.

While *Rush to Judgment* was in early release, two professors, Terry Morrone and John Attlee, urged de Antonio to make another film documenting government attacks on the official constitutional order and democratic ideals of the United States. They, like many in de Antonio's circles, wanted to see a compelling, critical and historical film that would offset the banal journalistic coverage of the fighting in Vietnam. De Antonio agreed to do it if they would raise the money. When it was apparent they could not, de Antonio rose to the occasion.

Again he reached out to New York socialites and "rich liberals" for backing. But rather than treating them like "pigeons,"[49] he appealed to a philosophical and political solidarity. American public opinion had not yet turned against the war policy as it would in 1968–69, but many objectors were being mobilized. One was Moxie Schell, mother of Orville and Jonathan Schell, both of whom were budding writers and Asia scholars. Jonathan was in the vanguard of awakening readers to the realities of the fighting in Vietnam, and later published the antinuclear classic *The Fate of the Earth*. Fresh out of Harvard, he had gone with the American military into battle zones. His articles for the *New Yorker* became two important books that were published just as de Antonio was raising funds for *Year of the Pig*.[50]

Moxie Schell organized fund-raisers in Manhattan where de Antonio spoke to groups of sympathetic patrons, many of whom were celebrities willing to lend their names to the cause. Shares in the so-called Monday Film Company were sold for $500. Donors signed onto the film's point of view, which de Antonio put to them as: "U.S. intervention in Vietnam is immoral, unjust, impractical and debasing. History and the facts speak out against it."[51] The several dozen supporters included progressives active in the arts (Leonard Bernstein, Steve Allen, Robert Ryan, Mitch Miller), the fashion world (Richard Avedon, several professional models), and philanthropists (Abby Rockefeller). The largest contribution ($12,000) came from Martin Peretz, the wealthy editor of the *New Republic*. Peretz would also be listed as executive producer of de Antonio's next film, *America Is Hard to See* (1970), for bankrolling that profile of Eugene McCarthy's 1968 antiwar campaign.

During this time de Antonio never abandoned his libertine indulgences in food, drink, travel, and womanizing. Yet he set about the making of *Year of the Pig* with a serious and deliberate vigor. He applied his intellectual training in a disciplined way. While reading, he said, more than two hundred books on the history and geopolitics of Indochina and Vietnam, de Antonio began creating a conceptual time line that became the structure of his documentary. Like a New York artist stretching a canvas in his loft, the filmmaker wrote out key historical events and concepts on an enormous sheet of paper. As he acquired footage and shot interviews, this became the blueprint that guided his cutting of the film, effectively serving as his storyboard.

As with *Point of Order* and *Rush to Judgment*, the opposition that de Antonio met in the making of *Year of the Pig*, and the lengths to which he went in countering it, testified to the polemical power of his film. His methods again make a striking contrast with those of the U.S. television networks. Because these companies were both largely defining perceptions of the war and archiving much of the existing footage of events in Vietnam, de Antonio's film was "at war" with television as much as it was with the Pentagon and the U.S. political establishment.

Once again, de Antonio found it difficult to obtain film from the big three networks directly. Much of the footage that wound up in *Year of the Pig* originated at ABC, but had to be purchased from the Sherman Grinberg collection. (ABC microphone flags are seen in many shots and a young Ted Koppel can be heard interviewing military men.) This source gave de Antonio some important scenes to build upon, especially the now-famous outtake in which Colonel George S. Patton III proudly smiles and tells a reporter that U.S. troops are "a bloody good bunch of killers" (a moment repeated by Peter Davis in his end-of-the-war documentary *Hearts and Minds*, 1974). Not content with what mainstream journalists had brought back from the front and from press conferences, de Antonio sought out forgotten material in film archives around the world.

After a year of searching, he assembled an amazing collection of documents that revealed the colonial history of Indochina, Ho Chi Minh's fights against occupying forces, and contemporary scenes of the war. The found footage represented many ideological viewpoints: the colonial arrogance of Western travelogues; French nationalists' coverage of the war in the 1950s; U.S. military records; newsreel of dramatic and everyday scenes; and views from the North, sympathetic to communist battles against the United States. Much of the material was gathered in Europe. In the German Democratic Republic (GDR), one of the world's largest but least accessible film archives was opened to de Antonio in exchange for his appearance on the GDR's radio propaganda broadcasts. He was a willing tool for such programs, both because he wanted access to film and because he supported a communist victory. (After the release of *Pig*, de Antonio appeared on Radio Hanoi with other American dissidents he met through John Towler, the Green Beret defector who appears in the film.) Among the major finds in the GDR was a filmed restaging of the Battle of Dien Bien Phu made by the globe-trotting Soviet documentarist Roman Karman.

After East Berlin, de Antonio harvested archival footage in Prague, where the National Liberation Front of South Vietnam had an office. British news archives also held material. But the biggest caches of film came through Paris, where the peace talks were being conducted. North Vietnamese officials gave de Antonio a print of a rare biographical documentary, *The Life of Ho Chi Minh,* which contained most of the existing footage of Ho's early career. The French military archives were a rich source as well. Although de Antonio was allowed to go through virtually the entire catalog of war films from Indochina, French officials did not admire his cause and so reneged on some of his buys. De Antonio claimed to have stolen from the archives a favorite piece of footage showing Ho flicking his cigarette overboard as he exits negotiations with French diplomats. In the United States, government sources—not surprisingly—were also uncooperative. Even letters of introduction from de Antonio's friend Senator Jacob Javits failed to open doors at the Department of Defense.

With his trademark collection of found, pilfered, donated, and scavenged footage in hand, the director began filming original interviews for his project. Some, such as former British Prime Minister Anthony Eden, backed off the project (de Antonio thought because of CIA harassment). However, a surprising number of talking heads from U.S. officialdom willingly sat for questions about America's role in the war. "Getting the establishment to undress for you"[52] was de Antonio's favorite interview device. By the time he had finishing shooting, the empire had no clothes. State Department officials, military officers, leading Republican and Democratic senators, as well as establishment journalists such as David Halberstam and Harrison Salisbury of the *New York Times,* all gave de Antonio ammunition for his film's thesis. Each offered statements critical of America's role in Vietnam. Getting Thruston B. Morton, the Republican senator who was leading Richard Nixon's 1968 election campaign, to compare Ho Chi Minh to George Washington was a coup. De Antonio also clearly relished Morton's verification of CIA involvement in Vietnam in the 1950s. To punctuate the cinematic moment of admission, de Antonio left in footage showing the clapboard marking the take with Morton. We also get a glimpse of the director himself and hear his off-camera voice prompting a response to "my letter to you, Senator." By getting other officials to confirm that the United States wronged Ho—"We betrayed him," one bluntly says—de Antonio's filmic essay mustered considerable strength from the establishment itself.

In the Year of the Pig also included extensive interviews with French writers and scholars whose knowledge had guided de Antonio's research. Yale professor Paul Mus, who had met Ho in his native Vietnam, became an important voice for the film's interpretation of the battles in southeast Asia. He, and other French writers on Vietnam (Philippe Devillers, Jean Lacouture) recount the achievements, status, and political philosophy of Vietnam's patriot-president. De Antonio's treatment was unabashedly romantic. He saw in Ho an idealized life, one that perhaps shamed his own uneasy mixture of leftist politics and indulgent lifestyle. The filmmaker's romanticization of his protagonist was only strengthened with the death of the leader in the year of the film's release. Two years later, de Antonio said:

> Ho Chi Minh was able to do what many idealist-patriots dream of—to liberate his country. . . . his life was so romantic. Shipping out as a cabin boy at the age of seventeen before he ever heard the words Karl Marx or socialism. His anger and rebellion and revolt against the French. The fact that he wrote poetry. The fact that he was sentenced to death by the French authorities. . . . That against all odds he won . . . that he had such exquisite grace and style. I love the scenes of him . . . with a group of young people and children and he raises his hand to make them sit down. The simplicity of his life was, for a Marxist, a most aristocratic kind of simplicity: the typewriter, the blanket, the few books, all this appeals to me.[53]

But *Year of the Pig* was no subtle paean to a poet/philosopher king. De Antonio used a variety of cinematic devices to hammer home his point about the injustice of the United States' military cause. Some of the film's effectiveness came from cunning juxtaposition. Speeches by generals Curtis LeMay and Mark Clark intoning about the "Oriental" mind ring hollow after the many representations of Vietnamese patriotism. Throughout the film, de Antonio effectively puts in question official discourses by juxtaposing the speakers with images that undercut their rhetoric. File footage of official press conferences is intercut with de Antonio's antiestablishment interviews, while General Westmoreland's claim that "Orientals don't value human life" is juxtaposed with elders mourning the loss of friends and relatives (another sequence Peter Davis imitated in *Hearts and Minds*). A nuclear weapons officer who was on duty during the 1964 Gulf of Tonkin incident contradicts the Pentagon's account. Other scenes, like the now-familiar but unforgettable images of a Buddhist monk burning himself to death in protest of the war, are powerfully described by eyewitnesses, as the images of the burning monks linger on the screen.

The film opens with an image of a Civil War soldier from the 163d Pennsylvania infantry. This image highlights the theme of a "good" war opposed to the "bad" Vietnamese war and was also a personal symbol for de Antonio, who had himself fought in World War II as a Pennsylvania soldier—another good war. De Antonio's opening montage also included an image of the statue of Lafayette in Union Square in New York, across from his office, with focus on the words: "As soon as I heard of the American Revolution I enlisted in its cause." *Pig* frames Ho Chi Minh as the George Washington of Vietnam and presents the struggle as a revolutionary war of national independence, parallel to the American Revolution. The opening montage also contains images of Boston's memorial statue of Colonel Robert Gould Shaw and the black troops of the Massachusetts 54th Regiment going off to fight the Civil War, followed by images of American involvement in Vietnam, such as the famous photograph of a young U.S. soldier with "Make War, Not Love" scrawled on his helmet.[54]

As the opening images unfold, frequently cutting to black, the sound track plays ever louder harsh metallic sounds, simulating the ubiquitous figure of the helicopter. In addition to the montage of visuals, the manipulation of sound became important to de Antonio to a degree it had not with his earlier achievements in compilation filmmaking. Several aural machinations stand out as punctuation marks in the film. The director seems to have been most fond of the musical "helicopter concerto" he had created for the *Year of the Pig* sound track. Composer Steve Addiss put together an electronic, Cage-like collage of whirring helicopter sounds from various pieces of sync-sound film. De Antonio thought the effect evocative of the technology that put American troops in the field. He dropped the sound over black screen in key moments of the film, using it as a signifier of America's deepening involvement in the jungle warfare. Later, his friend Martin Sheen would report that Francis Ford Coppola took *Pig*'s helicopter effects as inspiration for his treatment in *Apocalypse Now*.

In addition to these experimental uses of sound, de Antonio constructed many darkly comic or ironic moments that employed old-fashioned propaganda techniques to contrast picture and sound track. Over archival scenes of French colonials lording it over Indochinese rickshaws he plays "The Light Cavalry Overture," cobbled together from scratchy old phonograph records. After seeing a reenactment of General Xiap's defeat of French forces at Dien Bien Phu, we hear a pentatonic "La Marseillaise" played on native instruments—followed by shots of Charles de Gaulle and military gravesites. To similar effect, the film brazenly concludes with shots of defeated U.S. forces backed by a bamboo flute rendition of "The Battle Hymn of the Republic."

As cinema scholar Thomas Waugh notes of de Antonio's work, his films are primarily aural in orientation.[55] Even in *Point of Order* and *Rush to Judgment,* where little more than actuality sound track is used, the voices of historical figures and interviewees dominate the construction. De Antonio would build his images while editing the transcriptions of his audio. With *Year of the Pig* he moved into a more sophisticated use of aural technique. He continued to go against the grain of conventional documentary practice, neither practicing straight cinema verité nor voice-of-God narration. But while his Vietnam film stood out precisely because it lacked the "crude intrusive" voice of a Walter Cronkite or Mike Wallace, de Antonio could again make an exception for himself. In *Year of the Pig*, after the Dien Bien Phu episode, his own voice appears anonymously on the sound track. He delivers a cool, detached reading of articles from the 1954 Geneva treaty that forbade Western military presence in Indochina. Again, he is ironic, not explanatory. His voice blends with the others as the voice of History that testifies in favor of Ho and his people.

In retrospect, *Year of the Pig* can also be read as a quasi-autobiographical tracing of de Antonio's political life. The historical figures who populated his film oeuvre—Joseph McCarthy, Richard Nixon, and even Father Daniel Berrigan (who would become the protagonist of *In the King of Prussia*)—appear as villainous and heroic commentators on Vietnam. Only archnemesis J. Edgar Hoover is absent. Furthermore, in interviews de Antonio pointed out that the still image that opens and closes the film is self-referential. He likened the statue of a Union infantryman at Gettysburg to himself: a Pennsylvania soldier who reluctantly fought in a just war. As a veteran, de Antonio was clearly at pains to separate his critique of American foreign policy from the foot soldiers carrying out orders. *Year of the Pig* does not demonize the troops, saving the commanders and power elite for that (dis)honor. Some soldiers are even interviewed as heroic dissenters, such as deserter John Towler and David Tuck, a black veteran who testifies about the racist indoctrination of U.S. troops.

While the film includes television news footage of forces fighting on the ground, de Antonio ends by showing American soldiers to be victims of an imperialist war policy. Wanting to aim his movie at American audiences, he decided against concluding with scenes of victorious (post-Tet Offensive) Vietcong. Instead, de Antonio ended with film clips showing badly injured American soldiers being evacuated from the battlefield. One is led away, groping, with his bloody face wrapped in a blindfold. Disturbing as it was, he felt it was the most symbolic and appropriate image to end on. Indeed, the scene prefigured the eventual U.S. military defeat. But de Antonio was not without his misgivings. When he began showing *Year of the Pig* in the spring of 1969, the college circuit was one of his chief venues. Antiwar protests were reaching a peak. At Dartmouth, he found that audiences "laughed in the right places" for the most part. But at a May Day screening at Columbia University, de Antonio expressed ambivalence when spectators applauded seeing U.S. planes shot down. Yes, he wanted the North to win the war. As an Air Corps veteran himself, however, he could feel empathy for the airmen who were dying in the war.

Nevertheless, de Antonio's outrage against the war—spurred on by his distress at the election of Richard Nixon in November 1968—led him to present *Year of the Pig* as an unmitigated antiwar weapon (although he claimed to have declined a request by some activists to show a rough cut of the film at the time of the Democratic convention in Chicago). De Antonio raised funds—from a Wall Street stockbroker, no less—for a New York premiere. The film received more critical and press attention than his previous work. A *New Yorker* review by influential critic Pauline Kael helped focus public attention on de Antonio. "Taking footage from all over," she wrote, "he has made a strong film that does what American television has failed to do." Some cities ran the documentary in commercial theaters for several weeks, while others succumbed to protests against its showing. The staff of *Time* magazine, it was reported, studied the film at an office screening.[56]

Despite condemnation of the film's Marxist perspective, de Antonio had made another breakthrough documentary. It was unlike television's coverage of the war—which the director despised for making the war "quotidian," "sticking the burning village between deodorant and Cadillac commercials" on the nightly news. *In the Year of the Pig* put the Vietnam War in historical perspective. Also unlike TV, it took a clear but unpopular stand in doing so. Nevertheless, the film became an object of considerable didactic value. During the antiwar Moratorium of 1969, *Year of the Pig* gained wide exhibition through college and alternative political circuits. With sublime irony, even the establishment recognized the film. De Antonio took perverse delight in seeing Fred Astaire announce its nomination for Best Documentary Feature at the Academy Award ceremonies. With such an imprimatur, *Pig* even became a profitable commercial property. Publishing giant McGraw-Hill distributed the film for its college market and asked de Antonio to publish a book based on the film.

▶

America Is Hard to See: 1968 and the Crisis of Liberalism

The following year, de Antonio, with editor Mary Lampson, produced another compilation film about the political events that confounded the nation in 1968, one very much tied to the war. On July 31, 1969, de Antonio had lunch with Senator Eugene McCarthy in Washington. He and *New*

Republic editor Martin Peretz, who had supported McCarthy, proposed a fifty-minute film on the 1968 campaign. The McCarthy Historical Project turned over all of its film, tape, and campaign materials to de Antonio, who set out to get more footage and new interviews from participants and commentators.[57]

Borrowing its title from a Robert Frost poem, *America Is Hard to See* (1970) traces the origins of Eugene McCarthy's run for the Democratic presidential nomination in 1968, opening with an account of the Minnesota senator's distress with the Vietnam War and his decision to enter the primaries. The film documents McCarthy's successful campaign in New Hampshire, focusing on the mobilization of the idealistic young staff that produced an upset victory. Interviews with the corps of antiwar activists are interspersed with speeches, politicking, and events recorded inside the Chicago convention hall, providing a documentary record of the electoral politics of the 1968 Democratic Party. In the background, as McCarthy's fortunes in the Wisconsin and following primaries are depicted, Robert Kennedy contemplates his run for the nomination. The film captures his vacillations, the hope and energy that the McCarthy campaign was eliciting, Kennedy's decision to run, and the collapse of the McCarthy candidacy. Interviews with participants such as campaign manager Richard Goodwin and supporters Arthur Miller, John Kenneth Galbraith, and Martin Peretz, are interspersed with news footage.

America begins with a leisurely examination of McCarthy's early efforts, including substantial excerpts from his speeches. Such footage bears out the conventional wisdom, that McCarthy was too reflective, intellectual, and ironic to win the nomination. The film then presents a fragmented montage of the chaotic, extraordinary events of '68, sampling the well-known political highlights: LBJ's withdrawal, McCarthy's victories, the assassination of Martin Luther King, and RFK's assassination. De Antonio concludes with the moment that represented for him the failure of liberalism and the triumph of establishment politics as Vice President Hubert Humphrey accepts the nomination.

The film's editing strategy is atypical of de Antonio's work to this point. He combines interview material with documentary footage as in *Rush to Judgment* and *Year of the Pig,* but *America Is Hard to See* lacks the dramatic force and dialectical tensions of his previous films. Many of the transitions seem arbitrary and the film loses focus and momentum. Although the first part of the film is entirely favorable to Eugene McCarthy, the middle part becomes ambiguous, and McCarthy's presence fades away by the final reel. Yet there is surprisingly little drama presented in the assassinations of Martin Luther King or Robert Kennedy, and the film does not deal with the militant demonstrations at the August 1968 Democratic convention in Chicago. The clip of Humphrey's acceptance speech conveys a sense of banal politics as usual despite the momentous events surrounding it.

This reassertion of power by the old guard within the Democratic Party is the film's most significant theme. In a telling interview, Arthur Miller quotes Lincoln Steffans's observation that political parties are run by professionals, that they discourage citizen participation, that they are tools of the establishment. Pictures of Richard Daley exerting control of the Democratic convention in Chicago and of Humphrey taking the nomination showed the power elite regrouping to take control of the party. Thus, the film concludes with a strong condemnation of a bankrupt party system unable to respond to popular concerns.

On the whole, Antonio's films up to this point focus on exposure of the failures and evils of the established system, rather than on depicting forces of radical opposition. In the turbulence of the epoch, *America Is Hard to See* did not receive much attention and de Antonio himself rarely discussed the film. It has been revived much less often than his other works, in part because it lacked the aesthetic power and innovation of his best films. Furthermore, so many documentaries were made about events in and outside the Chicago convention hall in the summer of 1968 that his was lost in the mix. The extensive live television coverage and follow-up film reports that aired on the networks surpassed in dramatic value anything *America Is Hard to See* could offer. After its premiere in Hanover, New Hampshire, the film failed to get theatrical distribution. One of the few published reviews appeared not in Peretz's *New Republic,* but in the new alternative film journal *Cineaste.* Despite its leftist political orientation, the critique was singularly harsh.[58]

Nonetheless, *America Is Hard to See* is a valuable record of the McCarthy campaign. The film was de Antonio's attempt to explain the failure of the liberal challenge to power in the United States. It shows idealistic youth eager to realize the promises of participatory democracy confronted by realities of the status quo. In his account of the campaign, *The Year of the People* (1969), Eugene McCarthy concluded that "if one looks hard and long one will see much that is good" in America;[59] but for de Antonio, '68 was the Year of the Pig, with little good to be seen. However, his film's message—America is hard to change—was old news by 1970. Although his modest document was overtaken by the events of the era, de Antonio soon returned to form. With *Millhouse,* he produced a devastating portrait of the conservative president elected in 1968.

Chasing Checkers: Tricky de

In the political and cultural furor of the late sixties and early seventies, de Antonio was in his element and at his most productive. Even as *Year of the Pig* and *America Is Hard to See* were chronicling the events of 1968, he was at work on two other major documentaries. In 1970, making a considerable shift in modus operandi, he had begun a film about the postwar New York art world. But a series of events interrupted production of *Painters Painting* and led him to produce a scathing satirical attack on the sitting president, Richard Milhous Nixon.

Millhouse: A White Comedy, his mischievous portrait of the cold warrior, won de Antonio further international acclaim as an inventive compilation documentarian while also eliciting even more political scrutiny by the federal government. Although the film has its sober moments, it has far more comedic verve than his previous work. The title slyly plays on Nixon's middle name with its misspelling, connoting various negative associations (a millstone, a soulless factory). Its subtitle was a barb directed at television's bland genre of political documentary—the "White Papers" done by NBC News (the apparent source of purloined Nixon footage)—and highlights the whiteness of Nixon and his supporters.

Although *Millhouse* examined the history of Nixon's public life in a satirical way, de Antonio made the film in deadly earnest, outraged, he said, by the bombing of Cambodia and the killings at Kent State University. The story of the making of *Millhouse* is one cloaked in a sort of subversive mystery rivaling even Congressman Nixon's publicity coup surrounding Alger Hiss and the microfilm hidden in a pumpkin. Although he was necessarily sketchy about the details, de Antonio frequently reported that he obtained several hundred purloined cans of film with Nixon-related news footage on them.

In his journals, he wrote that while editing *Painters Painting,* he received a phone call from an acquaintance, Paul Johnson, brother of Students for a Democratic Society (SDS) activist Peter Johnson, who had helped de Antonio put together a pre-*Millhouse,* anti-Nixon publicity stunt just before the 1968 election.[60] De wanted to obtain a print of Nixon's 1952 "Checkers" speech ("to steal it, if necessary") and have the kinescope projected at movie theaters. "I wanted . . . to let a young public look at that cheap, phony, and effective '50s act." When he tried to get a print from the networks, they balked. De Antonio believed the Republican Party was suppressing the recording, conscious of how it could hurt the image of the "new Nixon." Peter Johnson got the *New York Free Press,* an alternative weekly, to run a cover story about the Checkers idea. It included a three-page spread, "Chasing Checkers," coauthored by de Antonio and Albert Maher (another rich, young leftist who was working on *Year of the Pig* and helping to fund it with his brother John).[61]

Although the piece caused little stir, it started the association between de Antonio, the rakish master editor of old TV footage, and his quest for film of the old Nixon. Paul Johnson's phone call led to a surreptitious visit to a film warehouse in Manhattan, where two anonymous sympathizers left hundreds of canisters of the president's cinematic past. The footage had allegedly been part of NBC's film morgue. De Antonio gave the bootleggers $1,000 and swore his editor, Mary Lampson, to secrecy as they set about making what would be his last full-blown compilation documentary. (Initially, he told quite a different story. During a press conference for *Millhouse* in October 1971, de Antonio said he had purchased most of his footage from WABC-TV in New York, "because ABC is the poorest of the three networks and you can get a better price." He told *Interview* magazine "about 70 percent" of the Nixon material came from stock footage libraries.)[62]

Tapping a few patrons, de Antonio raised money to shoot interviews and pay expenses. Journalists and pols who knew Nixon's checkered past were interviewed in Washington, Los Angeles, Chicago, and New York: Jack Anderson, James Wechsler, Joe McGinnis (*The Selling of the President*, 1968), Jules Witcover (*The Resurrection of Richard Nixon*, 1970), even Jerry Voorhis, the congressman Nixon had defeated in his first run for office in 1946. Given his idée fixe about exposing the Checkers material, de Antonio lamented the fact that he was not successful in getting an interview with Professor Albert Upton—the man who claimed to have taught Nixon how to cry for his TV plea. But between the new talking-head footage and the massive archive showing Nixon's entire public career, de Antonio and Lampson had far more than they needed to complete a feature film.

The finished product was surprising on two levels: it was largely comedic, and it was not entirely uncharitable to the character of Nixon. Comic treatments had been rare in the field of documentary, especially political ones. The freewheeling, farcical style of *Millhouse* certainly had not been evident in de Antonio's ardent political pieces of the 1960s. However, comedy was one of the few film genres de Antonio ever professed to enjoy. He often mentioned the subversive, antiauthoritarian powers of popular film comics such as W. C. Fields, the Marx Brothers, and Charlie Chaplin. His pleasure in joining that tradition was obvious. The film was even advertised as "a movie in the tradition of the Marx Bros."

The humor of *Millhouse,* however, is largely dependent on one's predisposition to laugh at Nixon's persona and what de Antonio ridiculed as "the essential creepiness of the man himself." The sound track begins with a tinny fanfare (from a high-school band playing at a Republican campaign stop in 1968) heard over images of a less than lifelike wax figure of Nixon at Madame Tussaud's. A few other cinematic tricks are used for overtly humorous effects—such as having Martin Luther King's "I Have a Dream" speech come out of Nixon's mouth during the middle of one of his banal orations. But, for the most part, de Antonio lets Nixon's words and images stand on their own. Although the film makes clear its biases and its desire to see Nixon as an unctuous and Machiavellian politician, long stretches of newsreel are left to show that on their own. For de Antonio, to simply show Nixon performing politically was enough.

Another way *Millhouse* mocks Nixon's career is to appropriate the thematic structure of the campaigner's book *Six Crises,* cued by de Antonio reading a passage from it. Rather than retrace the sitting president's political career chronologically, the film begins in 1962, and signals "flashbacks" to six infamous episodes. The year that Nixon's book appeared was also the year he followed his presidential election defeat with a disastrous loss to Pat Brown for the governorship of California. The film revels in showing the classic symptoms of Nixonian media paranoia and self-pity, replaying the famous "last press conference" sound bite: "You don't have Nixon to kick around anymore." From there, it retraces his Cold War career, from the first "crisis" (the Hiss case of 1948, where Congressman Nixon first emerged) through the Checkers speech, to Vice President Nixon's escapades in Latin America and the Soviet Union, and his loss in the 1960 campaign. Through most of this material, de Antonio restrains his hand, going for few overt laughs. With "Crisis Numero Cuatro," Nixon's disastrous reception in Latin America, the director uses some of the propaganda tricks seen in *Year of the Pig,* playing the Chiquita Banana advertising jingle over scenes of the vice president's tour. Detractors of the film pointed to such devices as sophomoric, "descend[ing]," as Jay Cocks wrote in *Time,* "to the level of easy derision."[63]

At other points in *Millhouse* de Antonio lays on the comic intercutting, ironic juxtapositions, and outtakes. While we hear candidate Nixon address the 1968 Republican convention, a crawl informs us that telling sections of the new edition of *Six Crises* have been "deleted by the author." As Nixon makes reference to President Eisenhower's heart attack, de Antonio intercuts scenes from the Pat O'Brien/Ronald Reagan film *Knute Rockne, All American* (1940), mocking Nixon's pep talk with shots of the Gipper's fever chart and the Notre Dame fight song. In retrospect, de Antonio was underestimating the propaganda value of such Hollywood hokum. A decade later the same material would help mythologize a new political nemesis, Ronald Reagan, whose image appears in several of de Antonio's films. Later the attack becomes more savage, as President-elect Nixon's law-and-order speeches are undercut by news footage and eyewitness testimony from black protesters encountering police violence during the Republicans' convention in Miami.

The closing images and sounds for *Millhouse* are clearly intended to show Nixon the cultural conservative surrounded by awkward and embarrassing icons of whitebread America. But, as many reviewers pointed out, they preach to the converted. Although de Antonio knew firsthand—and earlier than most—the corrupt practices of the FBI, footage of Nixon joking with Director Hoover does little to indict either man in and of itself. Bob Hope's burlesquey gay jokes during a White House event do a little more to ridicule the "new Nixon." But de Antonio draws the cultural and critical distinctions much more clearly in the film's finale. After shots of Dick Gregory denouncing Nixon's war policies and Pete Seeger leading a mass antiwar rally in John Lennon's "Give Peace a Chance" ("Are you listening, Nixon?"), *Millhouse* ends with the president offering a New Year's Eve toast to the music of Guy Lombardo, who played for V-J Day and would play "when we end the next war."

Despite the cutting humor and attempts to show Nixon's manipulative side, de Antonio's film also reveals a resourceful Horatio Alger figure. As de Antonio told *Artforum* during a 1973 interview with Tanya Neufeld (who did the graphics for *Millhouse*), he wanted viewers "to have certain sympathy for him, to understand this poor boy from the lower middle classes with the burning desire and energy. Everybody who wrote about [*Millhouse*] missed the Horatio Alger structure." Clearly the larger-than-life dissident filmmaker with the political bravura had a respect for his archenemy's longevity and realpolitik. He went so far as to tell the left-wing press in 1972, "Nixon is the most intelligent [read: cunning] creature this country has produced in the 20th century."[64]

Despite the respect for Nixon's dogged ascent to power, de Antonio's aims were clear. Although he was hardly the first artist or dissident to attack President Nixon, his film got special attention when it appeared in the fall of 1971. Ironically, the federally supported American Film Institute hosted the premiere of *Millhouse* in Washington, D.C. De Antonio was delighted to report that Nixon White House functionary Tony Ulasewicz was in attendance, taking down names of Washington luminaries in the

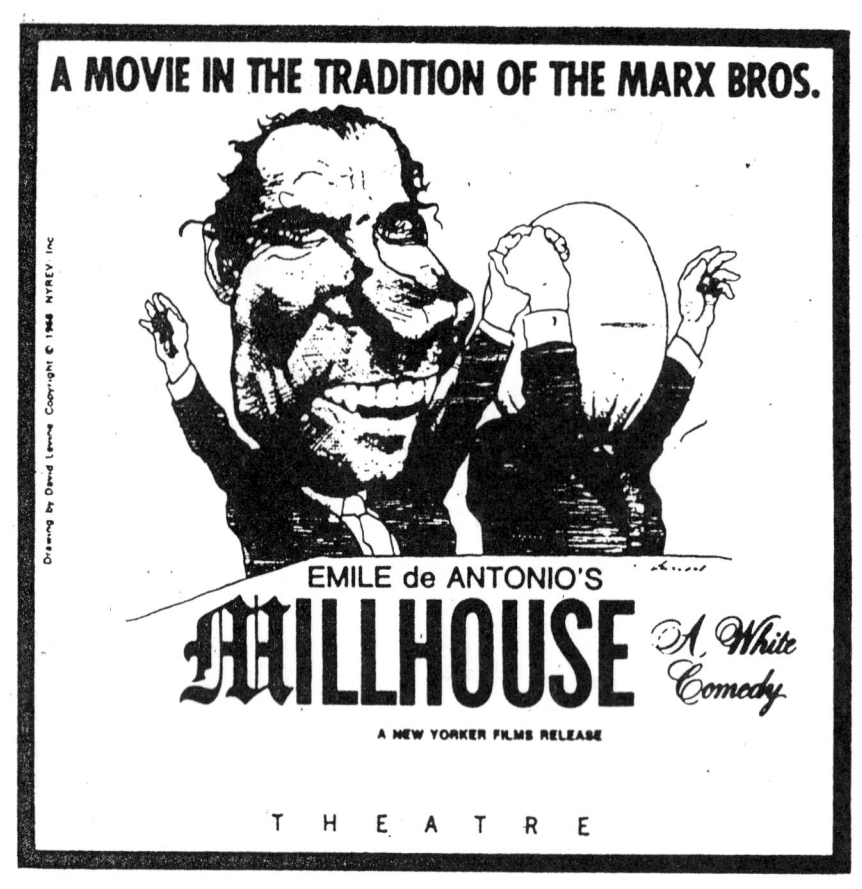

Figure 12. Ad slick for *Millhouse*.

audience. (A further irony: the *Variety* review appeared alongside one for one of the year's box-office hits, *The French Connection*—produced by G. David Shine, the former center of the Army-McCarthy controversy.)[65]

Sometimes the director suggested he never imagined the film having any actual influence on the president. But de Antonio once remarked that he fantasized about Tricky Dick overreacting to *Millhouse*'s exhibition. "I was aware of Nixon's paranoia and of the paranoia of those around him. I could foresee driving them into rash and criminal acts against me." Indeed, the White House did take notice, especially after the Hollywood trade press suggested the Democratic National Committee might be interested in *Millhouse*. On October 15, 1971, aide Jack Caulfield sent a memo to John Dean, recommending the release of "de Antonio's F.B.I. derogatory background to friendly media," and "discreet I.R.S. audits" of de Antonio and his distributor New Yorker Films (who were planning "massive college distribution" of *Millhouse* in 1972). Chief of staff H. R. Haldeman repeatedly tracked the film's status.[66]

Having been under FBI surveillance for four decades, de Antonio was hardly surprised by these moves. Yet the degree to which the White House would directly attack an independent filmmaker was perhaps unprecedented. Immediately after the Caulfield memos, pieces on de Antonio did appear in the "friendly media." But these were seldom as derogatory as Caulfield might have wished. After the *Washington Post* published the White House memos on *Millhouse,* Nixon himself came under more scrutiny. Many reviewers criticized the film's sometimes cheap humor, but only William F. Buckley's attack on de Antonio in the *New York Times* proved particularly vicious. ("I gather that the director-producer Mr. Emile de Antonio is not very bright.")[67] However, three years of Internal Revenue Service audits commenced for de Antonio, as called for in the memos. In later years, de Antonio boasted that he had been the only filmmaker on Nixon's infamous "enemies list." Although he was not on the same list as his friends Paul Newman and columnist Jack Anderson, the director had been the subject of White House memos and specific attacks. Even after Nixon left office, the FBI continued to scrutinize *Millhouse* for alleged criminal copyright violation because of its appropriation of the Checkers speech and other footage.

Despite the harassment and counterattack from the White House, *Millhouse* became de Antonio's most widely seen work. Its satirical edge made it more commercially viable than a hard-hitting essay like *In the Year of the Pig.* Some critics, including those in the alternative press, ridiculed the film and its tactics, but most praised its bravura.[68] In its way, the documentary that dared kick Nixon around was prophetic. Less than a year after the release of the "white comedy," the Watergate scandal broke. The two years of festering denial that came from the Nixon White House made de Antonio's film pale by comparison.

On the strength of *Millhouse*'s popular reception and the sympathies apparent in *America Is Hard to See,* de Antonio came nearest to influencing establishment politics in 1972. Although his own radicalism was well known, his gift for political image making attracted the attention of the George McGovern campaign during its latter stages. Documentary filmmaker Charles Guggenheim, a Democratic Party insider, met de Antonio at a Washington gathering in October. In hindsight, it seems remarkable that a mainstream political figure would have approached someone with such a radical résumé. Guggenheim asked de Antonio to edit together a sort of television debate, counterposing footage of incumbent Nixon against new scenes of the liberal challenger McGovern. De Antonio called the effort a "disaster," blaming Guggenheim for ruining his project by videotaping

Figure 13. De Antonio's favorite photograph was snapped at an antiwar protest at the U.S. Capitol in June 1972.

McGovern in a drab educational television studio setting. Compared to the politician he called "a master of packaging," de Antonio realized that McGovern came off looking worse than his rival. The candidate and the filmmaker screened the results together near the end of the campaign and agreed to scrap it.[69]

The Sights and Sounds of Modernism: Painters Talking

De Antonio's highly partisan and controversial films of the '60s and early '70s rank among the great artifacts of the political documentary. In the midst of this creative and turbulent historical period, de Antonio embarked on a decidedly different project. His wife, Terry Brook, suggested that he make a documentary about the New York art scene. An artist herself, she had performed in Claes Oldenburg's happenings in the early 1960s with

Figure 14. "The Art Girls." Terry Brook (right) and Barbara Rose in the 1950s. After her relationship with Frank Stella ended, Brook wed de Antonio in 1965. Rose, who became a prominent art critic, married Stella.

Henry Geldzahler and others. Brook knew many of the city's noted painters, including Frank Stella, with whom she had been intimate. De Antonio attributed his triumphs in the sixties to Terry's encouragement, so after initial hesitation he enthusiastically began work on *Painters Painting*. As he later recalled:

> I disliked films on painting that I knew. They were either arty, narrated in a gush of reverence, as if painting were made among angelic orders, or filmed with violent, brainless zooms on Apollo's navel, a celebration of the camera over the god. They revealed nothing at all about how or why a painting was made.[70]

By contrast, de Antonio intended to show the painters at work and to interview them in their studios, with their paintings. But he also needed to show their most famous creations. Henry Geldzahler's show *New York Painting and Sculpture: 1940–1970* at the Metropolitan Museum of Art in New York provided a perfect opportunity to shoot the art and painters that he was most interested in. Geldzahler collected 408 works by forty-three artists and de Antonio selected thirteen painters for his film, as well as a number of critics, curators, dealers, and collectors. He negotiated with the Metropolitan Museum officials to determine conditions for filming the exhibit and signed a contract giving his company, Turin Film, exclusive rights to film the show. Shooting at night, his crew brilliantly caught the color and vitality of the canvases. Ed Emshwiller, an established film and video artist in his own right, brought a pictorial sophistication not seen in other de Antonio projects.

Painters Painting stands as an extremely valuable film document depicting living artists and their work. Imagine a film capturing the great Renaissance painters at work in Rome or Florence, or earlier twentieth-century painters Picasso, Braque, and Matisse active in Paris. The postwar New York art scene produced the greatest contributions by American artists to world art and de Antonio was its privileged documentarian: a friend to many of its creative forces and an intimate participant in their culture. The combination of de Antonio's skill at filmmaking, the importance of his subject matter, and his intimacy with the protagonists produced a documentary film classic.

Utilizing modernist techniques of collage, de Antonio produced a unique cinematic document about the great American painters of his generation. *Painters Painting* contextualizes their work in its social milieu, enriching our appreciation of this immensely creative time and place. Showing the painters at work and relaxed in an interview situation, *Painters Painting* provides an excellent introduction to postwar American modernist

Figure 15. Two frames from *Painters Painting* (1972). De Antonio talks with painter Jasper Johns in his Manhattan apartment; Mary Lampson (right) records the conversation and ambient sounds.

painting and the interviews with the painters, critics, and collectors provide important documents in the history of American art.

De Antonio uses his now well-hewn collage technique to structure the film. From more than a hundred hours of interview footage and thousands of painted images, he cut the film to just under two hours. *Painters Painting* was the first of his works to use footage shot almost entirely by the filmmaker and his crew. For de Antonio, the formal structure was crucial to its aesthetic quality and he spent months editing. Yet he also followed spontaneous impulses that produced some accidental effects. His interview with Jasper Johns, for instance, blends a direct cinema approach with a Cage-like incorporation of sounds found in the environment. The crew records radio and street sounds as a background to the images of Johns being interviewed in his studio, a former bank. Uncomprehending reviewers criticized the seeming technical crudeness of these scenes, but they perfectly exemplify de Antonio's modernist aesthetic that incorporates aleatory and everyday elements into the work.

A conversation with Robert Rauschenberg utilizes a different kind of spontaneity, with Rauschenberg's assistant bringing him a fresh Jack Daniels whiskey during every reel change. The artist perches high on a ladder in his studio, a converted orphanage, and is filmed seated against the former chapel. With tenement buildings and fire escape behind him, the artist gets increasingly drunk as the interview goes on. The result, however, is some interesting dialogue and insight into Rauschenberg's personality, as well as his ideas on art. The day ended with a night of drinking and poker, documented by Marc Weiss, who filmed the poker game.

Painters Painting is similarly adept in setting up the interviews with other artists in the film. In many cases, his framing captures something of the ambiance, personality, and work of the painter involved. For instance, he frames his talk with Andy Warhol in a mirror with the painter's coworker

Figure 16. Brigid Polk (left), Andy Warhol, and de before the mirror in *Painters Painting*.

Brigid Polk sitting next to him. De Antonio also appears in the mirror frame, pointing to the combination of artificially constructed image, illusion, and mirroring of the mundane that characterized Warhol's art—just as the put-ons and self-deprecating joking in the interview capture Warhol's personality. The memorable image of Robert Rauschenberg slowly becoming inebriated while pontificating from atop a ladder, surrounded with city images and sounds, matches the spirit of Rauschenberg the urban artist and bohemian. It also suggests his ascendancy as a celebrity-star painter of international renown, a demigod of the art scene. The portrait of Jasper Johns sitting in his studio chatting with de Antonio and sound recorder Mary Lampson captures the urban ambiance of Johns's work, as well as his humor, seriousness, and close friendship with de Antonio. The scene of Larry Poons at work in his studio, pouring paint over a canvas stretched on the floor, reveals the young artist's dedication and unorthodox procedures that created a new kind of action painting.

In addition to depicting the painters' views, personalities, and works, *Painters Painting* illuminates both the economics and the politics of the art scene. De Antonio includes interviews with art dealer Leo Castelli, museum curators, and collectors Robert and Ethel Scull. The dapper Castelli, a longtime friend of de Antonio, frankly reveals the economics of the art market, alluding to the fabulous prices successful painters were receiving. The memorable interviews with Robert and Ethel Scull bring to life collectors who live vicariously through their relations with the artists. Interviews with art critics further contextualize the painters' work.

The exhibition's curator, Henry Geldzahler, situates the paintings in their historical ambience, offering analysis while standing in front of the canvases. Interchanges with Thomas Hess, Philip Leider, and formalist critic Clement Greenberg attempt to situate American painting within broader social and cultural currents, whereas the conservative *New York Times* critic Hilton Kramer is used as a foil for these more contextual and less elitist critics. The film effectively uses their commentary as voices in counterpoint, avoiding a singular narrator. *Painters Painting*'s texture is complex and dense, requiring viewers to work to make sense out of the film, to produce their own meanings and interpretations.

When it was released early in 1973, the film was generally received positively, particularly within the New York art scene itself. However, a few rival art critics blasted *Painters Painting*. In the *Village Voice,* John Perreault wrote that he was "insulted" by the film. "Artists should never be forced to explain their art," he argued. Worse still, he complained, de Antonio made the New York painters look bad. The *Nation*'s critique of the film was harsher still. Critic Lawrence Alloway claimed that the representation of the modern art world was out of date in 1973 (though de Antonio deals only with the exhibition of postwar work before 1970). Alloway also found the omission of sculptors a serious deficit, an odd criticism for a film called *Painters Painting*. Finally, he placed himself in the minority with an ad hominem assessment of de Antonio's skills as a filmmaker and art critic. "The interview as a form is not something for which he has any aptitude. He brutalizes every scene he enters, reducing the complex artists to stereotypes."[71] Alloway, who coined the term *pop art* in the fifties, was clearly grinding his own aesthetic axes, attacking de Antonio for privileging the views of Geldzahler and Greenberg.

On the whole, the film is a compelling document of artists painting and talking in their natural habitats, in the lofts and studios where de Antonio knew them best. Like the artists he depicts, de Antonio the filmmaker is very much a modernist, producing complex work that requires an active audience. This is no ordinary documentary homage to great men (and one woman) of the art world, but rather a dense tapestry that attempts to elicit a sense of the political, economic, cultural, and biographical forces that produced the most compelling visual art in the period under scrutiny. *Painters Painting* is also an autobiographical text in which the filmmaker attempts to make sense of his own cultural environment as he situates himself as a participant. Indeed, as a friend and promoter of many of the artists involved, he is part of the story of modern American art—a fact further documented in his 1984 book *Painters Painting: A Candid History of the Modern Art Scene, 1940–1970,* coauthored with Mitch Tuchman, and Ron Mann's 1995 CD-ROM edition of *Painters Painting.*

▶

Filming *Underground*

Upon completing *Painters Painting,* de Antonio entered a difficult personal period. Much of 1973 he spent recovering from radical surgery to remove a potentially fatal lymphatic cancer melanoma from his left arm. Movie projects on the American Indian, CIA agent-turned-critic Philip Agee, and other subjects failed to materialize. De Antonio had long resolved to make a film of his life, and was toying with combining fictional with documentary material, but this too was put on hold. He was forced to cope with his wife Terry's long and painful death from cancer. She eventually died in January 1975. After her funeral, he took a retreat, traveling to Israel with a group organized by Martin Peretz.

While trying to raise funds for the never-made film on Philip Agee, and despite Terry's lingering illness, in 1974 de Antonio became involved in a remarkable, secretive production of a documentary about the revolutionary Weather Underground. This small incendiary movement of the New Left grew out of a series of schisms within Students for a Democratic Society. The faction that became the Weather Underground Organization (WUO) turned to terrorism and militant revolutionary politics after what they saw as the failure of the democratic left. They began a campaign of bombing, first in retaliation against government murder of radical activists, and then against symbols of corporate and imperialist power. After the murder of Black Panther leaders in Chicago in 1969, they bombed police cars. Following the 1971 killing of radical activist George Jackson during a jailbreak, WUO members bombed the Office of California Prisons in Sacramento. After the invasion of Laos in 1971, Weatherpeople bombed the Capitol in Washington, D.C. They also set off explosive devices in banks, oil refineries, and corporate office buildings. By 1975, the Underground had carried out twenty-five armed actions, putting the Weather Underground on the FBI's Most Wanted list for five years.

In July 1974, the Weather Underground published *Prairie Fire,* a 150-page pamphlet decrying the global conditions of American imperialism. A second edition was circulated the following year, as was the first volume of the WUO publication *Osawatomie.*[72] These publications advocated revolutionary struggle against U.S. imperialism. Believing the publications represented a new, less terroristic strategy for the Weather Underground, de Antonio explored the possibility of making a film with the group.

Robert Friedman, a muckraking journalist in New York, had given de Antonio a copy of *Prairie Fire*.[73] Through Friedman, who knew Weatherman Mark Rudd while at Columbia University, the director let his interests in a film be known. The Underground sent word they wanted to read a "treatment." De Antonio wrote to them, describing his past work and proposing an interview documentary. In his journal, he later reflected:

> What did I want? I certainly did not share their tight, elitist, sectarian politics. They didn't kill like the PLO or the Russian Narodniki. No Nechayevs among them. They were American to the core, media people. The makers of headlines. From the beginning I saw the film as an extension of their activity. What the film did or what happened to the film would be a media action. Their bombings were dangerous. They were threats to society because they were successful media acts. The police response might be bullets. Living underground produces as many tensions as it does unity.[74]

In a cloak-and-dagger scenario, de Antonio was driven to Brooklyn, told to walk to a pay phone, where he was ordered to go to another pay phone, wait for instructions, and then stand on a street corner. After five tense minutes, he was approached by Jeff Jones, one of the leaders of the Weather Underground, who told him to go into a nearby restaurant to meet with other members of the group. Terms of agreement were hammered out, stressing that if subpoenaed by the government, the filmmakers would refuse to talk. After agreeing on Haskell Wexler as the choice camera operator, the WUO insisted that a woman be on the crew, so Mary Lampson was again recruited to work for de Antonio. Both Wexler and Lampson were reluctant, but after meetings with Weatherpeople in Los Angeles, de persuaded them to participate.

Haskell Wexler was already recognized as one of Hollywood's best cinematographers, having won Academy Awards for both his documentary and studio work. He was also a major player on the Hollywood left, having shot documentaries on labor and civil rights struggles, as well as on Brazil, Vietnam, and Chile. His direction of *Medium Cool* (1969) combined documentary and fictional footage to catch the drama of the 1968 demonstrations at the Chicago Democratic convention. Wexler also knew how to shoot interesting films that were little more than sit-down interviews, as he had proven in *Interview with My Lai Veterans* (1970), *Interview with President Allende* (1971), and *Introduction to the Enemy* (1974). Lampson, though not particularly politicized despite her work with de Antonio, got on well with the five young insurgents, all roughly her age. The group agreed to form a collective to make the film, to work closely with the

Underground, and to submit to "revolutionary discipline." But de Antonio played the lead role in conceptualizing and creating the film.

He and Lampson flew to Los Angeles to meet with Wexler and his son Jeff, who provided production assistance. Again they were given circuitous directions that eventually led them to their clandestine meeting place. Jeff Jones gave them sunglasses painted with nail polish so they could not see where they were going, a conspicuous gesture that de Antonio felt might call attention to their carful of passengers. After winding through the outskirts of L.A., they arrived at a nondescript "safe house" for the filming. The crew set up their equipment, then slept fitfully. De wrote in his journal:

> Haskell and I woke up, as usual, with first light. We checked the lights again and wondered who our actors would be.
>
> April 30, 1975, they walked in: Jeff Jones, leading Kathy Boudin, Billy Ayres, Bernardine Dohrn and Cathy Wilkerson. We never knew who bombed what, but Boudin and Wilkerson were camera shy and not very articulate, even in conversation. Tension heavy, barriers great . . . It would be hard to make a film rather than congealed rhetoric. I had always known it would be the problem. It was.[75]

The Weather Underground was understandably concerned with security so they insisted their faces not be shown. The filmmakers believed that masks would be inappropriate. They would create an image that was too inhuman and distort the fact that the WUO often worked above ground. So it was agreed that the photography would be done through a scrim that would hide their faces. A mirror in the background would reflect the filmmakers interviewing and shooting the film. The five fugitives began by introducing themselves, telling how they had been radicalized, and what they believed in. Through the course of the day they discussed their burning issues: Vietnam and world revolution, the importance of the movements of the 1960s, and struggles against racism, sexism, capitalism, and imperialism.

The interview situation was highly artificial and inverted the usual documentary process. Conventionally, filmmakers are invisible and the camera focuses on their subjects. Here things were reversed. The documentary camera usually focuses on faces, reactions, and interpersonal relations, but this time everything personal had to be blocked out. Their political positions were to become the center of the event. That night both groups met separately to discuss the day's shooting and both were frustrated with the setup. It was agreed that the gauze curtain be taken down. Wexler would shoot into a large mirror that showed the faces of the filmmakers and the backs of the Weather Underground, allowing the groups to face each other in a more dialogical situation.

De Antonio also convinced them that it would be better to discuss their personal lives and how middle-class kids had been radicalized, as well as more controversial topics, such as the Manhattan townhouse explosion that killed three of their members in 1970, their bombing of Congress in 1971, and their springing Timothy Leary out of prison—who then became an FBI informer and turned on them. After some hesitation, the Weather Underground agreed and these topics were discussed, although the Leary issue never made the final cut. In addition, Wexler asked them provocative questions about fear and living underground. The result was an engaging discussion for the final edition of the film.

At the end of shooting, the Weather Underground presented de Antonio with a quilt inscribed "The Future Will Be What the People Struggle to Make It," an artifact used as backdrop and prominently displayed at the end of the film. However, the fugitive activists proposed a third day of shooting, this time at the California state employment office, to demonstrate that they could operate above ground, that they were connected to the community, and that working people shared their perspectives. It was agreed that Jones and Boudin would interview people at the unemployment center, with Wexler and Lampson doing the recording. De Antonio would be left at the safe house. Despite his doubts, and unhappiness at being excluded, de Antonio conceded.

After shooting at the employment center, which did indeed produce ordinary people expressing radical sentiments, Jones and Boudin insisted on filming interviews at the Martin Luther King Hospital, where young black doctors were striking for increased community services. Police and hospital surveillance cameras at the picket line caught the group interviewing the doctors and recorded Wexler's license plate. Armed with this evidence, police began trailing and harassing the filmmakers.

Meanwhile, they needed to process the film and sound track, knowing that laboratories could turn over their material to the FBI. Wexler entrusted the film to his lab while de Antonio took the sound track to a small production house and supervised the audio transfer himself. The ploy seemed to work, but de Antonio and Lampson were distressed that their footage revealed the faces of the Weatherpeople. They were forced to obscure the identities of the subjects by blurring the images frame by frame. Later they learned that the sound lab had turned over a copy of the interviews to the FBI.

Government surveillance of the Wexlers and de Antonio and Lampson back in New York began at once. In early June, the filmmakers were presented with a subpoena, ordering them to appear in a district court in Los Angeles. They were enjoined to bring their film material with them and answer questions about the Weather Underground. A campaign was immediately put into motion involving the American Civil Liberties Union, the Screen Directors Guild, and major figures of the Hollywood left. On June 6, de Antonio, Lampson, and Wexler appeared at a press conference flanked by movie stars and defended by powerful lawyers Charles Nesson, Michael Kennedy, and Leonard Boudin (Kathy Boudin's father). Directors Guild president Robert Wise solemnly read a statement in favor of the filmmakers' First Amendment right to make any film they chose.

With coverage that night on the *CBS Evening News with Walter Cronkite*, de Antonio and his colleagues won an important public relations battle. The government dropped its subpoena, but threatened to reissue one at any time. De Antonio's legal team made a strong argument that prior restraint of a film in progress constituted an abuse of the grand jury system. Perhaps sensing that a verdict on behalf of these highly visible defendants might weaken government use of the grand jury method of interrogating radical groups, the Justice Department backed off.

Accordingly, de Antonio and his colleagues were free to finish the film. From the beginning, de Antonio feared that the interviews alone would not make an engaging film and began seeking documentary footage that would illustrate the points made in the interviews, music that would mobilize popular sentiment for their positions, and a complex montage/collage structure to organize the material. At the same time, a media campaign was undertaken to keep the freedom of speech issue and possible government suppression of the film in the public eye. Pacifica Radio stations discussed the project, while a lengthy *Rolling Stone* exposé in November 1975 reported the inside story of the production of the film, helping whet public appetite to see it.[76] *Underground* was released in May 1976, with a premiere in Madison, Wisconsin, a hotbed of political protest and home of the de Antonio archive.

The film opens with images of the crew shooting the film, accompanied by the sound of Nina Simone singing "New World Coming." Jeff Jones explains the film project and, as in the first day of shooting, the members of the Weather Underground introduce themselves, but in each case de Antonio and Lampson juxtapose documentary footage from key events of the preceding decade. The film illustrates the history of the Weather Underground, beginning with the Days of Rage in Chicago, October 8–11, 1969, when their antiwar demonstration turned violent, and continued listing, discussing, and providing documentation of their most notorious exploits. Discussion of the filmmaking process itself punctuates the narrative and the film concludes with the Weather Underground above ground. Acting as on-camera reporters, they interview people at the employment center in Los Angeles and on the picket line of striking doctors.

In editing the film, de Antonio tried to keep the pace moving, to avoid the dead end of rhetorical didacticism, to break up and enliven the interviews with historical montage, and to effectively combine his material into an organic whole. Consequently, de Antonio deployed his signature documentary technique, producing a montage of interviews and documentary images that constituted a history of the American New Left, putting the Weather Underground in the tradition of radical struggles throughout the 1960s.

Yet in *Underground* there is a lack of the dialectical tension that characterizes his best work in *In the Year of the Pig* and *Millhouse*. In these films, ironic juxtapositions—between the sounds of official pronouncements and the documentary images that contradict what the power elite say—provide a fissure of critical energy. By contrast, the compilation sections of *Underground* tend to illustrate what is said in the interviews, creating none of the critical tension between the archival footage and the original interviews that characterizes de Antonio's films at their best.

It is negative energy that most inspires de Antonio to exercise his sometimes savage wit and heavy sense of critical irony on subjects whom he holds in contempt. He is superior as a demythologizer, as a radical critic of the system, as an ironic modernist, rather than as a propagandist for political movements. Although there are definite differences between his own more populist and intellectual version of Marxism and the revolutionary extremism of the Weather Underground, this tension does not emerge in the film, except, perhaps, in subtle asides or distancing, as when de Antonio includes images of himself appearing bored, or standing off to the side of the proceedings when the Weather Underground is engaged in what he obviously sees as canned rhetoric and posturing. By contrast, Lampson appears to be deeply involved in the discussion, while Wexler appears as the "man with the movie camera," a figure in command of the technical apparatus.

Nonetheless, the making of *Underground* was a heroic undertaking, to which de Antonio dedicated high levels of energy and intelligence. By filming a group of revolutionaries on the FBI's Most Wanted list, he and his crew were literally risking their lives. All involved knew that, under similar circumstances the previous year, a SWAT team had killed members of the Symbionese Liberation Army—another terrorist group hiding from the FBI in Los Angeles.

Underground captured a political moment that was passing, one whose final adherents looked isolated. When ads for *Underground* appeared alongside those for the Watergate drama *All the President's Men* (1976), it was a symptom that mainstream Hollywood had made the *Millhouse* perspective commonplace. Yet de Antonio's natural constituency was divided about the merits of his film, just as it was about the WUO. The alternative film journal *Cineaste,* usually highly supportive of de Antonio, ran pro and con reviews: a favorable appreciation by a fellow activist and a sharp critique by senior editor Dan Georgakas. Again the left had split, leaving practitioners like de Antonio with a fragmented, dwindling audience.

The film itself had limited release, mixed reviews, and positioned de Antonio as a supporter of the hard left, pushing him even further to the margins of U.S. culture and politics. He had won the right to make a dissident film, but in making it he scared off much economic support. Even de Antonio's regular distributor, New Yorker Films, chose not to release *Underground* after its premiere—although it had initially agreed to do so. Hollywood producer Bert Schneider, who helped organize the movie industry's strong free-speech stand the year before, stepped in to distribute the film, but theatrical bookings were modest in number as the American media preoccupied itself with Bicentennial pageantry in the summer of '76, and chose to bury most reminders of recent militancy and conflict. (De Antonio sued Schneider's distributorship, rbc Films, for its handling of the film.)

As America drifted farther right, de Antonio lost more backers. For the first time, a major effort to raise money for a film failed with his anti-CIA Philip Agee project. For five years, de Antonio went without work on a major production. However, his legal entanglements with *Underground* led him to another important court victory over the federal government. Shortly before his interviews with the Weatherpeople, de Antonio filed a Freedom of Information Act request to obtain copies of his FBI files. When the agency withheld its mass of material, de Antonio prevailed upon Harvard law professor Charles Nesson to sue the FBI and CIA. In *Emile de Antonio v. Clarence Kelley* (1979), Judge John J. Sirica—who had once subpoenaed Nixon's tapes—ruled for the filmmaker. Thousands of documents emanated from Washington over the next several years.[77]

De Antonio spent those years working and reworking his own archive. He assembled many volumes of diaries, including material for a long-planned autobiographical project. He also promoted his past films, lectured on campuses, sat for interviews, and enjoyed retrospectives of his work. Several book projects went unfinished, but he published a number of essays and cranked out tart letters to the editor while engaging in voluminous correspondence. Even during this hiatus from moviemaking he remained under government scrutiny. In 1977, the public television station in Madison, Wisconsin, broadcast an interview with de Antonio after airing *Millhouse.* Alarmed by what he saw, a station manager phoned the FBI, who subsequently looked into the film's copyright infringement.[78]

With the Plowshares Eight in King of Prussia

Throughout the 1970s, de Antonio's politics had become increasingly militant, but his first film of the 1980s was made with a group of Catholic activists who were pacifists. Two priests and six laypeople were on trial for their 1980 attempt to call attention to nuclear madness by vandalizing the nose cones of atomic weapons and splashing blood on classified documents in a General Electric factory in King of Prussia, Pennsylvania. Led by Philip and Daniel Berrigan, the Plowshares Eight followed the biblical injunction to transform swords into plowshares and undertook dramatic actions to oppose U.S. nuclear policy and the production of atomic weapons.

De Antonio had known Father Daniel Berrigan since the filming of *In the Year of the Pig*. Berrigan had been one of the first Americans to visit Hanoi during the Vietnam War. When he returned, de Antonio went to Cornell University to film the antiwar priest. "I felt I was in the presence of an independent spirit," Berrigan recalled of their first meeting. Despite de Antonio's atheism, he and Berrigan maintained a long friendship and socialized in New York. Like many on the left, de Antonio had profound respect for the Berrigans. He admired their moral purism, their commitment to nonviolent resistance, and their spiritual devotion to social justice.

De Antonio encountered many difficulties in making the film. The initial plan was to film the trial itself in March 1981, but the judge permitted no cameras in his courtroom. De Antonio's appeal to the Pennsylvania Supreme Court failed. Moreover, it was difficult to raise money for the film on short notice. The liberal contributors who usually supported de Antonio were not eager to support Catholic activists whose positions included opposition to abortion and support of the Palestinian Liberation Organization.

Using his own money, de Antonio assembled a very low-budget production. He was forced to shoot primarily on one-inch videotape rather than 16mm stock. He brought in a young cinematographer, Judy Irola, whom he had befriended at a film festival in Spain. Having the Eight play themselves, supported by a few professional actors, de Antonio undertook a re-creation based on his edited transcripts of the trial.[79] For two days in July, the cast worked in a little theater space run by St. Peter's Episcopal Church in the Chelsea district of New York, a location also used by the Bread and Puppet Theater and other politically oriented troupes. Set designer Richard Hoover, working on his first film, built the sparse courtroom scenery. Irola and her assistant shot the performance using two cameras to cover the staging. The defendants, facing imminent incarceration, had little time for rehearsal. Daniel Berrigan recalled that he and his codefendants were glad to have the film done, but were preoccupied with more immediate concerns. The Plowshares movement was built on principles of direct action, grassroots participation, and spiritual communion; the labor-intensive, complex machinery of filmmaking was not a priority for them.[80]

Made under such severe constraints, *In the King of Prussia* may be de Antonio's least successful film. Its mission, however, was not to take documentary film to a new height, but to call attention to a cause with guerrilla-like immediacy and to militate against the Plowshares Eight's imprisonment. Released in 1982, *In the King of Prussia* combines documentary footage shot in Pennsylvania and trial scenes reenacted in New York, thus providing another variant of de Antonio's collage method. It was his first use of quasi-fictional material, his first use of videotape, and thus a continuation of his experimentation with documentary form.

The film opens with the cult graffiti artist Futura 2000 spray-painting the title of the film on a wall, accompanied by Jackson Browne's song "Crow on the Cradle." Vérité footage shows Plowshares supporters singing "Rejoice" as they leave the courthouse. The film then turns to a docudrama re-creation of the trial. Testimony by General Electric employees (restaged by actors) discloses that none of them knew they were working in a nuclear weapons production facility. Throughout the trial, Judge Samuel Salus (played by actor Martin Sheen), denied the defendants the right to present witnesses who would give evidence of the justification for shutting down the facility.

Documentary footage of a sidewalk press conference held during the trial, however, allows the Plowshares' expert witnesses to make their points. Nobel Prize-winning biologist George Wald argues that nuclear weapons threaten human and natural life on the planet. Engineer Robert Aldridge testifies that the G.E. plant produces first-strike atomic warheads that could trigger World War III, while legal scholar Richard Falk contends that first-strike use of nuclear weapons violates international law. Psychiatrist Robert Jay Lifton, who had researched Hiroshima survivors, tells the press that human beings lack the psychological capacity to survive a nuclear war. Judge Salus barred such testimony in court, but this indictment of atomic weapons constitutes one of the film's effective elements.

In the King of Prussia closes with the Plowshares Eight ordered to stiff prison terms. We see former Attorney General Ramsey Clark standing in front of Salus's courthouse, coolly reporting the one-to-ten-year punishments doled out in August 1981. He comments for the camera, "The sentences are an incredible miscarriage of justice and they show how dangerous it is to seek peace in America." The film ends with an abrupt cut to black.

Although de Antonio's attempt at agitprop may have had little direct effect on subsequent events in the case, the legal system did eventually amend the injustices of Salus's rulings. After a decade of appeals, in April 1990, another Pennsylvania judge resentenced the protesters to the time they had served before the trial. On this occasion Clark, Lifton, and Falk, as well as historian Howard Zinn, were allowed to testify that the actions taken by the eight were justified. After the first Plowshares protest in King of Prussia in 1980, dozens of similar demonstrations continued worldwide. However, few other Plowshares actions received significant press coverage. De Antonio's documentary was one of the movement's few attempts to work with mass media.[81]

In the King of Prussia was a highly experimental undertaking. Film festivals in Locarno and Berlin recognized its political heart and challenging form with special awards, but most opinion makers and audiences found it difficult viewing as a theatrical presentation. The uneven acting, imperfect sound recording, and other substandard production values proved too great a liability. The Plowshares Eight had no time to prepare for the filming and their performances were uneven. Reviewers complained that Martin Sheen went over the top in his performance as the hot-tempered Judge Salus, although de Antonio insisted that he underplayed the noxious judge, who was clearly contemptuous of the defendants. The documentary footage is often more engaging than the courtroom drama, and the juxtapositions do not always enhance the film's impact. However, *King of Prussia* was not trying to be a film of "quality." The trial restaging in particular, with its naive acting, minimal sets, and simple design, can be seen as an example of what Richard Hoover calls "demonstrated theater," an aesthetic of poverty with a direct, fablelike quality. For art-house audiences and documentary filmmakers, the aesthetic remains jarring, and for some, amateurish.

"The film was made to encourage people to act," de Antonio wrote to the *Bulletin of Atomic Scientists*. In some cases it apparently did. Daniel Berrigan, Martin Sheen, and de Antonio attended the premiere in Minneapolis, where an estimated 1,500 people saw *In the King of Prussia*. "It was used as an organizing tool," he continued, and helped mobilize civil disobedience in the aftermath of the screenings. "The next day we all went to Honeywell and demonstrated." The fact that more than 600 Minnesota protesters were arrested in antinuclear demonstrations in the days that followed, de Antonio argued, was in part due to the movement's use of his film.[82]

Despite a successful premiere in Minneapolis, the film got little theatrical distribution (though it was broadcast on European television). Father Berrigan's request that Cardinal Bernardin of Chicago endorse the film was ignored. Yet it did what the Plowshares Eight had hoped their trial would do: carry out a radical critique of U.S. nuclear weapons policy. The proceedings revealed that even workers in nuclear weapons plants and townspeople in the places where they were produced were not aware of what was transpiring. The Plowshares Eight and their supporters present strong arguments, making the film a valuable brief against nuclear weapons.

In retrospect, *Underground* provides an elegy for the American New Left that was disintegrating at the time of the film's release, while *In the King of Prussia* showed members of the left seeking new social movements and strategies. The highly skeptical and critical de Antonio never entirely sympathized with either group. Being much more pragmatic, he was unable to believe in moral absolutes or in a "correct" way to create political change. Moreover, as he conceded, there was an anarchistic streak in him that would not submit to any political discipline or line, and an individualist strain that drove him to seek his own political and aesthetic practices, to go it alone.

The breakup of the radical movement in which de Antonio had participated was dispiriting. After 1982, he never fully recovered his prodigious energies and ambitions, though he continued to attempt to find new projects and especially to tell the story of his life on film. Indeed, much of his energy went into writing a journal, which he began intensely around 1976 and continued up until his death in 1989, producing twenty volumes. De Antonio's journals constitute an impressive literary achievement. They are full of insights into his films, their genesis, funding, making, and reception, as well as his ideas on cinema, art, politics, and philosophy. The journals also contain engaging commentary on his life and times, presenting contemporary history from the point of view of a lifelong radical. De Antonio was an omnivorous reader who commented on major books and ideas of his time. Although there is one journal from the 1940s and a couple of journals in notebooks from the 1960s, most were written during his life with Nancy Mindlin, whom he married in 1978 and remained with until his death. Even though de talked for more than twenty years of writing a fictionalized autobiography, he never launched this project. Nor did he complete his book on Leo Castelli or the volume on George Bush he and former *Ramparts* editor Warren Hinckle were preparing. Instead, he directed his creative energies into his journal. Even there he practiced collage. Amid his many typed and handwritten pages he intermixed news clippings, magazine offprints, photos, postcards, letters, financial records, legal documents, FBI memoranda, and other miscellany.[83]

He did, however, manage to make one last film.

Figure 17. De Antonio gets a haircut from his wife Nancy in *Mr. Hoover and I* (1989).

Figure 18. At home in his kitchen, John Cage makes macrobiotic bread while talking with longtime friend de. Footage used in *Mr. Hoover and I* shot by Ron Mann.

▶
___

"A Middle-Aged Radical as Seen through the Eyes of His Government"

Although his output as a filmmaker slowed in the last decade of his life, de Antonio concluded his career with another surprising excursion into new cinematic form. With graceful good humor and a minimal budget (courtesy of the BBC's Channel Four), he made *Mr. Hoover and I*, an autobiographical swan song that deftly captured his political voice and vision in a revealing personal profile. It also provided an effective assault on J. Edgar Hoover, whose FBI compiled a 10,000-page dossier on him, chronicling events in his life that he had himself forgotten.

Released only months before his death, the film is disarmingly spare in production values. Gone are his predilections for archival compilation, interviews with power brokers, and the emphasis on montage. Instead, *Mr. Hoover and I* is constructed largely from four simple pieces of direct cinema. A handheld camera records composer John Cage making bread in his kitchen while de Antonio talks to him about art. The same informal style captures the director at home, talking casually while his wife Nancy cuts his hair. The offbeat selection of haircutting conjures up Andy Warhol's *Haircut,* one of the long-take études made just before the infamous *Drunk.* But de Antonio spoke of these personal, domestic scenes as contrasts to images of the rough, inhuman public sphere, the nurturing world of friends and lovers, food and drink, standing in contrast to the harsh, power-mongering world of politics. A third segment shows the director addressing a Dartmouth College audience after a screening of *Point of Order.* These scenes alternate with the footage that makes up the majority of the film: de Antonio himself standing before the brick walls of his Manhattan apartment, speaking directly to the camera about the shaping events of his life and their curious entangling with Hoover's pathological police state.

This unconventional documentary presents only a modest number of conventional documents (photographs, FBI files, a lone film clip of Hoover) to illustrate de Antonio's oral history. In their place, he offers up himself as evidence of a half century of official misconduct and government suppression. "I am the ultimate document," he says to the camera.

> And I am also the ultimate test of the First Amendment of the Constitution of the United States. I took on every single hard issue there was. And the government tried to stop me. And it tried to stop me in hard ways . . . everything from custodial detention (which is a concentration camp), to having theaters ruined, my films sabotaged. Anything that can be done to a filmmaker, short of killing me.

The words betray a megalomaniacal edge, but he delivers the dramatic rhetoric cogently. As is clear in both the intimate monologues and the footage of his public talks, de Antonio was a gifted speaker. With a rich, understated voice, a golden-tongued vocabulary, and the ability to make his pronouncements seem both natural and polished, he commands the screen like a Wellesian raconteur. Like Orson Welles, he was a cinematic innovator who struggled to finance his films, a connoisseur of the classics trying to work in a medium dominated by exploiters of popular formulas, and a highly inventive artist who combined his creative talents with a self-promotion made possible by a bigger-than-life personality.

Unlike Welles, de Antonio remained uncompromising, relegating himself to the fringes of independent filmmaking by insisting on making documentaries about things of political consequence. Making something for next to nothing remained an essential part of the ethic and aesthetic of his films. *Mr. Hoover and I,* he wrote in 1989, "is made of poor means but it is ambitious, more ambitious than *Batman*"[84]—Hollywood's latest blockbuster at the time.

Indeed, the film is ambitious on two levels. First, as a bold political summing up of a career and a period in history, the director declares on-screen: "This film, although it probably won't be seen by many people, is an attempt at subversion. This film is a film of opposition." Second, as a work of autobiography, *Mr. Hoover and I* reveals de Antonio's impressive ability to reinvent his formal sensibility even in the twilight of his career. It depicts de Antonio as a radical outsider who opposed the entire trajectory of the national security state throughout his life.

That the story of his life should also be a document of the political history of the Cold War era seemed inevitable. Although he had spent long periods in avowedly indulgent, nonpolitical pursuits, de Antonio became a lifelong subversive by state and self-definition. Joining leftist groups in his youth ensured the creation of his FBI file; making landmark antiestablishment films agitated the machinery of government surveillance. De Antonio compulsively recorded the events of his life, resulting in the substantial archive at the State Historical Society of Wisconsin. A complementary set of archives also documented his colorful life. Because of the ways in which J. Edgar Hoover ran the Federal Bureau of Investigation from 1924 to 1972, the minutiae of the life of Emile Francisco de Antonio were recorded in detail in thousands of pages.

The acquisition of these files merely confirmed and inflamed de Antonio's defiant political position. It also personalized the antagonism to a fairly obsessive degree. "I can't get over Hoover, ever," the narrator confesses at the beginning of the film. As a final act of comic revenge, he uses the FBI's documentation as a springboard for his cinematic autobiography. *Mr. Hoover and I* is quite literally an analysis of the parallel lives led by Hoover and de Antonio. The former, we are told from the beginning, is the "villain" of America in the twentieth century—the pathological head of the secret police, the destroyer of civil rights and liberties, the bizarre blackmailer, the anti-Semitic, racist hypocrite, the capricious and spiteful bureaucrat with unprecedented power, the master of deceit. Emile de Antonio is the defiant resister, the muckraker who exposes corruption in high places, the historian of the ugly underbelly of American political theater.

In this sense, the film reprises de Antonio's earlier cinematic explorations of American power. While describing the outrages of Hoover, he intermixes episodes about the cast of political players he had documented in his previous work. His on-camera history lessons tie the careers of these men to his archnemesis. He tells us: "J. Edgar Hoover was a close friend of Joe McCarthy's. They shared a tremendous amount. They were both liars. . . . Hoover fed him data," including lists of suspected Communists culled from the files. After cutting to a *Millhouse* clip showing the bureau chief making President Nixon an honorary FBI agent (the sole piece of archival footage used), de Antonio cuts back to himself. "Nixon and J. Edgar Hoover both lied . . . Nixon and Hoover were close . . . Hoover fed information to Congressperson Nixon." John F. Kennedy, too, is linked to this web. He was only able to win election to the Senate because his father allegedly "paid McCarthy to stay out of Massachusetts." De Antonio also displays a penchant for anecdotes that prick at the personalities of these figures. It was not enough that Hoover wanted to set up detention camps for ideological dissidents, he also skimmed money, freeloaded off the Mafia, closeted his sexual identity, and never let his chauffeur make left turns. At times these clandestine tales border on ad hominem jibes ("McCarthy frequently urinated in the pool"), but these are relegated to droll and joking asides.

Such comic counterpunches create one of the film's virtues—its sense of humor. Rather than simply paint a grim portrait of life in a police state, de Antonio shows Hoovermania run amok. Only by reading his FBI file, he tells us, did he discover that as a young man he answered the question "What do you want to be when you grow up?" by replying nonsensically, "I'd like to be an eggplant."[85] *Mr. Hoover and I* is most lively when the storyteller ridicules himself, finding it absurd that someone as marginalized as he could have ever been considered a threat to the nation. In a smooth stand-up delivery, he recounts to a college audience how his FBI dossier tried to paint him as "a major spy." "I'm not the right kind of person to be a spy." Later, in what is obviously a favorite line, he disputes the accuracy of an FBI charge that he "emptied his wallet" at a pro-Soviet meeting. "Anyone who knows me well knows that the only time I empty my wallet is in a bar." Cut to a scene of de getting his hair cut and joking with his wife Nancy about sending another batch of hair and nail clippings to his archive in Wisconsin—which, in fact, he did. Even the ashes of his cremated body were sent to his Madison repository, in a cigar can labeled "The Final Gesture." As if playing a prank on Mr. Hoover, de Antonio makes a mockery of the idea of official filekeeping.[86]

However, the fact that de Antonio sensed that a hybrid, autobiographical documentary was the next form that he needed to pursue hardly made him less innovative. *Mr. Hoover and I* testifies to his ability to shift gears creatively. Rather than remain limited to the "difficult," modernist methods of his earlier work, he found a way to remain honest to his clear political impulses while also experimenting with the new emerging conventions of personal documentary.

The film possesses stylistic qualities shared by modernist and postmodernist aesthetics. Theorists of both have pointed to the importance of self-reflexivity. *Mr. Hoover and I* extensively reflects on its own creation and production. Early in the film, de Antonio offers a philosophical justification for returning to the minimalist elements of *art brut*. Standing before a white wall, wearing a black turtleneck, he calls attention to the whir of the camera's motor, which is not blimped to silence it.

> I'm glad we're hearing the sound. Why should the process of any art not be included in whatever that art is?
> That kind of blind technical perfection which we seek so assiduously is what finally gives us a film—and a world of film—that winds up in . . . the garbage can of television . . . And that is what I'm uninterested in.

The movie also opens with, and continually deploys, the modernist device par excellence—the jump cut. It serves its Godardian function, erasing the illusion of seamlessness, but de Antonio also uses it more playfully. In his opening monologue to the camera, he tries to direct retakes of himself as the performer. His commands of "cut"/"don't cut" to the camera operator are exactly undone in the finished version we see. This is a serious film that has learned not to take itself too seriously. In fact, the director had considered making the film with a fictional veneer, having the great comic actor Rip Torn, another of his cronies, play the part of Emile de Antonio. This would have been truly inspired casting. Torn had just completed a peculiar hat trick, portraying the three U.S. presidents central to de Antonio's career: Nixon in the TV miniseries *Blind Ambition* (1979), Reagan in *Airplane II: The Sequel* (1982), and Lyndon Johnson in *J. Edgar Hoover* (1987).

The appearance of legendary composer John Cage in the film reinforces the playful postmodern posture. De Antonio often remarked that this friendship, which began in 1953 when both were unknown, was among the most important influences on his own life and art. (In 1982, he began shooting a film about John Cage, but it was aborted.)[87] The scene of the two together, talking casually while Cage shapes a green loaf of macrobiotic bread, reveals a tender side. This is de away from the podium and politics, indulging in the pleasures of everyday life, enjoying food and drink as much as intellectual conversation. One realizes too that it is important for de Antonio to have sophisticated, celebrated friends. Hanging out with John Cage is like the name-dropping in his journals. We first cut to Cage's kitchen after the director tells us, "I know everything about anyone of importance."

Again, the way in which the footage of the two is used in *Mr. Hoover and I* exhibits a modernist impulse but uses it in a tricksterish way. De Antonio intercuts the Cage scene in four seemingly random places. He prompts the composer to talk about his theories of chance operation and nonsyntactical art, essentially commenting on the way the film is being edited before us. However, de Antonio makes light of the seriousness by suddenly cutting away on comic beats. After his eccentric friend discourses on the mundane art of how to grease a loaf pan, de Antonio says, "At some point we're going to have to talk about indeterminacy and all that." Cage laughs, asking "What do you mean?" Cut to a photograph of Hoover and McCarthy posing in a backyard. Resume de Antonio's exposé of their crimes. Another non sequitur appears in the final sequence. After listening to Cage explain how he uses a computer program to devise random ordering, an off-camera de Antonio asks, "How is interval determined?" The puzzled-looking Cage says "What?" as we cut immediately to an empty space back in the de Antonio apartment. An impish de rises into the frame. Nancy takes a final snip at his hair. A quick kiss and de Antonio launches into his eggplant story. He is having fun making his final film.

Yet the form is new to him, albeit not purely original. The impression left after seeing de Antonio in his element and hearing him narrate his own life story is that *Mr. Hoover and I* fits well into the new documentary subgenres of autobiography and personal essay films that proliferated in the 1980s and 90s. "My father told me stories," he recounts at one point, a line that might characterize the sort of intimate diary films that have become a pronounced part of recent documentary. His film shares common elements not only with *Roger and Me* but also with the work of independent filmmakers such as Ross McElwee, Ralph Arlyck, and Chris Marker. Critic Phillip Lopate has categorized the work of these personal documentarists as "essay-films," movies that are intensely word-based, singular but broad-ranging in topic, and not image-driven.[88] Like Marker (*The Last Bolshevik*, 1992), de Antonio is part of the "old left," a dedicated radical and political modernist whose personal tastes in art run toward the literate, the complex, and the highbrow.

Like McElwee's *Sherman's March* (1986), de Antonio's film has a dual focus. Both movies mock the conventional biographical documentary. Both use a comic, sometimes wistful, first-person narration to chronicle the director's life. Yet both are also films that wind up being about something else too. *Sherman's March* pretends to be a film retracing the Union general's march to the sea, but becomes a road trip where one man looks for love (with a dose of no-nuke politics thrown in). *Mr. Hoover and I* manages to balance more carefully its twin goals, documenting the careers of its two subjects, while keeping political purpose front and center. It is also a more subversive treatment of the documentary format, replacing an organized narrative with a more fragmented and disjointed structure.

As the final sequence suggests, de Antonio was not so much following a contemporary trend as he was finally realizing the type of film he had tried to make about Bertrand Russell twenty-five years earlier—a filmed obituary. Like Russell, de Antonio was a rare breed who was capable of undertaking such a project: committed to ideas; strongwilled about talking them through; honest and insightful enough to see himself amid the historical forces of his time; articulate enough to tell the truth cogently and forcefully; and ultimately brave enough to face the camera and talk about his life just before his death.

But de Antonio chose not to end this final film on an elegiac or nostalgic note. As we see an audience exiting the Dartmouth lecture hall and hear applause die down, *Mr. Hoover and I* cuts to a last close-up of de Antonio talking to his camera. He clearly wishes he might have worked out a plan of political action that could have sparked a new activism against the Reagan/Bush reign. He speaks of social change, the fights against injustice, and the "high political moments." "We had politics in the sixties." But just as he seems to wax defeatist, he changes tack, exiting with words that are designed to inspire without sounding falsely optimistic.

> We no longer have politics. But I think we're on the verge of it. And I think that's why we're making this film. I think we're on the verge of a new kind of social change. History *doesn't* repeat itself. It only *appears* to repeat itself.
>
> The form of the new change cannot be predicted. We will be aware of that form as it takes place.

His words are deliberately reminiscent of the passage from Jean-Paul Sartre that de Antonio wrote in his World War II journal and which he reads aloud midway through *Mr. Hoover and I.*

> Man is absolute, but he is absolute in his own time, in his own environment, on his own earth . . .
>
> It is not by chasing after immortality that we will make ourselves eternal . . . but by fighting passionately in our own time, by loving it passionately, and by consenting to perish entirely with it.[89]

In leaving his last will and testament on film in this way, de Antonio aptly summed up his own contribution to film, art, and politics: fighting passionately and loving it.

Emile de Antonio died of a heart attack outside his Manhattan home on December 19, 1989. Although he did not live to see the theatrical release of *Mr. Hoover and I,* recognition of his lifetime of achievement surrounded its festival run. When it was screened at the Virginia Festival of American Film in November 1989, the director accepted an award for Excellence in Documentary Filmmaking (Frederick Wiseman having been the only other recipient). De Antonio had also been scheduled to appear with *Mr. Hoover and I* at the Sundance U.S. Film Festival the following January. Learning of his death, the festival organizers dedicated the documentary prize to de Antonio. "He contended and informed, and over the decades while doing so, changed our idea of how an effective documentary could look," said Sundance officials. "[De Antonio's] passing is a loss for us all, particularly if his notions of film are neither respected nor carried forward."[90]

▶ Denouement: The De Antonio Legacy

De Antonio's later films can be seen as noble failures, as experiments that dared to explore new territory but failed to attain the power and audiences of his earlier work. Part of the reason was financial. The increasingly isolated Marxist radical was unable to raise the funds he had gotten when attacking Joe McCarthy, investigating the Kennedy assassination, scrutinizing the Vietnam War, and taking on Richard Nixon—all of which were popular causes for liberal progressives. With the fragmentation of the left after 1975, he lacked the inspiration and support of powerful opposition movements to nourish his cinematic art. His own political passions continued to burn, but they received less and less sustenance from history itself. His legendary dissipation also contributed to his diminished output for a time, but he controlled his drinking during his later years. As production opportunities dwindled, he invested more control over his film library, promoting videocassette sales and film retrospectives.

In retrospect, de Antonio's films are divided between attacks on the power elite of Cold War America and exhortative depictions of oppositional forces, ranging from peace candidate Eugene McCarthy to the militant Weatherpeople, from the celebrated cultural dissenters of *Painters Painting* to the grassroots activists of the Plowshares movement. As an appropriate end point, *Mr. Hoover and I* brings the two together in a work of self-representation, posing the corrupt head of the corrupt establishment against the ultimate radical dissenter.

As cinema scholar Bill Nichols has suggested, contemporary filmmakers who have collectively lost the ability to articulate in "the voice of documentary" would do well to learn from the technique and political clarity of Emile de Antonio. His legacy, from the pathfinding *Point of Order* to his valedictory *Mr. Hoover and I,* offers a paradigm of alterity. To be sure, not all of his work displayed exemplary film craft. His lack of technical polish is sometimes off-putting to viewers. The primitive graininess of *Point of Order* might be made a virtue, but difficulty in synchronizing sound and image tracks nearly prevented the release of *Mr. Hoover and I.* Even in his best compilation work, de Antonio worked with footage that had been poorly reproduced, sometimes bootlegged. *Painters Painting* aside, his films lacked the surface beauty of his painter friends' creations.

Despite these difficulties, the success of his films creates a model for filmmakers who seek alternatives—formal, political, and economic. De Antonio, without the benefit of technical training, took the tools of documentary cinema and applied the aesthetic principles of the modern and modernist artists he admired and promoted. His method of synthesizing new and archival footage into forceful, historically informed arguments went against existing film practices. He challenged the newsreel's voice of God tradition and shunned the ambiguities of the new direct cinema, denouncing the myth of cinema verité at every turn.

A gifted fabulist offscreen, de Antonio often overstated the uniqueness of his films. Journalists and cinema scholars have often reprinted his claims. *Point of Order* and *In the Year of the Pig* have been rightly honored for their influence and editorial brilliance. But de Antonio did not invent the compilation film. Jay Leyda's book *Films Beget Films* appeared in the same year as *Point of Order* and chronicled the long history of the compilation genre.

Figure 19. Emile de Antonio, ca. 1987, in a portrait made for the Museum of Modern Art's film catalog. Photograph taken and provided by William Sloan.

De Antonio also doubly mischaracterized his status as the inventor of documentaries free of narration. First, he had many precursors: Robert Flaherty, Leni Riefenstahl, and Soviet montage artists such as Esfir Shub and Dziga Vertov used no voice-overs. The first generation of cinema verité also abandoned omniscient narrators—for reasons similar to de Antonio's. Yet he habitually disparaged fellow documentarians Frederick Wiseman, Marcel Ophuls, Richard Leacock, and the Maysles brothers. Second, de Antonio makes use of his own velvety baritone in most of his films—in the prologue to *Point of Order,* intermittently in *Rush to Judgment, Charge and Countercharge, In the Year of the Pig,* and *Millhouse,* as well as on camera in *Painters Painting, Underground,* and *Mr. Hoover and I.*

Yet his contributions to the formal aspects of documentary remain considerable. A self-described "radical scavenger," he constructed original works from neglected materials. "My method is collage," he wrote at the time of *Year of the Pig.* "Certain pieces of film make a new thing when they rub up against other pieces of film, something like (when it works) that the whole is greater than the sum of its parts."[91] As he sometimes suggested, de Antonio was obviously extending the ideas of Soviet directors Vsevolod Pudovkin and Sergei Eisenstein. As a Marxist, he was a logical heir to Eisenstein's principles of montage. He retained the term *collage* from his indebtedness to the noncinematic visual arts, but never developed a fully articulated film theory as his predecessor did. Rather than editing sequences for exacting cognitive response (montage), de Antonio more often achieved the indeterminate, open effect of a collage artist, cutting and pasting elements from disparate sources—kinescopes and newsreels, color and black-and-white stock, videotape and film, experimental music and old phonograph records, folk songs and high oratory, home movies and government propaganda.

At their best, de Antonio's cinematic experiments create ideological tension and narrative drama through the strategic juxtaposition of cinematic elements. Other attempts are less successful, striking the monotones of propaganda, as in *Underground* and *In the King of Prussia.* His most provocative films require an active audience to take the different perspectives and construct meaning, to negotiate the complex pieces of historical narrative. Ironically, those same films have become difficult for later audiences. Interpreting them requires historical knowledge of the Cold War. Films produced by de Antonio in the years of the pig were made as interventions in ongoing political battles. Their topicality means that their immediacy diminishes for viewers who lack that lived experience. Moreover, their subject matter has been submitted to many cinematic treatments and

Figure 20. Actor Martin Sheen (left), director Ron Mann (seated), and poet Tuli Kupferberg consult with de Antonio during preproduction for Mann's film *Listen to the City* (1984). Reproduced by permission of Art Gallery of Ontario.

the clichés of TV documentary. His pioneering representations stand to be overwhelmed by the images and narratives that have followed.[92]

De Antonio, however, respected his audiences and was willing to pay the price of losing some viewers in order to produce challenging works. Such an aesthetic strategy places his work in the tradition of modernism. It also puts de Antonio in a democratic documentary tradition that trusts popular intelligence to draw appropriate conclusions from complex work.

This democratic impulse led to another significant contribution Emile de Antonio left to an alternative sphere of cinema and other media. Throughout his career he hired, encouraged, and promoted young film talents who did not have access to jobs in the media industries. Many went on to make their own films or do other significant work in both independent and commercial production. Some of de Antonio's mentorships include:

- Dan Drasin. After making his first film at eighteen, he worked for Robert Drew Associates. He later coedited *Rush to Judgment* and continues to work in documentary.
- Robert Duncan, hired by de Antonio to edit *Point of Order* despite having virtually no experience, went on to work with the Maysles brothers and became a longtime producer-director for ABC television.
- Robert Primes, the commercial cinematographer who shot *Rush to Judgment,* went on to become a director of photography in

Hollywood film (e.g., *A Murder of Crows,* 1999; *Rumblefish,* 1983) and television.
- Mary Lampson, de Antonio's closest collaborator in the seventies, worked on Barbara Kopple's *Harlan County, USA* (1976, Best Documentary Oscar) before turning to educational television.
- Lynzee Klingman got her first film credit for reassembling *Point of Order* and other footage into *Charge and Countercharge*. She then expertly cut de Antonio's Vietnam film. From there she worked on the Oscar-winning documentary *Hearts and Minds* (1974) and became a Hollywood feature editor, earning an Academy Award nomination for her first effort, *One Flew over the Cuckoo's Nest* (1975). She remains one of the industry's top editors.
- Marc Weiss was an assistant on four de Antonio films and continued to work in independent documentary. In the 1990s, he was executive producer of the PBS series *P.O.V.*
- Cinda Firestone Fox, an assistant editor, went on to direct her own documentary feature, *Attica* (1974).
- Glenn Silber produced the documentaries *The War at Home* (1979) and *El Salvador: Another Vietnam* (1981).
- Allan Siegel, coproducer on *America Is Hard to See,* later made documentaries at Third World Newsreel. He teaches video production at the Art Institute of Chicago.
- Judy Irola, cinematographer on *In the King of Prussia,* has since become only the third woman invited to join the American Society of Cinematographers. She teaches at the University of Southern California and has won awards at the Cannes and Sundance film festivals.
- Ron Mann attributes his ability to break into filmmaking to de Antonio's active mentorship. He has since directed acclaimed documentaries, including *Poetry in Motion* (1982) and *Comic Book Confidential* (1988), as well as the CD-ROM version of *Painters Painting*.
- Peter Wintonick wrote about de Antonio in Canadian film magazines, befriended him, and produced a video documentary, *The New Cinema* (1983), in which de Antonio appeared. He and Mark Achbar later made *Manufacturing Consent: Noam Chomsky and the Media* (1992).

Often de Antonio gave such talents more responsibility than their experience might have warranted. But it was a way to produce films for very little money, relying on the enthusiasm and exploitability of youth. It also helped perpetuate the heritage of radical filmmaking into a new generation.

This method of production represents the model that de Antonio's career offers as an alternative to the big business of the motion picture industry and the conventions of nonfiction film. His documentaries were funded by a few like-minded individuals, never by government grants or commercial studios. The commission by Britain's Channel Four for *Mr. Hoover and I* was the exception. Costs were minuscule by industry standards because he eschewed standard production values, seeing them as a political compromise from the start.

Finally, as a Marxist, he might be expected to have sought alternative methods of collective production. De Antonio did repeatedly attempt to work with film collectives, but paradoxically and inevitably he insisted on imposing his maverick vision on any documentary he produced. Just as he supported the New American Cinema Group, he later lent his name to less successful efforts such as "The Film Collective, Inc." With Charles Burnett, Haile Gerima, Jacqueline Shearer, and others he wrote a manifesto promoting independent films of "low budget" and "high ambition."[93]

As this document and the list of names above demonstrate, de Antonio was considerably ahead of his time in actively promoting the careers of women and excluded minorities in the film world. Renee Tajima, in her *Village Voice* obituary, remembered him from her days at Third World Newsreel:

> For the most part we were young women of color making movies. The last person we'd look up to is a sixtyish, WASP male who still wore dockers and Oxford shirts. But De *was* the dean. He shared an irreverence for the same types (the establishment, cinema verité-ists, liberals) and had made radical filmmaking a respectable vocation.[94]

His collaborations on *America Is Hard to See* (on which he shared creative credit with five young activists) and *Underground* are further examples of his democratic practices. Ultimately, however, he was—as he often said—a bad party member. De Antonio exerted his independence in his film work much as he was unable to commit to political groups for long periods of time.

Always experimenting, the restless filmmaker left an impressive body of finished work and a wealth of ideas, many found in the interviews and writings collected here. Our Emile de Antonio reader attempts to make the connections between his films, aesthetics, politics, and life better understood. Although we have tried to present a useful biographical context to his work in documentary film, the force of his personality is difficult to capture. Words and images on paper can only suggest the charismatic presence and intensity that all who knew him acknowledged. "Just one of the most interesting people who ever lived," cinematographer Judy Irola said of de, with whom she maintained a "highly charged friendship" in the last decade of his life. "Making a film with him was no less than wondering. He was a very complicated man. He loved his own contradictions. That's what made him an intellectual."[95] We hope that his work will be viewed and reviewed, debated and appreciated as an important cinematic legacy, and that his art, politics, and life will receive the attention they deserve.

◆

NOTES

1. The most important studies of de Antonio films are Thomas Waugh (Summer 1976), Bill Nichols (1983), and Randolph Lewis (2000). The State Historical Society of Wisconsin (SHSW) houses the Emile de Antonio Collection in its Archives Division in Madison. The papers include his unpublished diaries (hereafter Journals, vols. I–XV), as well as correspondence, government documents, and extensive files on film production, including legal and financial records, scripts, production notes, and promotional materials. Among the nonprint artifacts are films (249 cans), audio recordings, and videotapes.

    Most historical surveys of film mention de Antonio, and describe his films as historically significant and aesthetically innovative. Kristin Thompson and David Bordwell (1994), for example, describe de Antonio as the politically "engaged filmmaker who consistently achieved [a] scale of commercial recognition" for feature-length documentaries. They credit him with pioneering a new "synthetic format" for documentaries, blending cinema verité, interviews, and compilation techniques in a way that inspired a generation of filmmakers to create exciting new films like *Harlan County, USA* (1975), *The Atomic Cafe* (1982), and *Common Threads: Stories from the Quilt* (1989). Bill Nichols's *Representing Reality* (1992)—a book dedicated to the memory of Emile de Antonio—makes comparable claims. In *An Introduction to Film Studies* (1996), Paul Wells concludes his discussion of documentary by citing de Antonio as an exemplary practitioner who "imbued his films with Marxist politics and fierce intellectual criticism of American institutional hypocrisy." While acknowledging his historical importance, such accounts treat the filmmaker's work only briefly. Even a study like Peter Stevens's collection of radical cinema criticism from *Jump Cut* follows this pattern. "A few major films from these counter-cinemas are widely known," Stevens begins, "for example, the documentaries of U.S. filmmaker Emile de Antonio, such as *In the Year of the Pig* . . . and *Millhouse*." Yet, after identifying de Antonio as North America's leading practitioner of counter-cinema, the book makes no further mention of him. Thompson and Bordwell, *Film History: An Introduction* (New York: McGraw-Hill, 1994), pp. 561, 645–46, 671–73, 692, 800; Wells, "The Documentary Form," in *An Introduction to Film Studies*, ed. Jill Nelmes (New York: Routledge, 1996), p. 188; Stevens, *Jump Cut: Hollywood, Politics and Counter Cinema* (New York: Praeger, 1985), p. 16.

2. Richard Barsam, *Nonfiction Film: A Critical History* (Bloomington: Indiana University Press, 1992). *The International Dictionary of Film and Filmmakers* goes so far as to dub de Antonio "the great precursor of scratch video and sampling"[!] (Chicago: St. James Press, 1990, pp. 196–97).

3. Georgakas (1990), 529.

4. Hertzberg (1964), n.p. In correspondence and journals, de Antonio signed (and typed) his name with the lone, lowercase letter "d." In published articles, his nickname has been conventionally printed as "De." Friends varied in their spellings of his name but most often used the lowercase prefix of his Italian surname, referring to him as "de." We therefore use that form—de—throughout the reader, unless quoting directly from an original source that does otherwise.

5. Interview with Madeline de Antonio, May 1977. Interview with Warren Green, July 1978; and Journals, passim. In the SHSW.

6. Emile de Antonio interview, ca. 1969. In SHSW file titled "I was born in Scranton . . ." De Antonio claims: "when I graduated from college, I became a longshoreman in Baltimore. The reason for becoming a longshoreman is probably hard to determine—the real truth of why I became a longshoreman. . . . Part of it was simply because I was waiting to enlist in the military, but the other reason was that, while I was at Harvard I became involved in radical politics. And it seemed to me sort of ridiculous, and hypocritical, to enter the normal world without

ever having had any experience in the working class world."
7. *Journals*, X.21 (January 1979).
8. Letter to Mel Novikoff, October 1, 1971. SHSW.
9. Ibid.
10. *Journals*, III. 111–29 (August 23, 1977), and his account of the event in the introduction to the book edition of *Painters Painting*. See also Calvin Tompkins, *Off the Wall: Robert Rauschenberg and the Art World of Our Time* (New York: Penguin, 1980), pp. 147–49. Documents detailing de Antonio's relation to the New York avant-garde are collected in the 1995 Voyager CD-ROM *Emile de Antonio's Painters Painting*.
11. *The 25-Year Retrospective Concert of the Music of John Cage*. Recorded in performance at Town Hall, New York, May 15, 1958. Three LP boxed set. George Avakian, producer, 1959. See Avakian, "About the Concert" (liner notes). Virgil Thompson and others compared the riotous event to the infamous premiere of Igor Stravinsky's *Rite of Spring* (1913; *Saturday Review of Literature*, June 1960). See also David Revill, *The Roaring Silence; John Cage: A Life* (New York: Arcade, 1992), pp. 190–91; Richard Kostelanetz, ed., *John Cage: An Anthology* (New York: Da Capo, 1991), p. 220. For an account of Cage's work with de Antonio's wife Lois Long, see Joan Rettacek, ed., *Musicage: Cage Muses on Words, Art, Music* (Wesleyan University Press, 1996), pp. 89ff. John Cage dedicated his "Music for Piano, nos. 69–84" to Lois and Emile de Antonio (May 1956) and his "Atlas Elipticalis" (1961) to Emile de Antonio and others.
12. Frank Stella named a painting in his Purple Series "D" (1961–63). *Journals* II.61ff. (January 14, 1977). Warhol and Pat Hackett, *POPism: The Warhol '60s* (New York: Harcourt Brace Jovanovich, 1980), pp. 3–4; Tina S. Fredericks, "Remembering Andy," in Jesse Kornbluth, *Pre-Pop Warhol* (New York: Panache Press, 1988), p. 13.
13. Quoted in Jean W. Ross (1986), p. 97. The script for the film was published by Grove Press in 1961. See also Blaine Allan, "The Making (and Unmaking) of *Pull My Daisy*," *Film History* 2 (1988): 185–203; David E. James, *Allegories of Cinema: American Film in the Sixties* (Princeton, N.J.: Princeton University Press, 1989); Jack Sargeant, *The Naked Lens: An Illustrated History of Beat Cinema* (London: Creation Books, 1997).
14. See the numerous references to this film pairing in the earliest issues of Jonas Mekas's journal *Film Culture*. Also, Parker Tyler, "For Shadows, Against Pull My Daisy," in *The Three Faces of the Film: The Art, the Dream, the Cult* (South Brunswick, N.J.: A. S. Barnes, 1967), pp. 105–20.
15. Mekas (1982), 8. Mekas recorded the camaraderie of the Group even in their leanest times. His journal noted that Christmas 1960 was celebrated by de Antonio, Peter Bogdanovich, Sheldon and Diane Rochlin, and himself with Daniel Talbot, eating kielbasa and drinking vodka in the offices of the New Yorker Theater. "Peter was imitating Dylan Thomas and Orson Welles. De got completely drunk. We all spilled into the street and continued our party outside."
16. "First Statement," *Film Culture* 22–23 (Summer 1961).
17. Peter Bogdanovich wrote program notes for Talbot in the early 1960s. He had also been a member of The Group and a prolific film journalist. He was the only member of this New York-based circle to go to Hollywood. Film critic Pauline Kael helped de Antonio distribute his films on the West Coast in the early 1960s. See their correspondence in the de Antonio archives.
18. Dan Drasin correspondence, June 26, 1998. Harold Louis Humes was also cofounder of the *Paris Review* and author of the novels *Men Die* (1959) and *The Underground City* (1958), both published by Random House. Correspondence with Immy Humes, July 1998. When a routine permit for Sunday afternoon folk-singing sessions in Washington Square Park was denied by the park commissioner, Israel Young led dozens of singers in a protest. Police overreacted as hundreds of people gathered to sing. The ban became a cause célèbre and a political football. Protest "sing-ins" grew throughout April and May until Mayor Robert Wagner overturned the ban. Opposition to the benign, amateur folk music performances stemmed from fears of the Village's beatniks, racial integration of the park, and class divisions between factions within Greenwich Village. In the 1961 *New York Times*, see "Folk Singers Riot in Washington Sq.," April 10, p. 1; "Morris Will Make Informal Survey on Lifting Ban," April 11, p. 1; "Revolt in Washington Square," April 11, 1961, p. 36; In the *Village Voice*, see "Sunday Serenade in Square," April 13, p. 1; "Cops, 'Beatniks,' and Facts," April 13, p. 7; "'Right to Sing Rally' Scores Ban by Morris; Ready to Fight," April 20, p. 1.
19. Drasin and Vanderbeek both received Ford Foundation film development grants in 1964. Drasin, working for the prestigious Robert Drew Associates documentary outfit, became the first cinematographer to shoot synchronous-sound combat footage in Vietnam. Dan Drasin correspondence, June 26, 1998; Daniel Einstein, *Special Edition: A Guide to Network Television Documentary Series and Special News Reports, 1955–1979* (Metuchen, N.J.: Scarecrow, 1987); *Film Comment* (Winter 1964): 36.
20. Although the two later had a falling out over the authorship of *Point of Order*, de Antonio's

version of the film's origins do not substantially contradict the details Talbot wrote in the *New York Times*, January 12, 1964, p. X9. (Talbot took no active production role, though he played a key role in handling the business affairs and promotion of the film.)
21. *Variety*, October 16, 1961; "TV Interviews as Theatrical Fare," *Variety*, October 18, 1961, p. 27; *Hollywood Reporter*, October 17, 1961.
22. *Film Comment* (Fall/Winter 1967): 3; "Notes on the Film of Fact," *IT: Festival Supplement*, ca. 1967, in Journals, XI.7 (February 5, 1980).
23. Robert Duncan reports that he and de Antonio wanted to include an episode they called "the chuckle scene." McCarthy and Welch engaged in a wordplay about whether or not McCarthy and Army Secretary Stevens had been serious or "chuckled" during their discussions about David Schine's military status. For Duncan and de Antonio it was evidence that McCarthy was playing entirely to the media public and had little true ideological concern about communism. The sequence was omitted because it did not fit into the film's dramatic structure. Duncan interview, July 11, 1998. See U.S. Senate, 83/2d, Special Subcommittee on Investigations, Committee on Government Operations, "Hearings before the Special Senate Investigation on Charges and Countercharges involving: Sect. of the Army Robert T. Stevens . . . and Senator Joe McCarthy, Roy M. Cohn, and Francis P. Carr," June 17, 1954, pp. 2960–63.
24. De Antonio artist-friend Larry Rivers painted a huge canvas promoting the festival on a Broadway billboard and designed the festival's poster. *New York Times*, August 21, 1963, p. 38; Andrew Sarris, "Films," *Village Voice*, September 5, p. 9; "New York's Film Festival Presents," *New York Times*, September 8, p. X9; "10 Cinemaniacal Days at Lincoln Center," *Village Voice*, September 12, p. 16; "Festivals 1963," *Film Quarterly* 17.2 (Winter 1963–64): 19; Parker Tyler, "The Atomic Age at New York City's First Film Festival," in *The Three Faces of the Film* (New York: T. Yseloff, 1960), pp. 105–20. It is clear from the both contemporaneous and retrospective accounts of the atmosphere that led to the production of *Point of Order* that de Antonio and his colleagues were part of the charmed cultural moment of "Greenwich Village 1963," a phenomenon Sally Banes documents so well in her book of the same name (Durham, N.C.: Duke University Press, 1993).
25. Stanley Kauffmann, "After the Ball Was Over," *New Republic*, October 5, 1963, p. 33. De Antonio claimed that festival organizer Richard Roud kept *Point of Order* out of the New York Film Festival because its TV origins meant it was technically not a film. But the Museum of Modern Art screenings were certainly part of the festival event.
26. MacDonald (1963), 77.
27. Sontag (1964), 292.
28. Daniel Talbot interview, July 2, 1998. According to Talbot, the deal enabled him and de Antonio to pay off the debt they had incurred in making the film. Short-term profits were small, but the film continues to be screened and was theatrically revived in 1998. More than 1,500 videocassette editions were sold to schools by Zenger Video. Sander Weiner interview and correspondence, August 1998. Eichelbaum (1964), 19; Grenier (1964); *Paris Herald-Tribune*, May 10, 1964.
29. *Firing Line*, nos. 86–87, January 19, 1968. Producer Warren Steibel provided gracious assistance in locating the transcripts. Quotations taken from no. 86, pp. 1, 9; no. 87, pp. 1, 11, 23.
30. ABC showed the film without commercial interruption sponsored by Xerox. Little attention was given to the telecast because TV journalists, viewers, and political commentators were focused on the assassination of Martin Luther King that had occurred the night before. Bill, "The Confrontation," *Variety*, April 10, 1968; reprinted in *Variety Television Reviews*, vol. 9 (New York: Garland, 1989).
31. In 1979, the Paul Newman edition of *Point of Order* was syndicated to local television stations. Ellen Oumano, "Interview with Emile de Antonio about Paul Newman," unpublished transcript, n.d., SHSW.
32. Michael Straight covered the hearings for the *New Republic*. See Michael Straight, *Trial by Television* (Boston: Beacon Press, 1954). In *Life*, see "The Men McCarthy Made Famous," May 17, 1954, pp. 47–48; "Cross-Examination with Jests and Jabs," June 14, p. 27; "Have You No Sense of Decency?" June 21, p. 40.
33. According to Talbot, the ending was de Antonio's conception. New Yorker distributed most of de Antonio's films until the 1980s, although the partners had clashed when de Antonio excised Talbot's screen credit ("Based on an idea by Daniel Talbot") from the original negative in 1963. It was restored to release prints. Robert Duncan, the film's principal editor, also complained of having his screen credit deleted in a New Yorker videocassette version of *Point of Order*.
34. Weiner, "Radical Scavenging" (1971), 9.
35. The divorce was unusually lengthy and acrimonious. De Antonio brought a suit against her subsequent husband, Arthur Solomon of Harvard Medical School, charging that he "wrongfully and wickedly debauched and carnally knew" Marilyn A. B. de Antonio, enticing her to leave him. De Antonio's attorneys tried to subpoena her passport to prove she

had traveled with Solomon while still married. But the subpoena and suit were dismissed on Fifth Amendment grounds. *De Antonio v. Solomon* Civ. A. No. 65–679, U.S. District Court of Massachusetts, 41 F.R.D. 447 (1966); 42–F.R.D. 320 (1967).

36. Callie Angell, adjunct curator of the Andy Warhol Film Project, Whitney Museum of American Art, generously shared her notes on *Drunk*, based on her viewing of the camera original. Correspondence, August 18 and 24, 1998. Film critic Sheldon Renan was present at the filming of *Drunk* and published a description of it in *Moderator* (Summer 1965), which was found in Warhol's Time Capsule #55 (Archives Study Center, Andy Warhol Museum, Pittsburgh), also provided here by Angell. See Emile de Antonio, "Point of Order (Hic)," *Village Voice*, January 28, 1980, p. 42; *New York Times*, October 17, 1971; Debra Miller (1994); Billy Name (1996). Telephone interview with Billy Name, August 14, 1998.
37. Journals, X.4–6 (September 25, 1979).
38. Journals, II.71–77 (February 6–9, 1977). In 1970, de Antonio's view of Schoenman was publicly vindicated. The dying Russell issued a lengthy memorandum separating himself from his former assistant, who had been deported from Britain in 1968. Schoenman had persistently caused trouble in international relations (and inside the British and American left) by abusing his power as Russell's supposed spokesman. Russell censured Schoenman in part because of de Antonio's letter of resignation from the Peace Foundation. "I feel," de Antonio wrote, "that Ralph Schoenman has captured the Foundation and turned it into a monolithic expression of his own limited interests. . . . I also find it painful to be unable to conclude the film about you which I have begun." "Bertrand Russell's Political Testament," *Black Dwarf* (September 5, 1970), p. 9.
39. Interview with Ben Sonnenberg Jr., June 30, 1998. Sonnenberg most aptly characterized de Antonio in saying, "de was a great fabulist—which is not to say a liar."
40. Weiner, "Radical Scavenging" (1971), 7.
41. Eventually Hill did tell her story again, making media appearances and publishing a book at the time of Oliver Stone's *JFK*. Bill Sloan with Jean Hill, *JFK: The Last Dissenting Witness* (Gretna, La.: Pelican, 1992).
42. Lane (1968); *Times* (London), January 30, 1967, p. 1.
43. Later, he regretted Lane's on-screen prominence and cut scenes from a video release version of *Rush to Judgment*. The move was as much personal as it was aesthetic, if de Antonio's harsh assessments of Lane are any indication.
44. *Film Comment* (Fall/Winter 1967): 3.
45. Terry de Antonio (1972), 20.
46. *Artforum* (March 1973): 79–83.
47. *Film Comment* (Fall/Winter 1967): 19.
48. Emile de Antonio, "Movies and Me" (1974). The film did not actually appear in the year of the pig (boar), which fell in 1959 and 1971.
49. Crowdus and Georgakas (1982), 27.
50. Jonathan Schell, *The Village of Ben Suc* (1967), *The Military Half: An Account of Destruction in Quang Ngai and Quang Tin* (1968), and *The Fate of the Earth* (1982), all by Knopf, New York.
51. "A Film on the War in Vietnam." Letter sent by de Antonio to investors in the film, June 26, 1968. SHSW. Also quoted in Asnen (1968).
52. Weiner, "Radical Scavenging" (1971), 6.
53. Terry de Antonio (1972), 19.
54. Shaw was the subject of the 1989 Hollywood film *Glory*. Barbara Correll (1991) offers perhaps the most insightful and thorough reading of *In the Year of the Pig* to date, contrasting *In the Year of the Pig* with *Glory*. She points to de Antonio's history of the Vietnam War as an exemplary anticipation of the theoretical ideas of Foucault's "genealogical" historiography and of deconstruction.
55. Waugh (Summer 1976), 33–39.
56. Kael (1969), 177.
57. EYR Campus Programs distribution publicity for the film (no date), SHSW. In a letter to Jay Murphy (March 30, 1970), de Antonio wrote: "The chinks in the system interest me and the film is about the rational liberal's last hope. I'm not that rational nor a liberal but [Eugene] McCarthy was impressive to me in the way he adhered to sweet and lovely liberal ideas about an America which no longer exists, in the way he resignedly watched the system crush him and because he is one of the few 'heads' operating in Washington. . . . [McCarthy and I] had a nostalgic, snowy weekend together in Hanover on the second anniversary of the New Hampshire campaign; he did, after all, knock out LBJ. Given today's Washington it almost seems like a ghastly mistake."
58. David C. Hohe correspondence, July 7, 1998. Despite his role in arranging the film, Martin Peretz scarcely remembered *America Is Hard to See* when queried about it. Peretz correspondence, July 23, 1998. See Mellen (1971), 28.
59. Eugene McCarthy, *The Year of the People* (Garden City, N.Y.: Doubleday, 1969), p. 261.
60. Journals, X.
61. *New York Free Press,* September 26–October 2, 1968. The *East Village Other* also interviewed de Antonio about the Checkers film at the time of Nixon's election.
62. *Variety,* October 13, 1971, pp. 1, 22; *Interview,* February 1972, p. 28. The kinescope of the Checkers speech (aka "The Fund Broadcast") was never copyrighted, but only a few copies existed between 1952 and 1970. When

de Antonio came into possession of the bootleg print used in *Millhouse*, New Yorker Films began renting 16mm prints of "Checkers" and continued doing so despite FBI investigations. Nixon kept his own print in his private film library and did not deed it to the government as he did his other prepresidency motion pictures. Although there is no evidence of a deliberate suppression of the film, only after de Antonio's handiwork did the visual portion of Nixon's performance become widely available. "Fund Broadcast" (the Checkers speech), MFF MPR# 168 MPPCA, recorded September 23, 1952, at El Capitan NBC-TV Studio, Los Angeles; 27 minutes, Nixon Library and Birthplace, Yorba Linda, California.
63. Cocks (1971), 87.
64. *Liberation News Service*, April 15, 1972, pp. 12–14.
65. *Variety*, October 6, 1971, p. 16.
66. Jack Caulfield, "Memorandum for John W. Dean on Emile de Antonio," the White House, October 15, 1971. Reprinted in *Take One*, April 7–23, 1975, p. 12. John Dean, *Blind Ambition* (New York: Simon and Schuster, 1976), p. 40. Caulfield became less concerned about *Millhouse* in subsequent memos when FBI agents assessed that New Yorker Films was run like an "amateur" outfit.
67. Buckley (1971), II-11.
68. Critiques of *Millhouse* include *Newsweek*, November 15, 1971, pp. 120–21; *D.C. Gazette*, November 15, 1971, pp. 8–9; *New York*, October 4, 1971, p. 63; *Nation*, October 18, 1971, pp. 381–82; *Washington Post*, October 21, 1971, p. C1; *Wall Street Journal*, November 11, 1971, p. 16; *Rolling Stone*, January 20, 1972, p. 58.
69. Interview with Charles Guggenheim, July 1998; Weiss (March 1974): 19.
70. Emile de Antonio, "My Brush with Painting" (1984), 10.
71. Perreault (1973), 32; Alloway (1973), 475–76.
72. *Osawatomie* took its name from a battle in which abolitionist John Brown defeated an army of slaveholders.
73. Robert Friedman edited the *Daily Spectator*, Columbia University's student newspaper, March 1968–March 1969, then worked on his own alternative journal, *UR: University Review*, until it folded in 1976. Copies of *Prairie Fire* had been left anonymously at *UR* and many other publications. During the making of *Underground*, de Antonio moved his office into the Union Square facility that *UR* was vacating. Friedman also wrote for *More* (an alternative journalism review), edited the *Village Voice* in the mid-1980s, and became assistant managing editor at *Life* magazine. Interviews with Robert Friedman (September 10, 1998) and Marc Weiss (August 1998).
74. Journals, V.7.
75. Ibid.
76. Biskind and Weiss (1975). De Antonio appeared frequently on WBAI-FM, Pacifica Radio's New York affiliate.
77. *Emile de Antonio v. Clarence Kelley* (1979), Civ. A. 75-1071, October 30, 1975. Also *Emile de Antonio v. William E. Colby and Central Intelligence Agency*. Nesson's cocounsel was Terry Lenzner, later a noted Washington investigator who worked for the Clinton White House. De Antonio met Fern Nesson on a trip to Israel with Martin Peretz in January 1975. She convinced him that her husband could help obtain FBI files via the Freedom of Information Act. Charles and Fern Nesson interviewed October 1, 1998. See also *Levitch v. CBS* 495 F. Supp. 640 (S.D.N.Y. 1980), in which de Antonio and twenty-five other independent documentary filmmakers unsuccessfully tried to sue the three major TV networks for conspiring to restrict their First Amendment rights by airing only documentaries produced in-house.
78. Peck (1983), 19.
79. This concept might have been inspired by the play and film written by Daniel Berrigan, *The Trial of the Catonsville Nine*, which provided a dramatic reconstruction of the trial in which the Berrigan brothers and others were convicted for the destruction of draft board files in Catonsville, Maryland, an act of protest against the military in the Vietnam War. When *In the King of Prussia* played in Germany in 1983, Berrigan's play was performed in conjunction with it.
80. Interviews in 1998 with Father Daniel Berrigan (July 8), Judy Irola (September 19), and Richard Hoover (September 27). Hoover described de Antonio as "a presence in the neighborhood" around St. Peter's. His film production office at Union Square and 17th Street was near the church and theater (on 20th Street).
81. James Munves, "Majority of 8," *Nation*, May 7, 1990, p. 621; Fred A. Wilcox, *Uncommon Martyrs: The Berrigans, the Catholic Left, and the Plowshares Movement* (Reading, Mass.: Addison-Wesley, 1991). Wilcox's book is one of the few writings about Plowshares or the Berrigans that mentions *In the King of Prussia*, saying only that the movement had failed to take advantage of "Emile de Antonio's powerful film" (p. xiii). Bob Hohler, "U.S. Strips Berrigan of Visiting Privileges after Woman's Sit-in," *Boston Globe*, April 1, 1998. In 1998, Philip Berrigan was again in federal prison for continued Plowshares actions. Although seventy-four years of age, he was not allowed visitors. He was released from prison November 20,

1998. Philip Berrigan correspondence November 19, 1998.
82. Letter to Steven McGuire, associate editor of the *Bulletin of the Atomic Scientists,* December 13, 1983; reprinted in *Film Threat* 12 (1987), p. 31. See also Gallagher (1983), 25, and interviews with Berrigan and Hoover.
83. Excerpts from his journals appear in the Voyager CD-ROM of *Painters Painting* (1995). Publication of more of his remarkable memoirs is forthcoming. De Antonio and Hinckle's book on George Bush was to have been published by Steven Schragis (of *Spy* magazine) at the height of the 1988 presidential campaign. But a disagreement developed with the publisher and the anthology of alternative press stories about Bush was the subject of a lawsuit brought by Schragis at the time of de Antonio's death. Kelly (1990), E1.
84. Emile de Antonio, "Mr. Hoover and I," unpublished manuscript, October 16, 1989, p. 6. SHSW.
85. This favorite anecdote of absurdity is also mentioned in Georgakas and McIsaac (1976) and Green (1989).
86. The story of de Antonio's ashes was offered by Donald Crafton at the film preservation symposium "Orphans of the Storm: Saving 'Orphan Films' in the Digital Age," University of South Carolina, September 24, 1999.

  With the entertaining mix of progressive politics and irreverent, self-deprecating humor, *Mr. Hoover and I* invites comparison with the better-known comic documentary, Michael Moore's *Roger and Me* (1989). Not only are their titles similar, they were released in the same year. There is nothing to suggest either director knew of the other's project. De Antonio's film had been in gestation for a considerable period of time and in production since at least 1986. Curiously, when invited to compare the films, de Antonio refused to see Moore's work. Rather than being heartened by the fact that a major motion picture with a leftist critique of corporate America was being released, he reverted to his perennial disdain for the work of most of his fellow documentarians. This blind spot was unfortunate, for it would be easy to see in *Roger and Me* the cinematic inspirations that satirical documentaries such as *Millhouse: A White Comedy* and take-no-prisoners agitprop such as *In the Year of the Pig* provided for Moore.
87. A Swedish television producer funded the start of a film to be directed by de Antonio. Videotape (in SHSW) was shot at the Whitney Museum of American Art in New York, with de Antonio interviewing Cage in a gallery where an exhibition of his drawings is about to open. Later, the director interviews illustrious friends (Robert Rauschenberg, sculptor Richard Lippold, and others) at a party for Cage at the museum. The filming is brought to an embarrassing halt when Flora Miller Biddle, whom de Antonio calls a "royal princess," shuts down the production during an interview with Merce Cunningham. The raw footage records a scene reminiscent of an encounter with power in a Michael Moore documentary.

  FMB: We did not arrange for this, if you don't mind me saying so.
  DE: Who is "we"?
  FMB: Well, I'm the president of the Whitney Museum and this is my party. It's a social party, for our friends.
  DE: At the same time, this party was arranged for by the Whitney. I received permission to come and do this. I don't walk into places with this camera and all this equipment as a lark.
  FMB: It's not fair to take advantage of our friends.
  DE: I knew Merce before you did. Socially, and every other way. I mean, that's *your* view of it. I'm not taking advantage of *anybody.*

88. Phillip Lopate, "In Search of the Centaur: The Essay-Film," in *Beyond Document: Essays on Nonfiction Film,* ed. Charles Warren (Hanover, N.H.: University Press of New England/Wesleyan University Press, 1996), 243–68.
89. Jean-Paul Sartre, "Présentation," *Les Temps modernes* 1.1 (October 1945): 1–21; "The Case for Responsible Literature," trans. Natalie Galitzine, *Horizon* (London) 9.65 (May 1945): 307–12. Abridged version published in English as "A Credo in Action," *Partisan Review* 12.3 (Summer 1945): 304–8, and copied in Journals I.29.
90. "Film Competition Dedicated to de Antonio," United Press International, January 6, 1990.
91. Letter to William Nee, December 21, 1969. SHSW.
92. Not only are contemporary viewers forced to read *Point of Order, Rush to Judgment,* and *Millhouse* in the light of a multitude of documentary treatments produced after de Antonio's, they must also weigh them against docudramas such as Oliver Stone's infamous *JFK* and *Nixon.* Furthermore, postmodern fictionalizations of history and media memory have further clouded the historical horizon. For example, in March 1998, while *Point of Order* was being revived at the Film Forum in New York, *The X Files* television series aired an episode titled "Travelers." FBI agent Fox Mulder sees his father on a videotape of the Army-McCarthy hearings. (Is he watching *Point of Order!*?) We then flashback anachronistically to 1952 (two years too early), where we hear that Joseph McCarthy is part of the communist

witchhunting of HUAC (although *Senator* McCarthy, of course, was never part of the *House* Un-American Activities Committee). The confusion of facts in drama is less problematic than the conflation of historical forces and political powers. In the postmodern age, de Antonio's historical films could be easily and unfairly caricatured as conspiratorial. The world of *The X Files* melds together the lore of the Kennedy/King assassinations, J. Edgar Hoover's secret files, Nixonian lies, misdeeds of military intelligence, the McCarthyite fear of "aliens," and antigovernment undergrounds—milking all of them for their paranoia-inducing dramatic qualities. In contrast, de Antonio's films responded to the materiality of these events and forces and were rendered in an intellectually rigorous, politically coherent manner. His goal was to demystify that which has now been remystified.

93. Charles Burnett, Emile de Antonio, Haile Gerima, Jacqueline Shearer, Allan Siegel, and Jack Willis, "The Film Collective, Inc.," ca. 1979–80. SHSW.

94. Tajima (1990), 86. However, with his Italian father and Catholic Lithuanian mother, Emile de Antonio would hardly qualify as a "WASP."

95. Judy Irola correspondence, September 12, 1998.

I De on De:
Overviews and Interviews

TERRY DE ANTONIO

An In-Depth Interview with Emile de Antonio (1972)

A poet and teacher of literature, Terry Brook was married to de Antonio from 1965 to 1975, the period he deemed his most creative. Her cogent questions here allow de Antonio to hold forth on his devotion to books—the "slavery," "domination," and "love of words"—and his ambivalence about cinema. The recondite journal Shantih, *a review of international writings, was published in Brooklyn from 1960 to 1979.*

What does film mean to you?
In the early days of my life, film had no meaning at all to me. The beginning of my life was literary. My father was literary. We lived in a house full of books. After dinner every day my brother and I sat by the fireplace and my father told us stories. And they were always stories of the classical myths or the great tales of European fiction or poetry or drama. Since we were Italian, of course a great many of them were Italian tales retold for us in my father's own style. Boccaccio and *Orlando Furioso* and Dante, as well as Homer. So that when I was a little boy I had a fairly good command of the vocabulary of mythology.

But bred into this same love of books was a contempt for the mass media. My father never listened to the radio, he rarely went to the movies, and that characterized my own attitude toward film. Obviously, I've made a one hundred and eighty-degree turn because books have no meaning to me anymore. I can't even reread the novels I once loved. Like *Ulysses*. All that I can read is a poem or a piece of a poem.

As I work on a film I try to learn all I can about the subject—all the factual material there is. And because information storage and retrieval is not yet perfected into tape, we still have to read. But books themselves have lost their significance for me. It seems to me that lesser people are writing them. Our major writers—like Mailer or Styron or Updike—are second-rate writers. Not one of them is first-rate. This is not the age of the book.

You think it's the age of film?
Well, I think that we are also at the end of film as we know it. We're on the threshold of a combination of television and the cassette in which every home will really have Malraux's museum without walls. It will have everything. Not just information—art, film, music, the whole gamut of human experience.

Will this change the nature of the experience?
There's no doubt that it *has* changed the nature of the experience. We are indeed proceeding toward a vegetable kingdom, and this is one of the things that interests me politically. This vegetable kingdom is dominated by the money-grubbers, by people like Paley and Sarnoff and their boards of directors and stockholders. As long as television and television time are regarded simply as commodities for sale, what you will have is the creation of a vast, passive republic.

And you see cassettes as being an extension of this vegetative world?
Absolutely. Unless there are revolutionary changes in our society. The French philosopher Barthes recently made the following point: In talking about the 1968 revolution in France, he said it's quite apparent that the government is perfectly willing to surrender the universities to the demonstrators and to the communists, the Maoists, because the universities are no longer sources of power or ideas, or of influence. But what the government will never surrender is its control of and use of the media because that's where power is. Power no longer resides in the universities, as it once may have, but in television aerials.

Is there any society in which the media are not an extension of the government?
No. One thing that the twentieth century has taught us is that revolutions develop along highly nationalistic lines. What we need in this country is the development of an American Revolution in our time. That means a revolution that is based on the Bill of Rights. The Bill of Rights implies a pluralistic society and by a pluralistic society I mean specifically in relationship to the media. It would seem to me that there should be a pluralism of ownerships or directions, a pluralism of control, and a pluralism of interest in relationship to television. We can open up an unlimited number of channels. If an unlimited number of channels are opened to the widely warring diverse voices from among the American people, this would become a way to advance the idea of democratic pluralism in an infinitely complex society.

Are you thinking, for example, of each community or locality having its own station?

Well, there's no doubt that I favor decentralization generally, but at the same time that would be self-defeating with television because it means there would be a certain professional slickness in the centralized stations and a kind of amateurish bumbling at the local level. What I meant is that you must have a pluralistic setup in which you have large, so-called national stations like the BBC. The trouble with the BBC is that it's freighted down with bureaucratic heaviness, but even so it does better work than anything we do in our television. You might even continue to have the private channels like CBS, ABC, or NBC—if you have three or four channels of equal size and power not dominated by the government or business. True, they would reflect the class aspirations of whatever society it was, but it would be an improvement over what we have or what we are about to have. And it could become part of a process of participation and revelation—participation by voices shut out from television today and revealing those things which are hidden today.

There are hundreds of channels which could operate at local levels. In a city like New York there is no reason why you shouldn't have a Columbia University channel which anybody could turn on, which could be as wild as anybody wanted. And there's no reason why there couldn't be channels which could be given over to the counterculture so that there would be a free choice.

Since we're talking about government rather than about film, you know this goes back to the one great media crime that is being committed today—like the burning of the library at Alexandria—the destruction of television tapes and film by boards of grubby, little money-minded men. The material is systematically being wiped or thrown away because it has no commercial value. *I Love Lucy* shows are kept forever because they can be sold.

Like most people, I don't trust history anymore, not written history. I once was devoted to the idea of history. Stalin and Nixon have both rewritten history. All winners rewrite it. I don't trust it as it's written, but I do trust the raw television tapes of events that have taken place over the last fifteen years. This is what is being thrown away.

If I were to make one appeal, it would be for the creation of an electronic archive. The networks which use our free air, that ether which belongs to all the American people, would be forced to support and maintain this archive in which everything would be banked and made available to anybody.

This gets me back to one of my films, *Point of Order,* based on the

Army-McCarthy hearings. The one lesson that those hearings taught the American establishment is that no complete hearing must ever be televised again on a national basis because it exposes too much of the guts of the system. In this pluralism of stations which I envision, one station would televise House and Senate proceedings and government special hearings or commissions. The tapes would become a statement of record and the *Congressional Record* could go on being the place where only Izzy Stone can find the truth.

I'd like to go back a minute to...
No, I want to make one more statement. Downstairs there are now at least twenty books covering Joseph McCarthy. Not one of them has the meaning that *Point of Order* has because there is something about the immediacy of a film image that enables the viewer himself to perceive something about the nature of process and the nature of character in a way that words could never do.

A footnote to your question about what films meant to me and my youth. I read a book when we were in Florida three years ago called *The Words* by Sartre which describes exactly the kind of dedication I once had as a young man, as a very young man at Harvard, to words and to the idea of the word, to the slavery of words, to the domination of words, to the love of words—all in the written form. It was because there was such an acceptance of the word—because of my father—that the word became an impossible thing for me to deal with. I had too exalted a view of what the world was, and it wasn't until I got older that I regained my perspective.

Do you consider yourself essentially alone in terms of style without precedent or forebears?
The loneliness of my style was thrust upon me for a variety of reasons. As I said before, I came to film in innocence, not having had any great experience in viewing films or any great interest in it. Also, the nature of my first film, *Point of Order,* was unique in that it was the first time a film was ever made from television. This was in itself a radical departure. It was also the first time that a long film had been made from one specific closed event—the Army-McCarthy hearings—and the sprawling, unregulated aspect of those hearings, which in real life lasted 188 hours, presented me right away with what I think is the real problem of film: structure.

It's what is crudely called editing, but it's not editing as the word is understood in Hollywood, but structure. Life is raw, disordered, and this was one of the jobs of making *Point of Order*: to take something that had no structure—no structure for many reasons, not the least of which was the desire of the government to dissemble what was really going on. In fact, the end of *Point of Order* has been written about by many critics as an exemplary cinema verité or documentary style ending, when in fact the ending was invented by me. In real life, the gavel was rapped rather hastily, and there was an attempt to sweep the whole thing under the rug. That last sequence is totally out of chronological context, it was structured from many segments, but it's the real truth and I think that this is what the film-maker has to deal with. The real truth is not all those discrete phenomena that lie about us in the world, but the imposition of order over them. The whole idea of cinema verité is bogus.

Is structure the documentary equivalent of aesthetic style?
No. Structure is one element.

But haven't you been saying that structure is the key to your work?
Well, structure is in part the key to my work, but there's another aspect of my work that nobody's ever mentioned, which is character. There's a revelation of character in all of my films that interests me as much as structure.

In *Rush to Judgment*—a film that has been attacked critically—one of the things that I'm proudest of is the development of character in a group of working-class Texans who testify about what they saw the day Kennedy was assassinated. These working-class witnesses from the railroad bridge were shy and hesitant in front of the camera, but something emerges in the film that makes these people as interesting as characters in a novel.

What do your films say about America?
My films are really a history of the United States in the Cold War. I've already talked about *Point of Order*. *Rush to Judgment* has to do with police over people and with official cover-up at the highest level in our history. *In the Year of the Pig* is our foreign and military policy run amok in pursuit of imperial aims, from backing French imperialists to creating our own brand of the imperial. *That's Where the Action Is* (BBC title, not mine) *is* the city, pollution, corruption, race and was done in 1965 before these issues became glosses and superficialities on U.S. television. *America Is Hard to See* is the failure of liberalism in the '68 campaign, the failure of an idealistic middle class and the young. It reflects their impotence before the reality of the system. With *Millhouse* we have one of the first attempts at serious, documentary comedy as well as the life of that man whose entire career was based on the Cold War. He antedates McCarthy. He is the original cold warrior. He discovered the archvictim of the Cold War in Alger Hiss.

Can you see yourself dealing with a subject which isn't American?
No. I cannot. I often think that people like myself, deeply conscious of their foreign origins, develop a special feeling about where it is they live.

But you were born here?
I was born here and I'm an American, but every day I went back to a family, my father anyway, who was not American, who came to this country in maturity, not as a child, who was totally formed in Europe. As a young man I knew as much about the Risorgimento, as much about the French Revolution, as I did about the American Revolution. My father probably knew more about Saint-Just than he did about George Washington and Nathanael Greene. I read about Washington and Greene, but my first hero was Napoleon because my father used to tell me all those Stendhalian tales of Napoleon.

Yet you once told me that the first work you considered doing was a novel about Scranton, where you were born.
Of course. I live here. It's not even a matter of choice. I'm interested in reality. Those people whose work I admire have a real sense of place. All I'm saying is that I was lucky as people sometimes are by not being totally absorbed into this place, my country, by having a certain distance from it. This does not mean that I am anti-American or even unpatriotic because, although I'm a Marxist, I regard myself as a patriot.

Would you ever live anywhere else?
No.

Pauline Kael called Ho Chi Minh the hero of In The Year of the Pig. *What did you find admirable about him?*
Well, I am a romantic. And my work, though hard and documentary, is essentially romantic work because beneath it there lies a hope that the world can change. I agree with a man I came to love in the making of the film—Paul Mus, a professor of Buddhism at Yale and the Collège de France—who said that when the history of the twentieth century is written Ho Chi Minh will be known as its greatest patriot and perhaps its greatest man. Ho Chi Minh was able to do what many idealist patriots dream of—to liberate his country—and there is no higher ideal than that. Particularly the liberation of one's country from a foreign oppressor, a colonial oppressor, a racist colonial oppressor. He led the first successful Asian revolution—before China—against the white imperialists.

In addition, his life was so romantic. Shipping out as a cabin boy at the age of seventeen before he ever heard the words Karl Marx or socialism. His anger and rebellion and revolt against the French. The fact that he wrote poetry. The fact that he was sentenced to death by the French authorities and in prison he wrote poetry. That against all odds he won. And, finally, since one of my failings is a concern with grace and style, that he had such exquisite grace and style. I love the scenes of him—given to me by the Democratic Republic of Vietnam—in *In the Year of the Pig* when he's with a group of young people and children and he raises his hand to make them sit down. The simplicity of his life was, for a Marxist, a most aristocratic kind of simplicity: the typewriter, the blanket, the few books, all this appeals to me. His was a life not only of devotion to his people, but a life in which all those sorts of boring possessions were stripped away.

Do you have a philosophy of life?
I can't answer a question like that. I don't know what that means.

What else do you like to do besides work and drink?
I'd like to say something more about film. The real problem in any form of expression is when the form becomes so polished and so gilded as to be devoid of content. It is always *those* films which I find most shallow and least interesting. Take a cult figure. The early Hitchcock—before World War II—is a brilliant filmmaker, technically and innovatively brilliant. The sound cuts in *The 39 Steps,* the moving train device of *The Lady Vanishes,* both of those are brilliant. But what happens to Hitchcock is that he masters the form, and Hitchcock is like Simenon novels: they're perfect and very bad. It's not just *Psycho—Strangers on a Train* may be an exception—but most of the Hitchcock films that are the object of cult worship are bad because they are so well made. And that's not a paradox. In the dichotomy between form and content, I suspect that work of any kind, unless it has content—by content I don't mean political slogans—but unless it has some subject, it tends to become evanescent or trivial.

What American movies do you like?
I like the obvious things. The trouble with John Ford's movies is that all the good things are exactly alike. *My Darling Clementine* and *Stagecoach.* They're both the same movie. And so I like one of them. There's no development in a person like Ford. He gets old, but his movies don't develop. There's a naive, primitive, reactionary view of life that is the same throughout all his films. That's one of the troubles with being an American. Auden once said that American writers usually have one book in them. We don't have enough of a cultural reservoir to fall back on. And this is what happened to Orson Welles. He made *a* movie. He made a movie whose failing is that it's synthetic and whose virtue is that it's a brilliant synthesis. But he never developed. Not one movie he made after that was ever as good as the first one. Also, of course, Welles suffers from the fact that he's an actor, so he has a large, inflatable ego to pump up, and the films in which he acts are in most cases deplorable—like *Mr. Arkadin.* Or Lear. [Welles's video

production of *King Lear* was unfinished at the time of his death in 1985. De Antonio is conflating Welles's other Shakespearean roles in *Macbeth* (1948), *Othello* (1952), and *Falstaff* aka *Chimes at Midnight* (1966).]

Where do you want to go with documentary?
I don't know. I'm at a critical point. I work very slowly. This is why Sartre's book *The Words* means so much to me. He speaks of sweat, nothing comes easy. Victor Alfieri, the Italian poet, had literally to be chained to his desk in order to work. I have that kind of problem. I love my work and I love working, but it doesn't come easily. People who know me socially see someone who can speak quickly. And I tend to have a quickness in perception. But the actual work—the people who work with me are oddly amused by it—I have solved some of the problems I deal with in film through what I call brutality, which is just looking at stuff over and over and over until you're exhausted.

This is the way *In the Year of the Pig* was ended. I had an ending, and we were ready to go to mix, and the ending was all right. But it was wrong. It would have worked, but failed to make the point I wanted. The editor and I stayed so late, she cried. It was a miniature nervous breakdown, but then I had what I wanted. My work has to do with sweat.

Would you consider making a film that wasn't a documentary?
Each time I think of doing fiction, I get excited by a documentary idea.

I've always responded to dares and challenges. Even as a boy, "I dare you" is the one thing that could get me involved in any form of insanity. My drinking a quart of whiskey for Andy Warhol—a quart in twenty minutes, on camera—was exactly that kind of thing. So I like the idea of making a fiction film. I'm over fifty. Nobody has taken up a whole new kind of film at that age. But the problems of fiction up until now have been less interesting to me. It's hard to talk about what you're going to do unless you're talking about product: how many sausages you're going to produce, or how many cars, or how many films to fill a theater.

Do you care about an audience?
You have to remember that my films are made from a minority point of view, independently, without corporate backing, each one as an individual enterprise. I never think of a distribution contract until the film is finished. On the other hand, anybody who makes films makes them to be seen. But while I'm making them I don't think about the audience. I have to like what I'm doing.

Are you afraid fiction would lessen your independence?
Fiction would mean finding a great deal of money from people who've had no experience with me in that form. This is a problem of filmmaking. I no-

tice that the more commercial directors are, the more they talk about high art and things that are pure bullshit, and that they never discuss money, while the directors who are involved with an attempt at real art talk about money.

The real problems in filmmaking if you're independent and free are financial. If you want to make films that you think should be made, you have to find the money to indulge in this luxury. It's not like sitting down and writing a book. If I want to write a novel, all it takes is a few thousand dollars and a typewriter and I don't drink vintage Burgundy. But once you pick up a camera you're spending a lot of money. In making the documentaries that I've done, critical of the United States in the years of the Cold War, I've spent a million dollars. And they were cheap to make by film standards.

In a recent interview, Stanley Kubrick said that his desire to become a director began with his love for the camera. You don't share that sense of the machine as part of the process, do you?
No. I'm no good at machines. I think it's only necessary to know what a camera can do, not to operate one. That same article also said that Kubrick liked to shoot certain sequences. I like Kubrick's work—I haven't seen *2001* or *A Clockwork Orange*—but I particularly like *Paths of Glory, The Killing,* and *Dr. Strangelove*. But *Strangelove* and *Paths of Glory* are marred by the one thing that tends to mar American filmmaking generally—a kind of insane technical perfection.

If there's any underlying aspect of American life that's sick over and above our politics, it is this mad passion for technique over substance. There's a problem with becoming too technically proficient—there may not be a problem in being a painter and being so proficient, because your hand to that canvas is a non-machine relationship. But when you're dealing with machines and you become too interested in the gimmicks, you have a problem.

Who are the filmmakers you really like?
I like many filmmakers. It's just hard to bring to mind any specific names. From the past, the work of D. W. Griffith. I don't like that many documentary directors. *Birth of a Nation* seems to me to be one of the best films ever made, although its politics is the opposite of mine.

This is always a real problem. It's one of my own problems with the so-called socialist countries. Because *Birth of a Nation* is better than any left-wing American film ever made. The work that I'm most sympathetic to is work that is artistically successful, that shares my own sometimes angry, sometimes cynical, sometimes sardonic view, and is at the same time romantic. Namely, the work of Renoir and Buñuel. *Rules of the Game* is one of the great films, and it is political. Renoir was a Communist at the time. It was the kind of thing that the Communists of France at that time were unable to understand.

I find I'm at home in Buñuel's world. Another thing that comes from my father, I suppose, is an almost professional contempt for religion and, at the same time, a deep fascination with it, which is what is in all of Buñuel's work—the atheist whose films are all cluttered with miracles and crosses and believers. Buñuel is the most interesting of all filmmakers because he inhabits the world that I find most interesting, including the early surrealism. And at the same time admixture of that with politics. People tend to forget that almost all the surrealists and Dadaists were politically motivated. The real trick is to be a political artist without being doctrinaire. Even Brecht was an artist first. This is what's wrong with Soviet painting. It's what's wrong with Chinese films. They're simplistic. I come from a culture that is plural.

What do you do for relaxation?
Talk and drink.

And chop wood.
And chop wood, yes. Swim. Swim in the ocean. I still love the ocean. After all, we swim in it in November.

Speak for yourself.
That's the papal we.

EMILE DE ANTONIO

Movies and Me (1974)

In May 1974, Britain's National Film Theatre held a retrospective of all of de Antonio's work, including the rarely screened 1965 BBC telefilm That's Where the Action Is. *This characteristic piece of de Antonio prose was printed as the festival's program. The bibliophile, who insisted he seldom went to the movies, here exhibits a fairly encyclopedic (albeit contemptuous) familiarity with the history of cinema. As was often the case in his writing, he includes even his personal allies (e.g., Pauline Kael, Peter Bogdanovich) as targets of his barbs.*

Movies: Movies were American mass production of a fix to make the blues go away. K. Marx a better critic than A. Bazin. What could have become mass art/mass weapon/mass information became nighttime poppy to dream away the alienated, drab real daytime work/no work. The more opium, the more money. *In principio erat dollar. The Godfather.* I & II.

Wars and Depressions: "Anything can be said as long as it signifies nothing." K. Jaspers. Even better if it seems to signify something. Death, poverty, sadness needed happy endings, glamorous ones. Breadlines, the dole, *les mutilés* faded into ermines, Dusenbergs, barons, The Old South. Children & animals for $ & heart-tugs. Flag-waving for even more $. The West was won and rewon and rewon, dead savages (treacherous) lay around the smoking wagons all along the Great Golden Plains. Front-office cynicism more $. Mr. Deeds. Mr. Smith. *It Happened One Night. Virgo intacta* + $.

Brecht: "Only boots can be made to measure." McLuhan wrong from pratfall to pratfall. Medium is not the message. Who owns the medium owns and is the message. Which is why TV programs *are* like movies. Cut to measure for grazing sheep to make them think, for 90 minutes, that they are wolves.

Exceptions: Vertov, early Chaplin, the Marxes, Fields, Keaton, Renoir, Buñuel, etc.

Auteurs?: A theory uncorked by A. Bazin to find some art in the bottom of the glass. To have art you need artists. Authors. Where were they in the Hollywood navel-orange assembly line? Bazin was personalist (dilute Catholicism developed by Jean-Joseph Mounier). *Personalist = auteur.* The real auteurs were bankers and promoters: Joe Kennedy, the Brothers Warner, Harry Cohn, Rank and Howard Hughes. Ford, Hawks, Hitchcock, Walsh, Capra were canonized by Bazin, but Harry Cohn dictated the final cut by the itch in his ass. Robert Chartoff, coproducer of *The Strawberry Statement,* told Mitch Tuchman, "Usually the director we pick we pick because we think their ideas are consistent with ours. . . . It's our material. It's not theirs." I have enough ego to believe that on any pictures we make there isn't any *auteur.* We don't choose to be the *auteur* . . . but neither are directors *auteurs,* I don't think.

Who really needed an auteur theory were the "running dogs" (Sarris/Roud) of the byzantine subindustry spun off from Hollywood: critics, festivals, flacks, TV interviewers, Bogdanovich, gossip columnists, Truffaut, ego creators. Pantheon? Like the beginning of the Trojan War. Actor gods/director gods. And hundreds of nonbooks by nonwriters used in colleges in noncourses.

Cinema verité?: Mindlessness with light sync-sound equipment. Repeat Jaspers. Best examples: Rock-docs.

I never saw *Gone with the Wind* and never will. I haven't seen *Last Tango in Paris.* Sex for the '30s and the burning of Atlanta; sex for the '70s and autism. Perhaps sex for Pauline Kael. As a boy I saw cops, robbers, cowboys, Indians, air aces. Except infrequently, I stopped going when I entered Harvard long ago.

I believe in movies as art and struggle. That movies can reveal actively as no other form can. I believe that movies can be the thing itself rather than *about* the thing. I believe in the independent working with total control over her/his material. I believe in audiences. I don't believe in Francis Ford Coppola, computers, movies/programs packaged for mythical mass audience taste. I believe in choice.

Point of Order (1963)

Film is anything that passes through a projector. Even white leader, if you're dull enough. What counts is on the screen and what it does to people. Raw material of *Point of Order* was shot by two network cameras in a fixed position grinding away for 188 hours during the 1954 Army-McCarthy hearings. The movie works because there are no tricks in it. It was stripped down to where it really mattered. The aesthetics was the politics, it was the character, the tone and voice, it was America. That's what movies are, not beautiful shots.

What interests me more than anything in movies is structure. The hearings themselves were untrue, as the historical present usually is. The structure not only makes a new kind of documentary—feature-length with a story and *no* narration; it also made a political truth. *Point of Order* was the first American documentary to play theatrically after World War II. *Louisiana Story* was sponsored and financed by Standard Oil.

That's Where the Action Is (1965)

A ride through the 1965 New York mayoral race marred by bootless BBC narration, used over my objection. Beame, Lindsay, Robert Kennedy, a cop, a black radical, a bookie, go-go girls, street politics, commercials, money. How to package a young congressman who looks like a movie star and make him into a mayor. All my films are stares at tricks and technique in political life, USA.

Rush to Judgment (1966)

First commercially released montage film made of TV, stock footage, shot material, interviews. Its subject: questions raised by the death of Kennedy which still remain. Movie is an attack on the Warren Report and the police system which blurred, suppressed, and distorted evidence. And lied. *Rush to Judgment* found witnesses whose existence the FBI denied. Demystification of the police world. U.S. TV today is creating a new myth about police. Heroes of the film are the people of Texas who spoke up and told what they saw when it mattered and when it was dangerous to do so. Interviews are lengthy because I wanted audiences to sense credibility of witnesses. Jump cuts to remind audiences that film is being manipulated. With *Rush to Judgment* I was promoted to U.S. Immigration Lookout Book. In addition to phone tap, the police noted entries and exits.

In the Year Of the Pig (1969)

With *In the Year of the Pig* I wanted to make an intellectual weapon to be used against our war in Vietnam. Everything I had seen aimed at emotion, attracting those who were already moved. To be against the war was not enough. Why were we in it? How did we get into it? To make a movie that was not a lecture, not a scream. The movie begins with French days, early '30s and goes down to the Tet Offensive of 1968. Sources: old newsreels everyone had forgotten; interviews; films from the DRV and NLF; but most of all, film from U.S. TV where the war was being hidden by making it part of daily news programming, sticking the burning village between deodorant and Cadillac commercials. By making it quotidian, TV made it go away. I wanted to bring it back, film history at 24 frames a second.

All my films are the history of my country in the days of the Cold War. Pauline Kael said of it, "Ho Chi Minh is the hero." She was right. Curiously enough, the film was nominated for an Oscar. Fred Astaire introduced it with a certain embarrassment.

America Is Hard to See (1970)
The 1968 campaign for Democratic presidential nomination seen from the POV of liberals and Eugene McCarthy. Failure of liberal, peace politics and why. Detailed material from New Hampshire and Wisconsin primaries which brought down LBJ. The intellectual in politics, Senator Eugene McCarthy. Chicago 1968 seen from inside Convention Hall rather than the streets. The McCarthy Movement prefigured what would happen in 1972, including the disastrous, bungled campaign of George McGovern. Also, McCarthy was tougher, smarter, and made the issues clearer. An intentionally sour note is Robert Kennedy's jump into the campaign after McCarthy's New Hampshire upset. The title line is from a poem by Robert Frost. Sources of material: newsreel, TV, interviews with the young who created the McCarthy campaign, Paul Newman campaigning in Wisconsin.

Millhouse: A White Comedy (1971)
Not an attack on the man who may withstand Watergate, but on the system which produced him. Vincent Canby of the *New York Times* said, "The easiest way to describe Emile de Antonio's *Millhouse* is as a satiric documentary, but that's a bland weasel-like definition for the exuberantly opinionated film. . . . De Antonio has no special interest in balanced reportage, which is as antithetical to his concerns as it is to those of superior fiction, and *Millhouse*, a study of the political career of Richard Milhous Nixon (as well as his career's various lives and times) is superior fiction, as implacable as *An American Tragedy*, as mysterious as *You Can't Go Home Again*, as funny as *Why Are We in Viet Nam?* and as banal as *Main Street*. By this I don't mean to say that it's not true, but rather that it shares with fiction the kind of truth that is greater than the sum of its parts."

Painter's Painting (1972)
Most of the Cold War showed the seams of U.S. society. U.S. painting in that period was something, alive, isolated, wild. I was able to film the biggest collection of it in museums, studios, galleries. I end by quoting myself: "I had known many of these painters for much of my adult life. I admired their work long before they had dealers or a public: Rauschenberg,

Johns, Stella, Warhol. I was there when they were changing the shape of American painting, when no one liked it and when the art world in particular thought it was a joke. It was precisely when we left the old oaken bucket and the trash can, the puerilities of Wyeth, the sentimentality and sexism of naked women, it was precisely then that we came to terms with European abstraction that we finally produced an American art, a high art that was made in New York."

Painters Painting (the painters include also Motherwell, Newman, Pollock, Hofmann, de Kooning, Poons, Noland, Olitski, Frankenthaler) was shot in both black and white and color, which is the way I see the world.

TANYA NEUFELD

An Interview with Emile de Antonio (1973)

Appearing in the prestigious glossy journal Artforum, *this piece gave de Antonio one of his largest reading audiences in the art world and a chance to discuss his new film on American painters. Although he had a "friendly" interviewer in Tanya Neufeld, who worked with him on* Millhouse *and* Painters Painting, *de Antonio was not reticent to disparage* Artforum *and its coverage of experimental filmmakers. He attacked the magazine for its "coy, arty, and academic way [of] searching out all kinds of crap in film" and writing about undistinguished experimenters "who seem to amuse Annette Michelson."*

Editor Michelson appended a pointed reply to "the very loose, lazy rhetoric of de Antonio's art-historical free associations." She noted that his dismissal of Hollis Frampton and Stan Brakhage was discouraging in its "lack of sympathy with those younger men, working in considerable difficulty, who might be regarded as his fellows in independence and integrity." Michelson concluded by charging that it was de Antonio who was lagging behind the avant-garde. Artforum's *"advanced" theory "provoke[d] discomfort" in him just as it had "in those official and largely journalistic film-critical milieus who have responded with enthusiasm to de Antonio's own work." The "montage tradition upon which de Antonio is largely dependent," she contended, was better questioned by a comparison of Eisenstein and experimenter Brakhage than by "rhetoric now outworn."*

Why have your films always been political in nature?
I have always looked upon documentary as belonging to politics as much as to art. Those documentary films which have survived, which have had meaning, which have been artistically interesting, have been political. These include Eisenstein's reconstructions, the work of Shub and Vertov, and the

documentaries made by Americans in the thirties, such as *The Plow That Broke the Plains* and *The River.*

In 1948, Robert Flaherty made his last film, *Louisiana Story.* It was the first American documentary film to be shown in theaters after World War II until *Point of Order.* I would like to attack Flaherty and the principles of his work, and *Louisiana Story* is exactly the opposite of everything that I have aspired to do in film—in the way it was made, in intention, and the way it was financed. *Louisiana Story* was financed by a $285,000 grant from Humble Oil Company. $285,000 in 1948 is like $500,000 today. It becomes one of the costliest documentaries ever made. It was a repudiation of the tradition of dissent and of such films as *The Plow That Broke the Plains,* made in the days of the New Deal, that questioned the rape of our country. That's what *The Plow That Broke the Plains* is about, the creation of the dust bowl. It was how the insane and insulting abuse of the earth created an emptiness in the center of America that forced people to go westward. But *Louisiana Story* is finally an accommodation between the oil map and the people of the bayou.

When you make a film like *Louisiana Story,* the film of a young Cajun boy confronted by the drilling rigs in Louisiana, and you've been commissioned to make this film by an oil company, you are already compromised. One of the reasons this film played so widely is because Humble Oil gave it away to theaters all over the country. Each time we look at anything, we change it. Seen today, Flaherty seems to stand for shallow aestheticism, a search for the artificially exotic. Flaherty's staged conflicts between man and nature were, in the first place, false, and in the second place, because of the brilliant execution and personal devotion, they deflected documentary into hopeless and unrewarding motions. The enemy out there isn't ice or the sea, but man. The Flaherty line leads directly to cinema verité. A line dead, blank, and empty.

At the time of *Louisiana Story* we were already in the Cold War, which is what my life in film is all about, including *Painters Painting.* What you had in that period was silence. The silent fifties. But the fifties weren't silent on the part of the United States government. The government in its various forms produced Richard Nixon and the House Un-American Activities Committee; it produced Joseph McCarthy; it produced a thousand films through the U.S. Information Agency supporting Korea and the Cold War. What you had was silence on the part of the people. There were very few documentary films, mainly those made by television, which were links of sausage, not films. Most of them sought after that illusory concept—objectivity—which is pure bullshit and in reality means no offense to advertisers.

Do you feel that the politically oriented film can serve an essential function to the community in much the same way that an annual theater festival in fifth-century Athens combined politics, religion, and entertainment into a single integral community event?

The theater of Aeschylus, Sophocles, and Euripides is essentially a theater of celebration. Even including the disharmony within the Athenian state, from what we know of it, and I have the most serious doubts about the validity of history as an idea, but from what we know of it, it always took place at a certain time of year under the auspices of the state. So even if Euripides was thought of as a subversive, the plays were nonetheless put on by the state in a state-operated and state-trained theater. In our time, the film documentary is the art of opposition. My films have been against the chief assumptions of the American state, and I think my films have succeeded in making a new kind of art form in film out of political material. This is precisely the problem that interested me. My films were made alone, outside the structure, opposed to the structure, opposed to specific activities of the United States government. When you put my films together, they constitute the history of the United States in the days of the Cold War.

Point of Order deals with witch-hunts in the broadest sense, and with McCarthyism, which was the dominant idea of domestic politics in the United States in the fifties. *Rush to Judgment* is not about the death of President Kennedy, nothing could interest me less. Nothing could bore me more than those USIA films like *Years of Lightning, Day of Drums* with Kennedy's coffin and weeping Jackie. What was of interest to me was the suppression of evidence and the elevation of the police to a superpower within the United States. That was the consequence of the death of Kennedy. The FBI and the Secret Service and the Dallas police had at the very least been remiss. They were covered up by a government commission of most august people. The film I made was out of outrage at the police and judicial conspiracy. One result of the Warren Report is that we are now living in a form of police state. *In the Year of the Pig* is a cry of outrage against our war in Vietnam. After Kent State and Cambodia, I stopped work on *Painters Painting* to make *Millhouse*.

Millhouse is historical in approach. It begins with Nixon's career and traces it throughout as comedy, as satire. Nixon is the Tartuffe of the Cold War from its beginnings to its most refined development in 1972. One of the things that happened from 1945 to 1970, the years covered in *Painters Painting,* is that the United States, in some curious way, for the first time confronting the whole problem of abstraction, produced a new kind of painting. It was the painting with which I grew up. I knew a good many of the artists personally, and it introduced me to a problem which lay in the back of my mind as I was doing all my other films, which is the relationship between art and politics.

The inconsistency of having left-wing politics, as I do, and liking the paintings of Jackson Pollock, Jasper Johns, and Frank Stella, is not to me contradictory. The film is largely supportive of what I consider the chief lines of American painting from 1945 to the present in the days of the Cold War. This is painting that is apolitical, that is concerned with painting, not with politics. This is painting that was concerned with paint, canvas, and objects. There seems to be an apparent schizophrenic separation between what I was doing on the one hand and what these people were doing on the other. It's a question I raise myself and there is no answer to it.

Could the art of the forties, fifties, and sixties have been produced without the political and economic structure that supported it?
That's the key question that has been worrying me all these years. This is why I go out of my way in *Painters Painting* to separate the painters from the collectors, the dealers, and the people who create the market, although they are an intrinsic part of the world.

What do you see for the future of painting?
One of the reasons *Artforum* is writing so much about film is that the fantastic movement that was going on in American painting has come to an end. I think the thing that worries the best young painters we have, like Stella, is that there is nobody behind them. They don't hear that herd of hoofbeats, that compression that you had with abstract expressionism followed by Johns and Rauschenberg, followed by Stella and Noland, followed by pop art, all these ideas, movements, ferments, one right after the other, bang, bang, bang. Suddenly, where are the guys twenty-five years old? I don't see them.

Aren't there more people making art today than ever before?
That's right, but most of it is not good art. And this is the key to the whole thing, quality. One of the reasons I made *Painters Painting* is that I was alive in the middle of this extraordinary period which was a kind of rush of talent, of ambition, of energy. Abstract expressionism, when Rauschenberg and Johns came on the scene, was exhausted. The second-generation abstract expressionists were for the most part very, very second-generation. One night I was playing poker with several of them in East Hampton and they were saying, "What are you doing going around with people like Johns and Rauschenberg? Are you some sort of fucking anarchist? They're not artists, they're antiart." I said, "Precisely, that is the point."

I'm not equating art with fashion. There was a compression of energy, one thing following another, but it stopped—by the time you get to Stella and Poons, it's over.

I think that one of the reasons *Artforum* is in such a coy, arty, and academic way searching out all kinds of crap in film is that most of the filmmakers you are dealing with are failed painters or filmmakers who think like painters or aspire to a painting "scene." People like Hollis Frampton and the people who seem to amuse Annette Michelson and film fleas like Jonas Mekas are essentially failed painters. They were choked off and cast aside into the development of another art form and came to film out of desperation. They are the tail end, and they have all the same feeling toward visual material that the painters had who succeeded in their art. They tried to translate their failure on canvas into some kind of cinematic existence; what they do doesn't work in film. When Jasper Johns paints letters it's art; Hollis Frampton's *A, B, C, D* film is something else. The idea of literally transposing exhausted painting ideas into film is a boring idea and most of the people doing this are painters manqués. These are the people who seem to interest art critics, which is one of the reasons why art magazines are devoting so much time to this sort of work. An issue of *Artforum* on Brakhage!

What of the young artists today who are putting their energies into other media such as videotape, Conceptual art, etc.?
When I began work on *Painters Painting* I went to Henry Geldzahler and got permission to film his show *American Painting 1940–1970* at the Metropolitan Museum. The camera crew and I spent ten nights there filming those canvases. Nobody will ever film those works again. Nobody will ever again bring together such a collection. First of all, modern painting is much more fragile than the old masterpieces. A Rembrandt holds up much better than a Rauschenberg. They were painted with better paint on better canvas. Then there are the present-day problems of shipping and insurance. Henry's intuition behind the choice of time span for his show was similar to mine for *Painters Painting*. No matter how many good paintings these artists go on to make, the original source of that information is finished for me. The younger artists are into nonpainting activity, which I regard as another world that is not necessarily a new world or an interesting world. Conceptual art is a symbol of exhaustion.

What motivated you to make Painters Painting?
As much as I distrust history, I live in it and I work in it. One of the things I wanted to do in *Painters Painting* was to make something, rather than doing a film about it as TV does it. TV uses a narrator to explain it, to tell you what it was about. I wanted to make a film which would be a thing in

itself, which would reflect what happened in those twenty-five years in which I lived, what I thought was important, what generated it. I wanted it in the words of the people who did it, rather than making a film *about* it, and I wanted to define who did it in the widest possible sense. The film includes the promoters, the dealers, the collectors, as well as the people who make the art.

It is perfectly obvious that when you have a man like Barnett Newman who was so extraordinarily articulate, whose work I happen to like tremendously, who had such a sense of the pertinent anecdote, and was able to tie that pertinent anecdote to a genuine point in the development of his art and to abstract art in America, you tend to use more of Barney than you do of many others in the film. This suggests one of the limitations in the kind of film I made—you were in a sense trapped by the projective capacity of those you film. There is an extraordinary sweet expressiveness about de Kooning; there's a steely passion in Stella; there's a fantastic ability to articulate and an intellectuality in Newman; there's an iron, logical precision, and a gift for speech, in Jasper Johns which are overwhelming. So you tend to be more interested in them because you are dealing with films as well as painting.

Would you have included more artists in Painters Painting *if time had allowed?*
I made the film as long as I wanted it. One thing about making the films I make is that I'm not responsible to anybody. I could have made the film eight hours long if I had wanted to.

I find that there is no written overall history of the art of this period which covers the field as thoroughly as *Painters Painting.* As I read the written history of American Painting in the twentieth century, I find remarkable shallowness that is highly journalistic rather than revealing.

In Painters Painting, *was the end result similar to your original intent?*
One of the reasons the film works is that most of the painters are articulate people. One thing about the birth of abstract expressionism, one thing about beginning at the bottom, being born in despair without acceptance the way modern American painting began, is that it created verbal expressiveness as defense. It forced an artist to become a theorist to defend his position. This is one reason artists, particularly like Newman, became brilliant at rhetoric. A question I asked during the interviews was, "How old were you when you had your first one-man show?" Willem de Kooning was forty-four, Barnett Newman was forty-five. Hans Hofmann was over sixty. Painters of the next generation were having their first shows in their twenties.

Do you feel that the decline in the quality of art is due to the partial elimination of the struggle, since there is now more money, more galleries, more public and private support than ever before?
The struggle was eliminated by the time Stella and Johns appeared. There are more galleries, but the successful galleries throughout the country are selling the work of these same artists.

    A big point of argument between Phil Leider and myself was that he thought that Earthworks and Conceptual art had a special social meaning. Originally, I did an interview with Phil about that but decided to substitute a later interview in the film. For me their social meaning was negative. I wasn't interested in Smithson's *Spiral Jetty*. Some post-Stella artists were tired of the whole gallery setup, which they considered bourgeois and proprietary, and they were trying to move their art out of the galleries. They started by having exhibits in their studios, which was not very different really than having an exhibit in a gallery. They still put up the pictures and had somebody come in and buy them. Some people will argue that the artists who moved art out into the landscape, like Michael Heizer and Robert Smithson, destroyed the buying and selling concept. How? You still had to have a patron: you had to go back and have a Holy Roman Catholic Church pay the bill or a Bob Scull.

How old were you when you made your first film?
I was forty years old when I started work on my first film, *Point of Order,* twelve years ago. Before that my life had been a sort of stew. How does an intellectual survive when he doesn't have anything that he really wants to do?

    The first job I had after I got out of college was as a translator, then as a longshoreman in Baltimore, and then into the army. After the army I went to graduate school at Columbia and was a barge captain at the same time. A barge captain is the only job for an unemployed intellectual because you have absolutely nothing to do. I used to read all day and get paid for it. But I was bored by everything.

    I saw an ad in the paper once that said "Wanted: economist with graduate degree," so I called up and said, "I'm an economist." All they did was check to see that I had a degree, but not in what subject.

    Then I taught at the College of William and Mary and at CCNY [City College of New York]. But that was never a completely engrossing activity. The interesting problem in teaching was to teach something for the first time, when you weren't sure of the material yourself, when you had to get up on your tightrope, and something about the excitement of that made you a good teacher. The second time it was already flat.

After teaching I flopped around into different things and then I became a combination peddler and idea man. It was very uninspiring but lucrative. I put people together who weren't very logical together. My first relationship with Andy Warhol was commercial. I got him a job painting a Puerto Rican theater in Spanish Harlem. Andy went to the theater owner and told him to paint it Puerto Rican colors, pink and gaudy. The man did and Andy got a fee for saying that and I took a piece of Andy's fee. It was kind of a joke. I was always astounded at how silly businesspeople were. At that time I never went to the movies, I really disliked the medium.

What finally got you interested in making a film?
I saw a film in 1958–59 which had a great deal to do with the art world called *Pull My Daisy*. There was a new spirit in the air—we were emerging from the '50s and there was a new questioning that meshed with my own mood. I'd been a radical at the age of sixteen, then I became quiet. *Pull My Daisy* was shot by Alfred Leslie and Robert Frank. Allen Ginsberg and Larry Rivers were in it. It was the most brilliant text that Jack Kerouac had ever done. I liked the film because it was a very grubby little film, very cheaply made. It was a very alive film and it had a great sense of black and white which I liked. I was suddenly looking at films, looking at films I should have seen before, and I was excited by them.

What motivated you to make Point of Order?
There was a hole, something that had to be filled. Dan Talbot and I talked about his problem of getting new films to show in his theater. He hadn't at that time been able to procure all the old films and start the great classic series that he did. So originally he had the idea of taking the footage from the Army-McCarthy hearings and showing it at his theater. That's the point at which suddenly something went click in my head, which was "No. We shouldn't do that—we should make a film. It should be an imposition of order over chaos. It should be something different."

Did you have any training in filmmaking at all?
No. I'd never seen a piece of film, I'd never seen an editing machine. I started from scratch. It's a brutal way to learn things, but a very good way to find out everything for yourself.

The sociological aspect of all this that I find entertaining is that my life is a reversal of the American Dream, which is that you work your ass off to make a lot of money and when you're forty you retire. I gambled with my life. I spent all my time doing all the things that people who wanted to retire hoped to do when they retired, but didn't have the energy to do. I knew a lot of women, drank a lot, played very hard. That's what I did when I was young. When I reached middle age I started working very hard, nonstop. Right now I'm in a state of exhaustion and boredom. So I'm about to strike out in a new direction. It's not the subject alone, it's not the fact that I've looked upon documentary as a way to right wrong, as a way to cry out against injustice, as a way to attack the social system: I still feel that all those problems remain and that films should be made about them. But I've done everything I can. I can't say anything else with force in the documentary that I haven't said before.

This is something that happens to everyone in every art form. "What are you going to do next?" You can't fall back on earlier ideas. They're boring. The crack of that whip is very loud indeed and it prevents you from going back.

Richard Roud, whom I call Richard Rude, the director of the New York Film Festival, thought *Point of Order* was very good but not a film. It was just far enough ahead of its time that a festival director was too blind to see it. Dan Talbot's New Yorker is a better festival than Roud ever promoted.

A film is anything that goes through a projector. I'd been saying that for ten years before I read it in *Artforum*. I heard it in defense of a film by Peter Kubelka in which he simply ran white leader through the projector. My definition of film is anything that passes through a projector and produces a filmic response in people. It doesn't matter where the material comes from. But the audience is part of it.

Point of Order was shot with two absolutely fixed cameras. It's lucky that all I had to work with was those two fixed cameras grinding away remorselessly for 188 hours. The film worked better because there were no tricks in it. It was stripped down to where it really mattered. The aesthetics in that film was the politics, it was the character, it was the tone and the voice, it was America. That's what film is about, not beautiful shots.

What interests me more than anything else in film is structure. The Army-McCarthy hearings themselves were untrue, as the historical present usually is. What I did was make them true because what appeared to be the truth, that which actually happened, included all the efforts to sweep it under the rug, included that weaselly little ending in which everyone wanted to run away and not acknowledge what had been let loose in the land. When I changed it all around, it became not only a new kind of documentary, but also the truth.

Will you define structure?
The Swedes in reviewing *Millhouse* said it was the best portrait of a statesman since Charlie Chaplin's *The Great Dictator*. I think it's different than fiction, but it is made up in a sense. What I wanted to do in *Millhouse* was

to create a portrait of a political figure, to make it very clear that I wasn't being objective, to make Nixon as round as he could be on film, to make him as round as a figure in Molière, to have certain sympathy for him, to understand this poor boy from the lower middle classes with the burning desire and energy to have the whole piece of cake. Who wanted to eat the whole thing and got to eat the whole thing no matter how many Asian peasants were to die for it. Everybody who wrote about it missed the Horatio Alger structure. *Millhouse* starts with Nixon in 1962, defeated for the governorship of California, after already losing a shot at the presidency. To put that together in such a way on film, the Vietnam War and everything else, and not to make it strictly chronological but to have theme and subtheme . . . it's a wholly different experience in documentary. Structure is all.

All my films are collage films and I've wondered if there was any relationship between what I was doing and the fact that I did know these painters who were doing collage before I ever made films. *Millhouse* is cut from millions of options; it's the marriage of all kinds of elements. I use collage in film to make a political point because it's a shorthand to the truth of the documents.

Is there anyone today making films that, in your opinion, are superior or significant?
Not too many. One of the great problems of being an American is that you are driven mad by all the technical garbage that goes on around you, and you become inordinately impressed with the significance of technique and technical things. Lots of people have gone that route.

What about Andy Warhol's films?
What Andy was doing, which nobody picked up on, was reproducing the whole history of film from the beginning. His first films were silent; Andy didn't know how to use sound. He didn't know how to deal with motion. His films were static. One of his first films was *Sleep*—about a guy lying on a couch. Another was a transvestite eating a banana. It was exactly like the beginning of film. Then Andy learned how to move the camera, so you got a little more action. Then he learned how to do sync sound. Although Andy didn't do much of this himself, there would be no Warhol films without Warhol. Without Andy, I doubt if the people around him could exist. Andy is the organizing force and intelligence. Whether he actually handles the camera himself isn't important. As he has moved closer to conventional film, the films are less interesting.

I was the subject of a film by Warhol so I saw him work, what I could remember of it. He made a seventy-minute film of me getting drunk. I drank a quart of whiskey in twenty minutes—that's very hard to do and stay alive. I noticed his technique was primitive (this was early in his film life). It was refreshing. That "Look, Ma, no hands" aspect of Andy's work was always the most interesting part of his work, whether it was in painting or in film. Again, it was the necessary and proper rebellion against the million-handed Hollywood monster. How else could you begin except the way Andy began or the way I began, if you were going to make serious films? He didn't cut anything. His films were just rolls of film spliced together. It was like he invented cutting as Porter and Griffith did. Andy got it reduced to a premodern minimum. What you saw in his life, taking place about every three months, was the whole history of film being redone.

What sort of material do you consider to be documents for your films?
My films are made with documents, whether I film the document or whether the document exists. The structure, the technique, everything else is invented. There are no actors employed.

An aspect of all this that I find interesting is the films of mine that have been commercial failures, like *Rush to Judgment,* 1966, which was the first film that began with a collage of events, newsreels, and interviews. A film that I really dislike, *The Sorrow and the Pity,* is an absolute imitation of my film, and is financially one of the most successful documentaries ever made. *Rush to Judgment* was seen in France by all the people in the film world. It had a run there before it ran here, and it was the first film made like that. *The Sorrow and the Pity* is the same film, sentimentally done and badly structured. It's more sentimental for New Yorkers because it emphasizes the Jewish question under the Nazis, and because we're already nostalgic about Hitler, World War II, and the Resistance. Also it doesn't offend anybody. It's very safe to talk about the Resistance and to take the mealymouthed position Anthony Eden does in that film. A liberal film. It's easy to get up and talk about the fall of France, or the Resistance, because it's all so alien to our culture or to English culture at this point, and it's so dim in the past. Hitler is dead and buried. But to talk about the assassination of John F. Kennedy in Dallas right now is still dangerous.

Are your films being rereleased now?
Yes. The American Film Institute did a retrospective of my films two years ago and since that time different countries have been doing it, the Swedes, the Danes, the Finns, the Norwegians, now the University of Wisconsin. No film of mine has ever been on television in the United States in its original version. Every film of mine has played television in Holland, Belgium, Sweden, England, West Germany, and at the commercial rates.

SUSAN LINFIELD

Irrepressible Emile de Antonio Speaks (1982)

Editor Susan Linfield's probing interview with de Antonio appeared in two consecutive summer issues of the Independent, *the journal of the Foundation for Independent Video and Film in New York. "Irrepressible Emile de Antonio Speaks" was followed by "De Antonio's Fireside Chat: Part Two," excerpted here. Part Montaigne, part "bear act," the irrepressible filmmaker/intellectual connects his ideas on philosophy, religion, and politics with thoughts on cinema.*

The whole collage technique you've developed has been called a kind of "counter-philosophy" of filmmaking.
The early Soviets had a kind of collage technique. This is what Eisenstein was doing, although I don't think he ever used the word *collage*. But what the Russian theorists talked about is the thing that I feel I got out of strictly American roots: putting two elements together in the editing process, if you do it right, develops something greater than the sum of the two parts. And that's what collage basically is, whether the collage was by Picasso or by Rauschenberg, or a musical collage by John Cage—the introduction of seemingly disparate elements not only provided a new insight, but became almost a totally different thing.

But the thing that made the collage thing live, that made my becoming an artist in film possible, among other things, was knowing John Cage. I met Cage in the early fifties. He and I both drank a great deal, and we used to sit up all night arguing.

This was before he was well known?
Oh, yeah, he wasn't well known at all. Cocteau once said that the ideal is to be brilliant, famous, and unknown, which is what John was: brilliant, famous to a few people, and totally unknown to the world.

John had already brought Zen Buddhism here from the West Coast. He was the first one. He was a lively, hostile person, which I liked. He opened up my mind and my sensibility, and it was through him that I met Rauschenberg and Johns. John was a collage artist. His music was collage.

When Dan [Talbot] and I were talking years later about the Army-McCarthy hearings, suddenly I saw the way it should be done. We both agreed that we had an intact historical experience. And the idea always was to make it organic and still a collage, although not an obvious one. Not a collage like Picasso, where you'd have a banjo and then something attached, but a very subtle kind of collage, like a fiction film. Not that I have any particular liking for fiction films; they're not better than documentaries, they're just different. But with that kind of organic wholeness you can go from the beginning to the end without having that crude intrusive voice, or smarmy, velvety TV voice, telling you what it is you're looking at while you're looking at it.

You've said that you think that kind of external narration is a fascist form.
I could see doing a film, say, on El Salvador right now, with narration. In those days, because I was inventing a new kind of film, I had to hate narration!

Point of Order *is in some ways your most organic film, because not only does it not have any narration, it doesn't even have any interviews, or anything outside of that one event [the Army-McCarthy hearings].*
Nothing. That's it. The other thing that I like most about it is that it was ugly. There was nothing worse than those TV cameras. First of all, it was kinescope. Secondly, they were fixed by senatorial rule and could not be moved. I loved the fact that I was going to make art out of junk, which is another thing that goes back to Cage and Rauschenberg.

Did you have particular political aims in mind for the film while you were making it?
Yes, absolutely. I've always been left-wing. Left-wing is like a flame. It doesn't burn constantly. You have to replenish it and refurbish it and recharge it. Like any belief, it has its ups and downs. There have been long periods when I've been depressed about myself and the world in which I've been a very poor left-wing person. And then in other periods I'm very up, usually when I'm working. That's a hell of a confession, because people will say, "Aha! Look at this hypocritical bastard: when he relaxes after a film he's nonpolitical, and he takes the artificial stimulation of politics to make him work." Well, people have the right to make that charge, though it doesn't happen to be true.

It was very necessary to make the point in *Point of Order* which no one got. It got the greatest reviews that any documentary film has ever had in this country. But they didn't understand it, the more they praised it. That idiot Jimmy Wechsler said [the film was] "a love letter to Miss Liberty." Those lines are meaningless. What is "a love letter to Miss Liberty"? The film was not a love letter to Miss Liberty—although I believe in liberty. The film, which no critic ever saw, revealed a kind of fundamental conspiracy of weakness before this harsh, cruel, totally ignorant man, who was a genius in one thing, who understood the thing that underlies all my work, which is that our culture is like the Homeric Cave of the Winds: it's about words boring through the earth: words, words, words. And McCarthy knew that he could dominate this country by lying consistently.

So I wanted the film to reveal something which had never been done on film, which is the downfall of a demagogue. The film has no hero. It wasn't Welch who beat him. Welch used the same shabby tricks McCarthy used! It was my belief then, and is still my belief, that if you put a pig on the air long enough he will reveal himself.

And that's why I didn't want a narrator saying any of that. This is the difference between a film that has artistic and political aspirations and the garbage that the entertainment industry spews forth: I wanted people to perceive for themselves what had happened. I wanted people to have an active role. That's what I've done in all my films. I don't explain. If I have to explain it, I don't want it in the film. I feel that audiences are much smarter than critics.

The person who makes a serious film is at such an extraordinary disadvantage. It's a disadvantage I prize and treasure, but a disadvantage nonetheless. We are conditioned as a people; we are the most brainwashed people in the world: TV going in and out of your minds from childhood to the grave. And what are you looking at? Stuff whose primary object is to sell products we don't need. But during the sale of those products you are also being sold, you're being absolutely excluded from any democratic process and cut out of life. You are totally passive.

Cinema verité films also have no narration, but there's obviously a big difference between your films and those of [Richard] Leacock or [Don] Pennebaker.
Yeah. Their contribution to filmmaking is substantial and valuable, because it has to do with the development of equipment. It has nothing to do with the art of film.

The great philosophical weakness of vérité is to ask: Whose vérité? Whose truth? Truth is a fugitive thing. Every time you look through a camera and every time you cut a piece of film you impose a point of view. Pretending not to impose a point of view is to impose the view of the state, or of whatever society you work in. You simply reinforce it.

Cinema verité is film which pursues a fugitive and hopeless lie, which is that the camera itself is capable of presenting us with a form of truth. No camera can present the truth. A person presents the truth.

So it's the illusion of objectivity to which you object?
It's the illusion of technical objectivity. The great flaw of our culture is this adoration of technique. The myth is that through some kind of fake technical objectivity we can reach an objective statement or image of society, or even of people. Untrue. Because those people caught in that second of time have history. And history is what destroys the very concept of cinema verité. It becomes a kind of masturbatory, self-indulgent, self-promoting fake idea of filmmaking that that moment you catch in midair is Life. But it isn't Life. It's a moment caught in midair.

Did you just gain your technical knowledge as you went along making films?
I've kept, by inclination, my technical command of film to a minimum, because I think there is a human idea that presupposes the shape of what's going to happen. And the technology should serve it.

If there's somebody who's really fucking up film, it's a guy like [George] Lucas. The end of *Star Wars* is exactly the same as *Triumph of the Will*. Luke Skywalker is walking down an aisle. He's going to be decorated, he has his two friends behind him, he's in front, and there are masses of people. In *Triumph* Hitler's walking down with the mass of Nazis on the side, and behind Hitler are Himmler and Hess. It's the same shot.

To begin with, his work is fascist, that celebration of the irrational, of military ardor. I saw the one that came after *Star Wars*, in which Alec Guinness plays the wise old man who has The Force. That's such a totalitarian concept, too. The transmission of the mystical. What it's doing, in fact, is making fascist ideology out of myths that weren't fascist. It's stressing the fanatical, the military. And it's not an accident that the name Darth Vader looks like Dark Invader, and that the character has a black voice. Those liberal scenes in *Star Wars* are the most despicable of all, where all the little monsters and animals are sitting together in the space bar having a drink, showing that we're all equal even though we're all little monsters.

How much of this do you think is conscious?
Not all. Absolutely not all.

What does it mean to you to be a Marxist filmmaker working in America in 1982?
Maybe I'm comfortable with the position of opposition, and it's probably the duty of a Marxist in anything to be in opposition to a government like those that we've had in my mature life.

All my films, including *Painters Painting,* have to do with the history of my country in my time. That's a suitable subject for an artist to address himself to. But it's always been in the light of opposition. And the painting question raises it emblematically for all the arts. The painter too is in opposition. Even if he paints abstractly, those abstract shapes are subversive, because the people who are heads of state think there has to be something wrong with it. I mean, that was Stalin's reason for suppressing [Liubov] Popova: that her work didn't glorify Stalin.

You were once thinking of making a film about your life.
Yeah. That's the best idea I've ever had: "A Middle-Aged Radical as Seen through the Eyes of His Government." I was so shocked when I got the first bunch of stuff through the Freedom of Information Act back in 1975. When I was a teenager I was already literally on a list signed by J. Edgar Hoover for concentration camps. This while I was doing my best to enlist in the U.S. Army. I read it and saw the whole country differently. I realized that there was sheer madness in it. I wasn't a serious revolutionary when I was a teenager. I mean, I was revolutionary enough to go and get arrested and be on picket lines, but I also wore black tie and went to parties and drank champagne. They should have seen me for what I was: a weakling.

The Freedom of Information Act was the greatest single act that this country's had since the Bill of Rights. In a technological society, where you have the capability to eavesdrop electronically, you have to bring the Bill of Rights up to date, you have to make it a twentieth-century Bill of Rights. The FBI and CIA never cooperated in the administration of that law. They abandoned it. They subverted it.

What do you see as the political trend in this country?
I think we're going to have a major depression. But at that point the military will take over. The more we play around with all this stuff, the more we look like a banana republic. I think the American military is perfectly capable, with the CIA and the FBI, of creating a genuinely computerized fascist society.

There is something so shabby about a clown becoming the president of a country. You know, the great line in film history is when somebody asked the old man Louis B. Mayer, who was approaching death, "Mr. Mayer, have you heard that they just nominated Ronnie Reagan for governor?" He said, "Oh, no no no, not for governor. Jimmy Stewart for governor: Ronnie for lieutenant governor!"

Can you talk about the case of the Plowshares Eight, the subject of your new film?
The title comes from the Book of Isaiah in the Old Testament: "They shall beat their swords into plowshares." It's the definitive antiwar statement of a warlike people, the ancient Hebrews. The movement itself stems from the actions of the Berrigans, going way back. They always get other people involved; in this case, a nun, a public defender, a priest, a mother of six children.

The group studied how most effectively to make a blow against the nuclear arms race. And they found out that the central GE plant among the ten plants in the King of Prussia, Pennsylvania, area, was Plant No. 9, which made one thing: nose cones for thermonuclear bombs. This nose cone shields the bomb from exploding and burning when it enters the atmosphere. Without the shell they can't use the bomb.

So they studied shift changes and everything else. They just drove in just before the shift changed, seven o'clock in the morning. They walked in, right through the doors. (The FBI went crazy, because those plants are supposed to have tremendous security.) They had hammers hidden under their clothes. Then they took out their hammers and smashed two nose cones—very fragile metal, very thin—put the hammers down, held hands, sang hymns and prayers. The cops came and arrested them. Then nobody knew what to do with them. The FBI was there, the U.S. attorney was there, the local people were there. Then they decided to let the local people prosecute them.

And then, different members of the Catholic left approached me and said, "You should really make a film about this." And I said, "You're wrong. I'm not a Catholic, I'm not a pacifist, and I'm not interested."

The people I knew were very honorable, tough people. They were more left than most leftists. And they kept pressing harder. And I thought, "Well, this will be an easy documentary, the kind I don't make. So I'll just get a camera crew and go down there and film it all and that will be the end of it. It'll take a month to edit and it'll be like some fucking TV thing."

But I can't do that kind of thing and the government didn't let me. I assumed that because of the new rules I could film in court. But they never allow you to do political stuff, just murders and things. So I went down to Norristown, Pennsylvania, where the trial was held. And I suddenly saw that all the stuff I was thinking about could come to be in this film. I suddenly saw the possibility of making a new kind of film, which I liked. I said, "Fuck the trial, I don't need it: I'll make a script out of the trial."

So you reenacted the trial?
Yes.

Did you write the script or just condense from verbatim transcripts?
Both.

Did the Plowshares Eight have the support of the people in the town?
Oh, no. The town hated them and the whole trial. This is the place that Haig comes from. It's a very quiet, WASPy, conservative place. They don't like troublemakers. They hated the Plowshares Eight, but even more, they hated the people who came down from Philadelphia and New York to demonstrate. Why make all this fuss and noise here? Let's "just go about our business of making atomic weapons."

It was a cruel trial. The town was very nervous and frightened. There were a lot of threats made against the film crew.

I admire the courage behind that kind of act, but I can't see how that type of action will stop the U.S. war machine.
I don't think the Berrigans do either. They don't think individual actions stop anything. The action itself is symbolic, it attracts attention, it makes people think about the arms race. And it also shows that there are people who are not afraid of those who run the arms race.

In the second place, when you do that kind of action, you have a public trial. And when you have a public trial you have stuff come out of it like this film, which tends to perpetuate the action, and tends to make the action seen. Already, we have a possible [European] audience of probably 15 to 20 million people.

In the trial, Dan [Berrigan] and [Father] Carl Kabat would get up and say, "Your Honor, we did that, we broke those bombs." In fact Kabot, who's not so articulate, said, "We got those nose cones good, Your Honor." He was proud. I mean, they didn't say, "guilty with an explanation." They just said, "We did it." The jury had to convict them.

One of their main points was the metaphor of what FDR said to the people of Germany in World War II. He said, "Destroy your concentration camps. Destroy the ovens. Risk your lives to do this." So the Plowshares Eight said that they feel it's the same thing in attacking this plant: that we, as Americans, have that same imperative laid down for us.

My father taught me to laugh at all religions. We hated equally rabbis, priests, nuns, and ministers. My father's favorite word was, "Ooh, look at that Jesuitical face," and it would be a conniving, smiling, cold face. Now there's a price on every Jesuit's head in Guatemala. They're killed on sight. They're all left-wing.

All the Helen Caldicotts in the world aren't going to change anybody—all those talky doctors, Physicians for Social Responsibility, all those people babbling away. You finally need people who will do things, who will put their lives out there. And the trial illustrates that. Had they won the case, that would have meant that private business and the government did not have the right to stop people from committing acts of witness against property. That could never be. The government had to find a way to jail them. Otherwise, they could have gone the next day to another plant.

Do the Berrigans share your pessimism about social change?
No. Absolutely not.

How did you get Martin Sheen involved?
A whole bunch of celebrities in Hollywood supported Mary [Lampson] and Haskell [Wexler] and me [during the *Underground* grand jury]. Among them was Martin Sheen. I met Sheen then and was very impressed with him. He's a brilliant actor, and I love him. I also believe in magic; maybe it's a substitute for religion. I had one of those magical moments in which I thought I would write to Martin Sheen. Why didn't I write to Jon Voight? I wrote to Sheen and said, "Look, I'm doing this film, and I need some help." Sheen is also a believer. There are not many believers out there.

In what?
In social change. In radical activity. And his is Christian radical activity. He wrote me a letter thanking me for giving him the opportunity to be in the film, and he ended it by saying, "And for allowing me to come as close to courage as I ever am likely to come in my life," meaning the courage of the Berrigans, of course.

How did shooting in video work out? Are you going to do it again?
Never. I don't like the image. Never, never.

I knew from watching TV films that those films that are shot by TV cameramen are boring, visually. A TV cameraperson is a fucking bug, because they're tied to a headset and some idiot so-called floor director is telling them what to do while the producer is telling the floor director what to do. So the guy at the end is like an insect. So I knew that I wanted a cameraperson from films who had never had any TV experience. I don't like that film *Northern Lights* very much, but I love Judy Irola's camera work. So I got hold of Judy and she saw it right away.

What are your political hopes for the film? How will it be distributed? Who will it reach?
I don't show things to anybody before they're finished, but I've already sold it to a major TV station in England, one in Holland, and one in Sweden. I'm going to have a big agent here go after this and try to get it.

I would like it to have a theatrical release. It's a hard film. There are no fake or meretricious or flashy moments in it. It's a trial film, basically. Trial films work when they have Charles Laughton and Marlene Dietrich, or even Joe McCarthy and Joe Welch. This has real people.

Dan Berrigan is a great actor. Dan does two speeches in the film, and I'm sure he'll be nominated for an Academy Award. Seriously. One of them is a showstopper. I sent Sheen a tape of it, which he showed in his house, and—this shows you how corrupt America is—the people who saw the film said, "Who's his agent?" [Berrigan subsequently was cast in *The Mission* (1986), with Robert De Niro and Jeremy Irons.]

Do you see the film as an organizing tool for support for the Plowshares Eight?
I never see films as organizing tools. I see films as films. It's like being a mother, in a way. Once a film is done, you sort of let go of it. I've got to do something else. I hope that people use it in a way that's productive. But I can't make that next political step that some filmmakers do, which is to spend three years working with the film. I couldn't stand it. I really want to make another film, not spend the rest of my life talking about this one.

What ever happened to your CIA [Philip Agee] film?
That was shot down when [CIA agent Richard] Welch was killed in Athens. Nothing worse could have happened to me than having Welch killed. It's the worst that could have happened to him, too, I guess. When Welch was killed, they claimed Agee was involved in naming him, which was totally untrue. I know Greek radicals who say it was absolutely obvious to anybody who lived in Athens that that was the CIA's house. So when you read those crappy letters about what a sensitive, witty man Richard Welch was, a classical scholar and all that . . . CIA guys are thugs! They are secret political police, and getting killed goes with the job, frankly. It's like being a soldier. But it destroyed the film. People are afraid to buck the CIA.

What about the film you were once planning on the Long March?
I had lunch with the new [Chinese] ambassador to Canada, an extraordinary Chinese lunch. But they were so bureaucratic and crazy. They said, "Why don't you just come to Peking, Hangchow?" I said, "No, I'm not interested in Nixon's trip; I want to do the Long March!" I wanted to intercut stuff

that I would shoot today with the whole history of that triumph, one of the greatest moments in the short life of socialism.

I could have made the film by taking two years off and proving that I was a sincere Chinese Communist. But I'm not a Chinese Communist. I'm an American communist.

How have you raised money for your films?
In the documentary collages, I've amassed enormous collections of valuable archives. So, in making the next film, I would say to a rich person, "Look, I have this tremendous amount of stuff on, say, Vietnam. As an inducement to invest in my new project I will sell you this for a thousand dollars. You can give it away and get a $100,000 tax deduction. Plus there will be a little permanent collection on Hanoi donated by you."

It's the boring responsibility of filmmakers to raise money. I myself don't like to ask the foundations and the government for money. I don't want to be judged by those assholes. I prefer to do my "bear act" (you know, I look a little like a bear): put on my bearskin and perform for people, tell them how wonderful it's going to be, and how brilliant I am. Then they write checks. It's worked up till now.

But you also have a long track record.
It doesn't hurt. I don't see much of a future [for independent filmmakers] unless you are willing to produce entertainment. And even if I were to make a fiction film, entertainment is not my first consideration. The film could be funny and sexy and even brutal, but those elements would not be there to sell tickets.

I probably am moving away from documentaries toward fiction. But I've always regarded all the people in my films as actors, which is maybe nonhuman and impersonal of me. Ho Chi Minh and Nixon, Roy Cohn and Joe McCarthy.

You've talked, and other filmmakers have talked, about the paradox of making films for social change which don't reach a mass audience.
Sure. The very nature of our society is that the mass audience is cut off from ideas and clearly indoctrinated by the ultimate brainwashing tool, American TV. Godard, who's the most innovative filmmaker since World War II, has no audience here. And there's no decent distribution for independent films now.

One of the most perverse aspects of our culture is that truth in American films comes out of comedy, where, under the guise of not being serious, you are actually much more serious. W. C. Fields's *It's a Gift* is the most radical film I've ever seen in America. It makes my work look conservative. Fields, an old right-winger, plays a guy in a hardware store during the Depression who reads an ad about orange groves in California. So he drives across the country in a rickety car, with his terrible wife and wretched children. In the end he is sold part of the town dump for an orange grove, and he's crestfallen, devastated—and then it turns out to be an oil well, so he's rich. In the last shot he's still with his terrible wife and disgusting children, but he has an English butler pouring him gallons of martinis. It's a devastating attack on the impersonal and inhuman aspects of capitalism. Marvelous thing.

JAY MURPHY

Red Bass *Interview:*
Emile de Antonio (1983)

Jay Murphy, editor of the literary review Red Bass, *later published two tributes to de Antonio:"Radical Politics and an Art of Quality," an obituary in the* Independent *(1990), and a memorial in the* Red Bass *anthology* Conspiracy Charges *(1991). Here Murphy allows de Antonio, "with all the crustiness of a barge captain," to harangue against President Reagan. De Antonio ends with a call for the new generation of filmmakers to skewer "the old mummer" and his republished memoir* Where's the Rest of Me? The Autobiography of Ronald Reagan *(New York: Karz, 1965, 1981).*

In the King of Prussia *is the first film that you have made that is part fiction; why have you chosen the medium of documentary film rather than any other?*
I chose documentary not because it is cheaper, although it is; not because it is easier, it isn't; not because it was a training exercise for a higher form of film. I chose it because the form itself was more difficult and more interesting; because I am political; because almost all the films being made in the U.S. when I made *Point of Order* were pretty and irrelevant. Pretty is commercial and deadly. Pretty films are anodynes, manufactured antireality.

Luck belongs to art as much as talent, will, ability. I had been lucky enough to be a friend of John Cage and Bob Rauschenberg. Both of them had used elements of cultural detritus in their work: Cage, odd sounds that were out there; Rauschenberg, odd objects that were out there. I discovered that to be art, film did not have to be well framed, well lit shots of Charlton Heston.

Movies had been boring to me; they were Barbie dolls for an audience that was assumed to be dim-witted. The logical conclusion of that vacuity was to elect an aged Barbie doll to the White House. That is the penalty of media domination. What mad director could have dreamed of a broken-down actor, out of work, playing real scenes with real generals and weapons on a stage where life itself could end? Was it an accident that Reagan's career began with "live" broadcasts of baseball games he never saw? Making them exciting to audiences which wanted to believe they were hearing the crack of a real bat. Then all those dull film roles and hustling workers at GE preaching that capitalism was good for workers. The old mummer is the president we deserve. Mummery a better teacher than Harvard.

My first film, *Point of Order,* was made of wavy-lined kinescope material from the 1954 Army-McCarthy hearings. It was the first feature documentary without narration and it played theaters successfully. It wasn't pretty; it was real; it was grainy and the sound was extremely uneven and it was art, had more emotion and politics than any Hollywood film being made. It opened in 1963 and I went to Cannes with it and saw *The Best Man* there. I knew I had the best film and all that Hollywood hokum was made by con men for boobs.

How have you survived as an independent filmmaker? Is it more difficult now to raise money for films than a decade or so ago? You have said that it has been harder to raise money for this movie about Catholic activists than any other; why is that so?

I have survived as an independent film director because I am a turtle. I lay my eggs carefully and hope they survive. It is harder now than at any time in the past twenty-five years. We live in a police state. The liberal rich who used to fund progressive films are scared. The Petroleum Broadcasting System is a cringing, servile, bootlicking toady before Gulf, Mobil, and Reagan's culture police. The networks are comfortable enough being well-paid hookers in expensive pads. Masterpiece Theater is pseudocultural pap for the middle class that used to belong to the Book of the Month Club. Alistair Cooke receives awards for fatuously telling us what we're looking at as we look at it. The greatest gift to the United States would be the complete destruction of television in its present state.

TV is a repressive tool. Think of the last twenty years from Jack Webb to Kojak. Why so many shows about cops? The Greeks peopled their theater with gods, heroes, struggles; Shakespeare with kings, romance, wars, and national destiny. TV: the cops, Kojak, Columbo, a cop in a wheelchair, a blind cop, *Mod Squad,* Angie Dickinson, *Hill Street Blues, CHiPs, Starsky and Hutch,* on and on. Always good, never brutal, always honest. Think of the show J. Edgar Hoover sponsored: *The FBI.* Does anyone who lives in the real world believe the police are their image? That's why it's hard to raise money.

As a lifelong Marxist, how has the time spent with the Plowshares Eight, with Daniel and Philip Berrigan, influenced your politics?
Finally, what matters is living what you truly believe, hoping first of all that you are lucky enough to be right. I have always been a Marxist without a party. I have known Marxists with eleven cars; Marxists whose taste in film, poetry, music was as bourgeois as Stalin's. Or Reagan's. Nancy and Ronald Reagan have the same exquisite taste Andropov has. The mind of the Pentagon when it is perceived resembles the mind of Soviet rocket generals. Daily we and they resemble one another more and more. Neither can bear dissent at home. They have Budapest, Prague, Afghanistan; we're bloodier: Korea, Vietnam, Chile, and now the great Central American peasant shoot. Reagan backs labor unions and democratic processes in Poland while he attacks and suppresses them at home. The old mummer is the finest hypocrite of our stage. And people are afraid here. Try telling a cop he's wrong. The FBI is as corrupt and murderous as the KGB, and the CIA is worse. We need a yardstick to measure the monsters that devour us. The number of the dead is not a bad place to begin the measure of the monstrous.

I support the Catholic left, the Christian left, because it is for peace with courage and honor. It stands for people and the extension of their rights. It is not a church of the counting house or the golf course. It tries to be a church of the people.

In retrospect, what are your reflections on one of the most interesting films you have made, Underground? *Despite the fact that the Weather Underground is regularly vilified in the left press now (an article in* In These Times *called them "criminal"), do you still feel that what they accomplished and attempted to accomplish is important in terms of political struggle today?*
The Weather Underground slowly lived out the end of a period. It was out of touch with the mass of people. It no longer exists. Its splits revealed its weaknesses. It was small. And yet, its larger assumptions, which it shared with much of the left, are correct: that we are racist and imperialist. These two words need to be defined and redefined through action. If they are "criminal," what shall we name Kissinger, Nixon, Johnson, the generals of death without victory, My Lai, the CIA programs in Vietnam? Surely the WUO deserves more from history than those.

Do you feel greater political pressure on you today, or less than in the Nixon era, when you were the only filmmaker on the enemy list? Has harassment from the government ever substantially interfered with your work?
In bad times, social art must be critical of evil. The personal arts such as poetry and painting are more idiosyncratic and can be what they want. But

not film. Repression is greater today. Pressure is greater. Time runs out. It doesn't affect me directly. I shall continue to do what I choose to do. Those who deal with my work talk to the FBI, they are inhibited, they are frightened. For me, being on Nixon's "enemies list" was a greater honor than the Academy Award. The list is also a text on the White House as madhouse. I have before me many memoranda on White House letterhead. Haldeman, John Dean, Fred Fielding, now counselor to RR, they wondered and wondered what they should do to me. They were as paranoid as their master. Bombing Cambodia, planning Watergate, the Huston plan, and there they were worried that Larry O'Brien would use my film.

In the making of *Underground* the government subpoenaed us. Our crime: exercise of the First Amendment of the Constitution. The FBI stole our sound track. A former FBI agent told me they planned to mug me to steal the negative so the film would never be made. I wasn't at all surprised. It is what a reasonable person might expect from the FBI. Don't forget that Hoover's greatest skill was blackmail. Publicity and blackmail, interrelated. JFK wanted to get rid of him, Nixon too, but Hoover had everyone's dirty underwear in his files, including the Congress. This is why [CIA director William] Webster looks like Dick Tracy: to clean up the act.

Do you know any filmmakers on the left that you feel are successful in using film as a tool for social change? How do you see the effectiveness of someone such as Godard?
Your last question raises more questions. . . .

I cannot see success without a party which has an impermanent, totally democratic vanguard. Correctly enough, no party will work here unless it is, and is perceived as, American. That is the lesson of Mao, Fidel, Ho, the Sandinistas. An American party for peace, equality, education, open media, one free from police intrusion and with a police responsible to the people and technology controlled by the people.

The "free media" are free to make money. They don't even pay the interest they owe on the debt to freedom and to us. The *New York Times* sells papers, pulp, airtime, and it is part of the government.

Neither Marx nor Lenin wrote sacred texts. The economic analysis seems correct to me. I see no party capable of implementing it. The duty of artists is to create new myths which will displace false ones—such as the melting pot. Our melting pot is a stew for fascists. The question of Central America is: Who was Sandino? And who was Somoza?

Artists are freakish and unreliable. Hacks who work for money alone, like Hollywood auteurs, are easier to understand. Most left-wing filmmakers flop around too much. The truth and its forms make hard demands in our police state. Those without politics invent historical substitutes which support the state. Hence Godard, who lived history in darkened movie houses and helped invent a theory of auteurs. Hence the foolish essays on Frank Tashlin, Jerry Lewis, and Alfred Hitchcock. But, fortunately, life is unpredictable. [Godard] made some very good films. He has not yet recovered from his pseudopolitical phase. Much can be learned from him, even from his pedantry and the uses of it.

A call at the end from an older person to a younger one: Don't forget, the old mummer isn't playing a Christmas comedy in a home for retired actors. The role he plays controls life on this planet. It's time for a new filmmaker to come out with *Where* Is *the Rest of You?*

JEAN-MICHEL BASQUIAT

Emile de Antonio with Jean-Michel Basquiat (1984)

A cartoon of country singer Dolly Parton graced the cover of Andy Warhol's Interview *magazine in July 1984, the age of what Teri Tynes has called High Reagan. Between glitzy photo spreads on Dolly and Muppet Miss Piggy readers found this incongruous encounter between Warhol's old mentor and his new protégé. Basquiat, the young artist who rocketed to brief fame before dying of a drug overdose at age twenty-seven, drew a crayola portrait of de Antonio for the publication. In vintage Warhol fashion, a photograph of the Marxist filmmaker and the cause célèbre of the art scene featured a caption advertising Giorgio Armani couture (figure 34).*

Elaine [New York restaurateur Elaine Kauffman] calls him the greatest documentarist in the world, and the greatest drinker. Emile de Antonio—anarchist, ex-professor, author, and the only filmmaker on Richard Nixon's enemies list—has spent the last twenty years making trouble for the big boys.

De Antonio lives with his sixth wife, a psychoanalyst, in an East Village townhouse, where two major projects are currently under way: a book on art empire-builder Leo Castelli, and an autobiographical labor entitled *A Middle-Aged Radical As Seen through the Eyes of His Government*, about his life and lawsuits against the FBI. Taken from that organization's five thousand-page dossier on de Antonio, the film will star Martin Sheen as the reeling rebel with the last word.

EMILE DE ANTONIO: My new book is called *Painters Painting*. It's based on a film I shot in 1970, then interrupted and finished in 1973. Henry Geldzahler did a show for the Metropolitan Museum centennial (which my book documents), and this was probably the only time in the history of this country or of any country that you're going to have a collection of major modern painting like that at one time. Modern [art] doesn't travel the way, say,

Figure 21. "Fur Hat," a drawing of de Antonio (right) by Jean-Michel Basquiat appeared in *Interview* magazine, July 1984. Compare with figure 34. Copyright 2000 Artists Rights Society (ARS), New York/ADAGP, Paris. Reproduced by permission of Artists Rights Society.

Rembrandts do. Modern is more fragile basically, like the painting of yours I just saw that's on pieces of wood. Some of those early Rauschenbergs are, and an early Jasper Johns was made with a bedsheet—his first American flag—the sheet he slept on. Anyway, it was an enormous show, and it filled huge numbers of galleries. I had to sign a lot of papers to get into the museum at night. I had to hire four Metropolitan Museum guards—ex-cops, so they would watch my crew and me to make sure that we didn't steal anything. It's very hard to steal a painting anyway when you're there in the middle of the night. I bought them beer and sandwiches, and after three weeks they were pretty nice.

JEAN-MICHEL BASQUIAT: *You're a very political person. Tell me about your film* Millhouse.
EMILE DE ANTONIO: After I shot the material for *Painters Painting,* the phone rang one day and some guy said, "Listen, we just ripped off the XYZ network, and we have all the Nixon material that ever existed, everything—Checkers, all this stuff that nobody was allowed to have." I said, "Why are you telling me this?" He said, "Well, we know your work; we'd like you to make a film out of it." I said, "I can't make a film out of it, I'm working on a film, and what do you want out of all this?" He said, "I don't want a penny. I just want you to make a film." These were passionate times in 1970. There was Vietnam, Nixon was in office, there was no way to ever get him out. I asked the guy for twenty minutes, and I thought, if I do it, I've got to put all this painting stuff aside, but I do want to do it because I am a political person. I hate Nixon, I hate the war, and I hate everything those people stand for. So when the guy called back I agreed. I said, "I'll give the super twenty bucks and you come here around midnight; there will be nobody in my place. The super will let you in, you put it all there and get out." I said, "You don't want to know me?" and he said, "No." The next morning I walk in and there were five hundred cans of film. There was enough film there to make fifty movies, probably. I went through it all. There was stuff about the Native American takeover of Alcatraz, there was a lot of civil rights stuff. I took all that and gave it to the Cubans.

The Cubans?
Castro's people. I gave it to those guys so they could make a film out of it themselves, and I kept all the Nixon material.

What did you give to Castro?
Native Americans taking over Alcatraz, that had nothing to do with Nixon.

I don't understand. Why the Cubans?
Because I'm sympathetic to Castro. We put three industries into Cuba: sugar, whores, and gambling. I'm not against the United States or the people of the United States, but I'm against interfering in Central America. I'm against our going into El Salvador and Nicaragua. We went into Grenada, among other things, because we lost the war in Vietnam. We finally found some small place where we could send in the 82d Airborne, Rangers, Marines. . . .

I mean, it's insane. But I was in World War II. That seemed like it was worth doing. See, the thing that bugs me about Reagan is that he's also destroying our language; there's no meaning. He went on television and said we did not "invade" Grenada—that was a word the press used, "invasion." It was an *invasion*. We didn't go there to make love, we didn't go there to dance, we went there with arms ready to kill people who would pick up a gun on turf that wasn't ours. This is the most inhumane government I've ever seen in the United States.

Is it scary to be you?
Sure.

You seem to be a very important—
Agitator.

No, journalist.
I'm not a journalist, I'm an artist. I make films that aren't like all the trash—

No, you seem like a very real journalist. Your business seems to be compiling information.
Most journalists deal with fiction, but I deal with the documents. *Millhouse* became a very successful film. It played all over the world. I'm the only person who put in a film what the black riots in Miami were about in 1968, when Nixon ran. That to me was just as important as Nixon getting nominated. People were killed there and the riot was by the police against the people. One of the things I did, for instance: Nixon almost begins to say in the 1968 convention acceptance speech, "When I was a boy I had a dream. . . ."

He said, "I have a dream"?
Not precisely those words. It had those resonances. It sounded like that. He said, "I see a boy and he hears the train go by at night," and it was exactly with the cadences of King. I love making people realize what the world is really about. People used to say to me, "D, how come you have all these left-wing politics and you like this decadent painting?" Most radicals don't like modern art, they don't like modern painting, modern writing.

Why?
Because so many radicals are conventional in everything but a single hard political line. And that's as boring as being like Nixon or Reagan.

So your book, Painters Painting, *is based directly on the film?*
What I find interesting about the book is the same thing that's interesting about the film.

Why make a book today out of a film you shot in 1970?
I thought the period of New York painting covered by the film was just as important as the Renaissance, or Paris in the second half of the nineteenth century. No written record of those times exists.

But Leonardo kept a lot of his own records.
Those are his own records, but it's not somebody pushing him and leading him into a conversation. I wanted a written record of de Kooning, Pollock, Stella, Rauschenberg, and Johns, and many others. I knew all those people, it was off the cuff, it was immediate. It's what they really thought about how and why they worked. There had been only words *about* them.

In this movie did you interview all the artists?
Yes, on film.

Who was in the show at the Metropolitan?
De Kooning, Pollock, Kline . . .

Pollock was still alive?
No. There were dead people in it, like David Smith and Pollock. But Stella, Rauschenberg, Johns, Lichtenstein, Ellsworth Kelly, some of the minimalist sculptors were there, Barnett Newman, who was a friend of mine, and Rothko. Rauschenberg has a building on Lafayette Street. I filmed him over there. Part of that building is a four-story chapel, and I put him on a ladder higher than this room, at the top of the skylight, and filmed up. He had a Japanese houseboy. Sixteen-millimeter film takes ten minutes a roll. So at the end of each roll the houseboy would hand him another big glass of Jack Daniels. He was so good in the beginning, but the end I couldn't use. . . . I loved their work. Their work is why I made the film. I liked being in the spaces where they painted and have them talk about what they did, how they did it, why they did it, when they did it. It's funny that a camera crew sees people differently. They're not like news crews or television crews who are bored as hell—they do the same thing every day. These are freelance people and most of them want to become directors themselves. . . . I was the only film director on Nixon's enemies list. When you think that the government had nothing else to do than look at movies I made against the president . . . There were all these memoranda, "To John Dean from Haldeman—subject: Emile de Antonio, *Millhouse* film; let us devise means to release derogatory FBI files of de Antonio to friendly news media."

Fake ones?
No, the FBI has many pages on me. I talk against the FBI at the drop of a hat. I thought it would be good to do a musical called *Johnnie and Clyde*,

about Clyde Tolson and John Edgar Hoover. Somebody ought to do one about these two middle-aged guys who were persecuting anybody who was having any fun in life whether he was heterosexual or homosexual.

Talk more about J. Edgar Hoover. I think he's interesting.
J. Edgar Hoover was born January 1, 1895. His father was a bureaucrat in Washington. His grandfather was a bureaucrat. He became head of the FBI in 1924, and he was still the head of it in 1972 when he died. He was in the saddle forty-eight years. Nowhere, not in Russia, not in Nazi Germany, not in the history of the world has one guy run the secret police for forty-eight years. . . . The minute he died, everybody in the FBI was ready to pounce on his files, because his files were all about John F. Kennedy and who he was sleeping with, it was about what Nixon *really* did, it was about what LBJ *really* did. . . .

That would make the great American novel.
That's the truth, he had it on everybody. His files, one at a time, would expose everybody in political life. He wouldn't care about de Kooning or Pollock and he wouldn't care about baseball players unless they said something. If Babe Ruth got up and said the FBI was full of crooks, then they would have had a file on him, too. . . . I don't know what J. Edgar Hoover knew about painters; I'm sure he knew nothing about painting. . . . Picasso was a Communist, that he knew. Picasso was a member of the Communist Party of France. He did the peace dove. The hardline Communists hated his paintings. They thought he did decadent, bourgeois painting. What those people have to say is economically not incorrect, it's artistically incorrect. They say art should belong to the people, whatever that means.

It does, though.
It doesn't. The fact that you make it at twenty-two is extraordinary, but most people twenty-two have never really seen a good painting, a real painting, and particularly not black kids. They don't understand a Picasso in relationship to your work or for that matter Barnett Newman's work. They don't even know the Picasso. You know, school is a drag, but you drag your ass through.

I never learned anything about art in school.
No, that's what I'm saying. When Frank Stella went to school he knew that he wanted to be a painter when he was about fourteen.

I knew I wanted to be a painter the whole time. I wanted to be a cartoonist, though, when I was eleven or twelve or thirteen.
Stella went to a very fancy expensive school.

Which one?
Andover, before he went to Princeton. They had a teacher there who taught art and had his own collection. He and his wife would take the better students down to New York to the Museum of Modern Art, the Metropolitan. They'd say, there is the painting, this is what this is. They didn't explain it away, they just revealed the presence of the stuff. It had a very big influence. Frank wanted to be a painter and it got him going.

I wrote to J. Edgar Hoover as a kid, did you know that?
No.

I sent him a drawing.
That's wonderful, and you got a letter?

I didn't get any letter back. It was one of the first art things I did. I must have been eight or nine.
He answered practically everything unless he thought it was insulting.

I got no letter back. It was a design for a gun.
That he might not have answered.

It was by a child, though. The bullets were really really big. . . . I know you don't go to other filmmakers' movies. Don't you think it would be interesting to see what others are doing? Don't you think your attitude is pretentious?
No. I see films of the past, I see works I regard as significant, but most mass-produced films are just like Fords. They're not art, they're not politics, they're just something to be consumed.

Are you interested in the new painters?
I stopped being interested because I saw nothing new until I saw your work and Andrew Lyght's. Now I think I'm going to look around some more.

All those names you mentioned before, the painters in your book and film, what do you think of their work today?
Well, I think inventive people remain inventive. New ideas come out. I don't think we're surprised that Picasso painted interestingly all those years. The trick is to survive physically.

JEAN W. ROSS

Emile de Antonio (1986)

Intended as an encyclopedic entry for the Contemporary Authors *reference series, this interview is notable for de Antonio's interjection of a powerful political statement he delivered in defense of sculptor Richard Serra's controversial work* Tilted Arc. Contemporary Authors *interviewed Emile de Antonio by telephone on March 8, 1985, at his home in New York City.*

You came to filmmaking—for you, a "mystical experience"—after being a longshoreman, an editor, and a college instructor, among other things. How did you discover film as the best medium for your talents and your views?

To begin with, I had always found distasteful most mass-produced films that were made in Hollywood. I saw them as industrial products. I liked certain of them very much; I loved early films in particular—D. W. Griffith and [Charlie] Chaplin and the Marx Brothers. American comedy I thought was good. But I thought when American films got serious, they tended to be industrial products. I loved certain European directors. Rossellini is perhaps the most important director in my life, because he tried what I have to do, which is to treat intellectual subjects in a mass medium.

The turning point in my life for film was seeing a film made by Robert Frank in 1959 called *Pull My Daisy*. It was about the Beatniks, and it had a brilliant text by Jack Kerouac. I knew almost all the people involved in it. The thing that inspired me most was the fact that so much material could be put into film in a very short period of time, for almost no money. The budget of that film was fifteen thousand dollars. I've never myself worked with such a small amount of money, but nonetheless that was to be a fantastically interesting idea, that you did not have to throw millions of dollars at the wall—in fact, that throwing millions of dollars at the wall tended to produce what to me were meretricious and boring films.

The way films were being made then, and particularly documentaries, is that they were words narrated by celebrities to rather easy images. I loved the idea that *Point of Order* was essentially kinescope, which means it was very tacky-looking film, that the production values were low. In addition to that, because the hearings were held in a very crowded Senate caucus room, the cameras were fixed; you had very little true camera motion, just a swivel on the tripod. I loved all those limitations.

I spent a long time—two years—working with this, because I'd never done anything like it. I'd never even seen a piece of film before. When it came out, lo and behold, it was a hit. It was picked up by a distributor with a very good advance. Four months after it opened in New York, I was in the Cannes Film Festival with it. It was a very giddy experience to go from never having made a film to suddenly being hailed in Europe as somebody who invented a new form of film.

What do you mean when you say you distrust history?
I think winners write history. Given the size of the two main countries of the world today, the U.S. and the USSR, we tend to write history for a tremendous part of the world, as the Soviet Union tends to write history for another tremendous part of the world. The subject of all my work is history. What I mean when I say I distrust history is that I distrust most official written histories. I think there's something that is so revealing about the film image in documentary, images that exist, no matter how much one is accused of manipulating them. In living out the history that is the subject of my films, the human face itself, in its attitudes and in the language that the face expresses, has a way of giving an audience a *feeling,* so that the audience can make up its own mind—no matter how much you manipulate it. And it's easy enough to manipulate it, God knows.

The idea really is that when you look at Joe McCarthy badgering and hectoring the lawyer Joseph Welch, you not only know that he's a bully, but you know that he has lost the American people. People in masses see only the big brush strokes, but to see McCarthy bully that old man and lie before a huge audience destroyed his career. Those are the moments I wanted to re-create, using that same material. I manipulate the material, and then I let history judge if I've lied or not. For instance, there's something that film critics don't see very much. The film ends with everybody walking out on McCarthy. If you look very carefully at those images, you'll see that the same people have different shirts on, because I made a collage of the endings of different days of the hearings. At the very end, when the credit comes on, there's no sound at all. There's just an incredibly moving shot of an empty room, that Senate caucus room that throughout the rest of the film had been filled with people shouting and screaming "Point of order!" and all the rest of it.

Do the early films continue to be shown widely?
They do, as a matter of fact, though not all of them. *Rush to Judgment* does not. I wanted to make that very bare and very much the way a legal case is developed. That's the film about the President Kennedy assassination. *Point of Order* plays all the time, all over the world and on television. I think it's one of the few documentaries that was actually televised uncut. It was played by ABC back in the late sixties; it was a network thing sponsored by Xerox. Since that time it's played on PBS. Swedish television seems to play it about every two or three years. British television is going to play it again this fall. So it has a very active life. It just played in a theater in New York six weeks ago.

Where are your best audiences now? Can you tell?
By the time a film is that old, the best audiences are universities. I lecture with my films from time to time. I don't like to do it much anymore because it interferes with my busy life, but I do like to do it infrequently just to be in touch. I spoke at Eastman House, where they did a few of my films and where it's an honor to go because it's the beginning of American film, in a way.

Of the countries besides the United States where your films are shown, where do they seem to be most popular?
It's different with different films, but essentially in the English-speaking countries. Curiously enough, my films do least well in the Soviet bloc. I've frequently been invited to visit Eastern bloc countries as a guest of their governments, and I've been a member of the jury for the East German Film Festival, which is the most important Soviet bloc festival. While I was there, I met a man who has a job equivalent to what Walter Cronkite did, or Dan Rather today; this was in the mid-1970s. I said to him, "Why don't you play *Millhouse*? Here you have a portrait by an American of the quintessential cold warrior." He said, "Ah, you don't understand at all, do you? Nixon and Brezhnev got together. We despise your Cold War liberals like Kennedy, but Nixon we understood because he understood us. We would never play a film that was against Nixon." The Soviets don't like the form of my films; they don't like films that reveal governments doing things wrong, even our government, because it could make people think, why don't we make films like that over here?

My films are meant to be subversive, and they are. I happen to live in America, and I also feel I'm a good American. I have the money to live wherever I want; I prefer to live here. This is my space, and this is why I'm interested in it, and this is why my life is devoted to making films about it.

I'm appearing at a public hearing in less than an hour for Richard Serra, the sculptor. It's been covered in the *New York Times* for three days. He was given a contract by the General Services Administration [GSA] to do this giant piece. They took three years to decide, because they knew it was a provocative piece. So they put it up—in 1981—and they looked at it. Now they want to tear it down. I helped him get together a lot of people, and even TV coverage, so he's asked me to go to the hearing. He's not going to like what I say, because he's *not* political. But I'm going to say this:

"Trust is the real bond between people and government. Our government is as trustworthy as the Soviet government—no more, no less. Freedom itself is not a Madison Avenue package. It exists or doesn't exist only when it is tested. It is now being tested by Mr. Diamond and the General Services Administration. Mr. Reagan, with great enjoyment and advantage, quoted President Roosevelt, who helped bring public art to our country. Mr. Diamond's proposed destruction of *Tilted Arc* is closer to Stalin's art criticism than to FDR's. New art, particularly good new art, lives at the edge of human experience and feeling. It is a challenge to old ways of seeing, performing, and living. This is why Stalin destroyed a great Soviet art. It is why the French middle classes sneered at Cézanne. It is why Hitler destroyed 'decadent' art. And it is why the yahoos of the GSA propose to move *Tilted Arc*.

"There is another point which has nothing at all to do with art: the contract between Richard Serra and the GSA. Mr. Diamond and the GSA bureaucrats propose demolishing law, trust, and intention as well as art. This is wholly in keeping with the new barbarism of this administration. The government that hires gangsters to murder women and children in Nicaragua cannot be expected to honor contracts made in trust with an American artist."

That's why I have five thousand pages in my FBI file. I've never broken a law; my only crime is exercising the First Amendment of the Constitution of the United States, and I think the Bill of Rights is the greatest statement that any country has.

Are you still aware of being followed by FBI agents? Is it that frequent?
Well, I've given up worrying about it. I sued the government and won. That's why they have all that material on me. And it's amazing material, because they were so stupid and so thorough that they literally put stuff in my file like reviews of films. If I were to come to your city with one of my films and speak, there would be a review of the film in the newspaper and

an article saying I spoke. The FBI would faithfully clip this out, Xerox many copies, and put it in different files. It seemed insane to me until I realized finally that that was J. Edgar Hoover's real strength—he was a great bureaucrat and it was a way to give employment to a lot of people who possibly could not be employed otherwise.

Throughout your film career you've criticized television for its presentation of news and issues. Do you see any improvement in the way they're doing it?
None. I think, for instance, that CBS didn't fight the Westmoreland case on principle; they fought it in a narrow legal way. [General William C. Westmoreland, commander of U.S. forces in Vietnam until 1967, brought a $120-million libel suit against Columbia Broadcasting System for a 1982 television documentary that accused him of conspiring to underestimate enemy troop strength in Vietnam in order to convince then-President Lyndon Johnson and the American public that the United States was winning the war. After a five-month struggle, Westmoreland withdrew the suit in March 1985.] There was a principle involved there, you know. We lost the war, and that's the thing we can't face. I think countries that can't face the truth are in trouble.

Film history and film technique are taught widely now in colleges and universities. Do you think some of the teaching is useful to aspiring filmmakers?
I think only to those who are gifted. I think that, unfortunately, most teaching of film is a scam. Almost every large university has a big film department, and it turns out to be expensive to go there, because using film equipment is expensive. Just processing film in a laboratory is expensive, to say nothing of steenbecks for editing and decent cameras. But there are very few jobs out there—there really are—and the unions are very retrograde about letting people in. Unless you go in as a writer or as a director, it's hard. If you're in a more conventional field like medicine, it's hard as hell to get into medical school, but if you get into medical school and you do your work, you get to practice medicine. But if you study film and learn it, that may not be true.

Do you enjoy the work of any of the mass-audience filmmakers?
Not very much.

One of the results of your association with artists was the 1972 film Painters Painting. *Did your friendship with artists grow out of an interest in art, or was the reverse the case?*
I've always been interested in painting since I was a little boy and my father, who was a doctor in Pennsylvania, would take me down to New York to look in the Frick Gallery and the Metropolitan. I still see those paintings as

clearly as I did all those years ago; I can tell you every painting in a certain room of the Frick. I've always loved painting. When I got out of the army in 1945, I also realized that I always was interested in my own time, in every place—in politics and in art and in poetry—and I suddenly became more interested in Jackson Pollock, of whom I did not know except a little bit. Then I became more interested in the work around me, and that intensified when I became very good friends with the people who are in the cast of *Painters Painting*.

I'm writing a book now about [Leo] Castelli—not only because Leo is an old friend; it's not going to be a puff piece—but because I'm really interested in power and money, and it's a book about power and money and the manipulation of the art market. Why does a Jasper Johns flag sell today for two and a half million dollars when I remember Leo had a hard time selling it for nine hundred dollars? I believe the flags are worth the price they bring today, because they are extraordinary paintings. But there also was a very careful manipulation of the market, and Castelli devised a whole bunch of new techniques for making American art win out in the world. Europeans didn't know a damn thing about American art. In 1964 Rauschenberg won the Biennale at Venice; he was the first American since [Alexander] Calder and the only American except for Calder, and it was like a revolution. The Italian and French presses attacked it wildly. The patriarch of Venice, who was the highest religious figure, thought that all those works submitted by the Americans should be condemned for heresy. It was amazing.

That fascinates me, and the fact that Leo is seventy-eight years old and still is looking for new people and new artists—he's a fascinating man, he speaks five languages perfectly, and he knows all the artists I know. My book is not a biography. It's a cultural history. I haven't finished it; I have a thousand pages and I'm not half done. I'm going to cut way back, but I always work lavishly.

For In the King of Prussia *you used the Berrigans and other members of* Plowshares Eight *as "actors" where you couldn't get actual documentary footage. Was there any precedent for that method?*
I think I invented that method, because in this one film the main thing is that real people play themselves and actors play real people. For instance, Martin Sheen and the other people in the film never saw the Berrigans until they walked onto the set. And we didn't have much time, so we immediately started shooting and acting! It was an amazing experience. Sheen and I are very good friends—in fact, he was here last week—and he and Rip Torn are going to be in my next film, which I'm writing as I write the Castelli

book. The film is called *Cassettes*. It's a low-budget science-fiction film that has no optical tricks of any kind. It's about science fiction in the U.S. right now, at this moment, except it won't be shot until the end of the summer.

Do you think there's any worthwhile film reviewing being done?
I think reviewing in the daily press can generally be discounted, unfortunately, because it's hard work. I mean, you have to look at twelve or fourteen films in a week. And then when you think of the different subjects of films, you have to be a world authority. To review a film like *In the Year of the Pig,* and then to review an old Doris Day film or whatever piece of fluff is out there, that's too much to expect anyone to do. So I think for the big-newspaper reviewing, like the *New York Times,* they should stop trying to be clever and just report what was on the screen—who did what and how it was done. When they try to do arty kind of criticism, like Vincent Canby in the *Times,* they fall on their faces.

The only critic I know who could do anything like that—and I read a tremendous amount, frankly—was George Bernard Shaw. Under the name of Corno di Bassetto, he was a music critic in England before he ever wrote a play. He made his living reviewing concerts two, three, four times a week. Those pieces have been collected, and they're absolutely brilliant. I don't know how accurate the criticism was, because we're talking about over a hundred years ago. But the writing is so polished and so witty. That just proves that good writers write well.

I think there are critics who are very good who write in quarterlies and in monthlies and who do books. But it's putting an impossible burden on a man or a woman to see twelve to fifteen films in a week and write as many as nine or ten reviews in a week.

Is there anything new you'd like to try your hand at—anything you haven't done before?
Well, I have a bad knee, but one thing I do is bodysurfing in the ocean. I like big waves, and I like it after a hurricane. I would like to go to North Carolina and do that off of Nags Head. But anything else? My time is very full. Once you get to a certain age, you live one day at a time. I'm interested in finishing *Cassettes* and the book on Castelli. I'm going to have to put the book aside for six months, so I won't be done with that until the spring or even the summer of 1986. That's a lot of work. I do incidental writing and a lot of political stuff. I appear for anybody in the name of liberty. I get involved in controversies. I like controversy. I'm a controversial person, so why shouldn't I swim in my medium, which is controversy?

EMILE DE ANTONIO

Why I Make Films (1987)

For the fortieth anniversary of the Cannes Film Festival, the Paris daily newspaper Libération *and the* French cinémathèque, *revising André Breton and Louis Aragon's famous question "Why do you write?" asked the world's top directors "Pourquoi filmez-vous?" De Antonio's answer, written on February 10, 1987, was as follows.*

I make films in opposition. I cannot be a good Nazi in Reagan's America. I also make films against that "industry" which every year produces thousands of hours of images and sound in Hollywood and New York. Its auteur is the dollar. A court of Moloch served by corrupt priests.

But I do not make films that are shouts and screeds. I make films to change the form of film. Godard said: all film is fiction. Equally true, all film is documentary. *Bedtime for Bonzo* is as much a document of American life as *In the Year of the Pig*. And took less invention.

It was not intentional, but by 1967 it was clear to me that I was making films of the history of my country in the days of the Cold War, not in an orderly, systematic way like Gibbon or Braudel, but in moving images and sound, disjunctively, intuitively.

One gore of the dilemma: hopelessly competing with *Rambo* and *Dynasty* for an audience which has been brainwashed beyond any Pavlovian dog.

Finally, we must make films to free audiences to find film as it should be, not as it is. That's the dilemma's other gore: cigars and deals at the Carlton in Cannes.

II The Films

Point of Order

Figure 22. Senator Joseph R. McCarthy during the Army-McCarthy hearings in *Point of Order*.

Figure 23. Robert F. Kennedy and Senator Stuart Symington during the Army-McCarthy hearings in *Point of Order*.

EMILE DE ANTONIO

The Point of View in Point of Order (1964)

De Antonio's influence in the New York independent film community is evidenced by his access to Film Comment. *Not only had he helped get Dan Drasin's* Sunday *(1961) on the cover of the magazine's first issue, he was allowed to author his own account of his own debut film. In his first piece of published writing, de Antonio exhibits the pithy, contentious staccato style that became his trademark. In this initial cycle of public pronouncements about* Point of Order *he was careful to include Dan Talbot's name as the coproducer of the film. Afterward, he increasingly represented the film as primarily his own creation. The essay also initiated his long-running attack on the concept of cinema verité.*

> *Metaphysics is the finding of bad reasons for what we believe upon instinct.*
> :: F. A. Bradley

The fact that Talbot and I wanted to produce a film based on the Army-McCarthy hearings was a priori evidence of a point of view in both politics and film. In fact, we made two decisions before we ever saw one frame of the 188 hours we bought from CBS. These decisions shaped much of the form and content of the film. They were:

1. Only footage from the actual hearings would be used. No stock footage. No TV biographies.
2. No preaching. We were both against McCarthyism, but theater was more effective than howl and wail.

Other decisions I reached in structuring (directing?) the inert, immutable, nine-year-old material were:

1. No narration, no explanation, no comment. Fifty-nine seconds for setting time, place and the charges are heard over black leader *outside* the film proper.
2. No attempt to follow chronological order. Picture is not a compilation or a synopsis. Actual hearings were 188 formless hours ending with a whimper. Film moves freely through all the material to make its points. The Form and the Truth are our Form and Truth. Senator Goldwater's might be much different.

Truth in art is internal, personal, and once committed in form offers itself for judgment. It is not discovered by a committee of reasonable men, however eminent. The assumptions were Talbot's and mine and, I suspect, mostly mine because I actually put the film together.

An English critic has called *Point of Order!* the only good example of cinema verité. I disagree. In fact, nonsense. Cinema verité is what Henry Ford called history—"the bunk." Cinema verité assumes a mindless cameraman pointing his integrity at the world. Point something else. A wasted exercise. "Fewer curses, more stones," shouted the gondolier as the works of Gassendi were chucked into a Venetian canal by the Inquisition.

Here are more assumptions behind *Point of Order!*

1. McCarthy was not a fascist. Fascists have ideology and organized followings. He had none. (Cohn and Schine?)
2. McCarthy was complex, interesting. Most vital American political figure since FDR. Superb sense of theater. Master of mass media. Triumph of technique over substance. Singularly American failing—like Madison Avenue.
3. McCarthy was not only caused; he was permitted. And the permission came from the top of the Republican party. Senator Taft et al.
4. McCarthy has to be credited with charm, energy, insight into the American mind, and political temper. Otherwise, how to explain his rise and power?
5. McCarthy did have a case against the Army and the shadows behind the Army. The film is about complicity, a shared complicity.
6. Neither the hearings nor the film is a good guy/bad guy situation. All are implicated since he "made it." The Army had truckled, the White House had been silent, the Senate had cowered, the press printed more and more, the victims were offered up, and the peeps of protest were very small until near the end.
7. The hero is not Joseph Welch (a great lawyer and great actor) but the camera. No political figure of the modern world was ever

looked at so thoroughly as McCarthy was between April and June 1954.

Back to cinema verité. The phrase is silly if we look at the cutting-room floor. If all 188 hours were the whole vérité, then any cut would make for less or no vérité. The vérité, as well as the prejudice, is Talbot's and mine. And there is enough material to make fifteen different movies, including one that would make Roy Cohn look like Tennyson's Galahad.

Our prejudices are the film. Without them it would not have existed.

JUDITH CRIST

Re-creating the Incredible McCarthy Days (1964)

Emile de Antonio was a consummate New Yorker. His cinematic reputation was not harmed by his proximity to the New York film critics who so dominated the journalistic discourse on movies throughout the 1960s and 1970s. Judith Crist, though less influential than her colleagues Crowther, Kael, Canby, Kauffmann, and Sarris, had a wide audience. At the time of this review, she had just become the film critic for the Herald Tribune, *after nearly twenty years as a reporter. Crist had also become the movie reviewer for NBC-TV's Today Show (1963–73), where she later brought* Rush to Judgment *to viewers' attention. As a film critic for* TV Guide *(1966–88) and many other publications, she had a vast readership.*

Crist's review nicely captures the dramatic structure and intentions of Point of Order. *Like most mainstream responses, however, it sees the film as a safe, latter-day record of the triumph of American "decency" over the coarse politics of McCarthyism.*

A full-length feature drawn from the Army-McCarthy hearings of 1954, based upon an idea by Daniel Talbot, coproducers Emile de Antonio and Mr. Talbot, presented by Point Films, Inc. Running time: One hour and 37 minutes.

The jolting reality about *Point of Order!*—a 97-minute-documentary of excerpted highlights of the 188-hour televised Army-McCarthy hearings—is one of time. Was it only yesterday, only ten years ago, rather than in another century and a far-off land, that this political morality play, this dramatic revelation of the face of demagoguery and of its collapse, took place here?

It was—and therein is the impact of this film culled from kinescopes by Emile de Antonio and Daniel Talbot. For it was indeed only in the springtime of 1954 that the face of Senator Joseph R. McCarthy was shown in all its aspects to the public in a day-in, day-out controversy, and the public sat in judgment. And it was in a Senate caucus room that the man who had, in four years, risen to a position of apparent invulnerability, issued his ultimate defiance of democracy. No fictioneer, no pamphleteer, no dramatist or satirist or pleader of causes could have created the characters or dreamed up the events that the camera recorded during those April into June days.

Credit the producers with letting the cast introduce itself and the events speak for themselves; the camera needs no assistance, as witnesses talk around and about the matters at hand and the tables slowly turn. At the outset and at the end there is the haranguing whine of McCarthy self-confident in its diversionary tactic at the beginning, straw-grasping and frantic in its fade-out with an emptying caucus room and only a stenotypist to record the bombast of the smearer charging "smear."

In between there is the charge and countercharge (the Army accused McCarthy and his staff of using improper pressure in behalf of David Schine, and McCarthy counterchrged that the Army attempted blackmail and used Schine as a hostage), statement and counterstatement, digression, diversion—a "misleading" chart, a "doctored" photograph, a presidential memorandum, a J. Edgar Hoover letter Hoover denied writing. The McCarthy laughter and smile give way to a quarrelsome anger; nerves show through, senatorial politeness fades and the climactic moment of Special Army Counsel Joseph Welch asking McCarthy, "Have you no sense of decency, sir, at long last?" comes with heartbreaking power. And finally Senator Stuart Symington's "Senator, let me tell you something. The American people have had a look at you for six weeks. You're not fooling anyone either."

Certainly, remembered highlights have been captured and much has admittedly been omitted. The producers have excerpted a superdocumentary instead of creating one of their own. The excerpts exert their initial fascination, but for those with short memories or without the experience of the contemporary context of the hearings, one wishes that the producers had provided an epilogue, [that they had] concluded with the Senate's censure of McCarthy that December or a reference to the career that petered out even before his death on May 2, 1957. For the astonishing thing *Point of Order!* demonstrates is that you had to live through the incredibilities of the McCarthy era in order to accept their reality today.

The initial service—of letting the people see and thereby judge—was done by television: Mesrs. de Antonio and Talbot have furthered it by capturing the essential moral and enduring parable of this political experience succinctly and dramatically. For *Point of Order!* is not only a testament to the ultimate—albeit belated—triumph of democratic decency over demagoguery—but also a grim reminder of what had happened here.

TIME MAGAZINE

McCarthy's Last Stand (1964)

Time's *respectful review of* Point of Order *shows how safe McCarthy bashing had become by the 1960s. The reference to de Antonio's "intelligent and impartial editing" perceives the careful construction of the film's montage but misses de Antonio's partisanship. Although* Time *attempted to safely bury McCarthy, his ghost and offspring would continue to haunt the body politic.*

Point of Order
The Army-McCarthy hearings were superb political theater. In this fascinating film, a 97-minute précis of what television audiences saw at the time, the theater is heightened by intelligent and impartial editing.

The reason the Senate held the hearings is explained in a terse foreword: the Army charged that McCarthy and two members of his staff, Roy Cohn and Frank Carr, had sought special favors for Private G. David Schine, one of McCarthy's assistants. McCarthy and Cohn countercharged that the Army was holding Schine as a hostage to prevent their investigation of subversion in the Army.

Then the drama begins, and it is constructed like a prizefight. In the early rounds the opponents politely feel each other out, and there is time for the referee to provide low comic relief ("Am I running this committee," Senator Mundt splutters intellectually, "or am I not?"). In the middle rounds the opponents get down to serious slugging, and both take damaging blows—the evidence demonstrates that McCarthy attempted to blackmail the Army and that the Army then attempted to buy McCarthy off. But in the later rounds, McCarthy begins to swing wildly, and Joseph N. Welch, the Army's counsel, delicately cuts him into paper dolls. His methods are exposed as stupid, his morals as prehistoric. "At long last," Welch cries in revulsion, "at long last, sir, have you no decency left at all?"—and the spectators burst into sustained applause.

In the end, the other senators on the subcommittee turn fiercely against McCarthy. "No one is afraid of you—in or out of jail," bellows Senator McClellan, and Senator Symington hoots: "Go see a psychiatrist." Even Counsel Cohn looks as though he longed to desert the sinking ship. As for McCarthy, he just sits there with a strange and frightening look on his face: a smile that is somehow vicious, a grin like the grin of a wounded and desperate hyena. The look is the look of a very sick man, and it did more to damage McCarthy's case than any evidence introduced against him. When the hearings were finished, McCarthy was finished as a force in U.S. political life.

EMILE DE ANTONIO

Letter to Hubert Bals and Wendy Lidell (197?)

Of his several accounts of the making of Point of Order, *this letter from de Antonio's journals is the most thorough. Bals founded the Rotterdam Film Festival, which he ran until his death in 1988. Lidell has been a long-time advocate for international alternative film distribution, founding the International Film Circuit and other programming organizations.*

Dear Hubert Bals and Wendy Lidell,
    I'm sending a copy of this to Daniel Talbot. It is a brief history of *Point of Order,* which may have been the first political documentary in the U.S. after World War II as well as a documentary which, in opposition to prevailing trends, also changed the form of documentary.
    By the time *Point of Order* was in production in 1961, there was already the hope, at least in my mind, that it would achieve more than filling theater seats and TV screens. What follows is probably a "mélange adultère du tout" of ideas about film and politics present while the film was being made and retrospectively after it was made.
    The concept cinema verité begun in France and advanced here by Leacock and others, although it employed new techniques and equipment, seemed to me even then to be the enemy. Whose vérité? It assumed an impersonal godlike stance before human events that was alien to me and my ideas of society. It was an echo of an obsession with technique as an end in itself.
    My long history with John Cage and Bob Rauschenberg enlightened me about the uses of junk, the detritus of modern industrial society as a source for the materials of art, of political art in film.
    My father was an important influence. He was already old when I was born. He had a European intellectual's contempt for film, save for comedy which he perceived to be a social weapon. Not just Chaplin but also Fields,

the Marx Brothers, others. I entered Harvard young and never went to films. In the military, I avoided films except for those I was forced to see such as anti-venereal disease films.

Later, after the war, certain films meant much to me. Eisenstein, Lang, Renoir. But basically I was not a film person. *Open City* was an important moment in my life. It was fluid, cheap, quick, and political. I couldn't relate it to what I was doing, a young war veteran studying philosophy and literature. I also loved *Birth of a Nation*. The politics of it is what it is: puerile, bad, racist, naive, inborn.

I joined the New American Cinema being formed by Jonas Mekas. I met Lionel Rogosin, Shirley Clarke (she and I did a long interview together one day in my studio overlooking Union Square in those days. It is scabrous and confined to my archive), Ed Bland, Lewis Allen, and others. I already knew Alfred Leslie and Robert Frank.

I met Henry Rosenberg and Daniel Talbot at the same time in 1959 or 1960, about the time the New Yorker Theater opened. I thought it was Dan's theater. I soon learned it was Hank's and Dan worked for him.

I had been a friend of avant-garde painters and musicians of New York from long before the New American Cinema. I knew John Cage, Merce Cunningham, Jasper Johns, Bob Rauschenberg, Frank Stella, and many others before they had galleries. I knew little of the film world and did not like what I knew. I had been a Marxist since I was sixteen years old, but it's very tough occupying that space with intensity over a long period of time, particularly in Stalin's day. I wasn't a professional revolutionary at all but an artist looking for his art.

I saw Robert Frank's *Pull My Daisy*. Robert knew many of the people I knew.

To come full circle, I have just finished acting in his new $1,000,000 fiction film. *Pull My Daisy* was a strange and important moment for me. I loved it for being stripped bare. I was not a fan of Kerouac, whom I knew. I thought the sound track of *Pull My Daisy*, which he wrote and spoke, was the best thing he ever did. Better than *On the Road*. I was tremendously excited and wanted to make a film.

All time is blurred, it was more than twenty-six years ago . . . Dan and I were friends. The programming at the New Yorker was important and it was very tough for Dan and Hank to book films. The big companies were uninterested in an uptown theater lacking Sodom and Gomorrah fancy. Dan and Hank had the courage to play *Triumph of the Will*. It was then a Jewish neighborhood, and the Jewish post of the American Legion picketed the theater.

Dan was pressed for "product." He asked me for ideas. One I suggested foreshadows dimly *Point of Order.* I told him to play *Operation Abolition,* a right-wing film made defending the House Un-American Activities Committee hearings in Berkeley and San Francisco. Dan said to me: how would I get it?

I said: I'll get it from the company that made it and wanted it seen. And, on the same program you have to show the film made by radical students by stealing the HUAC print, doing a new sound track, with film of their own. I suspect it was the first time these films were ever shown together. During their brief play, many radicals, old and young, came to see the films.

Finding playable material for the New Yorker screen continued to be a problem for Hank and Dan. We frequently ate pastrami sandwiches together and drank beer at the end of a night at a Jewish family restaurant, the Tip Toe Inn. Note: conversations are made without quotation marks because they are not precise but recollections.

One night Dan said to me (and he knew the answer, it was a rhetorical question): what was the most exciting event that ever took place on American television? I said: The Army-McCarthy hearings. He said: absolutely. He wondered how we could get them on to the New Yorker screen.

I don't think that Dan would object to anything that has been written so far. The nub is at this point. I am a materialist. I don't have visions. But as I spoke I saw the film I wanted to make: made of junk like Cage musical pieces or Rauschenberg's work, stripped of the phony and dubious aestheticism of the Hollywood film. I saw it lean, bare, cheap, and without narration. I think Dan was looking for a program to put into the New Yorker and I wanted to make a film. Films should never, absolutely never, carry a credit: "From an idea by X." Ideas lie on the floors of all the saloons of the world. Films, like books are made, written, worked on. The organizing of it and raising the money devolved on me from the beginning, except for Hank Rosenberg, but that comes a little later. First of all, did the footage exist and who had it? We formed a corporation—Dan, Hank, and I. I was its president. Hank was in real estate, Dan was running the New Yorker for Hank. I started looking for the footage. Who owned it? Was it available? The corporation was Point Films, Inc.

I found that CBS had it. I wrote to the president of CBS News, a notorious right-winger, Sig Mikelson. Mikelson wrote to me and said: We don't have any footage, and besides, why bring up that old issue?

The film was dead in the water right there. And then, I found out that Mikelson had been replaced as head of CBS News—the myth of corporate telecasting is that the news divisions are separate and pure entities quite distant from soap operas and sit-coms—by Dick Salant. I had no illusions about Salant, but I decided to give it a shot. He was interested and after thinking it over a few months, told me the footage was lost and could not be found. Mind you: this original footage was 188 hours of kinescope negative with separate picture and track or 376 hours of film to handle. Hard to believe it could have been lost.

I had a friend, a casual friend whom I had known since the time each of us left military service after WWII, Dick Ellison. He had been a seaman. In 1961 he was editing a minor internal magazine for CBS. A Madison Avenue job with a clerkly salary. I asked him if he could prowl in the archives and files without jeopardizing his job. He said he would. He was a decent liberal who went on to produce the PBS liberal view of the Vietnam War.

Ellison found the footage rather quickly. It was where it should have been: at the CBS storage warehouse rented from Bonded Film in Fort Lee, New Jersey. CBS was now in a quandary. It was beneath the dignity of CBS News to sell anything, let alone its probity or a huge hunk like the Army-McCarthy hearings. So, the project was turned over to Murray Benson of CBS Promotions. He was at 485 Madison Avenue. He ran the merchandising department of CBS. He sold dolls, toys, and games based on the culturally uplifting CBS programming: like *Wagon Train*. His office was a marvel stuffed with artifacts, dolls, spacemen, rockets, etc. He was nervous but not a fool.

Reality intervened. We had a New York corporation; we had Hank Rosenberg's $5,000; and I had the desire to make a film. We had no money. Hank and Dan looked at me. I went to see an old acquaintance: Eliot Pratt, the grandson of a Rockefeller partner, an older man of inherited wealth who had been a left-wing liberal all his life. He used to run sheep on his Greenwich, Connecticut, estate and I was told he stated under the caption OCCUPATION on his tax forms: sheep farmer. Eliot was ardently anti-McCarthy. He ardently believed in civil liberty. He was a good man and slightly afraid of me. I was unbearably arrogant in those greener days. He suggested we have lunch near his town house.

We went to the original Allan's on Third Avenue and 71st Street. We had a hamburger and one drink each. The bill was $6.00. Eliot left a 10 cent tip. He agreed to give me $100,000. Eliot, like CBS, was reassured because Hank owned the New Yorker and other cinemas and Dan had a steady job working for Hank. He knew me as a freelance radical who seemed to live well without working at regular jobs.

From the moment we had that first money, Hank became uninterested in the details of what was to happen, and Dan began a campaign directed to the notion that I could not make the film because I didn't like films and had had no experience. He set up the files. I was shaken when he told me he was going to cable Orson Welles and ask him to make the film. What could I say to that? Nothing. I didn't. I waited.

The lawyer of any new corporation who had worked for one principal of that corporation has enormous power. Bernie Sorkin worked for Columbia Pictures; he was our lawyer; he had worked for or with Hank; he knew Dan as a result. I was a cipher and whenever we met, it was clear Sorkin was representing what he deemed to be Hank's and the New Yorker Theater's interests.

Welles cabled. He could not do it. (Dan must have all this. If he does, as president then and still president of Point Films Inc., I am legally entitled to those files. I had not realized at the time how important files were. Dan can have the xeroxes.)

Back to the beginning. Again, Dan played on my own nervousness at undertaking such a project. Dan became very loyal to Eliot's money and ingratiated himself with Eliot. He proposed that we ask Irving Lerner to come east from Hollywood and ask him to make it. Dan prized Lerner because he was famous for making good, tight very low-budget films. I protested.

Interruption: back to CBS. We are in Murray Benson's office with all the sales trinkets. We had many meetings hammering out the contract between CBS and us. CBS was terribly uptight. First, $50,000 up front non-returnable. Then, a proviso that if the name CBS was ever used by us, the contract was null and void and CBS kept the $50,000. And more outrageous, CBS was to own half the profits forever.

Hank and Dan were amused because I always turned up in a blue button-down shirt, khaki trousers, and tennis shoes. One day we were quibbling over $25,000. Again, don't forget: $25,000 then = $100,000 or $125,000 of today's Reagan dollar. I said: Murray, let's toss for it, double or nothing. Murray said: D, you're kidding? I said: no, let's toss.

We didn't, of course. Hank said to me after: d, who would have paid for it if you lost the toss? I said: I wasn't going to lose. The CBS contract was signed April 6, 1961. A key provision was that we would obtain a $1,000,000 indemnity policy.

Irving Lerner: We put him up in the Algonquin Hotel and then went to East Hampton at my friend Tina Fredericks's house. It was the first time Dan and Toby Talbot had seen that part of eastern Long Island. Lerner was an interesting man but he did not understand the project. Rosenberg wasn't there, chiefly because Dan kept him as far away from me possible. Dan told tales of Hank's grossness, of his strange Hispanic hookers, etc., of his insensitivity to film.

It was obvious to me that Dan was playing Uriah Heep to Hank at the same time and setting him up for a deal whereby he could buy freedom and the New Yorker Theater from Hank for a modest amount. The theater was making money. Dan's booking was wonderful, but his true gift was publicity. He had the genius to invite critics, film writers into the New Yorker as guests, to arrange free private screenings of whatever they liked, etc. He invited the whole lot from the *New York Times* to the avant-garde. It was intelligent and an investment.

It was then that I tried to get Dan and Hank to agree to let me do the film.

I was voted down, wheedled down, it was always thrust upon me that I had never made a film. So, we hired a very good, well-known editor named Paul Falkenberg and his wife as well. Falkenberg never understood my idea: that the film had to be free of other material; it had to be narration-free. TV was making documentary more boring by adding its roster of famous journalists to the documentary. Cronkite, Murrow, etc. Their voices told and explained and destroyed whatever filmic qualities that might have been there. The no-narration, political documentary after World War II had its beginning with me in *Point of Order*. That's the end of the story.

Back to Falkenberg. His idea was simplistic, it was also Dan's. Take the great moments and have a brilliant narration and it's easy. It would have been easy and it would have looked like CBS, not film.

I appear weak in this chronicle, giving in at every point. And I suppose I was, but always the bugbear was dragged out: you have never worked in film, how can we risk all this? Falkenberg asked for narration. The best-known book on McCarthy at that time was by Richard Rovere, the *New Yorker* magazine's Washington reporter.

Dan and I drove upstate New York and asked him to do it. We paid him a lot of money. Rovere was careful to state he wasn't radical. It was obvious, and it was also known to me that he had once been a Communist. What he wrote did not work. We hired another writer whose name is in my archive at the University of Wisconsin. He wrote a narration which pleased Falkenberg.

At this point I had been a friend of John Cage for a long time and he and I talked about my problems. John said: be Zen. Just let it ride. You will be doing the film within months. I saw that myself. I also knew that Falkenberg would have to take his best shot and it would be over. So, I asked my friend Mike Wallace to read the narration. He did it. We paid him $2,500. Two hours work. [Mike Wallace contends he was never paid. Interview with Dan Streible, July 16, 1998.]

We screened the Falkenberg cut. It had a Vermont church with an American flag in it. This, I suppose, was a signal to the press that the makers of the film were patriots and free of Marxist taint. It also had a wedding scene, Joe marrying Jean. Bobby Kennedy was in it.

I knew I had won. John was right. Eliot, Hank, Dan and I, and others screened the film. It was a disaster. There was no money left. I said to Dan: okay, from here on out, either you do it or I'll go it alone. Dan said: d, you know that's not fair. I have a wife, children, the theater to run. My answer: tough. You or I. He said: there's no more money to pay you.

I said: fine. It was a mistake. We paid everyone else and I worked on it for eighteen months without pay. When the film was finished, it was what it is today. Dan didn't like speaking with the film because he didn't know very much about either the film or the history of the period.

Dan didn't even understand the politics of insurance. Two months before the film opened at the Museum of Modern Art prior to commercial release, I had a knee operation. Without consulting me, Dan gave an interview on the film. The reporter asked: What about Roy Cohn: Will he sue to stop the film? Dan's reply: We have a $1,000,000 insurance policy. I hope he does sue. This article appeared in *Variety*. The Fireman's Fund Insurance Company, one of the largest in the film industry, canceled our policy, hence there was no more film since that invalidated our CBS contract.

Dan then begged Bob Montgomery, already a great name in film law, to steady Fireman's Fund and Montgomery was able to do it. He saved our insurance coverage. He also went on to become Dan's lawyer even down to the day that the FBI appeared in Dan's office and asked Dan to cooperate in an investigation about *Millhouse* and me. But that's another tale.

To end this one, Dan and I met with attorney Sorkin to settle the problem of the credits. Dan was adamant that the top credit read: From an idea by Daniel Talbot. I gave in. Sorkin said: how can you direct stock footage? I shrugged and my credit was Editorial Director. Eliot Pratt was given the title of Executive Producer. That was fair. He put up the money. I think Hank Rosenberg's name disappeared.

The real credits are:

Point of Order: a film by Emile de Antonio
Produced by Emile de Antonio and Daniel Talbot
Executive Producers: Eliot Pratt and Henry Rosenberg
Editor: Robert Duncan
Director: Emile de Antonio
COPYRIGHT Point Films, Inc.

That's Where the Action Is

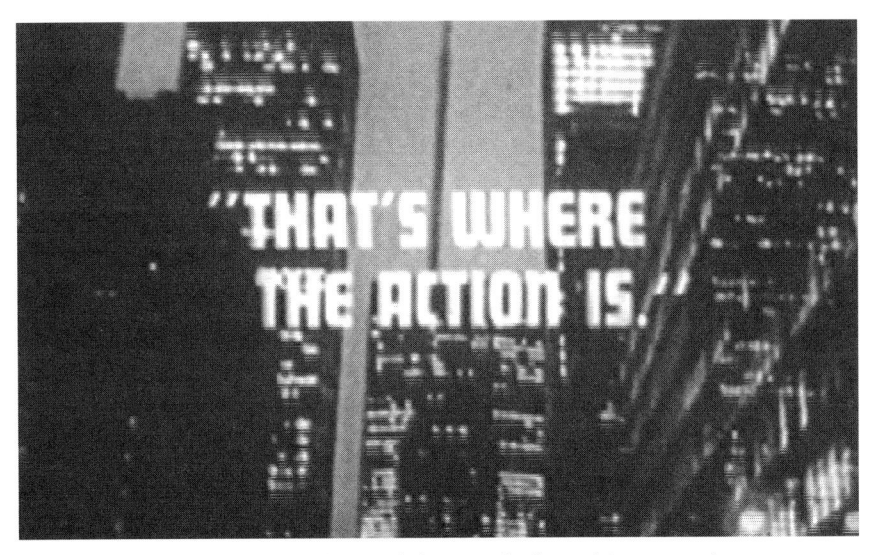

Figure 24. The Manhattan skyline and the sound of marching snare drums open de Antonio's BBC film about New York mayoral campaigns.

EMILE DE ANTONIO

Running to Win, Outline and Letter to BBC (1965)

Running to Win—*which the BBC retitled* That's Where the Action Is—*has been virtually unseen since its broadcast on British television in 1965. The film detailing the New York City mayoral campaign was revived at London's National Film Theatre in 1974, but has never been distributed. This structural outline and editorial instructions submitted with de Antonio's letter to BBC producer David Webster remain the best available evidence of the film's content and the director's conception for another political documentary collage sans narrator.*

NOTES: 7-14-65

Running to Win (1965)

A 50 minute document on John Lindsay and the 1965 New York mayoralty Race. *No narration.*

Voice will be voices of the real people.

Most of comment will be Lindsay's voice.

All the historical background and detail will be undercut with Lindsay today.

All the questions that remain unanswered in the normal campaign will be covered in two in-depth interviews with Lindsay. One at the beginning of the campaign and one after most of the footage is shot. From these interviews only Lindsay's answers will be used.

Opening Shot—"My name is John Lindsay and I'm here to get your vote." This will be used throughout in a variety of different circumstances since it has become John Lindsay's trademark.

Material from the past to be intercut—

> Mayoralty formerly a political dead end, now a stepping stone to national office.

The Past: The Mayor as merchant prince.

> The Mayor as Irish breakthrough (from ward and saloon to the urban top), Honey Fitz and Jimmy Walker.
>
> The Mayor as urban reformer—LaGuardia.
>
> The Mayor as hipster—O'Dwyer. It works; it may be bad, but it's ours.
>
> The Mayor as disengaged—Wagner.

John Lindsay—The mayoralty as national springboard—urban problems now national. First time mayoralty used as jumping-off place. How do you run as a Republican in a Democratic city?

Lindsay and Goldwater—stock footage.

John Lindsay and style—Does he have it? What kind? Will it develop under a rough campaign—Buckley? The Negro issue?

John Lindsay and how I moved from underdog to favorite. Money.

John Lindsay and his supporters—Price? Javits? Rockefeller? Ray Bliss?

John Lindsay and the issues—his voice over visual material. The Negro, beautification, crime in the streets, poverty, is the city governable? water, education, traffic, budget, industry, etc.

John Lindsay—the candidate as WASP.

Johnson and the election.

Overall aim of the film is political theater. To shoot the *tensions* of all the foregoing.

> How? Stock footage of other campaigns and Lindsay material already shot—*Meet the Press,* on the beach, etc.

A ride with Lindsay—Lindsay narrates.

His congressional campaigns.

Family and personal life.

Dear David—

1) Thanks for the Ballantine's [chocolates].

2) I have called Marian [Javits] again about the commercials and campaign music.

3) John Fearon today shipped you some more footage, including, he believes, [Abraham] Beame victory footage.

4) Some general notes on structure.

In an early letter of mine, I mentioned the idea of the mayoralty as Irish breakthrough—from saloon and ward to the urban top. I do think we might get a few feet of Jimmy Walker in his heyday. *MacKenzie,* after all, is going to have to cope with the fact that *this* campaign is different, that Lindsay and the liberal wing of the Republican Party are running for more than the mayoralty. That once upon a time the end of urban politics was city hall, the machine, the gravy, that the city was a usable, containable element in a greater whole. But that today is itself more than it was and a stepping stone to the highest office. Jimmy Walker's mayoralty addressed itself to the local only. Lindsay's campaign is addressed to the nation, for the city's concerns are the national problems.

Beginning: Since the English audience will be unfamiliar with many of the faces and what they represent, I do think the beginning should contain a cast of characters going from motion to the frozen frame and without lip sync. The sound should be a key sentence and one which should recur later in the picture. I suggest that all those who stand for themselves be included (Beame, Lindsay, Johnson, Buckley, Moynihan, Jesse Gray, Sammy Davis Jr., R. Kennedy) and that those who simply illustrate a position (a police sergeant or pats [patrol officers]) be omitted from cast of characters. I would proceed, for example, as follows with the cast.

A. [Mayor Robert] Wagner—for cast of characters, porch at Gracie Mansion is too static and would demand lip sync. For image I would use him walking a few feet at Baruch House, freeze frame at point where he is mobbed by autograph hunters, and for voice use one key line from your interview, for example, the line about culture.

B. For Lindsay I would use either on horseback and freeze or boardwalk at Coney Island, walking along and then freeze. Voice would be a key line about the great city. It's my belief that using non-sync pix/track makes viewer focus/listen more attentively.

C. For Beame, walking in the market and for track one sentence from victory speech.

D. Jesse Gray—not in car but speaking at street corner, then freeze and one hot line from track. In all cases I would identify each character

with a line of type at bottom: e.g., Jesse Gray, radical Negro leader, etc.
E. Moynihan at Rappaport's and freeze with a line from interview which would be picked up later, "City ready to explode."
F. Dubinsky, walking at cocktail party, freeze and line.
G. Sammy Davis jumping on bandstand, freeze and add line from your interview.
H. Buckley entering rally and getting on stand at Conservative Party meeting, freeze and one big anti-Lindsay line.
I. Walter Thayer and Bobby Kennedy ditto.

Another letter follows in six hours with more structure.

Love,
d

THOMAS WAUGH

That's Where the Action Is (1976)

"Emile de Antonio has set the pattern for the new documentary, and embodies its inspiration and its contradictions more than any other," wrote film scholar Thomas Waugh in his notable essay, "Beyond Verité: Emile de Antonio and the New Documentary of the Seventies." His analysis, which first appeared in Jump Cut *and was reprinted in Bill Nichols's* Movies and Methods, *vol. 2, An Anthology (1985), includes a discussion of* That's Where the Action Is. *"Beyond Verité" identified the "ex-academic culture hobo" as the leading documentarian of his time. Like others, the writer was as much taken by the man as by his work. "As one encounters him presiding over this New York office-studio, one is struck by the battle taken up by this congenial man with enormous energy, roving conversation, and a robust sense of outrage. . . . The overall impression is one of deadly seriousness and moral fervor, and in this, his role in the perpetuation of past traditions of documentary conscience, his place in the continuum of causes, ideals, and outcries that is his legacy as a documentarist is a clear one."*

Because That's Where the Action Is *was never theatrically distributed nor given a video release, Waugh's commentary represents the sole analysis of the film yet published. Although he correctly assesses the BBC film as a minor work, he concluded that it was an expression of "the rich creative energy, the obstinate commitment to rationality and to change, and the clear-sighted historical consciousness" that made de Antonio "one of the major American filmmakers."*

Emile de Antonio has set the pattern for the new documentary, embodies its inspiration and its contradictions, more than any other. As one encounters him presiding over his New York office-studio, one is struck by the incongruity of a battle taken up against the whole U.S. establishment by the congenial man with enormous energy, roving conversation, and a robust sense of outrage.

Of course the question can arise whether de Antonio's appeal to a broad-based liberal audience is consistent with the Marxist principles he professes. It is a question not easily resolved. Is his divergence from the reformist ideology of the sixties more a theoretical one than an actual one, his analytical methodology merely a style based on a theoretically constructed model of an ideal spectator who doesn't actually exist? Does de Antonio's recent interest in the Weatherpeople mean that his earlier faith in "democratic didacticism" has been reversed? He claims not, yet the contradictions persist. They present themselves sharply indeed in de Antonio's next film after *Point of Order, That's Where the Action Is*, a fifty-minute BBC television assignment dealing with the 1965 New York mayoral race between John Lindsay, Abraham Beame, and William Buckley. The artist's first experience with a camera crew and his first encounter with an ongoing event, the result is his most journalistic film. It is also most remote from the acerbic tone of the "radical scavenging" for which he was to become famous, and the least inclined to escape from the confines of the bourgeois problematic within which it is posed. Compared to the other films, it has, predictably, the impersonal air of an assignment about it, but it is executed with skill and verve nonetheless.

The film interpolates a British perspective of an American election (a BBC voice-over introducing parties, candidates, and issues was probably unavoidable) with a running discussion of the urban problems which were the issues of the campaign. The vivid mélange of vérité footage of campaign activity, and interviews with both voters and candidates, lay and professional commentators, is flawlessly assembled. The most impressive aspect of the film is its continuation of the theme of media critique begun with *Point of Order*. De Antonio wittily undercuts the electoral system by including television spots by both major candidates, complete with unabashedly empty rhetoric and tasteless campaign songs (by Ethel Merman in the Lindsay spot). There is also prolonged scrutiny of the candidates' platform demagoguery and a caustic critique of the Lindsay style by also-ran Conservative Buckley. On the whole, *That's Where the Action Is* (it's the BBC's title, not his own) is a modest and promising second film; however, it fails to heighten the satirical bemusement in its view of electoral politics to any serious level of interrogation, and furthermore, seems content with the classical sixties-liberal problematic of urban decay in its treatment of big-city problems (relying heavily on Daniel Moynihan for its commentary in this area). And ultimately the film's analysis of video politics is itself weakened by its own susceptibility to the charismatic attraction of candidate Lindsay. The photogenic, aristocratic liberal emerges relatively unscathed from the film, seeming to get the better share of the camera's attention (at one point he offers it a gigantic close-up hot dog). And in the long run he succeeds in charming the film's audience, despite the director's attempts to undercut his appeal, as much as he charmed most American liberals that year (as well as the majority of the voters).

However, if the film is unquestionably a minor work, it constitutes an important step in the artist's career. If *Point of Order* served as a manifesto of general aesthetic principle (democratic didacticism) and strategy (collage) expressed in their most basic form, *That's Where the Action Is* and de Antonio's subsequent film *Rush to Judgment* (1966) point clearly to the complex form of cinema, the "document-dossier," which the four following "mature" works [*In the Year of the Pig, America Is Hard to See, Millhouse,* and *Painters Painting*] were to imitate and refine.

Rush to Judgment

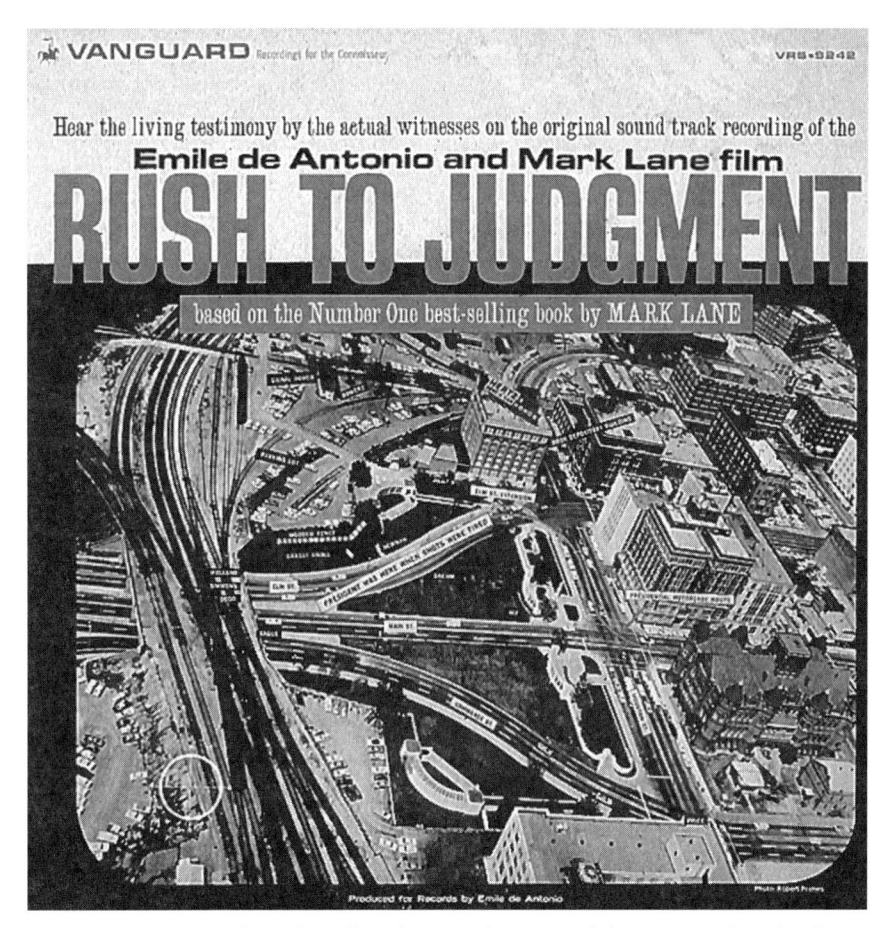

Figure 25. An aerial shot of Dealey Plaza on the cover of the LP sound track of *Rush to Judgment,* Vanguard Records, 1967.

Rush to Judgment: *A Conversation with Mark Lane and Emile de Antonio (1967)*

The first major film to raise doubts about the investigation of the Kennedy assassination, Rush to Judgment *was the principal subject of* Film Comment's *issue on JFK documentaries. The journal's cover featured a photograph of the "pristine bullet" that the Warren Commission said Lee Harvey Oswald had fired into the president's back. A lengthy interview with de Antonio and gadfly Warren critic Mark Lane (presented here in abridged form) was illustrated by frame enlargements of the many dissenting witnesses filmed by de Antonio.*

Rush to Judgment is:

    A. The first time a film specifically attacks and confronts a major government position: the Warren Commission and its Report.
    B. Not only a courtroom drama and a detective story but also the first time in which an actor in history becomes an actor in film: Mark Lane.
    C. The first time a film is a plea for the defense: Lee Harvey Oswald.
    D. A film with a precise activist goal. That goal is: by exposing filmically the errors, omissions, and distortions of the Warren Commission, to press for the reopening of the case, with Mark Lane as counsel for Lee Harvey Oswald.

        —Emile de Antonio, director, *Rush to Judgment*

DE ANTONIO: This is the first time in the history of film, to my knowledge, that a documentary has addressed itself to a frontal attack on a major report by an existing government. This is one of the major importances of the film. We have a picture that Mark and I both intentionally wanted to be spare, unsparing, didactic. It's a kind of Brechtian cinema. It's the theater of fact. It's the theater of argumentation. It's the theater of judicial investigation, the theater of attack on the Establishment and government. This is a very hot potato.

We might go to England and have a winner with this picture, but we face distribution problems here. I find this personally disturbing, and Mark does, too, because we are Americans and this is an American experience, and American film, an American issue. This is where *Rush to Judgment* belongs.

This movie in a sense concerns how Lee Harvey Oswald was executed, and then tried without a defense attorney. In a real sense, this film is his defense. And so we are not impartial. A defense attorney does not have to provide a second theory; he simply has to indicate that the facts leveled against his client are not consistent.

LANE: We don't really know who killed President John F. Kennedy. We all have our own guesses, but they are not in my book and they are not in the film. They have preempted the field. Our position is merely to present the testimony of the witnesses. When one hears what they have to say, one cannot believe the Warren Report.

DE ANTONIO: We have twenty-eight hours of negative right now, and if we had another $100,000 we could produce a twenty-four-hour film. We could match the Warren Report. We could at least produce a typescript document, which could be as detailed. But in this kind of production you simply have a terrible time getting money, and we were operating on very little. The money came from extraordinary sources—from private individuals, friends of Mark's, and people in England—Oscar Lewenstein, the producer of *Tom Jones,* who is now doing a film with Truffaut. And John Osborne and John Arden, the playwrights. Tony Richardson, the director. And some well-to-do young people in England.

It's a very low-budget picture, about $60,000. One reason it's low-budget is that, like everything that Mark and I have been involved in recently, we don't pay ourselves. We have a theoretical salary of $120 a week, but it's pure theory. We've been having a hard time getting the money.

LANE: What we are going to do when we've completed the film is to write a letter to every member of the Warren Commission, send them a print of the film and say, "This is the film we've made, and we will add ten minutes to the film of your answers to any point in the film, each of you, and we'll run that unedited, exactly as you present it to us. And if you'd be willing to do it, we'd be happy to come and film you."

DE ANTONIO: We uncovered whole worlds down there in Dallas that the Warren Commission with its vast apparatus missed. It had access, after all, to the whole majesty and power of the federal government. We uncovered people in the underworld there who had connections, who know about Ruby and Tippit and who testified on film. We had to go out and dig stuff.

In the beginning we weren't even sure that we could shoot down there in Dallas. So we aimed at stock footage, plus whatever shooting we could get. But our shooting in Dallas was so successful, and we acquired such massive material, that I would say now that the picture is 80 percent original material and 20 percent stock footage. It's black-and-white 16mm, and will be blown up to 35mm.

When I say we had a West Coast crew, don't misunderstand—it wasn't a Hollywood crew. They were young people who had done commercials— a company called Cosmopolitan Films, but operating as individuals. With Mark and myself and an assistant, it was essentially a six-man crew.

One approach we used was that most people think all this belongs to history. The Report came out in September 1964. We said, "It's history now. It's no longer controversial." The lack of money turned out to be a break for us. If we had gone down there a year ago we simply wouldn't have gotten it. This is the earliest that anybody could have done this in depth, frankly.

LANE: I'd been to Dallas before. I saw some people, but I never filmed an interview in Dallas before De and I went there. We had many members of our citizens committee—amateur investigators who had gone to Dallas and interviewed people we subsequently saw. But by then I was so well known—in Dallas anyway—that it seemed fruitless to approach witnesses who would know who I was. Most of the witnesses were reluctant to talk.

In Dallas we went to the Tower Motel. I registered in the name of Robert Blake. I talked to Domingo Benavides, who was the witness of the Tippit killing, who probably called the Dallas police—the two homicide fellows told De that Benavides had called. The police were interested obviously in De and Robert Blake. I don't think they knew that I was Mark Lane at the time. The next night we checked out of that motel on the advice of Penn Jones, editor of the *Midlothian Mirror.* We remained in Arlington until we left. All phone calls were always made either by De or by Robert Blake. We never told any of the witnesses who I was. It was merely a question of doing a documentary film on the assassination.

DE ANTONIO: People respond to film more than they do to ordinary types of interrogation. You'd think that they'd resist the idea of invading their houses, but in fact . . .

In making the film we uncovered witnesses who weren't available to Mark in writing the book, or witnesses who the Warren Commission had said did not exist, as in the case of one of the witnesses of the Tippit killing, a woman called Acquilla Clemons. The Warren Commission said this woman does not exist—and we have her on film telling exactly what she saw.

We filmed in Dallas about a month. We kept very much undercover, except when we actually had to go to a person. The witnesses had been intimidated. One of the main witnesses to the actual assassination—I don't know if we should put this in print.

LANE: It's in my book so . . .

DE ANTONIO: Mrs. Jean Hill, a schoolteacher in Dallas. A friend of hers was probably as close to the presidential car as anybody. Her friend, Mary Moorman, was actually taking a still photo at the precise time the president was shot. She angled in such a way that the Book Depository Building was in the rear of the photo. The FBI seized that photo on the site and never returned it to her. Now, Jean Hill maintains an absolutely different story than the Commission's version. Yet when we went to see her it was like some bad mystery story. A kid answered the door and said, "My mother doesn't want to talk to you. She's asleep." We started off and suddenly she came to the door and said, "Okay, I'll talk with you." So we sat down and talked to her for a hell of a long time. She said, "I'm a liberal," the only liberal we talked to down there. But, she said, "The principal of my school said the next time I am in the papers or anything is written about me, my job is finished." So we can understand why she was leery to do it.

Her testimony before the Commission was completely contrary to the Commission's conclusion in two respects. Number one: the shots came from behind the fence. She said there was no question about that. Number two: there were at least four or five shots. The Commission said there were only three because with the antiquated rifle they said they found on the sixth floor of the Book Depository Building, tested by the FBI, only three shots could be fired in the period of time which elapsed. Here was a witness close to the president who said that the shots came from behind the wooden fence, not from the Book Depository, and that there were at least four shots. Maybe as many as five or six.

She said, "I told the truth for two years. This country doesn't want to hear the truth. I know the Warren Report is a lie. But I've two small children to support. I'm a public schoolteacher in Dallas, and I just can't do anymore."

LANE: She said, "You know, Mark Lane called me." I was then Robert Blake in this interview. I had called her very early when I heard of her name. This was one of the tape-recorded interviews I conducted by phone.

"After Mark Lane called me the FBI was here all the time, practically lived in my house. I could not get rid of them, and so I can't do it anymore."

DE ANTONIO: A lot of these people have extraordinary guts. They knew what they were doing. They were being filmed by us, and we were very clear about what we were doing. We were not hoodwinking anybody. They did it, having been told by the FBI or the local police, or by relatives, or by a combination of all of these, not to go into this.

We thought about how it was possible to spend a month in Dallas without great trouble. My conclusion was that anything they did to try to stop us would be helpful. Publicity would be helpful, and killing us was out. That would be almost an admission of guilt.

Penn Jones of the *Midlothian Mirror*—somebody threw a firebomb into his office and blew it up. He's promised a long series of articles about the Warren Commission. He raises the point that a number of people have died who were connected to the events around the assassination.

After the police visited me in Dallas, one of the crew from San Francisco wanted to go home. He was sure there'd be trouble. Every day the crew waited for me to open the door of the car. They were waiting for me to turn the key in the car. . . .

I talked to General Walker five times. In fact, one of the people we filmed is the man called Warren Reynolds who was, I think, a right-wing sympathizer, an extraordinary person. His story didn't quite jibe with the Commission's and with that of the Dallas police.

LANE: He was in court because he saw a man leave the scene of the Tippit killing, saw him at rather close range. He did not identify that man as Oswald.

We found one witness, a Negro active in the Negro Community Free Movement in Dallas, who was arrested by Officer Tippit because he was the chef in an after-hours place where there were white and Negro girls.

DE ANTONIO: Of course, he provided the girls. And when this fellow was arrested, he sat in the front of the car driving into the jail with Officer Tippit, and sitting with him, going along for a joyride, was Jack Ruby. And the Commission's entire investigation called upon the FBI, CIA, and the Secret Service and they could show no relationship between Ruby and Tippit. Yet here was a guy who told us on film that he saw Ruby and Tippit together, and they were close and friendly.

We had another witness, [James] Tague, the only other person who was wounded on November 22nd. Kennedy was killed, Connolly was wounded, and a bullet hit the concrete and sprayed up and caused blood to flow from the face of an observer, Tague. This is very embarrassing to the three shots theory.

LANE: It was an absolute miss. Either fragments of the concrete or the fragments of the bullet struck him to the face. He reported this to a Deputy Sheriff Walters right on the scene.

We thought we'd finished with every witness when we had this police officer, this Negro named Napoleon Daniels. Daniels had seen Jack Ruby enter the police building basement, walk right past the police officer beside a sign to keep people out. Daniels said, "The police officer must have seen me look right at him, and Ruby had his hand in his pocket. I thought he had a gun there, quite frankly, then he went down and he shot Oswald."

DE ANTONIO: It's rather consistent among people who knew Ruby that Ruby knew hundreds of police officers. The Commission accommodated itself to Chief [of Police] Curry's guess that it was twenty-five to fifty. They accepted that statement, although the FBI questioned perhaps 25 percent of the Dallas police officers in reference to other matters who said, "Yes, I know Jack Ruby. I've known him for years." The Commission published in its twenty-six volumes the statements of seventy-six Dallas police officers who said they knew Ruby well—seventy-six! Yet the Commission itself said that Ruby knew no more than twenty-five to fifty, paying no attention to the FBI report that had been submitted to them. And so the terrible thing, I think, is the way the Commission functioned, seeking to fasten itself upon a theory....

And then we also interviewed Nelson Delgado, Oswald's friend in the Marine Corps. If you read the Report about Delgado, it says, "off the record." He gave us on film what he said he told the Commission off the record. The reason we got all this was due to Mark's research. No one had ever gone through this with such thoroughness. Most people who worked on this thing don't even know who the hell these witnesses are. This includes the books that share our point of view.

Even the books that share our point of view are not done properly. If you mention the name of Nancy Perrin Rich to the average specialist in this field, it would be meaningless. Yet Perrin was hired by Ruby the day she arrived in Dallas because the Dallas police took her there.

About the errors of the Warren Commission: the FBI, the Secret Service, and the Dallas police were the only groups to supply facts to it. The Commission had no fact-finding body itself. It had seven lawyers and some advisers, but the basic material fed to the Commission was incestuous. It came from the very agencies who might come under attack. If there was no conspiracy, if Lee Oswald alone had killed the president of the

United States, then, goddammit, at least the FBI was negligent, because the FBI had Oswald on its list as potentially dangerous. . . .

LANE: We have no conclusion. I have no conclusion in my book, and the film has none, except that we present what the witnesses told the Warren Commission, what they saw, and what they said they saw. We show how the Commission has ignored that which the witnesses told them if it did not conform to the Commission's preconceived conclusions that Oswald did it and did it alone from the sixth floor of the Book Depository Building. Or, if they did not ignore it, they distorted it.

Let me give you one example. Lee Bowers was the railroad employee who ran the tower, which was set perhaps seventy-five yards behind the wooden fence. He had a view of the fence. And he testified that "At the time the shots were fired something attracted my attention to that fence, something that . . ." And then there's a dash in the [Warren] record. . . . I asked Bowers, "What would you have said?" And he replied, "Well, I would have told them that something attracted my attention to that fence at the time the shot was fired—a flash, a flame, a puff of smoke, something like that—and that's why I centered my attention on the fence."

DE ANTONIO: You know the clichés about Texans. There was S. M. Holland, a lean, taciturn type. He seemed such a decent citizen, a beautiful man. He said, "I love this country. If we can't tell the truth here, let's give it back to the Indians."

LANE: Holland was a railroad employee who had worked for some forty-one years. In fact, he was a deputy sheriff. He was a great witness, he'll be great in the film—a Gary Cooper–type Texan, kind of tall, slim, lines in his face, and he wears a Texas hat. A very attractive witness. He was the employee chosen by the Dallas police that day to see that no one other than railroad employees got on the overpass. The overpass is maybe sixty yards from the fence. Holland said he told the Commission: "I heard the shots, I looked up, I saw the puff of smoke coming off of that wooden fence, and I ran behind the fence—"the Commission counsel cut him off.

We were there behind the wooden fence after we interviewed Holland. He said he liked us very much, and he would do anything he could to help us. He was on the overpass and showed us exactly the various areas where he heard shots and saw the smoke. He led us behind the wooden fence. And all this on film. One of these sheriffs came up to us in a ten-gallon hat, a tall fellow with a gun in his holster. He walked over and said, "What are you filming back here for? I've seen fifty or a hundred cameramen in this area, but they are all taking pictures of the sixth floor of the Book

Depository Building. The window is there. What are you back here for?" I was thinking of some lies to tell him about the sun glare on the window or something, but Holland said, "I'll tell you why: they want the facts. They know the shots came from back here." And the sheriff said, "Well, OK, I see. Would you mind moving your camera so I can get my car out of here?" That's all.

DE ANTONIO: Holland said, "You are the first people who ever asked me all these things, including the Warren Commission. There were five people who worked for me who were on the overpass with me. The Warren Commission never introduced any of these people." These weren't bankers or anything. They were ordinary Texas people who had no ax to grind, who weren't for or against any vested interests—the conspiracy theory or the single-guilt theory. The fact that they were omitted, as if they had never lived, is implausible.

When Mark and I arrived in Dallas, at first they weren't going to allow us to do the film. In fact, on the third day, two Dallas policemen came to see me, members of the homicide squad. Mark had uncovered a great witness, Benavides. That was their excuse. Since the witness was a Mexican, they kept referring to him as "boy." They said, "I hear you're going to interview this boy." Both [policemen were] very good-looking boys in civilian clothes. I had them identify themselves, and they produced both identification and a calling card. They said, "We're just protecting Benavides. You know, he was worried that there might be fraud." I said, "Well, if you're worried that there might be fraud, why are *you* here? You're the homicide squad." And they said, "Anything that has to do with the murder of Tippit has to do with us." Then Benavides disappeared as far as we were concerned. We were never able to film him. He was one of the few people we lost.

LANE: There was absolutely no tension at all on the scene of the assassination. We were there three hours. All the tension is where Tippit was killed.

DE ANTONIO: That's right. This is the key to it. This is the only witness we could not really get, Benavides. Benavides was one of the witnesses to the death of Tippit. He's a Mexican auto-repair worker, just a bystander. He was driving a pickup truck. He was fifteen feet from the guy who killed Tippit. And he disappeared.

If you were to ask me, "What would you do if you had $100,000?" my answer would be that we would go back to Dallas and we would break our asses to get Benavides.

We would also try to get this other thing, which I find the most mysterious part of this whole business. There is a "shadow Oswald" mentioned in the Report which should be fantastic in film. Part of it we were about to take up with CBS, then they withdrew the stock footage.

It really hinges on three things. There is first the shooting-range incident. A man who looked like Oswald on three different occasions turned up at a newly opened shooting-range just outside of Dallas. Once he put three bullets in [a target] at one hundred yards; on another occasion he put a bullet right in the center of somebody else's target, drawing attention to himself and mentioning his name. He also had this rifle bore-sighted and a scope put on it by a boy who works there. It turns out this was Oswald, allegedly. It is mentioned in the Report, but mentioned as something which is not accurate, that it was not Oswald. But then the question arises, "Who in the hell was it?"

And there's the incident of a young man around the first of November 1963, who went to the Lincoln-Ford Agency and said, "My name is Lee Oswald. I want to buy a car and if I can't get it I'm going back to the Soviet Union where I can get one." He said, "I'll have a lot of money in two or three weeks but I would like the car now." And then he test-drove the car and obviously drew attention to himself as he drove the car seventy to a hundred miles an hour down the freeway. The government then proved that Oswald wasn't even around that particular day. So again we ask, "Who in the hell was it? And why?"

And now there's a third "shadow Oswald." We'd like to find this lady named Sylvia Odio, who lived in New Orleans and Dallas. Her father is a prominent anti-Castro, Democratic-liberal type, who is now in a Cuban jail. She said that when she was living in New Orleans three men came to see her one night [in September 1963]. One announced that he was Leon Oswald. The others didn't announce themselves. The Leon Oswald type said, "You know, someone has got to kill Kennedy, because he is supporting Castro." She also said that he said he was an expert rifleman. Miss Odio saw a picture of him and said it looked very much like that man. The Commission said it couldn't have been Oswald, he was in Mexico at the time. But someone went there using Oswald's name, saying he was a rifleman, saying he was an ex-member of the Marine Corps, and saying that the president should be assassinated. Who was it, if it wasn't Oswald? The Commission just dropped it.

LANE: I don't think Kennedy was killed by Oswald. I don't know who killed him. But what Kennedy stood for prior to his assassination—as compared with where the country has gone since his assassination—is a clue to who killed him.

DE ANTONIO: The Report was an anthropological exorcism. It allayed and soothed the fears of the American people. The Warren Hearings [transcript] is very long, twenty-six volumes, plus the briefer Report. There are only 2,500 copies, apparently. Who the hell is going to go through those volumes—even people who are interested? Can you imagine how much work Mark did tracking through twenty-six volumes?

LANE: At least two people were involved in the killing. At least one shot came from the rear and at least one shot came from the right front, indicating at least two people. I see no evidence that either one was Oswald. I think there is evidence that shots were fired from two different areas, but who was involved I don't know. Either Oswald was involved two months in advance of the assassination, which both I and the Commission doubt, or someone planned to set up Oswald in advance. Or both. Maybe Oswald was partially involved. There's that possibility.

DE ANTONIO: We are avoiding all speculation in the film as to what may have happened. Besides, Mark and I do not have unanimity of opinion, for example, about Oswald's role, although our major conclusions are about the same. But the film is not setting up conjectures.

We have a tension between two points of view: there is the Warren Report and there is our point of view. My reading of direct quotations in context from the Warren Report says that there exists no credible evidence to believe that shots came from anywhere other than the Book Depository Building. I read that line and then—bang! You'll have six witnesses and other material indicating at least some doubt about that. Everywhere it is possible, we make a frontal attack on the Warren conclusion, when it can be done filmically.

I will speak this narration offering the Warren point of view. We were going to get an actor, but on second thought it seems that an actor—in a completely documentary situation—detracts from the atmosphere of facts that we create. Although Mark and I more or less share the same point of view, since it's our film, I will read the other side, off camera. This does not mean that I adhere to those conclusions. As a matter of fact, I adhere to quite the opposite conclusions.

Appearing visually is material that buttresses and explains the excerpts from the text of the Warren Report—a shot of the Book Depository Building, a shot of the fence, a shot of the presidential cavalcade—sequences put together out of stock footage.

Of the Warren Report, we obviously cannot present the entire work, but we present it wherever it impinges on our material—presented in context, in direct quotation. We don't redo their lines; we take the lines that are relevant and put them in the film in that form.

We have stock footage of Mark shot by the networks. Never shown, but shot. Back in December of 1963 and January 1964. Mark had initial doubts about Oswald's guilt before there was any Commission.

There is one great stock footage shot we can't get. [Earl] Warren is there surrounded by the august members of the Commission presenting the Report to Johnson—I saw it on TV live, it's great—and Johnson takes it and says, "It's very heavy." We can't get this footage. We went to the Grinberg Library, and they said, "You know, there's a lot of footage we can't get anymore."

In trying to get stock footage here in the U.S., we found that with NBC the answer is always no, and with ABC and CBS the answers were, "We're working on a show of our own." This is a legitimate response, but we suspected that they weren't really working on a show of their own that could be related in any way to what we were doing. The thing sort of trundled on that way. Mark was in London working on the book and dealing with Bodley Head, the publishers, and I went there to direct a show for the BBC about American urban problems. Mark and I discovered an enormous amount of stock footage in Visnews, an English stock-footage house, and at a very low price. So we started acquiring stock footage—as you do in these films with a little bit of money and promises. We came back here in Christmas of 1965 and found out that suddenly we could get access to the entire Sherman Grinberg Library of ABC, which is not all of ABC but enough to make a film.

Then CBS opened up, and something happened which I find absolutely shocking, because of my own personal dealings with CBS on *Point of Order*. They called Mark and me—the woman I dealt with on *Point of Order*. She said, "De, you know, we did a show in September 1964 call 26 *Witnesses*, which dealt with twenty-six witnesses in Dallas. We have seventy-five hours of outtakes, and if you and Mr. Lane would like to look at them, that would be great. They're for sale. You'll have to come at night because we're very busy." So Mark and I went one night (at ten dollars an hour) and looked at this stuff. Six hours. We found some fairly incredible material. We found some of the imaginary Oswald material, which the Warren Commission later admitted is imaginary. So we were very pleased after six hours of looking. The next morning I called and said, "Great. We'd like to just keep going." And she said, "Oh, De, I've made a terrible mistake. I've just been told by the head office that CBS is not allowed to sell this work."

I know this was simply untrue. I also know that they are going to destroy the footage. This to me is part of the basic frivolousness of the media, because here is the raw material—which they created in a sense, they went and talked to these people. They created it and they're simply chucking it down the drain. There is no other record of it. The people they interviewed are going to die. In fact, cab driver William W. Whaley died in 1966. He allegedly drove Oswald on November 22, 1963. These people are going to disappear as time goes on, and they're not going to want to talk again. This material can never be retrieved. It's simply material lost to America and to history and to the world.

For another project, I had to go through an interview to get some Nuremberg footage. I finally got this introduction to Senator Jacob Javits, but I had to see a State Department guy. He introduced another guy who said he was from State. I immediately suspected he was from the CIA. He talked to me for an hour and asked what my opinion was of Vietnam. Of course, this film had nothing to do with Vietnam. He asked me in a roundabout fashion what my political beliefs were. I wanted to make the film like hell, so I didn't lie to him. But I kept it all very cool, and I said precisely what I had felt about all these things. To lie would have been the end of it. Of course, it was the end of it anyway, because the people who were backing it decided the world didn't need such a film.

LANE: The outstanding example of the irresponsibility of the media was a story written by Anthony Lewis for the *New York Times*. Lewis said [the twenty-six volumes of evidence] prove conclusively that the Commission was right, that Oswald was the lone assassin . . . But Lewis wrote this article the day the volumes were released. . . .

This has really been the role of the media, of complete acceptance of the Commission, saying, "This is correct," when they could not possibly have any basis for that statement.

DE ANTONIO: The nature of subtle intimidation in the media is also remarkable. Take the case of Seth Kantor. He is a very important witness, a trained journalist who worked for Scripps-Howard for three years in Dallas. Now he's a congressional reporter for the chain in Washington. He said [to the Commission], "I was in Parkland Memorial Hospital in Dallas shortly after one o'clock. I felt a tug at my sleeve and turned around—there was Jack Ruby. I knew Jack Ruby very well because he'd given me about ten stories since I'd been in Dallas."

I called Kantor up and said, "May I come down to Washington to film you?" He said, "Sure, when do you want to come?" I called the next day to confirm the time. I said, "I'll get a car and a camera crew and drive down and I'll see you about 2:30 at the Scripps-Howard Building." Half an hour later he called and said, "Look, my wife would be really upset if I saw you tomorrow because we are having people in for lunch and cocktails and all. . . . Why don't you write me a letter and tell me who you are." I simply can't believe he changed of his own volition. I think he called somebody in the FBI.

The press and film world in this country have never properly treated the subject of the assassination and the events subsequent to it. Television has done an outstanding disservice to truth, as television almost always does. Almost without exception, in dealing with any controversial issue, television seems to take an Establishment point of view.

I think that the great disservice to this country is that we are trying everywhere to get a unanimity of opinion. But the only way democracy can function is to have a diversity of opinion. I don't know what the answer is with television because the noncommercial channels are too gutless, and the commercial channels are simply too interested in money. So it's a wholly depressing prospect.

For instance, they will now treat the topic of certain drugs but they avoid the issue of the rights of individuals who take marijuana, which is demonstrably less harmful than alcohol and probably less harmful than tobacco. Yet marijuana is treated in these television documentaries as if it were a great social terror. There is always the implication that it leads to something else.

Whenever the government comes out hard on an idea, the television medium backs it. I don't think this is the function of television.

Yet, in a curious way, it's in television that we need more government scrutiny in order to make for more diversity. One answer is to have an independent television authority as you have in England, but run by private individuals, maybe operated with government funds, given carte blanche to produce twenty hours of television per day of any kind and even seek out real controversy.

I think that if the Federal Communications Commission would bear down on the television networks it would make them face up to their public responsibility. The networks treat the air as *their* air, *their* time. The biggest phony phrase in the U.S. today is "free enterprise." I mean, who's free? what enterprise? Three networks control most of our air, but it's *our* air, the air of the American people. And yet Stanton and Paley and Sarnoff and Goldenson have got their mitts on the stuff.

As long as CBS looks like General Motors, you are not going to have decent programming. They pat themselves on the back because of *Death of a Salesman*, but what else has CBS done in a year? CBS is proud of the fact that it has the ten top ratings in daytime television. Do you know what this means, when you look at the *New York Times* to see what daytime television is about? My answer to that is fuck them. Those people have nothing to do with me. They have nothing to do with the world that interests me; nothing to do with art; nothing to do with politics—real politics. Nothing to do with controversy. Nothing to do with excitement.

LANE: ABC-TV decided to have a great debate between me and Melvin Belli, who was Ruby's lawyer and who believes the Warren Report. Les Crain was to be moderator. All of a sudden Les Crain calls up and says, "Geez, Mark, can't have you on the show." I said, "Why?" and he said, "Meet me in the bar," and I did and we spent about two hours talking. "ABC-TV said you can't debate Melvin Belli. You would confuse the audience because you would have affidavits and facts and things like that. So they decided that Melvin Belli would debate Marguerite Oswald.

Oswald's mother retained me to represent her son's interests before the Warren Commission, but I remained independent of her and investigated on my own. We aren't in this for the money. Congressman Gerald Ford of the Warren Commission sold his book for a great deal of money to Simon and Schuster.

DE ANTONIO: Mark had a book nobody would take. Nobody in this country would touch it. Although I wasn't involved at all in writing the book, I worked a little bit on trying to sell it. We saw important publishers here, and in most cases they didn't want to look at it. But Holt, Rinehart and Winston is making a major production out of the book. They spent a tremendous amount of money on advertising and promoting it. It's going to be a very, very big book.

The strength of the book is that most of it comes from the Report and the evidence that the government offers, in its own words. Mark's book treats this evidence. By his painstaking and brilliant analysis, he restores things to their original juxtaposition. The film uncovered people in some cases never heard of before by anybody, including the government. In other cases, [we] interview them more thoroughly than the government did.

There's a technical problem in the film, as yet unsolved. The Commission resorted to some of the wildest stuff in its reconstructions, like putting rifles on the sixth floor, with camera attachments, and taking footage and trying to fire exactly 178 feet and film it, time it, check it. We don't have the equipment to reconstruct it, nor the money or the people. So I thought to do something way out of the documentary field, to ask somebody like John Hubley to do animation for us. Since we are going to leave the world of fact anyway, just to set up a chart of what could happen—with different clocks going. I think you could almost get to be more real with this animation, better than any re-creation since re-creations are antinatural. But there's always a problem of money with a film like this.

This is not cinema verité. I don't accept cinema verité as a concept philosophically. Nobody is God. Nobody can do this thing with total objectivity. Mark and I do have a point of view. We are not objective. We are a plea for the defense. We hope we're honest. Objectivity is something we allow the gods to have, but not mere mortals. The most a man can hope for is that he does his best to be honest.

My experience in films has been within the last five years. I came into this new medium as an intellectual, as a former university teacher and editor, as a "word" person who taught philosophy and literature. I went to documentary films because it was the only way a person my age could begin making films.

I think it is much harder to make a fiction film—the kind of fiction film that I would like to make—which would have to do with the world in a different way, in which visual images would be different from those in Hollywood film. I couldn't have done it, even if I had the money, five years ago. I have learned something about filmmaking through the documentary. I am working on a semidocumentary right now.

There's no money for documentaries. The one I'd most like to do, I'd give up anything in the world to do, is the subject of the American Indian. I've been collecting much material and have a tremendous file on this. To do it right is a $300,000 picture, the ultimate statement on the American Indian, who is worse off than the American Negro. The American Indian is the one race being exterminated from the face of the earth, like the Nazis were doing to the Jews. The Indian who is left is still being robbed and cheated by the U.S. government. I'd like to make this long and tough and beautiful. The only people who would sponsor this would be a foundation, and foundations want too much control. I haven't gone to anybody.

The intended Indian project is somewhat related to my earlier film, *Point of Order,* [and] is about what interests me philosophically: the failure of American culture. . . . The dramatic interest of *Point of Order* lies in its characters; we have no such characters here in *Rush to Judgment*.

Rush to Judgment has a different problem because, in this film, the main problem is one of total credibility. I don't mean we invent credibility, but to sacrifice everything for credibility, to sacrifice even dramatic interest to make the points [is a problem]. We hope that drama and credibility can be done together; at least this is the optimum situation.

LOUIS MARCORELLES

Homo Americanus (1967)

This translated excerpt appeared alongside Film Comment's *lengthy interview with de Antonio and Mark Lane in an issue devoted to films about the Kennedy assassination. Originally published that April by* Cinéma 67 *(Paris) as "*Rush to Judgment *and* Force of Evil,*" the longer essay compared the documentary to the 1948 noir classic by blacklisted Hollywood director Abraham Polonsky. Marcorelles, a friend of de Antonio, later published an interview with him in* Cahiers du Cinéma *(1976).*

Two authentic films of the left, two films of extraordinary talent, two unequaled witnesses of American society, have just appeared on our screens in the midst of general indifference and the apathy of a literally exhausted criticism. Because these two films make no call to demagoguery, because they are "straight" like real bourbon, they have been purely and simply ignored. Let us attempt to repair the neglect.

Emile de Antonio, director of *Rush to Judgment*, professor of literature by training, but also an enthusiastic experimenter, associated with a number of avant-garde undertakings in the U.S. (most prominently those of the choreographer Merce Cunningham and composer John Cage), represents in the cinema one of the last authentic adventurers, a man always ready to take all the risks.

His *Point of Order* had earlier expressed his obsession with documenting American society and putting into question the foundations of this society. The film was characterized by the same surgical concern, the same desire to analyze how people *really* think and speak, how things *really* happen.

De Antonio, in a short written preface, terms his film "art brut"—that is to say, raw material of a reflective and poetic import, but not reworked, not dramatically and plastically remolded, as the canons dear as much to

Jean Mitry and Philippe Esnault as to the two Françoises, Truffaut and Chevassu, require. We are up to the neck in what I like to call, in what must more and more be called, the "cinema direct," that also of Richard Leacock, unequaled master of the modern film, and of Pierre Perrault: a cinema that catches at life with its lightweight equipment, where, contrary to what almost all my compatriots imagine, the question is not to shoot no matter how, but where the spoken word illuminates and plays a primordial role. If there is a crisis today in cinematography (in the Bressonian sense), if structuralism well apprehended is going to oblige us to rethink radically all our evangelical truths, it is through such works as *Rush to Judgment* that truly constructive reflection can be exercised.

The real problem—does this type of cinema have a public? as Karel Reisz, absolute admirer of *Rush to Judgment* as the equal of a Chris Marker film, said to me the other day in London. In the current climate of intellectual laziness, in this cultural desert where everything resembles everything and therefore nothing, I would not know how to reply. I only know that television, whether French or American, rarely would have or will have the self-assurance to bring into question the values of the society which creates it.

Nowhere else have we been offered a document as prodigious in invading the collective and therefore individual thought, with its corollaries concerning the omnipotence of the police on all levels and the ontological conformity of Homo Americanus, a conformity demonstrated repeatedly as the film shows witnesses offering evidence contradicting the Warren Report but aligning themselves with it in order to keep their consciences clean. Every Preminger will pass, and also the current Hollywood, while *Rush to Judgment* will retain its impact and will deliver to posterity a historic judgment.

Perhaps it is time to rethink the cinema in view of new exigencies formulated by films like *Rush to Judgment,* and above all by the great Canadians and New Yorkers—Groulx, Brault, Perrault, Leacock, Maysles, de Antonio. We realize that a new way of feeling and of perceiving for the cinematographer is in the process of being designed, if not of being decisively affirmed. This does not imply that all dramatization is to be rejected . . . rather, the spectator must pose to himself the new exigencies, must ask himself what he expects from the cinema.

EMILE DE ANTONIO

Liner Notes for Rush to Judgment *LP (1967)*

The second of four de Antonio films adapted for long-playing phonograph albums, Rush to Judgment's *sound track was released by the prestigious jazz, folk, and spoken-word label Vanguard. De Antonio's incisive liner notes were reprinted for the film's press kit. Here he reiterates a favorite philosophical point: media technologies are never neutral ("neutral like a gun"!) and neither are his films. His willingness to knight Mark Lane as a modern-day dragon slayer cloaks the contempt he later expressed for the writer. However, de Antonio's self-important desire to compare his own work with Zola's* J'accuse *demonstrates his affinity for European traditions of belles lettres and political dissent.*

The record *Rush to Judgment,* like the film from which it is made, is not an impartial study. It is not a study. It is advocacy, argument, a plea for the defense. The media, the FBI, the Dallas police, the Warren Commission made the case for the prosecution. As a defense, we present one side only—the other side, that side which did not accept Oswald's trial on television, which rejected the conclusion of the 888-page report based on the hasty assumptions of the police. Our side could not accept the call to national tranquillity when the national honor was at stake.

Example: Ninety witnesses were interviewed by the local and federal police. Fifty-eight said the shots came from the grassy knoll. Most of those who said so were never interviewed by the Commission or its lawyers. J. C. Dodd wasn't. James Leon Simmons wasn't. Only part of S. M. Holland's testimony was used and that out of context. As you hear them on our record, listen well. For you are the jury. Are they credible? Listen and decide for yourself. The Warren Commission decided this way (page 71, Warren Commission Report): "In contrast to the testimony of the witnesses who heard and observed shots fired from the Depository, the Commission's investigation has disclosed *no credible evidence* [italics mine] that any shots were fired from anywhere else."

Editing film and tape: Film, tape, the camera, the recorder, and the moviola on which film is edited are neutral—when not in use. They are neutral like a gun. Or a typewriter. In Dallas we shot over twenty hours of film. In New York, London, Dallas we looked at all the TV footage we could find. When we began editing there were thirty hours of 16mm footage to cut. The finished film is two hours long. In the trek from thirty to two, we were guided by belief and conviction as well as by the facts acquired in two years of research.

As a film and as a sound-track recording, *Rush to Judgment* is unique. But only because it is a film and a record. In fact, it belongs to a long tradition of dissent and of skepticism before the Establishment. If Zola were attacking the anti-Semites who framed Dreyfus today, I would like to believe he would use today's weapons to bring his *J'accuse* before the world.

A note on Mark Lane: The modern quest myth isn't peopled with dragons, moats, and maidens. Today the monster is the media. They are more efficient. Click clack. Click clack. Deserts of silence. The fires of half-truth. The fog of conformity which robes us in tranquillity. Today's quest is just as lonely; just as arduous; just as dangerous. And through tenacity and courage, Mark Lane has prevailed in his quest to the point where we must ask the president and the Congress for a new investigation—not one directed to domestic tranquillity but to find out what really happened in Dallas, November 22, 1963.

EMILE DE ANTONIO

Letter to Jean Hill (1966)

In 1979, de Antonio found this letter he had written to "grassy knoll" witness Jean Hill among the several thousand items in his FBI file. "She is the paradigm for the cover-up," he wrote in his journal, "a major witness to the crime of the century," first harassed, then ignored, by federal investigations. Despite his initial contacts with Jean Hill, she never sat for a Rush to Judgment *interview (although in 1992 she published her own account,* JFK: The Last Dissenting Witness, *after Oliver Stone's 1991 film* JFK *used her as a character). The "creep" to whom de Antonio's letter alludes he later identified as Jones Harris, son of Broadway producer Jed Harris and actress Ruth Gordon (Journals X.78, December 14, 1979).*

Box 1567
New York 17, N.Y.
CI6-4460
4.14.66

Dear Mrs. Hill,

    Our last talk was like dust in the air suspended—on my part. "Fama qui volit per urbe a nocte" is the way Vergil described the half-truths and nontruths purveyed by that ineffectual and dreary little creep.

    As I told you that night in Dallas, we have you on film from WFAA-TV; and it's good but I still would like the whole story. I'm interested in the truth and whether we make money or not is peripheral. I don't want time and indifference to bury what really happened in Dallas on that Friday in November. We have filmed all kinds of people, most of them from the Report, and we have already in process a film which will shoot a lot of holes in the Warren Report, in the official lies and stories; which will fill in the chinks of omission. Only madmen believe they possess absolute truth;

what we have is a stab at it, a little letting in of light, a hope that more can be done.

I've been a filmmaker for only a few years but I hope that what I've done (and here I am giving you a curriculum vitae) will convince you that I'm not a shady confidence man. To begin, I was a classmate of John F. Kennedy's at Harvard and I knew him. Since Harvard days I've been an editor, a longshoreman, a flier, a university teacher, graduate student, etc. In films I've done the following: produced the short *Sunday* which was about the riot in Washington Square between the folk singers and the police in April 1961. *Sunday* has won twelve international awards and I think it treated a rough theme honestly. I then coproduced and directed *Point of Order*, a 100-minute feature based on the Army-McCarthy hearings of 1954 and which was called "best picture of the year" by the *Herald Tribune*, generally acclaimed by critics, and the only American document to be shown at Cannes Film Festival. Last year I directed for the BBC a one-hour program about urban politics based on the 1965 New York mayoral election. The picture has not as yet been shown in the U.S. but it was a hit in England. The Kennedy-Oswald film is next and we're four months away from completion.

My call to you is based on many notes, not the least of which is the fact that of all the people I talked to in Dallas you are the only one whose views could be construed as even closely related to my own. All I ask is that you come here when your school is over and look at what we've done. It will not be too late then to add a few minutes of your testimony.

Mark Lane, of course had to be Bob Blake. Even Earl Warren registered in Dallas under a nom de guerre. In our case Mark was concerned that his true identity would force witnesses to conform to his ideas and Blake seemed obscure and objective enough to elicit truthful and neutral responses, which were what we wanted.

I hope you will agree. If you won't, will you write or call me collect and let me know your objections? The stories told to you by that lost, mixed-up, unhappy creep have another side.

At any rate,
best wishes,
d

EMILE DE ANTONIO

Journal Entry on Rush to Judgment (1980)

This cynical if frank account reveals how de Antonio and Lane ("rogues both") conducted their Judgment Films Corporation, living both indulgently and on the cheap.

A history of a part of a film, written by its checks with some help by its maker.

I never loved *Rush to Judgment* enough. Its crudeness was intentional and I love it. I had to push the film and push Mark Lane. His genius consists in knowing that there was a great distrust of all our institutions with the death of JFK and his uncanny and unique ability over the many years to find suckers—the young, frustrated middle-aged women, and marginal leftists—to believe in the holy cause of himself.

[In Dallas] . . . we knew something was wrong. But no one knew what. Our rulers must have been puzzled by the polls they had ordered, created, and influenced when 70 percent of our people, after the Warren Report, did not believe Lee Harvey Oswald alone killed JFK. He didn't and there was a conspiracy to change and destroy the facts, the witnesses, and the evidence.

Judgment Films Corporation
c/o Mr. Emile de Antonio
July 21, 1966—Mark Lane $150
July 17, 1966—Peggy Cooper, legal expenses, $75

Mark and I agreed to pay one another modest salaries while the film was being made. $150 a week is modest enough. Mark dropped into the cutting rooms in the Movielab building at 619 W. 54th Street and picked up a coffee and chatted and went on to promote his lecture career. . . . Peggy Cooper, a good-looking, young black activist lawyer wandered into our payroll. Sure, we were generous with the money I raised and would have to repay. And I was a sucker. And suckers feel low and mean and never forgive. I have taken mine from the company and the film. Mark never saw much of it except what he stole in France. And that's fair enough.

Peggy Cooper, August 28, 1966. $100
Chelsea Hotel, April 21, 1966. $282.60
Chelsea Hotel, n.d., $200

The Chelsea Hotel was hustle center. A suite for a prince of the left. Mark Lane and [his wife] Annalise stayed there when they didn't stay at one of my apartments or travel. We were all low on dough. The book wasn't out. I was making the film. He had an edge. I had stolen $3,000 from the company as a bonus for raising money. He claimed a piece, too. Rogues both, but with differences beyond my prejudices for myself.

We had parties at the Chelsea. Food and drink. Judgment Films paid. Not novel, even in the documentary film. One is always so pleased when a pigeon has been cornered and coughs up the ruby that glee calls for booze and good food. Mark learned about that too. I invented a spaghetti *à la de Antonio* for him and Annalise. Greens and Italian tuna fish with very good parmigiano.

And lonely widows.

Madeleine Goddard, February 13, 1967. $21.83

Madeleine Goddard had a small income. She loved Jack Kennedy. She thought Mark a knight *sans reproche et sans peur*. She gave him money. She was his pigeon a bit for the film. I told him no, not Madeleine Goddard. Are you sure she can afford it? Yeah, sure. Okay. She also worked at the rinky-dink group he set up at 156 Fifth Avenue, the Committee of Inquiry. Many middle-aged women in love with JFK trudged there to do free work, writing, stapling, mailing, etc. Slaves of master Lane. Madeleine finally invested $1,200. I was opposed but she insisted on becoming a pigeon. We paid her back, however. I paid her back. The check [$21.83] was for small office chores she did for me and expenses. The checkbook was in my hands with Mark's signature on a bunch of checks. At one point I took a jointly signed check and put it into a new account with one signatory: me. Mark was never there. He had no idea what the film looked like until I brought it to Paris. He hadn't seen it. Dan Drasin and Peter van Dyke were editing it for me. They were okay, journeymen American youths.

The real part of the film is made somewhere beyond the cameras and moviolas . . . otherwise any technician could make *Rules of the Game*. . . .

Truth is like Greek grape leaves: its wrappings are many and a huge industry grew out of JFK's assassination. The point, finally, was that there was a truth and its champions were tacky schemers, gulls, fools, peddlers, and hacks. Among all of them—some honest, some passionate, and some even in possession of the facts—the truth came through, beyond the death industry, to produce enough material to make the American people know that its government had lied. Today we have a congressional committee going into the assassination business. Quacks began it and now that so many are dead, so many facts buried by time and professionals, the congressional investigation can only plop around.

It seems that Clio's revenge is irony: what Mark made up was the truth and now that it is buried, the Congress will look for it.

It was that which attracted me to Mark more than anything in the beginning. The small-time charlatan—like the Shakespearean actors in *Huckleberry Finn*—was more interesting to me and, yes, more useful, than the rich and the grand and the powerful. Knowing them, I also knew that my style, my background, my contempt were too obviously a problem—for them and for me.

In the Year of the Pig

Figure 26. The famous "Make war not love" helmet from *In the Year of the Pig*.

PAULINE KAEL

Blood and Snow (1969)

"We don't want films the color of roses," the New American Cinema Group's manifesto declared in 1961. "We want them the color of blood." More than any other signatory, perhaps, de Antonio got his wish when the nation's most influential critic appraised In the Year of the Pig *under the heading "Blood." ("Snow" referred to another film under review.) This commendation of* Year of the Pig *in the* New Yorker *magazine secured de Antonio's critical reputation as a filmmaker of importance. He had a considerable correspondence with Kael, dating back to her days as a San Francisco film programmer and his as an enterprising art film distributor peddling prints of Josef von Sternberg's* The Blue Angel.

In the Year of the Pig is an assemblage of news footage and interviews that presents an overview of the Vietnam War; Ho Chi Minh is the hero, and the theme is not, as might be expected, the tragic destruction of Vietnam but the triumph of Vietnam over the American colossus. The movie is not a piece of reporting: Emile de Antonio, who gathered the material, has never been to Vietnam; his footage comes from a variety of sources, not specified on the screen but elsewhere acknowledged to include East Germany, Hanoi, the National Liberation Front offices in Prague, Britain, and some American companies (ABC, Paramount News, UPI, Pathé News, Fox Movietone News), and there is a Russian-staged reenactment of the battle of Dien Bien Phu. But, taking this footage from all over, he has made a strong film that does what American television has failed to do. It provides a historical background and puts the events of the last few years into an intelligible framework. Though the television coverage has often been covertly antiwar, and though watching the Americans behave like the bad guys in Hollywood war movies has undoubtedly helped turn the country against the war, the general effect of years of this has been a numbing one—constant horror but no clear idea of how each day's events fitted in, and growing uncertainty about the meaning of victories and defeats beyond the day's events. We now feel helpless to understand the war; we want to end it, and the fact that we can't demoralizes us. We seem to be powerless. Because this film makes sense out of what's been going on, even if this sense isn't the only sense to be made of it, de Antonio's historical interpretation becomes remarkably persuasive.

The movie does not claim to be "objective" (except in the way that every documentary implicitly claims to be, because it uses photographic records and, despite talk of media sophistication, "seeing is believing"). One could certainly argue that *In the Year of the Pig* (the title, I assume, does not refer only to the Chinese calendar) is merely restoring the balance by showing "the other side"—that if it attempted to be "objective" it would turn into another of those essays in confusion, like the network specials, that balance everything out until they get a collection of the disparate facts and platitudes that are considered "responsible" journalism. However, while the commentators' face-saving gestures and revelations have made us aware of the tacit commitment in that kind of coverage, we may be less conscious of the games being played with this footage. Some of them are obvious, loaded little tricks, like the film's crude beginning (a body in flames, still moving, followed by satiric glimpses of Hubert H. Humphrey, John Foster Dulles, President Johnson), and there are pranks (the insertion of a close-up of a toothy photo of Joseph P. Kennedy, and one of Arthur Schlesinger Jr., looking like a lewd Dracula). This is schoolboy stuff: de Antonio's judgment is erratic. But in the main line of the narrative he plays a highly sophisticated game, using the pick of the archives and recent interviews, expertly (and often very sensitively) edited, and with unusually good sound-editing.

What de Antonio has done is to present the issues of the war and American policy and the American leaders as Hanoi might see them, and he has done it out of our own mouths. He has gone to what must have been enormous effort to put the film together so that the words of men like Dulles, Dean Rusk, Joe McCarthy, and Wayne Morse and of experts and journalists like Roger Hilsman, Paul Mus, Harrison Salisbury, Jean Lacouture, and David Halberstam tell the story. They provide his polemic, without any additional narration. This makes it more credible—and more of a feat. De Antonio calls the film "political theater," and the counterpoint of words and actions involves so many heavy ironies it becomes too much of a feat. He's almost too clever, and his cleverness debases the subject; the method is a little obscene. But one tends to accept the line of argument, not just because it's a coherent historical view but because emotionally it feeds our current self-hatred.

The Americans make it so easy for de Antonio to build his case. When you listen to Mark Clark and Curtis LeMay, the war really sounds like a racist war. They're war boosters out of the political cartoons of an earlier era; their dialogue would make us laugh at how old-fashioned the satire was if we read it in a Sinclair Lewis novel. When one hears LeMay's vindictive tone as he talks about how every work of man in North Vietnam should be destroyed if that is what it takes to win, and when one hears Mark Clark say of the Vietnamese, "They're willing to die readily, like all Orientals are," it's hard to believe that the war they're engaged in is the same war that's still going on.

I saw this film on the afternoon of Monday, November 3rd, and after sitting there and thinking how far away much of it seemed—Eisenhower with President Diem, the dragon lady Mme Nhu, Dulles and the domino theory, the American leaders explaining how we were going to help the Vietnamese help themselves—I came home to hear President Nixon's speech, which seemed to belong to the same past as the speeches in the movie, though the new rhetoric is smoother and more refined. The continuity of the war that evoked the earlier crude justifications with the war that's still going on, even though hardly anybody believes in the justifications anymore, makes one susceptible to de Antonio's argument. In the context of the movie, even the casual stupidities of American soldiers sound meaningfully racist. When some American soldiers relaxing on a beach say that they miss girls, they're asked what's the matter with the Vietnamese girls, and a silly, grinning boy replies, "They're gooks. You know, slant-eyes. They're no good," and we're revved up to think, "The pig! And our leaders are trying to tell us he's there to keep the Vietnamese free!" In another context, we might simply think that this silly, lonely soldier was trying to find acceptable male slang for not being interested in girls he can't talk to. It might even mean that he wanted *more* than sex.

In this context, America is represented by clips of our leaders at their most repellent, of an American soldier who stands by smiling as a helpless, bound prisoner is kicked in the groin, of Mark Clark and Curtis LeMay, and of young George S. Patton III saying of his buddies, "They're a bloody good bunch of killers" (also a line that would sound very different in the context of, say, a Second World War movie). De Antonio finds a soldier who likes defoliation work, because it seems a step toward ending the war; Morley Safer, it may be remembered, interviewed a GI who said that he didn't like "riding the people's gardens down." No doubt there are both kinds, and certainly they're both destructive, whether they like the work or not. But by selecting Americans who do like it, by selecting Curtis LeMay and the others, de Antonio obviously means to suggest a basic rottenness in Americans, and in America that is antilife. After one watches the movie for a while, the Americans in it begin to look monstrously callow, like clumsy, oversized puppets.

De Antonio has not merely made a protest film documenting the "downward spiral" (as the North Vietnamese Pham Van Dong described it) of American policy, though that is the film's most valuable aspect. He has attempted to foreshadow the fall of the West—and not just in Vietnam—by presenting the Vietnamese as a people solidly behind Ho Chi Minh, who represents their goals and ideals, and as a people who have been ennobled by war and who must win. In his own way, de Antonio seems to support Mark Clark's view of Orientals; the movie suggests that the Vietnamese are willing to die because they are united in a common purpose, and that if they die, their dying still somehow stands for life, while we are dying though we live. The tone of the latter part of the film is almost mystical; the ability of the tiny country to go on fighting against a great power is not presented in practical terms of how much more difficult it is for a supernation to fight in a divided, decentralized country than to incapacitate a modern, powerful, centralized state but, rather, in terms of our inability to defeat the mystical spirit, the will (and perhaps the destiny?) of Ho Chi Minh's people. It is, in other words, as patriotic and jingoistic and, in its way, as pro-war as American wartime movies used to be about *our* mission and destiny and in this reversal it is the Americans who have become dehumanized.

ALAN ASNEN

De Antonio in Hell (1968)

As a longtime denizen of the East Village, the dissident filmmaker was an apt subject for the Village's alternative press, including the Village Voice, *the* Free Press, *the* East Village Eye, *and, in this interview, the* East Village Other. *This excerpt focuses on the release of* In the Year of the Pig, *though it was published on the fifth anniversary of the Kennedy assassination.*

You're releasing a movie, In the Year of the Pig, *which is a historical documentary about the trouble in Vietnam. Since this issue has been churned over for years now, what is your feeling about the time delay?*
It would be very difficult to make a film about the war in Vietnam ten years ago, or two years ago, because the war is not simply about American soldiers and Vietnamese soldiers in combat. It's about something that goes all the way back, as my film tries to show. The roots are in the Cold War, and when did the Cold War begin? The roots are in French colonial policy; then our attempt was to buttress the French in Vietnam in return for their joining NATO in Europe.

I don't say all this in film, obviously, but it's implied. For this reason the film also deals with John Foster Dulles and the Eisenhower administration in 1954. There are things I learned in making the film that are simply not "filmic" and were impossible to put in the film. Now, I don't think anybody knows what I'm about to tell you. In making the film I interviewed a Marine Corps colonel who was also a CIA man. He told me that there were fourteen American officers with the French at Dien Bien Phu as advisers in 1954. This was before there were any Americans there, in any capacity. There were fourteen American officers, field rank and above, who were with the French forces during the siege upon Dien Bien Phu. This is why I have Secretary of Defense [Charles] Wilson in the film, talking about giving the French help in 1954. I mean, all of this is part of a picture whose sense is evoked only by telling a substantial piece of it in time. And, if the war should end next month, which I myself consider quite unlikely, the picture would still be valid because it would still reflect that aspect of American political life in practice, there would still be something to learn about it, and it still is a kind of theater. To me the picture is a kind of black comedy and it has no audience yet because I haven't shown it anywhere. Well, actually the only audience was at Dartmouth College, where the students laughed in all of what I would consider the right places. But if the work has any validity, it has a validity outside of the moment, whether the bombing pause goes on, or whether the war goes on. I mean, these are simply extensions of a great many years of history and a great many sorts of commitments that this country has made and that other countries have made. The film assumes that most of those commitments are immoral.

I noticed in the film that the interviews were mostly with what one would call "doves," and the film clips were of people you could consider hawks. Was there any trouble getting interviews with the so-called hawks?
Well, hawks don't speak to people like me, so we've got them on film. One of the things I enjoyed most about making the films was the long contretemps I had with the United States Department of Defense. Senator Jacob Javits wrote to them for me asking them to cooperate, and I got back letters which I have here, containing such gobbledygook—two pages from a Commander Rohder asking me what it was that I was really doing and explaining that it wasn't the government's policy to give film away, when in fact the government gives and sells this film to many distributors. I can take a walk down this street and buy some of it. But the film I was looking for, of course, wasn't for sale and I don't suppose the average person gets to see it. This is part of my gripe against the government and the media. Who is it that the government takes this film for? I don't expect the government to help me in any work that I do. If they did, I suppose the work wouldn't be any good.

There's been a lot of talk rehashed again now that they're going to step up the Paris peace talks and the bombing has "ended." Many people think, optimistically that the war will be over soon, but a while ago you said that you don't believe it will even be over in a month. Why do you feel this way?
I believe that at this point peace is in the best interest of the people of Vietnam and the people of the United States. North Vietnam has taken a tremendous shellacking, yet they have beaten us on the ground. It's a very complicated confusing setup and logically it would seem highly desirable if the war would end. It would seem to serve the better interest of the United States and the Democratic Republic of Vietnam. But history does not work

logically and I suspect what will happen is that the present corrupt South Vietnamese government will be used as an excuse to get out of any meaningful negotiations and that the war will continue. I do not think that Ho Chi Minh and Pham Van Dong and the government of the Democratic Republic of Vietnam can give away what it gave before in March of 1946 when they made their first peace with the French, or what it gave away in 1954 at the Geneva Conference and Treaty. In both cases, it was the so-called Communist Power that was willing to concede and be conciliatory, and in both cases they were betrayed. I don't think that Ho Chi Minh can afford to risk this kind of betrayal. But he's in a very rough spot, because, if we simply do what General LeMay is talking about, which is to bomb the dikes, Haiphong, and Hanoi, we have then stepped the level of the war up to a position where it may become intolerable for them. Harrison Salisbury told me that there would be as many as five million casualties if the dikes were bombed properly with really heavy bombs and at the right time of the year, in the spring, when there's a flood tide anyway, you would just inundate millions of acres, destroy the food-producing capacity as well as drown millions of people.

You say that the Saigon government will be used to halt the peace talks. Recently, with the United States' new policy on the Paris peace talks, wanting to admit the NLF, the Saigon government has been opposed to it and has said that they won't participate. Do you think that this is a sort of under-the-table maneuver on the part of the United States forcing the South Vietnamese to say this?

No, I don't think that conspiracy works that way. When there's no need for a conspiracy there simply isn't one. It's simply Thieu's neck and Ky's neck and the necks of the corrupt government of South Vietnam that are at stake here. They cannot in any way agree to a treaty or to a meaningful meeting with the NLF and with Hanoi, because the first condition of any such meet would be that they would be thrown out. So as long as we humor them or cater to them in any way, we ourselves have already built impediments to meaningful peace talks, namely, Thieu and Ky. The complicating factor in this, though, is that only a few weeks ago General Minh was brought back into the country. Minh is known as "Big Minh" and was one of the leaders of the coup d'état against Ngo Dinh Diem in 1963, and was the man who probably would have won the election in 1967—the United States government-sponsored elections—if he'd been allowed into the country. But he'd been forced out of South Vietnam. Now, this is no democrat, it's just that he's simply a different article than Thieu or Ky. And the fact that he's been brought back now leads one to suspect that perhaps we might be getting ready to dump Thieu and Ky and put in Minh. Minh might be acceptable at the moment for Ho. Thieu and Ky are absolutely not acceptable, because they really are traitors to their country. When Ho Chi Minh was leading the Viet Minh in their struggle for independence from the French, Ky was in the French army bombing the Algerians with the French air force. General Ky is a traitor to the whole concept of the Afro-Asian revolution, and Ho will never accept Ky or Thieu as spokesmen for any part of Vietnam. Don't forget that it was President Eisenhower himself in 1956 who said that if the elections had been held as they were supposed to according to the Geneva Conference, Ho would have carried 80 percent of the vote in *South* Vietnam. I asked Than Van Dinh, the former South Vietnamese ambassador to Washington, what he thought Ho Chi Minh's percentage would be today in South Vietnam and he said 99 percent.

Do you think that it's possible that maybe one of these days the United States will come to the realization that they are never going to win over the people of South Vietnam?
Again, this is part of a bigger picture. The real hawks in our military aren't all that worried about Vietnam. They are convinced that they can beat Vietnam any time they want to step up the game. But in their curious, distorted, mysterious, mistaken, and imbecilic minds, they have equated the NLF in Vietnam with China, and China is the enemy. This is why in the film, as well as in their writings, the people like LeMay and General Clark are always talking about China. Now, China has shown remarkable restraint and has never entered into this war. Nor has Ho ever asked the Chinese to commit themselves. But what we are talking about here is more than just the war in Vietnam. What we are talking about is the position of the United States in all of Southeast Asia. We're talking about our stake in world empire, we're talking about the really big game of which Vietnam is a major part, but still just a part. And it depends on who you talk to. General LeMay is talking now and has been talking for five years about preventive war. In four or five years the Chinese are going to have the ability to deliver thermonuclear weapons, and this is a different game. This is why they want a war. I'm sure this is why people in the Pentagon would like to incite China to cross the border into Vietnam, so that we could then bomb them and their nuclear installations. This would leave only the Soviet Union and the United States to do whatever they want to do.

Sidetracking a little, it's ironic that while the Westerner thinks of the Oriental as always trying to save face, the whole United States position in Vietnam has been one of saving face. Can you see anything in this?

Well, part of the operation is called Save Faces, but the other part is Keep Power. In fact, the nature of our commitment is such that face-saving may not even seem remotely accurate. And in the true sense of "Face-Saving," the most face-saving thing we could do would be just get the hell out. This would show that at some point we learned something about what the nature of the war is. But killing people to save face is first of all stupid, and second of all, we are really involved in an exercise of our power and not just in face-saving.

The movie was made after you formed the Monday Film Corporation and the corporation made a formal statement which I'll quote: "Those who originally formed the partnership, the Monday Film Production Company, share the following convictions: that the United States intervention in Vietnam is immoral, unjust, impractical and debasing. History and the facts speak out against it." Will this be a continual policy in all your movies or was this corporation formed solely for the production of Pig?

It's fairly difficult to make radical films, so each time you make one you start a separate corporation, you have a new set of investors, and backers. The lines you just read were said to every one of the investors in this film. The investors are interesting people. They include three Rockefellers, Paul Newman, Robert Ryan, Steve Allen, Leonard Bernstein, Mitch Miller, a good many people who I think don't ordinarily invest in films. My next project will probably be a fiction film. Everything I do has something to do with the life of the country in which I live. I suspect that even though it's fiction, it will be political.

In conclusion, throughout your three movies, as you mention, you always deal with the state the country is in at the moment. Have you ever considered having a more international theme, dealing more with mankind in general?

I prefer to work with what I know best. I've also done films in addition to the three we've talked about and they too are similar to these. When you say international, I believe that most of my work will deal with America and Americans because this is the world that interests me the most, and of which I'm a part. I think the Vietnam film and *Point of Order* both have something to say about mankind. Words like *mankind* are sometimes fairly difficult to use, they're so big. I think if you tell it right, where it is, where you are, you say something about the nature of how it is everywhere. In my fiction film, although it won't be a message fiction film, I can't see how it won't carry a message. To me, all art is political, finally. I think this is why American painting is coming to an end, because American painting is in itself a political expression simply because it avoids everything this world has to do with, its ultimate statements are statements which are simply decoration. And these are statements, I might add, that are very, very congenial to U.S. government and big business, both of which endow and support painting. When film, like mine, is endowed and supported by big business and government, then we will know that the films are no good. The first time I get a government grant, I'll know that I've copped out. The state of our world right now is such that the voices we need are voices that question, voices that express doubt about what it is we're doing; because what we are doing is ugly, without life, and without direction. We are like some kind of giant engulfing animal that seems to be gobbling and gobbling everything in the world. *The Year of the Pig* does not refer to the police in Chicago. It was a title I had before Chicago happened. It is a metaphor which only in part describes what the French did in Vietnam or what we did there. It has to do with the kind of thing which underlies our lives now, and which I find revolting. Like most people who have a strong feeling about this country, which I do—a strong positive feeling—I'm a pessimist. I think we need a revolutionary change, but we won't get it.

LIL PICARD

Inter/view with Emile de Antonio (1969)

The first of three conversations with de Antonio published by Andy Warhol's Interview *magazine, this idiosyncratic profile was done by a French art critic.*

I'm writing about a movie I saw November 13th, one day before Moratorium Day. I saw a documentary, *In the Year of the Pig*, directed and produced by Emile de Antonio. Up on 88th Street and Broadway in the New York theater I sat in the afternoon between about fifty other people watching and listening to the images and voices of modern warfare.

Since I am miraculously still living after having had my experiences with fascism in Europe before WWII, I make it today my task to help to end violence and war and to bring about a change. The film of Mr. De is doing that too and so I asked him for an interview, which he agreed to give me.

We had planned it for a special day. But it happened that the film got repressed in Philadelphia and Emile de Antonio had to cancel the interview for that day to go to Philadelphia to talk on TV. We finally met November 19th at [the] Movielab [building], 619 West 64th Street, Room 64, where Mr. De has his headquarters.

I had never been in a movie lab and every new experience in "journalistic discovery" is for me an exciting adventure. I went to Hitler's speech before the German industry in the Berlin Funkhalle in 1933 and now I am still kicking to fight for seeing and viewing reality and truth at the source whenever life gives me a chance. I was very excited to talk to a man who—what a rare gift in our time of "fin de sixties"—is filming truth and reality. I had been kind of apprehensive to meet Mr. De, the famous moviemaker, and as security measure had taken along the magazine *New Yorker*, in which his movie had been reviewed.

Mr. De charmed me the moment he shook my hand.

Mr. De: "Let's go down to the coffee shop, where we can talk and have a cup of coffee."

He took my tape recorder and as a gallant gentleman of the old school carried it for me. He looks European to my European eyes. Tall, on the heavy side, easygoing and his eyes are the eyes of the artist, the painter-reporter. The movie *In the Year of the Pig* is in my opinion the work of a literary, schooled, extremely knowledgeable artistic painter-reporter-documentary filmmaker.

Here we get all the noises of the coffee shop.
The noise is very good. That's reality and my voice carries very well and you will surely understand it. I run this as a test. Shall I speak?

Yes.
November 15, 1969, the *New Yorker,* price 50 cents, a dreary middle-class magazine, which gave a not uninteresting review of my film with some fairly mad points in it. I think that's enough to run a test.

You told me you had to go to Philadelphia, where your film had been suppressed?
In Philadelphia the film had had the unusual experience of opening a new cinema there and the police came and said the fire exit is no good. Close down the cinema, and then one of the police said, it's because of one of those Vietnamese pictures you are playing; then the police gave 'em a license and then they closed it down again, with an audience there and they forced them to return the money and the patrons in the theater left and now they hold the theater closed for two more weeks.

And your film will not be shown now?
No, my film plays now in another theater. I was on television on Monday and we discussed this all in great detail.

What did you say on TV?
If you make radical films, you don't expect the same treatment as people who make films that they play in Radio City Music Hall. I mean, I expect my films to be censured. I don't expect conventional films to be censured, but I expect my films to be. My films are against the government.

Your film on McCarthy, Point of Order. *Did that film also have difficulties with the police?*
No. The only difficulty with the McCarthy film was in the making of it. CBS, because it had a monopoly position, charged me $50,000 for this material and finally, they had and still have 50 percent interest in the film. 50 percent what happens—they get. So it's not censorship, but it's a kind

of censorship. They could have prevented me from having the material, but once they decided to give me the material they charged an exorbitant extortionate rate. And these are the same people who complain that Vice President Agnew attacks them.

Mr. De, what interests me, you said you are glad I do this interview for Andy Warhol's inter/View *film magazine because you know Andy a long time. Do you think A.W. has a hidden political interest?*
No, I think Andy's politics are on the surface. I mean Andy pretends he has no politics.

But I think he has.
Andy denies it. But he does have politics. I think it's very hard to be a son of Czech immigrants, when your father was a manual worker, living in Pittsburgh, not to develop some political ideas. But because in Andy's case they're other ideas that enter into the context, I think working in fashion as long as he did tended to diminish his political ideas. You know, I was a friend of Andy when he first began to paint. Andy used to show me his paintings and ask me what do you think of this, what do you think of that?

Was that in 1957?
No, 1960. I think I gave him his first critique of the "Coke Bottle." I lived near to him and one day he asked me to come to his house. I went to his house all the time and he asked me what I think of two paintings of Coke bottles. One was a pure painting of a Coke bottle and the other one was a painting of a Coke bottle with many harsh slash marks that looked like an abstract expressionist drawing and he asked me what do you think of it? I said, one is interesting and one is terrible. The simple Coke bottle, like pop art, is interesting and the one with the marks is boring, because it's a combination of de Kooning and many other people.

When I listen to you now—how much you care about art! As you know, I write on art also, for European publications, so it's very interesting to listen to your ideas on art.
Last night I had dinner with Rauschenberg, Castelli, and Frank Stella, who is a very old friend of mine. I own eight or nine of his works. I know all these artists from way back, before they had galleries.

Does your friendship with all these artists influence you in your filmmaking?
No, not at all.

So why do you have painter friends? Is it a human need or is it interest in art?
At one time my interest was commercial. I made deals. Before I became involved in filmmaking I was a kind of agent without representing anybody.

I made deals with these people and we were also friends. We shared somewhat similar views of the world—I wasn't always as political as I am now. But I became political and each year as the U.S. becomes worse, I become more radicalized. And now, I have this film *In the Year of the Pig* playing around the country.

Was that the title from the beginning?
The title has nothing to do with Chicago and the police there. I don't choose the title first. First I make the film. Then the title emerges. Because *In the Year of the Pig*—this title relates it to the Confucian philosophy, Vietnam like China is a Confucian country and the Year of the Pig is like the Year of the Frog, the Year of the Rat, that makes it clear, that is, Vietnam and Pig represents for me also the idea of French colonialism and the American war. We are the Pigs, the French were the Pigs.

You are an American?
Certainly, I was born here and served in the United States Army. I'm a political person.

Is your film objective or did you approach the subject with a preconceived idea?
I don't believe that any filmmaker is objective. I think that objectivity is impossible unless you do abstract work. If you deal with the human image in your work, you cannot be objective. Whenever you point a camera, you make a statement. Whenever you cut a piece of film, you make a statement. I'm not interested in objectivity, I am a man who believes. I'm a man of political belief. I was absolutely convinced before I made the film that the U.S. was wrong. That the government of South Vietnam was a government of puppets created by us. I was asked this question (of objectivity) many times and I'm tired of it. It sounds flippant, but it's nonetheless correct: only God is objective and he doesn't make films. I'm not interested in God. I'm interested in films and I'm not objective and I hope I even never think of being objective. The most that a documentary filmmaker can hope for is that he is honest. For example, when my film *In the Year of the Pig* was shown in Harvard before the meeting of the biggest American society of Asian scholars, who all are concerned with the history of Vietnam, these scholars could not detect in my film a lie, they could not find out that I was a crook in my work, nobody could see anything untruthful, even those who defend the U.S. position could not say you doctored the evidence. Because I invented a kind of film which is like political theater like plays, *In the Matter of J. Robert Oppenheimer,* for example; those plays which are all taken from *Point of Order,* because as

you know, today the film comes first, the theater follows. The theater is boring, hopeless, nothing happens there. If you want the real difference, the way it happens, you look at my film *Point of Order* and then you look at the play.

Does the film Point of Order *still play in the U.S.?*
It plays in New York several times a year in the movie theaters and also all around the country. I'm very lucky as a documentary filmmaker. I may be the only one whose pictures play in theaters. *Point of Order* played in four hundred theaters the year it was out, and I'm not including colleges and television.

Do you think that we have today a similar situation as at the time of McCarthy?
Worse. Much worse. I don't think that there is anybody in American life today who is as dangerous as McCarthy was in 1954, but I think the American government today is so much more dangerous than the American government in 1954. I think we are living in a kind of police state now. It's a different kind of police state than the Nazi Germany or the Soviet Union, but it's a police state. We have a Federal Police now that is, you know, like the Geheime Staatspolizei was, and the FBI is exactly that, only it's much more clever, it's not as brutal, it has electronic eavesdropping, it has the advantage of all the recent advances of science. We now have two laws for the U.S., one law for the police and one law for people. And that is part of a police state. You see all these people out there and their cars with the slogans—"Support Your Local Police"—and those flags and stickers—"Honor America"—on buses, police cars, trucks—this is the beginning of fascism. It's an American form. It will not look like Mussolini nor like Hitler. But I mean Nixon and Agnew are not mistakes, they represent what the American right wing believes.

Did you ever think to do a film about the Negroes?
Well, to begin with I use the word the Blacks.

I do too. So did you think of making a film about the Blacks?
I really think a Black must do such a film.

Would you work together with a Black on such a film?
Certainly. In fact I spent a day recently with a Black man who came from Africa and he wanted me to come to Africa to work on a film. But I feel I'm incompetent to do that. I know nothing about Africa. That's one reason. And another is that I have work I'm committed to do that takes me through April.

Have your films been shown in Germany?
Oh, yes. *Rush to Judgment, Point of Order,* and *In the Year of the Pig* were all shown in the Deutsche Demokratische Republik (DDR) and *In the Year of the Pig* won the main prize in Leipzig in 1968. In West Germany *In the Year of the Pig* was shown and it will be shown on West German television.

When?
I don't know, we are just signing the contract. In 1967, *Rush to Judgment* was shown in the Mannheim festival. I refused that *Point of Order* be shown on West German television because they wanted to dub it. It seemed absolute insanity to dub the voices of McCarthy and Roy Cohn, it's so intrinsically American. It showed lack in sensitivity on their part. They offered a lot of money, but I refused.

When you did your Vietnam movie you never went to Vietnam. Why?
It's unnecessary. Because not only art, but also facts are in the mind. Just think of all the millions of reporters who go to Vietnam who are idiots, who see nothing. Immanuel Kant lived in Königsberg and he wrote the *Critique of Pure Reason* and he never left his small town. The housewives could set their clocks after his walks, because every morning he took a walk from his house to the church and back, and in his mind was, you know . . . and now, I am a very thorough worker. When I did the *Year of the Pig* I read everything I could find in French and in English before I even did anything. I spent over three months reading ten hours a day. I read every book that exists in English and French on Vietnam. I have 250 books at home in my library on the subject of Vietnam. I read these books how people dig a ditch with the same unending drive and as I read I took notes, I created a chronology, I took quotations, I wrote down things to look for, things that were said by President Johnson, things said by John Foster Dulles, and all the others who appear in the film, and I began a very methodical research in all the film libraries everywhere. It's the biggest collection of films which I got together that exists anywhere. It includes all the works of the Democratic Republic of Vietnam, all the works of the National Liberation Front, and it also includes the work of ABC (American Broadcasting Company) and the great old material of Paramount News, Fox, UPI. I have literally hundreds of thousands of feet of 16mm films, which I'm now donating—giving them to somebody. It takes me a long time to make my movies.

How long did it take you to make the film In the Year of the Pig?
Fifteen months. Fifteen months without stopping, seven days a week.

When I saw the film, I scribbled down all along during the screening in the dark some notations, for instance, the one with which the film begins. What is it?

Yes, you mean: "AS SOON AS I HEARD OF AMERICAN INDEPENDENCE MY HEART WAS ENLISTED IN ITS CAUSE"—that's by Marquis de Lafayette, who fought in the American Revolution. To me the war in Vietnam is a revolution for freedom on the part of Ho Chi Minh, there is a statue on Union Square, right where Andy's factory is, and on that statue are those words which I filmed.

The next note I made when seeing the film is about the noise. What kind of noise do you use in the film?

It's helicopter noise. The music of America today is the helicopter in Vietnam. That's "music concrete." You know that Bob Rauschenberg, Jasper Johns, and I produced the biggest concert of John Cage's music [in] 1958 at Town Hall. The music, the noise you hear in the film is really a helicopter concerto, it's written by a young man, who studied with John Cage, his name is: Steve Addis. Columbia Records produces his records.

Then I have a note about the coffeehouse with white uniformed officers, sitting at small sidewalk coffee tables and being deposited by rickshaw drivers there.

This coffeehouse is mentioned in many European countries as the essence of colonialism. They are sitting there, brought to the coffeehouse with the bodies of the Vietnamese in rickshaws and by the rickshaw driver, and the captain in the café snaps his fingers and sends the boys away. This is what it's all about. The white man sits and drinks his apéritif and the other man pulls him and waits on him. That's why we have the revolution to bring to the world.

I have made a note of a very important sequence of the film that struck me as especially well seen and photographed, village life in Vietnam. The peaceful landscape and in strong contrast to it the war machine with helicopter noise, the hardware, and then again the picture of Professor Mus talking in a quiet room surrounded by works of art.

That's Professor Mus, professor of Buddhism, he died this summer. He represented General de Gaulle. He spoke Vietnamese, he was born in Vietnam, came from the ruling classes of France who were in Vietnam in 1945. He had parachuted into Vietnam and negotiated with Ho Chi Minh on behalf of General de Gaulle. He is the man who said: "When the history of the twentieth century is written, Ho Chi Minh will be known as its greatest patriot." I use conservative people. Paul Mus is a conservative French scholar. It's too easy to use a communist or somebody who shares my own point of view. My method is always to find somebody like that, because it's more interesting that Paul Mus says it than the leader of the SDS, because the leader of the SDS is totally predictable, nobody is interested in him, everybody knows exactly what he is going to say. Paul Mus was professor of Buddhism at Yale and the Collège de France.

I find here a quote, starting with the words, a thumb-square of rice...
Paul Mus was saying that in 1945, September 2, when Ho Chi Minh began the Republic of Vietnam. Ho Chi Minh said to the people: what they must do is work, because "a thumb-square of planting rice is more valuable than a thumb-square of gold," and in that he meant that the people have to work and plant rice. It showed that Ho Chi Minh thought like a peasant. First he was a socialist and second a communist.

Ho Chi Minh is called in your film the George Washington of Vietnam.
That was said by a conservative Republican senator, Thruston B. Morton from Kentucky. I can give you a lot more material on all these details. The French magazine *Cahiers du Cinéma* brought out recently also an interview on me.

What does the passage in the film mean when Ho Chi Minh uses the comparison of the circle and the square in a talk with Professor Mus?
Oh, that is very beautiful and very rare. Nobody has seen this on film before. Not in Europe nor anywhere, except on my film. It's from a film from Hanoi and it shows Ho Chi Minh explaining the parable the circle and the square. In Confucian philosophy the circle means the imaginary, the dream, and the square represents the real, the tangible, the earth. What Ho Chi Minh wanted to say to Paul Mus when he was doing the circle with his hand in the air was: tell me about this treaty you were talking about, is it real or is it just a dream?

I have here as a reminding note the word hatred. *To which passage in the film does that belong?*
In 1945 Ho Chi Minh is saying: "I have no army, I have no director of public affairs, I have no finance minister, I have only my hatred," and he means his hatred for the French as his colonial oppressors.

Am I right with my observation that you had a very definite idea from the point of art making opposites? Nature in contrast to the hardware war machine?
That's very well observed.

The landscape looked to me like the one on old Chinese paintings.
That's meant to be so. That's exactly what I wanted it to be.

The pictures you showed look to me like those beautiful landscapes in fog with the grey skies with reeds, grass, trees, clouds, boats.
I hope you will write that. You are the first person who saw that, that's very good. I mean, I spent weeks looking for that material.

The sailboat and the piece of nature.
Like pre-Sung paintings.

The human being is very, very small and nature is overwhelmingly grandiose.
I remember in my film how big the mountains are and the people so very small.

Changing then to the hardware, the aircraft, the guns, it came on like a phalanx, a monster, with the terrific noise of the helicopters and the bullets.
That's it.

Yes, this absolutely terrifying frame, all black, just streaks and streaks of bullets and the sizzling agonizing whirling noise . . .
The imposition of an artificial environment.

And here I have another note of some part of the film that impressed me. "An island in a red sea" . . .
That's Joseph McCarthy who said in 1954: "And unless we win the war in Indochina we will be an island in a red sea of communism." It was insane in 1954 and it's insane in 1969.

May I to the end of this talk give you one more question, which I jotted down during the screening of the film in the dark auditorium of the New York theater: a new pathological power, police state 1956–1960, economical miracle . . .
Yes, that's a joke, that's an idiot who is still in the Congress, he is the majority leader of the Republican Party in the Congress, Jerry Ford, who said, Diem was an economical mirror. As you raise this question, let me say one thing: My essential method and technique is irony—it is the placing of one image against another, never with any explanation. This is my contribution to documentary film, in *Point of Order* and in this film. *Point of Order* was the first documentary made that had no narration, no explanation. The work explains itself, just like a theatrical work, like a dramatic work, there is no explanation and the perception must be with the eye and the mind and the ear. It's not told to you. This is what you are seeing, *you see it*. And everything in that film is very carefully plotted and there is always an irony between the truth and the lie. There is always irony. The old Soviet filmmakers used to say, "Between two frames is always the third frame which is not there, but people will perceive it."

JONAS MEKAS

Movie Journal (1969)

The leading advocate of New York independent cinema, Jonas Mekas had known de Antonio since their days organizing the New American Cinema Group in 1959. Mekas's own journal, Film Culture, *had published the manifesto that had declared de Antonio one of the Group's key instigators. But it was through his weekly "Movie Journal" column in the* Village Voice *that Mekas chronicled his experiences at underground screenings. After seeing* In the Year of the Pig, *Mekas visited de Antonio in his Movielab editing room, where he was already at work on* America Is Hard to See.

This week I saw two films on Vietnam. One was Newsreel's *Hanoi Film* [by] Norman Fruchter and Robert Kramer. The film concentrates on the people of North Vietnam, on their resistant spirit. We see them working and fighting. It is an unpretentious, direct film, like a letter from Vietnam. A letter which should be read by everybody.

The second film is Emile de Antonio's *In the Year of the Pig*, which opened at the New Yorker. It's a much bigger film. It concentrates on the political folly, on the speeches of the politicians and the generals. In collage form it traces the American involvement in the war. As such it is an important and unique document.

I visited de Antonio in his editing room where he is putting together a film on [Eugene] McCarthy's presidential campaign.

You have become a specialist and authority on a kind of political documentary where the filmmaker is involved with huge amounts of material which he then reduces to presentable length. In all such films usually there is this question of credibility. You have all these bits of film, this 100-minute collage, but every bit is out of the original context. You have edited them according to your own political stand.

I considered this problem, obviously, very seriously. It's really a philosophical problem first: is objectivity possible in the kind of political film that I do? And my answer is that objectivity is impossible. Because I begin with a set of passions and feelings. I don't think you can be objective about the war in Vietnam.

Obviously. It's also obvious that the saying "the camera eye doesn't lie" is just a saying. The camera eye will lie as much as the filmmaker behind the camera will lie. My question was more directed to the ways of presenting already existing footage.
I aim for a kind of collage where, by the way you make it, you achieve an element of reality which is more real than the real material you started with.

Your materials always seemed to me to be perfect materials for my own dream document film. I would use the same footage you did, only I would make neither collage nor montage with it. I would simply string pieces together, very scientifically, with an introductory frame, the way D. W. Griffith used to do, telling the name of the speaker, place, and date. Then we would have a collection of irrefutable bits of historical evidence, almost like notes that could go with textbooks. As it is now, the film can always be dismissed as propaganda.
Yes. But I am more interested to work the way I am working. Vietnam exists in history. All other films on Vietnam leave that out. They may have more passion, more emotion. But I am interested in the political theories, in the mass of facts. I am interested in establishing a line of thought. You can't arrive at the sort of linear, factual explanation in a film that you can in a book. Not even a single book contains it in any intelligible way. But I think that because of certain peaks within the film that point at what happened, you have revelations. The film reveals what really happened.

I liked the materials. Some footage is funny gallows humor. The generals, for instance. I have never seen such a bunch of morons. You see them, in the film, they are there for real, and you know they are there in charge of this war, and you see their faces, you listen to them, and my God they are morons. They are murderers and morons.
Most of the people I interviewed have seen the film and they agree that they have been used in a straight way. The film has been screened for Asian scholars. It played at Harvard and similar places, and nobody objected to its history aspect.

How much footage did you have to begin with?
You can only work by compression with collage technique. In all cases I had so much negative material that I was almost at the point of going insane.

Usually, I make two selections. I saw some material in Prague, some in East Germany, the ABC footage here in New York. I saw everything the National Liberation Front made in film and everything that Hanoi had on film, etc. etc. First, I look at everything they have and while I do that I make the first selection. From the thousands of hours of film I ended up with 100 hours. Then I started shooting interviews and getting other materials. The form starts evolving as I go.

Most of the films on Vietnam have little meaning for me, because I am not interested in refugees and staged battles. We had too much of it, so that we almost became insensitized to it. It doesn't do anything to us.

What I was interested in was the intellectual line of what happened. It tells us more about what happened, I think. I am not interested in demonstrations or anything of that aspect. I am interested in the establishment side, because that's the important side, frankly. That's the side we hope *leads* to demonstrations.

What's the McCarthy film you are working on?
It's not so much a McCarthy film as a study of why the campaign failed. Is it possible to work within the system? The assumption of the film is that Eugene McCarthy was the last best hope of working within the system in a national election.

When you said you were coming here I remembered one of the first times we met—because I don't see you anymore very much. But we were together when the New American Cinema Group was founded ten years ago. We all went in different directions, which is fine. But it was a very curious beginning. I think it was a very important moment in film because nobody was really confronting Hollywood or the big phony European companies, and most of us had never even made a film yet. Shirley [Clarke] was preparing *The Connection* and you were shooting *Guns of the Trees*. It was in reaction to your film that I started *Point of Order*.

But some very good works came out of the period, and it's almost time for some theater to come up with a retrospective of the entire period of the New American Cinema, ten or twelve works. The earlier ones, because I think—and you know I am interested in history—I think it's terribly important.

To look back, to survey, to sum up, and then make another step forward—
Because when we started there was very little happening and there was very little hope at the time.

You said we all moved in different directions. But on the other hand, we are all connected. We are all trying to deal with certain realities.

I think the connections would become clearer with such a retrospective. Because everything that has been done since then was done outside the existing system, I mean, politically, financially, artistically, every aspect. And there was no underground yet. But now you know that the underground no longer can be contained in that concept. Because some of the underground people are playing now in regular theaters or at universities.

So we are at some point of another beginning now.

EMILE DE ANTONIO
BILL NICHOLS

"De Antonio: Year of the Pig *Marxist Film*" and "Nichols Replies" (1978)

In April 1978, the film journal Jump Cut *ran an article by cinema scholar Bill Nichols, who noted that the radical collective Newsreel distributed its work in ways that bypassed the theatrical and university exhibition circuits that booked de Antonio documentaries. Bristling at the thought of being perceived as a "liberal," the director seized the opportunity to document his left-wing bona fides.*

Nichols's sympathetic reply would be followed by one of the most appreciative readings of de Antonio's modernist aesthetics. In "The Voice of Documentary" (Film Quarterly, Spring 1983), Nichols hailed de Antonio's montage technique as an exemplary application of Marxist historical principles. De Antonio sent the article to his Point of Order *video distributor, Sander Weiner, with the note: "This is a very good piece by the best person writing on film documentary in English, Prof. Bill Nichols."*

▶

By de Antonio

I want to reply to two lines in Bill Nichols's "New from California Newsreel."

> These films have their greatest value in ongoing political struggles to organize and mobilize the working class and Third World peoples. It is important to bear this in mind as a fundamental quality for it places them in a different context than left-liberal films that circulate predominantly in a middle-class, educational context (colleges, high schools, public libraries), such as *In the Year of the Pig* (Emile de Antonio, 1968).

In the Year of the Pig was/is an organizing weapon, a collage/history of the people's struggle in Vietnam. That collage was made with the help of the DRV [Democratic Republic of Vietnam], the NLF [National Liberation

Front], French Marxists, film and television friends of the Czech Democratic Republic (1967), the German Democratic Republic, U.S. deserters, antiwar veterans, and the antiwar movement itself. It was made when the Movement was young, large, high on struggle and emotion, and without knowledge of what had happened in Vietnam, when it happened and why. No U.S. protests were shown in the film because it was the other addressing itself to us, frequently in our words and images. It was also the way we saw them from the mid-1930s to the Tet Offensive. It was a Marxist, historical line, not free from error.

Its audience was varied, intense, in some places even wide. It played European television but never U.S. Not even now. It played the U.S. and Europe theatrically. Theaters were attacked. Screens were painted over with hammer and sickle (Los Angeles, among others); bomb threats to the theater in Houston; in Paris during a long, successful run, the cinema was systematically stink-bombed. It was used as a tool by the Moratorium; it was a benefit for the Chicago Seven at the opening of their trial; the Australian antiwar movement used it as its primary film weapon; it played GI coffeehouses; it played teach-ins. I still meet people who say, "Your film turned me to antiwar activity." And yes, it still plays colleges.

It was the first U.S. Marxist film to be nominated for an Academy Award. That didn't mean as much to me as the ring a DRV officer solemnly gave me in Leipzig where the film won a prize, a ring made from a plane shot down over the DRV.

If we forget history, we are only a convulsive twitch to today's media output. That output is false, bad, and works to blot out yesterday's reality. The struggle is always the same; the ultimate goal is always the same; but the currents, the cast, the emphases, the disguises change. I am not a left-liberal and neither is the film.

"Nichols Replies" (by Bill Nichols)

The Los Angeles screen I saw was painted "PIG"; our own screen in Kingston, at the National Film Theatre branch here, was severely slashed (in 1977!). De Antonio is right. His film emerged from the heat of the New Left, helped mobilize many, and fully deserves the support it's received. *In the Year of the Pig* was also a little different from Newsreel's films. Newsreel was an ongoing collective making films for circulation primarily within the community-based New Left (antidraft groups, GI coffeehouses, war resistance groups, the Black Panthers, the Young Lords, prisoner support groups. Specific defense efforts like that around Los Siete in San Francisco, the

Chicago Seven, etc.). Until *The Women's Film* in 1971, Newsreel never even attempted theatrical release, seeing that as step toward co-optation within the commodity system of circulation that sucked the political life from leftist films. Films that entered that system were left-liberal to Newsreel. Much debate went into this position, some even arguing that no Newsreel film should ever go out without a Newsreel member to help lead discussion, most agreeing that discussion in some form should occur whenever a Newsreel film was shown. Again, failure to insist upon the necessity of discussion around films when they are shown and to make explicit provisions for it seemed a liberal lapse, trusting aesthetic power to do what only political organizing could actually achieve—an ongoing, self-sustaining struggle to change our political and economic system.

But that was then. Today Newsreel's films circulate in a manner not radically different from de Antonio's films. The label "left-liberal" does not adequately describe the difference now, nor does it do full justice to de Antonio's films in any case. Its use continues a political position that grew up in a climate of confrontation and polarization and sometimes failed to distinguish friends from the myriad enemies. The question of how a film is distributed—by whom, at what rates, to what groups, shown in what context, with what kind of discussion or supporting materials—remains a vital and perhaps somewhat neglected one. It is not a question that should be glossed over; hopefully, all leftists actively engaged in the use of film and its related media, including both Emile de Antonio and Newsreel, will continue to contribute to an understanding of how to make the best possible political use of the context in which films are shown.

America Is Hard to See

Figure 27. *America Is Hard to See* (1970). De Antonio's most conventional mix of archival footage and talking heads captured Senator Eugene McCarthy's failed campaign for the 1968 Democratic presidential nomination through post mortem interviews with the candidate (27a) and his supporters, TV news excerpts (27c, from NBC's *Meet the Press*), and images from the campaign trail (27b and 27d).

DEAC ROSSELL

From Joe to Eugene:
To Hell and Back (1970)

Writing in the alternative Publick Occurrences & Boston After Dark *on June 2, 1970, Deac Rossell gave this rare notice to* America Is Hard to See *after attending its debut at Dartmouth College. Although the review (abridged here) seems to miss the documentary's more critical vision of the McCarthy campaign, Rossell (later author of* Living Pictures: The Origins of the Movies, *1998) offers insights into de Antonio's personality and his "quixotic idealism."*

Since the days when English filmmaker John Grierson fought for the recognition of his own work and that of Robert Flaherty, Len Lye, and Humphrey Jennings, the film of fact, or documentary film, has been associated with the film of persuasion. Grierson's commitment to social change has conditioned the mainstream of documentary filmmaking.

Emile de Antonio, in his own distinguished career in the United States, has continued that mainstream tradition, while expanding the cinematic language of the documentary. De Antonio's films have the impact and authority of a filmmaker who draws his material from actuality and who is not only willing to take a stand in interpreting the events around him, but considers it his artistic duty to do so.... In his new film, *America Is Hard to See,* de Antonio examines the most crucial political campaign of midcentury America: Senator Eugene McCarthy's unsuccessful bid for the 1968 Democratic presidential nomination.

McCarthy's defeat at the 1968 Democratic convention was not simply the victory of professional politicians over an outsider to the system, but the defeat of a political style, a style of reflection and thoughtfulness. Politicians, media, and public alike could not easily grasp McCarthy's aloof and reflective stance. He did not fit into the mainstream of a nation preoccupied with social mobility, moral relativism, and progress at any price. The

American scene today resembles a giant treadmill. McCarthy stepped off that treadmill of rhetoric and slavish repetition, and brought a fresh perspective to politics. The primary message of his campaign was that he didn't want just to change the results of the political machine, but to change that system's very organization and order. McCarthy has a strong sense of perspective, a sense of existing with a historical context. Before taking action he will look around a bit and think the consequences through. Ironically, it is the same struggle to pry into the kernel of an idea and discard the chaff, which pervades the career of Emile de Antonio, and undoubtedly brought him to make *America Is Hard to See,* which stands out in the director's career as his first optimistic, or at least uncritical, film.

De Antonio, working with material culled from thousands of feet of newsreel [and] combined with his own interviews, has put together a film which not only grasps the essentials of McCarthy's campaign, but also becomes a jumping-off point for reflection on the future ramifications of McCarthy's unsuccessful bid. Even though McCarthy loses in the end, the amount of hope and support that the coolly intellectual senator generated is the overwhelming impression of the film. When he began in New Hampshire, no one recognized him as he went from table to table shaking hands. But he won, and kept on winning. By the time of the convention, McCarthy had built a national organization and was a genuine contender. To emphasize the effect McCarthy had on the race, de Antonio constantly intercuts footage of the senator's political competitors: President Johnson discounting the New Hampshire primary, Senator Robert Kennedy suddenly "reassessing" his position about seeking the nomination. By the end of the film, McCarthy is seen to have been the catalyst for the political drama of 1968.

It is because the film does such an excellent job of describing how McCarthy built up tremendous political momentum outside traditional party machinery that I have come to think that de Antonio made only half his story. The night I saw the film, in an overflowing Hopkins Center at Dartmouth College, with Senator McCarthy and many of his coworkers present, it became clear that the vacuum created when McCarthy was defeated in Chicago was just as significant a political event as his miraculous campaign. McCarthy became a major national figure who presented an alternative. As de Antonio's film made this clearer and clearer, it became more and more depressing to reflect that no other political figure has risen to provide any alternative of national scope. True, there has been no presidential contest, but the sad thought lingers that McCarthy created something unique, something that was crushed definitively in Chicago.

Yet this personal view is not shared by the film's director, who stated forthrightly that "Most of my films have been critical of some aspect of

American politics, and *America Is Hard to See* represents a dramatic change in my work because it is a very positive statement about one man and his work in America in the 1960s." De Antonio is evidently convinced that McCarthy provided a viable route for change in America. The director ends the film with McCarthy's personal comment that although the traditional political system won this time, there is still hope for change.

My own reservations come from observing a number of similarities between McCarthy and de Antonio that raise questions about why the director made such an optimistic picture. Both men have constantly gone against fashionable kinds of thinking. Both are loners. Both are independent and abstract thinkers. Both are intellectuals. De Antonio likes to describe himself as a minority politician, a man who refuses in principle to support a majority position. Late one night at Dartmouth, walking down a deserted corridor of the Hanover Inn, I asked de Antonio whether he would have continued to support McCarthy [had he won]. "Probably not," was his reply—an answer I had expected, knowing the director's dedication to idealistic lost causes.

De Antonio is a man of great energy and intellect, a former professor of philosophy, and he constantly uses his energies with quixotic idealism. I honestly don't think the director is being perverse in his optimism; he has just been magnetically drawn to another idealistic intellectual who lost a well-fought battle. Perhaps that is why *America Is Hard to See* stops in Chicago, why the second half of the story—the depressing half—has not been told on the screen. But then again, optimism, expecially about the national political scene, is terribly out of fashion. It is certainly in character for de Antonio, again like McCarthy, to stand against fashion and make his first optimistic film.

JOAN MELLEN

America Is Hard to See *(1971)*

Joan Mellen, a prolific author of film books throughout the 1970s and beyond, was one of the few critics to examine de Antonio's little-seen film. Appearing in the radical journal Cineaste, *her harsh critique of* America Is Hard to See *reflects the commitment to cinematic realism by many on the left and the failure of such critics to grasp de Antonio's more complex cinematic and political strategies. Far from providing what Mellen calls "bandwagonism" for Gene McCarthy, the film critically portrays the collapse of McCarthy's campaign and the triumph of establishment politics.*

Although he claims for himself "honesty" in his films, Emile de Antonio has produced in *America Is Hard to See,* as in his previous film, *In the Year of the Pig,* a tedious and entirely disingenuous look at his subject—this time the 1968 presidential campaign of Eugene McCarthy. Just as *In the Year of the Pig* skirts any questioning of why the United States occupies Vietnam, *America* refuses to explore in what way Eugene McCarthy could represent a significant alternative to his supposedly more conservative antagonists in the Democratic Party. Nor does *America* use its camera for a sociological view of McCarthy's support, what was expected of him, and how his defeat affected the participation in American politics of his supporters.

De Antonio relies upon newsreel footage of McCarthy's attempts to win the primaries and, in so doing, inadvertently comments on why McCarthy could not hope to succeed—the footage (taken largely from television coverage) is unbelievably dull and repetitive. Interspersed throughout the news footage are interviews, generally with de Antonio's wealthy liberal supporters (Martin Peretz, etc.), who also contributed heavily to McCarthy's campaign. As commentators on the McCarthy phenomenon they are bland and self-serving and would have had no place in the film had their money not been used to buy them a "role" in praise of their protégé. So the unimaginative and unstructured editing of *America* cuts endlessly from one droning speaker to another, each reciting cliché and cracker-barrel philosophy weakening our sense of McCarthy's conviction in his own ideas. We gain very little sense of the man's perspective other than a grudging tactical retreat from overt domination in Vietnam.

Hiding behind the opaque nature of its newsreel quality with its claim to credibility, *America Is Hard to See* provides little insight into "what made McCarthy run." The news coverage and interviews are intercut at random with disconnected platitudinizing by McCarthy himself and so the candidate, too, emerges a colorless, essentially unperceptive man. With the perspective of almost four years behind us, it is a pity that we should be treated again to the stale image of a vague reformer, perhaps a poet, but hardly the bearer of a new direction in American politics. A film whose opening shot shows Leonard Bernstein introducing Eugene McCarthy with formula political jokes is made for the benefit of the liberal establishment. It could hardly provide an honest exploration of the latest liberal heir to Woodrow Wilson, FDR, and Adlai Stevenson.

The only moments of feeling in the film come in the brief sequences dealing with Robert Kennedy: his embarrassed reading of a ghost-written introduction of Lyndon Johnson as "the chief repository of our hopes and fears," followed by his refusal to shake hands with LBJ, and later the hushed silence of the funeral train carrying his body to its final rest. The two views of Kennedy, as crass politician and as fallen hero, cancel each other out, belying de Antonio's intention of using Robert Kennedy to justify the view that Eugene McCarthy responded to American needs unperceived by more vulgar opponents.

Perhaps the grossest distortion of all in *America Is Hard to See* is its attempt to equate the McCarthy campaign with the antiwar movement per se, all the more exasperating as McCarthy's purpose was to liquidate this movement by absorption—to get antiwar sentiment out of the streets and into the Democratic Party—a point well demonstrated in the film itself as McCarthy is seen self-righteously asserting that "Ho is no way comparable to Adolf Hitler." De Antonio's flattery and aggrandizement of McCarthy is embarrassing enough without his suggesting that a standard politician is a daring rebel.

Refusing to deal "honestly" with the McCarthy phenomenon is the failure of de Antonio in *America Is Hard to See*—a film which, finally, amounts to little more than a bandwagonism gone out of date.

Millhouse: A White Comedy

Figure 28. Vice President Richard "Millhouse" Nixon, as seen in the "Checkers" broadcast of September 23, 1952.

GLENN O'BRIEN

Interview with Emile de Antonio Director of Millhouse (1972)

In his second conversation with Warhol's *celebrity-driven tabloid* Interview, *de Antonio holds forth on the imbecilities he perceived in America's politics and popular culture, ranging from Richard Nixon's love of O. J. Simpson and sports to "the phony tones" of Walter Cronkite. Appearing during the theatrical release of* Millhouse, *the piece captures de Antonio at the peak of his public notoriety. Surprisingly, the avowed radical here announces that "healing" of factions is "my theme." He criticizes the "insane" violence of the Weathermen, although three years later he would treat them sympathetically in* Underground.

I've heard that Millhouse *is going to be seen in four hundred theaters across the country.*
Something like that. I hate opening an interview talking about money, but money is a measure of whether you're reaching an audience or not, in one sense, and *Millhouse* has had some remarkable successes when you remember that it's a documentary. We've broken the house record at the New Yorker Theater and we're in about forty theaters around the country. And there are several hundred more engagements contracted.

What's the reaction to Millhouse *been in smaller cities?*
Well, it hasn't played conventional small cities. It's being booked into small cities that have universities attached to them, New Haven, Providence, Princeton . . . And the old-fashioned commercial theaters there simply function better than sowing it in the college situation. I'm going down to Dallas with it. I prefer not to travel with the picture, but I'm going to Dallas because I once made a film in Dallas and because Dallas has a reputation of being fantastically right-wing and I'm left-wing. So the idea of that confrontation is interesting to me personally.

You did Rush to Judgment *in Dallas.*

Yes. Dallas was the first and only time that I've ever experienced fear in filmmaking. I went down there alone originally, without a crew, without Mark Lane. In fact Lane had never talked to a witness in Dallas until he was with the film crew. But I went there to research what the TV studios there had for sale and I knew I was being followed and they knew who I was and what I was doing. It's a fairly eerie feeling when you're alone. I remember I used to test myself by forcing myself to walk home through a lonely freight yard, across railroad tracks, and a police car would be behind me. I was wondering what they'd do, but I'm here talking to you so they didn't do anything. The first day I was in Dallas with the crew I was briefing them, telling them I was interested in head shots of a certain kind which revealed character, and that I really wasn't interested in atmospheres because I thought we were, in a sense, making a brief which attacked the credibility of the Warren Commission and of the FBI, and of the local police. And as I was telling them this there was a knock at the door and two hard-looking young men in business suits and Stetson hats came in and presented cards identifying them as members of the Dallas Homicide Squad. They started questioning me. And right there you have the fundamental decision. Do you tell them to fuck themselves and get run out of town and there's no film, or do you go ahead? So I answered their questions, which were innocuous enough. What are you doing here? Who are you working for? What's the name of your company? Until there was a change in their voices which was very dramatic. They said, "We hear you're down to interview this *boy* Benavides." In Texas, when it's a Mexican-American or black it's always boy. So I said, "Yes, I'm here to interview Mr. Benavides tomorrow morning." And they said, "Well that's why we're here." So I said, "Why's that?" They said, "Fraud." I said, "Why are you from the homicide squad if you're investigating fraud?" And they said, "Anything to do with the death of Officer Tippett has to do with the homicide squad." Benavides wasn't really important. He was simply the person closest to Tippett when he was killed. I never did get to see him. It was short-circuited. In fact, Benavides's brother-in-law was killed. But what happened was that the camera crew quit right then. They said, "We're finished." I'd told them it was going to be rough, but I had to spend most of the night convincing them that it was safer in Dallas than flying back to California, saying that if anything were to happen here it would surely be an admission on somebody's part that something was queer. But one day we were filming on Dealey Plaza and a truck was coming down the hill and it backfired, and the soundman simply threw the Nagra on the ground and fell down flat. That was the kind of feeling. So I'm sort of anxious to go back to Dallas.

How long did you work on Millhouse?
About a year. The film involved an immense amount of pure research of a nonfilmic nature. The only way you can know what to ask people, what to look for, what to shoot, is to really know everything that's happened. So I spent a great deal of time reading books about Nixon, looking up back issues of the *New York Times,* going through magazines. I hired a researcher in California who went through the press from 1946 to the present. So we uncovered people there whom we filmed, like the woman who went to the senior prom with him.

Did you have any problem getting access to the newsreel footage and kinescopes and so on?
No, we were very lucky. The trouble with doing the kind of film that I do is that everything is owned by the three networks who constitute a monopoly, and they can dictate prices. Whenever you deal with a monopoly, you're dealing with a world of gangster economics. That's not a dramatic statement, that's a plain fact. My first experience with that was in *Point of Order* with CBS. It was through our own research that we knew that CBS owned the complete Army-McCarthy hearings, all the negatives, and CBS alone. When I first talked to CBS they denied owning it, and this was not because they didn't want to sell it. They just didn't know. They simply had so much stuff that it was bureaucratic inefficiency. But once they did find out that they had it, the negotiations were as stark and as brutal as anything that I've ever undergone. And CBS's price was $50,000 in front plus half of the profits in perpetuity. That's like having a gun stuck up against your head, but there was no way out. I wanted to make the film, and it was either do that or not get the material. And the same was true in the Nixon film where about 70 percent of the material comes from stock footage, UPI or Paramount or ABC or Pathé, and you don't have much argument because these people know what they have and they know what you want. Hearst, for instance, refused to sell any footage to me. That was on a political basis. Then I threatened them with legal action. You can't discriminate as to whom you will sell footage. So they got out of the whole thing by saying that they were preparing a film on Nixon, therefore they would not sell anything on Nixon because it would compete with what they were doing. If they're making a film on Nixon, I wonder what kind it is.

Did you miss anything crucial?
No. Because our research was complete and thorough, we accumulated the largest storehouse of material on Nixon that exists anywhere. What I do with all this stuff is donate it to university libraries. With *In the Year of the*

Pig I gave Cornell what must be the largest collection of film on Indochina. And the Nixon material we have is really complete.

I imagine you had a lot of good material you couldn't use because of length.
Mary Lampson, the editor, and I were heartbroken over many scenes that simply didn't lend themselves to the film. One of the things that we all talk about with Mr. Nixon and the point that I made at the beginning of the film was the footage from Madame Tussaud's Wax Museum, where we had Nixon being created, a head being stuck on a torso, that's the Mr. Plastic motif, a true motif, and it's an expression of his inability to ever meet on a one-to-one basis with another human being and look him in the face, to deal with him on a human, personal level. But something that was left out that I found fascinating was Nixon in Vietnam. There was a bunch of GIs, infantry looking battle-weary with their rifles, and Nixon got out of a jeep with a high-ranking officer and walked up to a black soldier and said, "Where are you from?" The soldier said Buffalo. Nixon said, "The Buffalo Bills. Just think: O. J. Simpson, 6 feet 2, 220 pounds, can run the hundred yards in 9.2." The soldier looked at him blank, open-mouth, as if to say, "Who is this lunatic reading off sports statistics?" He wasn't able to make any human relation. Also, it's a part of Nixon's sports hang-up, which we covered in the film.

It's the same as the incident that occurred at the Lincoln Memorial during the Moratorium.
Right. It's one of those curious aspects of Nixon's mentality. Sports was the scene of his major failure. He was unable to make any team. As a banker in California told me, it wasn't that he was light, but that he was the most incredibly badly coordinated young man trying out, so there was no chance of his making any of them. Nixon is the only person I know who speaks out of sync. He speaks out of sync normally. His gestures come at the wrong moment every time. This failure in sports is the reason that so many of his metaphors and images have to do with success in sports. That's why I open the film with the quote "I guess you might say that's the world of sports, you might say it's the world of politics, you might say it's life itself . . ."
And during the Moratorium he watched a football game rather than confront the young demonstrators.

It was a great scene where Ike has the fly rod and Nixon ducks out of the way so strangely . . . then he stumbles through the stream . . .
Again, that's his lack of coordination. I took the corniest music I could find for that scene, as there was no sound on the original. I took Beethoven's Pastoral Symphony, the part entitled "By the Brook." Beethoven meant that

as programmatic music, but it never worked as programmatic music. But suddenly, as you have Nixon clumsily wading through that stream with the trout fishing gear, that music takes on another dimension. Of course, as you see from the poster of the film, there was never any pretense of objectivity. Objectivity to me is a totally nonreal concept, an unattainable concept, and this is why Nixon's name is misspelled in the title and why the picture is called a white comedy. White comedy has a lot of meanings to me. It makes it very clear at the outset that there was no pretense of objectivity.

I think that's very important, especially with documentary, where filmmakers perpetrate this sacred truth of documentary, this absolute objectivity.
The greatest single phony concept in film is the concept of cinema verité. The idea that the filmmaker is uninvolved with what's going on. Particularly the American filmmakers that call themselves vérité filmmakers, because I know how much they've staged. I know they never pick really boring people to film. It's a bankrupt concept as well as being dishonest. I suspect the point is that nobody, unless they're totally empty-minded and passionless, can confront the problems of our time without having some preconceptions. Cinema verité and the networks both share this bogus illusion that objectivity is possible. The networks do it because the networks are interested solely in making money. They are objective simply because they're deballed. The true castrati of our age are the networks who can't afford to offend the sponsors. This is why if you look at network news over a long period it evens itself out. This is why Agnew's criticism of the networks is valid, though he does it from the wrong point of view. The problem of the networks is that they avoid problems and they defend this whole concept by pretending they're objective. They're about as objective as a soap opera. Television is simply a sales tool to produce money for the monopoly capital class of this country. Cinema verité is more complicated because those people are working for themselves and they should be capable of treating something properly. One of the great weaknesses of the United States is our concern for technique, which is all cinema verité is, and they've perfected it: the use of terribly sophisticated equipment very skillfully handled, to say nothing or perhaps a lie. There are no lies in my films, but there is a point of view. I'm proud of my point of view and I flaunt it. I begin in the wax museum to make it abundantly clear that this is not a CBS documentary in which the phony tones of Mr. Cronkite are going to pretend to speak objectively about the president. What the television stations have said about the president in the last four years is nothing. With all that material they've finally managed to say very little. When he preempts prime time himself, he gives himself away better than they can treat him.

Do you know if anyone on Nixon's staff has seen the film?
I think given the fact that the film is a success and given the fact that the press has treated it hugely, and given the fact that the *New York Times* is reviewing it twice, with Buckley answering Canby, to get a view from the right, though Buckley's not really the right, he's just a dilettante; because of this the administration has played it very intelligently by ignoring it totally. I wrote the president and asked if we could go and interview him, that we were making a film. And although I'm sure he's never heard of me, people around him have heard of me, and without having delusions of grandeur, I think that a line was established at the beginning that the only intelligent way to handle the film was to ignore it.

So you never got any answer.
No. I would have used the answer. If he'd said no, I'd have put it on the screen. But then I write letters to Nixon from time to time. I wrote to a lot of people asking for money for Dan Berrigan when he was on the run, and sent copies to Hoover and Nixon, asking them for money. It amuses me.
I get an enormous amount of junk mail and I write "Fire J. Edgar Hoover" on it and send it back to them. A good many people get to look at it and it cost them ten cents to get their envelope back. Over the years I must have sent thousands. It's childish but I find it amusing.

JAY COCKS

Minor Surgery (1971)

Journalist and critic Jay Cocks went on to greater fame as a screenwriter collaborating with Martin Scorsese. His Time *magazine appreciation of de Antonio as a shrewd caricaturist was obviously not the sort of press the Nixon White House was seeking when, on October 15, aide Jack Caufield's memo to John Dean suggested supplying "friendly media" with "derogatory" information on de Antonio.*

Emile de Antonio is a specialist at cinematic acupuncture. In such documentary essays as *Point of Order* (about the Army-McCarthy hearings) and *In the Year of the Pig* (a cynical chronology of the Vietnam War), he needled some popular historic myths and a few political reputations. Now, in *Millhouse,* de Antonio has employed his usual technique of matching fragments of news film with quick on-camera interviews to produce an unflattering but funny likeness of the thirty-seventh president (whose middle name is Milhous, not Millhouse, but let that go). To be sure, de Antonio's jubilant bias sometimes plays him false. Nixon is too often seen stumbling over a foot or a phrase, and sometimes satire descends to the level of easy derision, as when scenes of Nixon's South American visit in 1958 are accompanied by the old Chiquita Banana jingle on the sound track.

But when it works, de Antonio's sense of juxtaposition can be lethal. News film of Nixon's 1968 nomination acceptance speech ("Let's win this one for Ike") is intercut with footage of Pat O'Brien in *Knute Rockne* advising his lachrymose squad to "win one for the Gipper"—their hospitalized teammate, who, with anachronistic irony, was portrayed by Ronald Reagan. De Antonio is also shrewd enough to know when Nixon is his own worst enemy, and he devotes a long section of *Millhouse* to the Checkers speech alone. Reciting his list of assets, attempting to sound humble and folksy ("Pat doesn't have a mink coat, but she does have a respectable

Republican cloth coat"), all the while struggling grimly to look natural, Nixon seems to emerge as the kind of bunko artist of whom W. C. Fields always ran afoul.

Millhouse touches on everything from the campaign against Helen Gahagan Douglas to all six crises, and includes some unfamiliar footage like J. Edgar Hoover making Nixon an honorary FBI agent. Subtitled a "white comedy" [see figure 12, the Levine drawing used in advertisements for the film—ed.], the film is hardly likely to win praise for fighting fair. But at its best, *Millhouse* has the impact of a David Levine caricature.

WILLIAM F. BUCKLEY JR.

Leave Your Wits at the Entrance (1971)

As America's best-known conservative pundit, William F. Buckley hardly needed instructions to defend President Nixon against his left-wing critics. The appearance of his attack on de Antonio in the Sunday New York Times *might not have been a result of a White House initiative to smear the filmmaker. De Antonio considered Buckley something of a nemesis: filming him during his run for mayor of New York in 1965, debating him on two episodes of* Firing Line *in 1968, later calling him a "fey prince" and an inflator of "jabberwocky balloons."*

Although Buckley was dismissive of de Antonio and his film, he found it necessary to blast them both. The columnist dashed off this ad hominem piece in advance of his own magazine's pan of Millhouse *a few weeks later (see David Brudnoy,* National Review, *December 3, 1971). The piece is remarkable for its personal venom, characterizing de Antonio as stupid and imagining him reduced to "nuclear ash."*

The current anti-Nixon documentary (it is called *Millhouse* for anagrammatic reasons which, like the penetration of *Oh! Calcutta!* are not worth the archeologist's time) is, of course, an insult to the intelligence, but of course insults to the intelligence can be fun. Not necessarily praiseworthy fun, but who said fun had to be praiseworthy? If Dwight Macdonald could have fun seeing *MacBird!*, you can have fun seeing *Millhouse,* and your neighbor can have fun reading the Black Book of the John Birch Society.

I gather that the director-producer Mr. Emile de Antonio is not very bright, which suggests a divine success in the distribution of talent which we mortals can only seek vainly to emulate. If Mr. de Antonio had been created bright, he would not have blown the opportunities he had to discredit Richard Nixon, which is the intention here. He rolls along, with his anti-Nixon collage, piling anti-Nixonism on anti-Nixonism, until the audience begins to groove with him, leering with pleasurable contempt at, for instance, the (very nearly intact) Checkers speech, the McCarthyite Nixon campaigner of the early fifties, and so on.

Then de Antonio brings in, of all people, Alger Hiss, with the clear suggestion that Alger Hiss was framed by Nixon ("Hiss was the bad guy. His guilt was predetermined," comments Fred Cook, whose judgment on Alger Hiss is as valuable as Mussmano's on Sacco Vanzetti). Poor Mr. de Antonio. His desire to torpedo Nixon is total, but not enough so to cause him to give a little prudent berth to the Hiss case. It is as if a Republican WASP had given us a long, eloquent, sincere, overwhelming documentary on why it would gravely injure the United States if we should elect John F. Kennedy as president, and ended it, "Besides, Kennedy is a Catholic."

Everyone has his weaknesses, and as one plods through *Millhouse*, after the Hiss bit, one thinks, well, maybe Alger Hiss is de Antonio's wife's brother, a passing exoneration of whom was a nepotistic imperative. But no, before the film is over, Mr. de Antonio is giving us the motivation for the Vietnam War, and you will not guess, no—I promise you, you will not guess what it is. The motives for our involvement in Vietnam are the commercial interests of a hundred or so American concerns whose products play a role in Vietnam, everything from Firestone Rubber Company to Colgate toothpaste, it being left to the viewer to assume that anyone in Vietnam who uses rubber or brushes his teeth is doing so in order to further American imperialistic interests.

By the same token, the war on poverty is the chauvinistic enterprise of United States Plywood and Bayer Aspirin, and Albert Schweitzer was a scout for the medical cartels. Odd that men who have a natural affinity for drama should be so easily tripped up by ideological ambushes. I remember the war movie by Carl Foreman in which, in order to drive home the paradoxes, he found it necessary to film the execution of an American deserter to the music, blaring forth from the PX's nickelodeon, of "Have Yourself a Merry Little Christmas." Needless to say, the execution took place on Christmas Day. De Antonio's execution of Mr. Nixon is intended to suit the convenience of the spontaneous shopper. It is only required that you leave your wits at the entrance: and, as I say, why not? Wit can be a nuisance.

Mr. de Antonio's film has some wonderful things in it which isn't surprising. The reviewer for the *New Yorker* remarked, after the famous Edward R. Murrow film of Senator Joe McCarthy, that the kind of documentary journalism which Mr. Murrow had just consummated presented quite extraordinary opportunities to the caricaturist. On that celebrated occasion Mr. Murrow began by showing Senator McCarthy belching. If you have available several hundreds of thousands of feet on somebody, the chances are reasonable that you can find a shot of him belching, and not altogether unreasonable that you can find a shot of him cursing, and, with a little luck, a shot of him urinating behind a tree.

So it goes in de Antonio's *Millhouse*. And of course he catches Mr. Nixon in moments unattractive, laying open the question whether they are typical; i.e., does Mr. Nixon, typically, belch?

Well, Mr. Nixon most certainly guarantees, single-handed, the price of corn, no doubt about it. In the Checkers speech he spoke the words, "Because, you see, I love my country and I think my country is in danger. And I think the only man that can save America at this time is the man who is running for president on my ticket, Dwight Eisenhower." And, sixteen years later, it hadn't greatly changed. "Sixteen years ago, I stood before this convention to accept your nomination as the running mate of one of the greatest Americans of our time or of any time, Dwight D. Eisenhower."

And there is fun in catching Mr. Nixon up on the Broken Campaign Promise. "We're going to stop the rise in prices . . . we're going to balance the federal budget." . . . "I will see to it that these laws will be enforced. We are going to make America free from fear again." I rather like that kind of thing, even as I like to run my fingers every now and then over the Democratic Party's convention pledge on Vietnam ("Our most urgent task is to end the war in Vietnam by an honorable and lasting settlement. We reject as unacceptable a unilateral withdrawal of our forces which would allow aggression and subversion to succeed"). And anyway, I believe in a little secular impiety, where presidents and princes are concerned, so much so that I like it when I see on the screen candidate Nixon saying, "Let me make one thing very clear . . . If there's going to be unemployment next year, it's going to be the ones who got us into this mess that's going to be unemployed." Jolly good. I am a paid-up member of the Anti-Beatification League.

But is there in this film a relative assessment? Here is the most damaging of Mr. de Antonio's anti-Nixonisms. Nixon on the stump: "Hubert is a loyal American. Hubert is against the Communists. Hubert is for peace. Hubert is a good speaker. Hubert is a very plausible man. He's a very pleasant man. He's a good campaigner. But Hubert is a sincere, dedicated radical." Sounds bad. On the other hand, in a wholly other connection, Mr. de Antonio permits us to have a glimpse of Adlai the Good, and he is saying, in his 1956 campaign against Eisenhower, "Every consideration, the president's age, his health, the fact that he can't succeed himself, make it inevitable that the dominant figure of the Republican Party under a second Eisenhower term would be Richard Nixon."

Interesting that Adlai, the prophet, was wrong in that Eisenhower's health proved to be better than Mr. Stevenson's, who pre-deceased him, that Eisenhower's health was altogether serviceable during his second term, and that Nixon proved not by any means the dominant figure of the Republican Party while Eisenhower was president—so what? De Antonio was so anxious to cash an anti-Nixon chip, he didn't even notice that it was counterfeit.

Adlai Stevenson went on: "Now I say to you, do you trust this gentleman to be fair? (Crowd yells no)—[as Mr. de Antonio's script records]. Do you want him as commander in chief to exercise power over war and peace? (Crowd yells no.) Do you want to place the hydrogen bomb in his hand? (Crowd yells no.) Do you believe that Richard Nixon has the confidence of other countries? (Crowd yells no.)" Poor crowd. One wishes that Oscar Wilde hadn't ruined it by saying it so definitively, "I hope you have not been leading a double life, pretending to be wicked, and being really good all the time. That would be hypocrisy."

You will understand then, why Nixon is such a wicked man, and how it must torture de Antonio not to have been reduced, long since, to nuclear ash.

DAVID THORSTAD

Millhouse (1971)

Appearing in the socialist newsweekly The Militant, *David Thorstad's review typifies the positive reception de Antonio's work had among the left. For Thorstad, this "white comedy" revealed itself to be a "horror film" that documented the monstrosities of the ruling elite and the "mediocrities" who were permitted to govern.*

> Nixon's the one, yes, Nixon's the one,
> To build a brand new wonderful world.
> He's the undisputed voice of the thinking man,
> He's everybody's choice for a better plan.

If you think this bit of pompous Americana is unreal in the revolting way the school songs sung at football games are, then you get the point of *Millhouse*. *Millhouse* is not only about Nixon (the title is a play on Nixon's middle name), but it is about the America that makes a phenomenon like Nixon possible. It is infuriating, as it intends to be.

Emile de Antonio, whose last film success was *In the Year of the Pig*, has done to Nixon more or less what he did to Joseph McCarthy in *Point of Order*. Starting out with newsreels and interviews with participants in and observers of Nixon's political career, de Antonio skillfully uses flashbacks, cuts, juxtapositions, and double entendres to tell the Nixon story. It is a real Horatio Alger story. It is proof that the American Dream comes true—but only for mediocrities who don't deserve it.

The film opens at Madame Tussaud's Wax Museum, where the wax figure of Millhouse is being put together. By the end of the film—after all the lying, rigged TV performances, fabricated witch-hunting of "subversives," slanderous campaigning for public office, searching for Communist plots in pumpkin patches, and eagle-spread victory salutes to the aging and mindless delegates to Republican Party conventions—it is clear that the "new" Nixon is really the same old phony he always was. Those who still tell public opinion pollsters they think the president is doing a good job have in mind the wax figure, not the real McCoy. This film gives them the real McCoy.

It traces the seemingly irresistible rise of Richard Milhous Nixon from the red-baiting 1946 campaign against California Congressman Jerry Voorhis, through the Alger Hiss hearings ("It was the Hiss case that was the thing . . . that made him," says Fred J. Cook); the 1952 Republican convention where Nixon became the vice presidential candidate (especially, according to Ike, for his "ability to ferret out any subversive influence wherever it may be found"); giving the famous "Checkers" speech, where he tries (successfully) to save his political career by going on TV to paint himself, in true soap-opera style, as a pauper ("Pat and I have the satisfaction that every dime we've got is honestly ours. I should say this, that Pat doesn't have a mink coat, but she does have a respectable Republican cloth coat and I always tell her she'd look good in anything. . . ."); almost tripping over the fly at the end of his line while fishing with Ike; addressing a convention of the Daughters of the American Revolution with a mammoth American flag floating like a giant sting ray overhead ("The only thing worse than atomic war today," he tells the patriots, "is surrender"); getting mobbed in Latin America; with Diem; being made an "official member of the FBI family" by J. Edgar Hoover; ignoring the November 15, 1969, mass antiwar demonstration in Washington; posing with his cabinet. And throughout, de Antonio lets Nixon for the most part tell you who he is in his own words.

Some of the footage in this film would be valuable to see even if it hadn't managed to find its way into this devastating indictment of the president of the United States. The House Un-American Activities Committee hearings on the Alger Hiss case, for instance. Nixon would not be president today were it not for the successful smear job he did on Alger Hiss ("verdict first and testimony later tactics," Hiss accuses Nixon of resorting to), and it is interesting to see the participants in this, one of the more sordid chapters in Nixon's career; besides Nixon and Hiss, they include Whittaker Chambers, who looks and sounds like a parody of Alfred Hitchcock. Seeing Nixon hold up for the press a few frames of film negative found in a pumpkin patch and claim with a straight face that they contain secret Communist documents is rather telling: you can see that Nixon didn't believe it himself. The remarkable thing is that so many other people did, and that it sent Hiss, not Nixon, to jail.

One of the more raucous sequences in *Millhouse* is the one on Millhouse the Intellectual. Jules Witcover, author of *The Resurrection of Richard*

Nixon, says that on several occasions Nixon "described himself to me as an intellectual. He called himself at one point the egghead of the Republican Party. . . ." De Antonio then immediately cuts to an evening of the Bob Hope show at the White House, with an audience of dignitaries, among them Nixon, who wallows with obvious glee in the cultural barbarism that has made Bob Hope rich (the program contains not only the kind of anti-homosexual jokes which still draw laughs for Hope, but also go-go girls in a zealous rendition of "Nixon's the one, yes, Nixon's the one"). By this point, you'll agree he's the one, all right.

Considering its subject, this is actually a horror film, in spite of the fact that de Antonio calls it a comedy "in the tradition of the Marx Brothers." After all, the Marx Brothers just made films, they didn't run the most powerful country on earth. And they weren't mediocrities. The question this film really raises, though of course only implicitly, is, How could someone like Nixon, who had nothing but his success as a Wall Street lawyer to recommend him, and who so often seemed out of the picture, reach the top? It says a lot—none of it good—about the social system in the United States that someone like Nixon is able to become president. Even when such heroes of the system are down and out—as Nixon was many times—they apparently never die, they just bounce back.

The fact that Nixon has bounced back in the middle of a mass radicalization where he is like a fish on dry land may add a note of optimism. But when Nixon gets the coup de grâce (and may it be the antiwar actions November 6 that help do it!), the system will still be there. This film can only help fan the flames of the discontent it will take to get rid of it.

CINDA FIRESTONE

"The Real History of Our Times Is on Film": Filmmaker Emile de Antonio Talks about Nixon, the '50s, and Now (1972)

In the midst of Millhouse's *theatrical run, young journalist Cinda Firestone (granddaughter of tire and rubber manufacturer Harvey Firestone) interviewed de Antonio for the alternative* Liberation News Service. *Many interviews with him were conducted by people who were already his creative collaborators (see interviews by Mekas, Neufeld, Weiss, Biskind, Silber, Tuchman, Segal, Sheen, and de Antonio). Firestone's case was the reverse. After publishing this piece, she learned filmmaking by working with de Antonio. Soon she directed her own acclaimed political documentary about the infamous prison riots in New York. In turn, footage from Firestone's* Attica *(1974) wound up in de Antonio's* Underground.

How did you get into films?
That is a question that I've been asked a lot and I'm always embarrassed by it. I wish there was a clear, straightforward, truthful answer about why I got into films. But there isn't. In a sense I almost backed into it. I went to the movies very rarely. I supposed I got interested in film as I got interested in politics again.

I had once, when I was very young, been a communist, at Harvard. Then I became apolitical. At the same time I was backing into film by mistake I started becoming interested in political events. And these things fused in *Point of Order*. But even that's not the truth because it was not that clear. It took a long time; it was complicated.

I worked on the docks when I got out of Harvard. I worked on the docks for eight or nine months in Baltimore, which was a very rough waterfront. I became a longshoreman because I decided since I was preaching left-wing theory as an undergraduate I ought to find out what the hell it was like, because I hadn't really done it.

When did you become apolitical?
Well, the military during World War II tended to have that effect on people. First of all, in the military you were totally isolated from anybody who was political. Where I was and what I was doing, there were almost no people who were even liberal. When I got out of the military I went to graduate school and there was that period of readjustment and disillusionment and a period of my life took place largely in Greenwich Village. There were a lot of people who were like me. It had to do with a lot of drinking and trying to make up for those three years lost. I may sound dramatic but it was a simple fact.

As the Cold War started, the government at this point was very efficient at supplying large chunks of Cold War rhetoric. One thing that people forget, when you get into the early '50s, is that it's not just Senator Joseph McCarthy. There already was HUAC (the House Un-American Activities Committee) going full blast. The government was producing the whole rhetoric of the Cold War.

There were so few voices, there were so few people who you could "repair to" in the year 1952 because this country was very frightened. The war in Vietnam made everything much more clear—the issues became clearer. It's too bad it took a lot of dead Vietnamese and dead Americans too to make those issues clear, but the conflicts in our society obviously became more apparent in the '60s than the '50s.

They were there in the '50s but there was no organization, there were no magazines, there were almost no writers, there were almost no films. There wasn't any place where ideas and people could meet. The clout of the government was enormous. In universities that was the beginning of the great CIA takeover. There were a lot of guys who were pigs and did the takeover but I knew a lot of guys who were OK people who were taken over and didn't even know they were taken over. The campuses—instead of demonstrations, they had panty raids.

What were you thinking about?
In my mind I withdrew. I became apolitical. I didn't believe in what was going on. I was outside the system but I was outside by myself—there was no community. You saw the thing happening and you were impotent. The feeling of impotence is finally the most devastating of all feelings. You saw the trade-union movement, which I helped to organize when I was sixteen years old, becoming racist, elitist. You saw a union like the printers union already setting it up so that sons would get jobs—excluding not just blacks but other ethnic groups too. There was no voice raised against this.

You've made two movies about two reactionary politicians—Point of Order, *about Senator Joseph McCarthy, and* Millhouse, *about Nixon. How would you compare the two men?*

If anything, I developed a slight sympathy for McCarthy because of the way the system was railroading him. Don't forget that McCarthy was railroaded. When McCarthy was useful, the system used him. McCarthy was given the chairmanship of a major Senate committee—that never would have happened to a junior senator unless his machinations as a chairman of that committee would have been helpful to the Republican Party.

But he started to run crazy. He started saying that the government was full of communists—and it was his own party that he was attacking. His own party was, in 1953, running the country—they were in the White House and had a majority in the House and Senate. That's when he was crushed.

This is the fundamental thing about Nixon. Nixon and McCarthy were very close. They were very dissimilar in style but when we were working on *Millhouse* we tried to find the famous speeches that McCarthy delivered in California in 1950 for Nixon when he was running. The film clips show McCarthy coming to California to speak in Nixon's behalf in Nixon's congressional campaign, yet Nixon was part of the team that dumped McCarthy.

There was a group that met in the White House that included Nixon, William Rogers, who's now the secretary of state, Henry Cabot Lodge, who was then U.S. ambassador to the UN, and Clark Clifford, who was a Democrat. These people got together and said, McCarthy is wrecking the country, McCarthy is wrecking the army, McCarthy is wrecking the administration. It was they who decided to run the Army-McCarthy hearings.

McCarthy was done in because he broke the rules of the game, the rules of the establishment. And this is one reason why, though McCarthy stood for fascist ideas, he himself was a drunkard, he had no party, he had no group around him. When you think of a fascist you immediately think of cliques and organization. Though McCarthy was power-hungry; he was money-hungry; he stole; he was supported by all the fascist elements in the country, including President Kennedy's father, and the Texas millionaires; he represented fascism more than he was a fascist.

He and Nixon did the same things (like running for office on anti-communism), except that Nixon did them first. Nixon did it in 1948 and McCarthy started in 1950. Nixon did it better, Nixon did it more intelligently. The one thing I feel strongly about is that Nixon is the most intelligent creature this country has produced in the twentieth century. I may find him personally and politically repellent and abhorrent, but he is somebody who was down and out in 1962 and who is now in the White House and who has managed to pull off all the things he has pulled off without doing anything. He is killing more people in Vietnam, yet many people in the U.S. feel the war is winding down.

What he was able to do in the Alger Hiss case, for example, is the key to what Nixon is all about. He took one case. This is what we wanted to get into the film but couldn't. (There is no footage of it.) This is the one case where Nixon is caught red-handed in an outright lie. Not an equivocation—a real lie in it; literal definition. He says in *Six Crises* in talking about Hiss, "on August 17, 1948, when Whittaker Chambers went before HUAC, the names Alger and Donald Hiss were mentioned. That's the first time I ever heard them mentioned."

Whereas for one year Nixon as a congressman had been getting secret information about the Hisses from a Catholic priest in Baltimore who was in with the FBI. For one year he had been preparing his case. The difference between Nixon and McCarthy. McCarthy shot his mouth off. McCarthy said all those things that were so crazy that people stopped believing him. McCarthy said of Eisenhower, "We had twenty years of treason under Roosevelt and Truman and now under Eisenhower, twenty-one." McCarthy was saying that the CIA was full of communists, that the hydrogen bomb plants were full of communists. Whereas Nixon just said Alger Hiss, and fingering Alger Hiss he prepared his case very carefully; he did a brilliant job. He got Hiss sent to prison and he himself into the White House.

A large part of Millhouse *focused on how Nixon used media—which he didn't as well as Kennedy, for example. Why didn't you try to make the point about Kennedy, who was so mythologized?*
The answer to that question is in your question. Kennedy used the media in a much more subtle way than Nixon. Also there was much less media coverage of him than Nixon. If you're making a film in which you use found material like stock footage—there simply isn't much stuff about Kennedy because film libraries didn't have anything. Nobody filmed Jack Kennedy until almost 1959. He was just another senator and not a very distinguished one. He was just a good-looking young senator.

The film libraries weren't even created, except CBS's, until after 1963. There just isn't the material.

There's a second question in that Kennedy was superficially such a likeable man. He was smoother, upper-class. The reason why Nixon is such a brilliant politician is because he's so unlikeable—he doesn't look like anything. His manner is so jerky compulsive nervous, yet still he's able to win an election. The myth—the Kennedy image of Camelot—that's what's left in the film libraries. There's nothing left in the film libraries that could enable you to pinpoint—that's a book, not a film.

One of the reasons Nixon was of interest to me personally was because there has been only one major figure in American life who runs the whole length of the Cold War and ends up in power. Nixon ran for Congress in 1946 for the first time on Cold War issues. He charged that the guy who ran against him—Jerry Voorhis—was a Communist. He started all the smear techniques. He ran on the Cold War in 1948, the Hiss case. In 1950, he said Helen Gahagan Douglas was a Communist; in 1952, Eisenhower was forced to choose him because he was the choice of the extreme conservatives in the Republican Party. He was a hard-liner on Communism, he was a hard-liner on China, Korea, the Soviet Union, and later because he was a hard-liner on Vietnam and everything else.

And he's smart—the Checkers speech was taken out of circulation by Nixon—it was suppressed. We got it from the movement. That's the only reason it's in the film *Millhouse*. Nobody has seen Checkers from 1952 to 1971, because Nixon bought it up. I tried to get it in 1968. When I called the networks and asked, Can I get a look at Checkers? And they said, Oh, sure, we'll send it over. Then the guy called the next day and said you can't have it—it turns out a client owns it and nobody can look at it. I said who's the client? And they said the Republican National Committee, so I called the Republican National Committee and they said you can't have it, Mr. Nixon owns it.

I think Nixon is going to be a lot different the next term than this one. I think that Vietnam proves we can be Nazis without jackboots. And we have our concentration camps in Attica and San Quentin. And what we're going to do is vote Nixon in and we're going to become the first nation in the world to vote fascism in. I think that when Nixon appointed Rehnquist and Powell to the Supreme Court it was a glimpse of what the future holds for us.

If you feel that way, do you think you would do a movie about the signs of coming greater repression?
No, because those are vague ideas in my head. I don't know what those signs are.

What about a film with footage of [recently appointed Supreme Court justices William] Rehnquist and [Lewis] Powell, for example?
There aren't that many film clips of people like Rehnquist. The reporters couldn't even find enough of the words, enough of the witnesses, when Rehnquist was trying to keep blacks from voting in Arizona. They couldn't even find enough people to which this had been done, even. There's no film

of Rehnquist and Powell, and now that they're there, they're not going to talk to anybody. They'll give a formal interview to CBS on "My Legal Philosophy," which just makes them look good.

The real history of our times is on film, on tape—the words just don't do it. I think there should be a national electronics archive financed by the three networks that make such a profit off our air. And anything that's in it should be made available to everybody at cost. First of all, the networks are destroying what they have. Tape is expensive but they keep *I Love Lucy* because they can peddle it, but they will wipe tapes, they will destroy footage. There are committees at each of the three networks who once a month decide what to throw away. And what they're throwing away is the raw history of our country, and our world and our times.

Painters Painting

Figure 29. *D*, by Frank Stella (1963). Copyright 2000 Frank Stella/Artists Rights Society (ARS), New York. Reproduced by permission of Artists Rights Society.

EMILE DE ANTONIO

The Agony of the Revolutionary Artist (1971)

Traveling the campus lecture circuit in 1971, de Antonio spoke at Western Washington State College in the remote burg of Bellingham. Writing for the alternative paper Northwest Passage, *Bernard Weiner parlayed his encounter with the director into several publications. His first interview for the student press led to a longer version published in* Film Quarterly *("Radical Scavenging," Fall 1971), which remains one of the best profiles of the filmmaker. A few months later his review of* Millhouse *for the modest* Passage *was reprinted in* Sight and Sound.

"The Agony of the Revolutionary Artist" is a portentously but aptly titled transcript of remarks on modern painting and politics that de Antonio delivered to an art class. In addressing the question that always plagued him—how to reconcile his Marxist politics with his preference for apolitical abstract art—he paints himself into an intellectual corner. Acknowledging that his own creative freedom would not be allowed in the Chinese Revolution he otherwise admired, de Antonio confesses paralysis before the fantastic hypothetical "What if Mao asked me to 'get rid of' that 'fascist' but brilliant poet T. S. Eliot?"

The film is about the period 1946–70, which is the great period of American painting. *Painters Painting* presented me with several problems personally. I regard myself as a Marxist. I regard myself as a critic of the existing social system in this country. I regard myself as an exponent of change and revolution. And the painters and the way in which they work are essentially manifestations of a very conservative aspect of America. The painting itself is not conservative, but it's part of a machine which runs this country. A big Rauschenberg painting today costs forty to fifty thousand dollars. There aren't that many people who can buy a Rauschenberg. The people who buy Rauschenbergs are either very rich or the huge corporations. The latter reveals another reason why American paintings have become so big. American paintings become vast because it's public painting. . . . It belongs in a bank or a corporation. . . .

American painting today is immensely expensive. The American painters today are immensely successful. The successful ones become immensely rich. They are collected by a small group of people—not more than a thousand out of 200 million—and by a group of corporations that does not exceed two hundred. And these are the people who set the canons of taste and fashion in American painting, namely, the American corporate world and that class which owns our country.

I personally am torn by all this because these people are my friends. It's complicated, because each one of these people regards himself personally as a critic of what's going on in this country. Frank Stella gives away a couple thousand dollars each month for peace causes. De Kooning gives away money. Jasper Johns and Rauschenberg give away money. Andy Warhol gives away money. But their work is something else. Their work, in my opinion, is totally uninvolved with the nature of the social struggle. . . .

Where I feel hypocritical is that I like these paintings and I still know these people. I'm personally hung up, because I've known these people for most of my mature life. My closest friend is Stella, with whom I celebrated his birthday the night before I flew out here, and his work is the most apolitical work that exists. I mean, stripes. Tell me the politics of a stripe. . . .

The older painters (like Jackson Pollock, de Kooning, Franz Kline) had some social consciousness in their work, without being deeply political. Those people did paint some realist painting. But the mainstream of American painting, they maintain, is away from the realistic tradition, and instead went into a totally abstract tradition. And if you're totally abstract, you're not saying anything about the nature of society. I mean, even if you strain in the most labored way, you cannot say that a de Kooning abstraction or a Frankenthaler doodle or a Stella line [has to do with the] world. It has only to do with themselves. . . .

And so if I have to make a choice between American painting and the attempt to turn men's minds and the search for a collective soul or collective mind—the collective man—then I'm more interested in what Mao's doing than in the art of my friends. And I'm personally forced into a position where you can't have them both. There are those who will say, "I prefer a society which allows Jasper Johns and de Kooning to exist, and is somehow more complicated, more sensitive, more interesting." That's their choice. I, on the other hand, have made another choice. I recognize the genius and the gifts of the people that I've mentioned, but I repudiate them.

Being my age, it's hard to come to this kind of decision. Because for ten years, or more than that, I was apolitical. I lived with these people and knew them and saw them every day, and admired their work. I liked their art and bought it before the critics and the collectors and corporations liked it. And now I can't say that I still don't like them and their work. That would be a lie. But I have to sacrifice my life with it, my interest in it, and many of my relationships revolving around it. Because I simply can't accept the political assumptions. . . .

Art is one of the main reasons given for excusing elitist societies in the past, as well as our own society. I'm really looking for something more fundamental, which is a revolution for the soul and minds and bodies of men, which will do away with injustice and will do away with all that is evil in our own society. In saying this, I'm perfectly aware that I would never have the right in a society organized along the lines of Mao to do the kinds of films I do, because my work would have to hew to a very precise line. But I think that I also have to be willing to repudiate my own work. Which I would do. Because the need for social change is so great; the amount of injustice in this country and the world is so great, that much will have to be sacrificed. And as Mao said, "A revolution is not a tea party." Much will have to [be] scrapped and junked. In every revolution, something's been scrapped and junked. . . .

[On Socialist Realist art in China]: It's not people's art. It's garbage art. Which is a mistake, but as the revolution progresses it will find an art form. The Chinese, after all, have the oldest civilization extant in the world today. The same people there on the Yellow and Yangtze River basins going back at least four or five thousand years. And they've produced a series of cultures which have disappeared. I'm sure that they will produce a people's art form in the Chinese People's Republic, which may not be in my lifetime but which will be there.

It's just bad art now, not people's art. The paintings stink. The films are lousy. They're just unbelievably dreary. . . . They're trying to make an art for the revolution of the Chinese People's Republic. And I don't think they've succeeded. Just as I don't think they've succeeded in other countries. We're not talking about Heaven. We're talking about the Chinese People's Republic, which is full of errors. It simply seems to me that what is being tried there is the most interesting experiment, and the biggest experiment, and the most exciting experiment, that has gone on in society for at least two thousand years. In my own mind, it is more significant than the work of any American painter who titillated me during the fifties and sixties. . . .

The regrettable truth is that is socialist countries—Cuba being the exception (Cuban film is interesting, the Cuban novel is interesting, and the Cuban graphics are terrific, and Fidel has encouraged all that)—but in most socialist countries, it is just appalling. I mean, in East Germany the Brecht theater is like a mausoleum. . . .

I think all art has to serve the revolution. You finally have to make your own kind of judgment about it. But I think painting (and all the arts) can serve the revolution and become great painting again. The Russian Revolution between 1917 and 1924 produced the most exciting work that was going on in the world—in architecture, painting, sculpture, theater, film. And then something happened called Stalin (and a few other things more complicated than that) and just cut it off . . . It was the beginning of a socialist kind of art and it died. I think in Czechoslovakia that maybe something was about to happen. And that was killed, of course. . . .

The same dilemma exists for me in writing. I used to teach poetry and philosophy, and I think the two great poets for me in English in the twentieth century were both absolute fascists. It wasn't that they were apolitical; they were fascists. One is T. S. Eliot—Eliot to the point where he actually wrote two or three anti-Semitic essays—and [the other] William Butler Yeats. . . .

That's the real question about art, and I don't know if it has an answer. Because I see everything in terms of politics. But how do you reconcile yourself to your admiration for their art? I've been struggling with that a long time. I can see myself in front of a group who share my politics, from a different country, and saying I like T. S. Eliot—and I don't know what I'd be saying by saying that. If Mao Tse-tung said to me, "Alright, get rid of that guy (Eliot)," I don't know what my response would be.

LAWRENCE ALLOWAY

Films: Painters Painting (1973)

The British-born art critic, curator, and historian Lawrence Alloway (1926–90) established himself in the New York art world in the 1960s. Credited with coining the term pop art, *he was preparing a major show and a book on the subject (*American Pop Art, *1974) when* Painters Painting *was released. Alloway's angry review in the* Nation *reveals a proprietary feeling about the New York art scene. The film was very well received on the whole; its severest critics were those inside the art world with rival claims on history and criticism. Alloway complains that de Antonio's documentary focuses on the 1970 Henry Geldzahler exhibit and therefore fails to portray newer, trendier art movements. He objects that it is the passé formalist critics who are allowed to contextualize the work. However, Alloway ends on a point that de Antonio himself conceded: the seemingly apolitical celebration of abstract art found in* Painters Painting *stands in contradiction to the intensely political nature of the filmmaker's own work.*

Painters Painting is a documentary film about the New York art world based, as Emile de Antonio admitted in an interview, on an exhibition at the Metropolitan Museum of Art four years ago called *New York Painting and Sculpture: 1940–1970*. In the interview (*Artforum,* March 1973) de Antonio characteristically gets it wrong and calls it "American Painting 1940 to 1970." The slip warns you of what is to come. The exhibition is buried in the body of the film but Henry Geldzahler, its curator, gets footage which is the show-biz equivalent of an acknowledgment. The original exhibition was flawed inasmuch as it presented the art of the period without benefit of later knowledge and research. Similarly, *Painters Painting* fails to come up to date, although the material was shot recently.

The argument begins like this: a heavy voice-over prologue (which turns out to be by Phil Leider) deals with the theme of national identity in the United States, about how the American Scene painters got it wrong and how the abstract expressionists, by taking up the issues of European modern art, made it. This section includes verbal contributions by various artists and critics, but unless you are acquainted with the 1940s–50s phase of the European/American agon it is a burden. Willem de Kooning, who came here from Holland about half a century ago and still doesn't speak English very well, says that Europe seemed small compared to American movies. Barnett Newman says, sure he's American but isn't art universal. Geldzahler links Jackson Pollock to Navajo sand painting, a topic that has expired in art criticism, but after all he has a big new audience so why try harder. Clement Greenberg says, yet once more, that Pollock must be judged like Rembrandt and Velázquez, because it's all the same at the top. The argument is never visualized: there is just a bunch of people repeating for the camera what they said years earlier to smaller and more informed audiences who have now stopped listening to them.

After this incoherent exposition of New York's centrality, de Antonio turns to a later generation, those artists who continued abstraction and those who kicked it. I will take his handling of the latter group first: Jasper Johns, Robert Rauschenberg, and Andy Warhol are all treated as characters, as personalities. Johns is part expository, part nervous barking laugh; Rauschenberg is shown sitting boyishly on top of a ladder addressing the lowly camera; and Warhol evades in uncharacteristically clumsy style while de Antonio, on screen, fidgets. One realizes the trouble: de Antonio is more used to editing existing material than shooting new footage, to cutting than keeping people talking. The interview as a form is not something for which he has any aptitude. He brutalizes every scene he enters, reducing the complex artists he talks with to stereotypes.

After Johns, Rauschenberg, and Warhol, Greenberg appears again to pronounce pop art "minor" and "easy," unlike real art, which is "difficult." Given this view, he has to pretend to like pop art so he can impute triviality to it as too likeable. After this the film settles down to what de Antonio seems really to esteem, more or less Greenbergian abstract artists: Helen Frankenthaler, Kenneth Noland, Frank Stella, Larry Poons, Jules Olitski. Noland allows that "judgment is crucial" and then equates judgment with "taste" and Olitski, standing before one of his expanses of sludge, discusses "drawing." Their interchangeable comments are stretched out to inordinate length. Indeed, in the case of Poons, de Antonio's poor judgment leads to such bathos as the artist saying, in reference to the effect of gravity on poured paint, "I've kinda gotten used to this floor," and when cropping a colossal picture, delivering the momentous line, "Let's take an inch off the left side."

Films, because of one's concentration on a lighted field in the dark and because of the coordination of sound and image, convey an absorbing sense of the present. In *Painters Painting,* however, this sense of the reality of the moment is compromised because the film rests on an obsolete view of the art world. There is a false present; for instance, the figure of de Kooning is real and the conversation takes on some of his presentness, but the subject of the talk is largely retrospective. The impression of authenticity is thus a cover for nostalgia. The sound recording is so loud and harsh that one feels that the physical reality of speech is being overemphasized to compensate for its remote content. Something similar happens with the younger abstract painters: the intensity with which each of them occupies a filmic present cannot be considered as representative of the art scene in New York now. They are certainly present in it, but they do not summarize its possibilities as they seemed to do a few years ago. Thus the topicality of the film is a put-on.

De Antonio is on record in the *Artforum* interview as placing his own work in the documentary "tradition of dissent," meaning he prefers *The Plough That Broke the Plains* to *The Louisiana Story.* However, his treatment of the art world of the recent past shows none of the political commitment supposed to inform the work of a man who made a scathing exposé of Senator Joseph McCarthy, admittedly six years after his death. Perhaps a reminder of de Antonio's other films is needed here: *Point of Order* was the McCarthy film, *Rush to Judgment* was about the Warren Commission, and *Millhouse* was about President Nixon. Indeed, he records that the impact of Kent State and Cambodia made him stop work on *Painters Painting* and make *Millhouse.*

Why is it then that the interaction of art and politics in the last few years escapes him? Why is Helen Frankenthaler the only woman in the film? He dismisses both Earthworks and Conceptual art because "their social meaning was negative," though he does not say anything about Noland's political significance. In the same loudmouthed interview, he proves his lack of competence in this area by expostulating: "Where are the guys twenty-five years old?" Actually, no one in *Painters Painting* could be called young except for Poons, and he is thirty-six. The fact is that de Antonio is out of touch with the art world, which is why his film is a nostalgic, abstract expressionist-based, Greenberg-oriented, politically backward perpetuation of the 1950s and early 1960s.

STANLEY KAUFFMANN

Films: Painters Painting *(1973)*

Stanley Kauffmann, who remained the New Republic's *movie critic for more than forty years, gave consistent praise to de Antonio in reviewing most of his major films. His recommendation of* Painters Painting *typifies the polite reception the documentary received outside of the infighting art world. Kauffmann displays little familiarity or resonance with contemporary painting, but he is sensitive to the role that the persona of Emile de Antonio played in the film and the way this personal relationship with the artists helped open them up.*

There are plentiful documentary films about painters—mostly short—and books of interviews, so Emile de Antonio has not precisely broken new ground in *Painters Painting,* but he has plowed it very well. This is a two-hour anthology of interviews with thirteen contemporary American artists, along with three critics, two curators, a dealer, and two collectors. The material is edited with modest deftness, shot with nice informality, recorded with—at times—too much informality. The interviews are in black and white, the paintings are in color. This was presumably an economic move, but it works out OK: it makes the frequent color shots of the paintings a series of climaxes and explications.

The secret of a film (or book) of this kind is the questioner, particularly when the subjects are veteran interviewees like famous artists. De Antonio, an experienced filmmaker *(In the Year of the Pig),* obviously has the respect of all the people he spoke to, as well as—in some cases—their long friendship. That was the crux, not his filmmaking skill. He is visible in some shots, invisible and unheard in others. He asked good questions, surely, because the overall impression of the film is that these painters are highly articulate. It's a common comment (or plaint) that much new art seems made to be written or spoken about. Not only by critics, apparently.

Barnett Newman (since deceased), Willem de Kooning (very witty), Robert Rauschenberg and Robert Motherwell and Frank Stella (a grave Woody Allen) are five of the most impressive. Jasper Johns seems coyly supercilious, and some others don't do themselves much good by public appearance. Andy Warhol is the only one photographed in an odd manner—from behind, seen in a mirror. (His own devising?) He is the least talky but not the least communicative. Whenever I'm tempted to believe that the Devil does not exist, I remember Andy Warhol. His brief interview here confirms a quiet satanism.

As to the content I note only that de Kooning says it was American films that brought him to America—their quality of light, particularly in silent comedies; and that the question remains very open as to whether these painters represent a great era or (as Hilton Kramer says in the picture) a mopping-up operation on some European movements. The two hours are fascinating, even if one wavers between the poles as I continually do. I can't imagine anyone remotely interested in contemporary art who would not find this film a lovely gift.

EMILE DE ANTONIO

My Brush with Painting (1984)

De Antonio embarked on several book-length manuscripts in the last two decades of his life, a biography of art dealer Leo Castelli and a stalled autobiography among them. The only one he was able to complete was the 1984 book adaptation of his 1972 film Painters Painting, *coauthored with Mitch Tuchman (a journalist and devotee who had interviewed him for the* Village Voice *in 1976). De Antonio's abridged version of the book's introduction appeared in* American Film.

Long before my 1973 film *Painters Painting,* there was my life in which I met the characters of the film. This is how it happened:

In 1946, as millions of Americans marched out of uniform, the arts were in the air in New York as they had never been before. Ex-soldiers found time and money to make art (all the arts) on the GI Bill—expenses were paid and a living allowance as well. In painting, legends were already sprouting: Pollock, de Kooning, Kline. Crowds drifted after them to the bars, the Cedar and later to Dillon's. We were out of one war and into a new one: Greece, the Marshall Plan, Korea, witch-hunts. The heroes of Stalingrad were now our enemies. And none of it made any difference to the new Bohemians who burst into Little Italy and beyond.

I joined that ex-GI Bohemian world. Not de Kooning's, not Pollock's. Picassoid forms swirled where I was, on Thompson and Spring Streets. Glass in hand, I squinted at enchanted, inauthentic abstraction and realism—the canvases of my friends, young veterans. The idea of being an artist rather than making art had caught them. The talk was high, the spirits free, the drink plentiful. Painters, even derivative painters, were tactile, had the best spaces, cared about good food. Anything was livelier than graduate school, where William York Tindall chased footnotes and Lionel Trilling studied gentility. Painting was chic. Did you see Picasso with his Afghan hound in *Vogue*?

Lois Long, after sharing a breakfast of old-fashioneds with me and a softball game with the Italian kids in the playground at MacDougal and Bleecker, said, "D, what the hell, why don't *you* become a painter?" I knew what she meant. I couldn't. I preferred being an artist without an art, a perpetual student.

One day in 1955, John Cage said, "D, I'd like you to meet two friends of mine. This is Bob Rauschenberg and this is Jasper Johns. They are *both* very good painters." They lived together in a loft downtown on Pearl Street when it was dark, narrow, and winding rather than dull and broad, as it is today. They were the first painters I knew whose work I also knew from the beginning and of whose gifts I was absolutely and immediately certain. I began visiting their studios frequently, we dined and drank together, and they took baths where I lived, both in Rockland County and the city. (Their loft was tubless—loft living in pre-boutique Soho meant whore's baths.) We talked constantly of painters and painting and food and drink. Once Jap (as Johns was known) made a dinner of mallards and wild rice. I brought Jack Daniels and invited some uptown people—Condé Nast editors, a few collectors—hoping to find Bob a gallery. Bob moved the big combine paintings so that Martha Jackson, who had an uptown gallery, could see them. She fell asleep, nodding and snoring quietly as a combine went by.

Most of the dealers I knew were sluggish in ideas, greedy, blind, and looking for complex and dramatic versions of the master-slave relationship with painters. I except Leo Castelli and a few others.

At the time, many second-generation abstract expressionists were puzzled and outraged because I preferred Bob's and Jap's work to theirs. During a poker game in East Hampton at Paul and Mimi Brach's (Helen Frankenthaler had invited me), these artists accused me of being an anarchist, a Dadaist, a wrecker. Maybe I *was* an anarchist; but that in no way lessened the fact that Rauschenberg and Johns were making a new art and a beautiful one. New art never threatens the past, only the present that is yesterday.

Jap called one day and said, "D, what are you doing next Thursday, the one after this one?" I said, "Why Jap, you know perfectly well I have no idea what I'm doing that far ahead. Why?" I went to see him that Thursday. All the paint cans, rags, old clothes, coffee cups, and papers had been cleared away. Floors mopped, walls painted white, more beautiful than any gallery. And on the walls were the works that were to sweep the art world before them: encaustic flags, plaster casts in boxes over targets and flags, a green target, numbers. I had seen all the works singly, but this showing was different. Bob was as happy as Jap that it was beautiful and that I loved it. The relationship between them was one of wit, affection, solicitude. Each spoke for the other, defended the work of the other. By 1970, Bob and Jap were separate and hostile. Once they had been their own club, but success stretched the friendship until it tore. Rauschenberg was older; success had come to Johns first.

I had struggled long in the space between my politics and my enjoyment and support of contemporary New York painting. I loved the painting and tried to live my politics. In 1969, my wife, Terry (she died in January 1975), suggested a film whose subject would be the New York painting of my time.

I disliked the films on painting that I knew. They were either arty, narrated in a gush of reverence, as if painting were made among angelic orders, or filmed with violent, brainless zooms on Apollo's navel, a celebration of the camera over the god. They revealed nothing at all about how or why a painting was made. Dislike of other films is not a bad place for a film to begin. There were problems nonetheless. The works were strewed across the world in different collections, and I didn't fancy trekking to Los Angeles, Japan, West Germany, and Italy to find collectors who thought "art" was collecting.

Henry Geldzahler and the Metropolitan Museum of Art solved that problem in 1969 with an exhibition for the Met's centennial called *New York Painting and Sculpture: 1940–1970*. Henry collected 408 works by forty-three artists. The press called it "Henry's show" and treated it like a campy scandal, which made it look like one. It wasn't. It was the best show of modern New York painting ever hung. Contemporary works of such quality will never again be brought together on such a scale and in such appropriately grand space, perfect for filming: Modern art is more fragile than that of the Renaissance and insurance costs are too high; the paint and parts are inferior, particularly in the early works of many painters; the big works don't move easily, and the big collages contain elements never made to move.

The show's opening was October 18, 1969. There were rock groups; the fashion world danced around David Smith sculptures. When I later filmed Andy Warhol, I asked about the opening.

> DE ANTONIO: What did you like best in Henry's show?
> WARHOL: Well, I never did see Henry's show.
> DE ANTONIO: You never went?
> WARHOL: I went to the opening but I didn't go inside. I pretended to be Mrs. Geldzahler and invited everybody in.

I met with Henry and Ashton Hawkins, also of the Met, and we agreed that my company, Turin Film Corporation, would have the exclusive right to film the exhibition. Two stipulations on their part: we could film only at night, when the museum was deserted, and had to pay to have three armed museum guards watch over us to preserve works from desecration. We spent many nights filming, and the guards successfully prevented me from stealing *Aristotle Contemplating the Bust of Homer*.

I had always liked black-and-white film better than color. I liked its tone, shades, limits. I decided to film all the artists in black-and-white 16mm and all the paintings in 35mm color. The film crew for *Painters Painting* was Ed Emshwiller, camera; Mary Lampson, sound; Marc Weiss, assistant camera. Hundreds of hours were spent lighting and filming the works I chose.

Modern painting is more difficult to film than older work because often the frames are metal and under intense film lighting they cause "hot spots" that distort the image. All the beers and sandwiches I provided the guards proved useful in the late hours of the night as Emshwiller and I attached gaffer tape over frames to neutralize them. The guards looked away.

Frank Stella had come to New York in 1958 and we became friends. He was fascinated because I knew Jap. Frank wanted a gallery, and he asked me to bring down Eleanor Ward of the Stable Gallery. (The Stable Gallery was a magic space—wood in the steel-and-stone city. Long before, the rich had stabled their horses there. There were no stairs, but a ramp between floors and the smell of horse piss on damp days.) Frank's loft was very small. He brought out the black paintings. Eleanor whispered, "D, why did you bring me here? I hate this; let's go." We left. Within a year Frank joined the Castelli Gallery and was in Dorothy Miller's show at the Museum of Modern Art, *Sixteen Americans*. Frank was twenty-four years old.

Frank's studio, where we filmed him in 1970, was on West Houston Street near Varick. He was congenial and organized. A sense of history and a Cuban cigar make for better footage than ahistorical staring at the floor. He could be edited without force because he knew where he had been and where he was. We filmed Frank before a work in progress, one of the "Protractor" series. When the image of the work dominated, I used color and Frank's voice; when Frank's voice and gesture worked better, I switched to black and white.

I had met Andy Warhol in 1958 through Tina Fredericks. When she had been art director at *Glamour,* Andy appeared with his portfolio. Tina looked at it and said, "Mr. Warhol, you're very gifted. I see gifted people every day. I need some drawings of shoes. I need them tomorrow morning at ten o'clock. Can you do them?" (Little did she know the wellsprings she had stirred. Andy not only loved shoes, he loved feet. His house was full of shoes. The first day I was there I picked up a pair. "What are these? A prop of some kind?" They were Carmen Miranda's.) The next day he appeared at *Glamour* with a stack of shoe drawings that propelled him to fortune: the I. Miller catalog, the *New York Times Magazine, Vogue.* He was famous in these circles before the public knew him. He bought a town house and collected paintings. He hid the paintings, but showed them to me: Johns, Rauschenberg, Fairfield Porter, two great Magrittes. Andy is New York and America, the coal miner's son who dines with the golden. I love his work and don't like his friends: old Hollywood stars of dubious parvenu politics. But, then, Dostoyevsky beat his wife; Stendhal and Balzac were toadies.

When I first knew Andy, he lived in a house at Eighty-ninth and Lexington, next door to the National Fertility Institute. He came to my small dinner parties at which I served smoked salmon, Dom Pérignon, and grass. Andy did extraordinary menus that were the size of paintings, big enough to frame. I introduced him to a fashion model whom I later married. Andy was fascinated—he stared at her and said, "Why, D, she looks just like David. Why don't you marry David?"

Andy remembered everything; he read every gossip column. He wrote fan letters to Tab Hunter. Of course, he had always wanted to be a painter. He masked his past. He denied he ever went to college. But he did; he graduated at nineteen. I helped Andy; I enjoyed it without regret.

We filmed Andy in his studio at 33 Union Square—a long space, most of a floor with floor-to-ceiling windows on the east and west. I knew long before the crew arrived exactly how I wanted to film him: Andy and I on a park bench between the two mirrors, Emshwiller standing behind us, shooting over our heads into the mirrors. Andy improvised by adding Brigid Polk to the scene. Andy lived in mirrors. (He was the prince of voyeurs. Not a peeper at all. People came to Andy to do whatever it was they wanted to do so that Andy could watch or film.) Thus, in long shots, Emshwiller could be seen filming; Mary doing sound; and Brigid, Andy, and I talking on a park bench. As we filmed and talked, Andy audiotaped everything. At the time he was audiotaping his entire life with others: Tennessee and Edie, Baby Jane and Nureyev. There is a social history of strange times in Andy's tape collection—enough to make five writers rich and famous. The atmosphere at 33 Union Square was so odd that the crew didn't enjoy Andy as it had Frank. Andy's brush with death a couple of years before, his chic, his quiet voice, his eyes that revealed so little—all this made them ill at ease.

The crew loved Barney Newman, with his monocle and mustache. Even the camera loved him. He was more American than Myles Standish.

Impatient, he had waited long for success and he didn't give an inch: in the thirties he had run for mayor of New York on the Trotsky ticket. Newman didn't need critics; he didn't need museums; the beautiful old walrus had triumphed. We loved his camera presence, his sense of himself, the flash awareness of what he was saying and giving, his pride, his quick anger, his glass of what his wife Annalee assured us was water, and one cigarette after the other with his emphysematous wheeze.

He died a few weeks after we filmed him, and Mary worked hard to cut out the wheeze without wrecking the rhythm of his speech. She did it, too. His painting was majestically lean. After his death we filmed the work in his downtown studio.

In 1973 I wrote the introduction to a catalog for an exhibition of New York work traveling to the Moderna Museet in Stockholm. Pontus Hultén was curator there. I had first encountered his name in an article entitled "Three Great Painters: Churchill, Hitler, and Eisenhower," which he had written for Alfred Leslie's magazine, the *Hasty Papers*. I knew that someday I would become the friend of the man who wrote such a piece. I did, and we went sailing in the Baltic. I finished my introduction to Hultén's catalog with two lines that still express my belief: "As for the dilemma between art and politics, I still believe in an art of quality and radical politics. The two are not incompatible."

Underground

Figure 30. Cinematographer Haskell Wexler framed de Antonio interviewing five Weatherpeople on May Day 1975. Frame enlargement from *Underground* (1976).

EMILE DE ANTONIO

How It Began (1976)

The director's acquaintance with the legendary record producer Moses Asch led to the release of two de Antonio sound tracks on the Folkways label. The "voice material" from Millhouse *was produced in 1979, a double album with a complete transcript. Folkways released* Underground *during the movie's theatrical run and included a reprint of the* Rolling Stone *exposé (Peter Biskind and Marc N. Weiss, "The Weather Underground, Take One," November 6, 1975) about the making of the clandestine documentary. De Antonio's liner notes give a succinct account of his political evolution from the hedonist who was "out to lunch" in the 1950s to the unabashed revolutionary who was willing to join forces with radical outlaws.*

I have been making political films since 1961 when Dan Talbot and I planned *Point of Order*. My active political life had begun long before—in the late thirties when I was a student at Harvard. The bang that ended World War II sliced my Marxism right down the middle. Praxis fell away. Without a party, without a machine for action, I hugely and self-indulgently savored the contradictions of Cold War capitalism, its piety and hypocrisy, the opulent click of the putter in the White House. I was out to lunch. My hedonism and egoism weren't aberrational. A Marxist in the USA during the fifties was like a Martian; no base, no solid space. Real change and revolution seemed a light-year and a day away. Meanwhile, on with the party.

In 1960, my politics, revived and twice-born, coalesced with my work in film. A series of films, analytical and critical, were the result: *Point of Order*, 1963; *Rush to Judgment*, 1967; *In the Year of the Pig*, 1969; *America Is Hard to See*, 1970; in 1971, *Millhouse: A White Comedy*, a political biography which got me on the "enemies list"; and in 1972, *Painters Painting*, real questions: art and politics, art versus politics.

And then Watergate. Watergate was a crime in which the thief was paid to slink away; business; an internal affair of the U.S. ruling class. The more things seemed to change, the less they did. Watergate proved the system worked, proved that it worked [for] imperialism, racism, sexism, oppression anywhere. I felt tired.

Until 1974 when I read *Prairie Fire: Political Statement of the Weather Underground*. The Weather Underground? Our perception of them was formed by the media. McLuhan got it wrong. The message really is: whoever owns the media owns the message. So what we saw in the *Times* and CBS were trendy Wonder Bread reality sandwiches. Artifical coloring added. One-sided, sensationalist, all about "crazed terrorists" and bombers. But the people who wrote and distributed *Prairie Fire* weren't crazed terrorists. Their voices were strong, analytical, rational.

I wanted to make a film with them, collectively. And to find people who would be interested in making a new kind of didactic, revolutionary film. We formed a collective, Mary Lampson, Haskell Wexler, and I. Forming is easier than being. Haskell worked as a cameraperson for four or five days; the collective dwindled to two and Mary and I spent most of a year making the film. With a lot of help from many people.

This record is not the official voice of the Weather Underground; their writings are that. This record is the sound track of a film which we shot May 1, 1975. Since then, the Weather Underground has undoubtedly changed its position on certain issues, shifted slightly on others. Good signs, signs of acknowledging contradiction, of growth, of learning to try to make the revolution by passing through error by criticism/self-criticism. August 25, 1976.

GAGE, JIM, AND REBECCA

Mallards and Trombones by Lake Mendota: An Interview with Emile de Antonio and Mary Lampson (1976)

The Dada title was suggested by de Antonio as he noted the sounds backing this interview conducted on the lakefront campus of the University of Wisconsin. De Antonio often visited Madison, not only because the State Historical Society of Wisconsin agreed to maintain his personal archive, but because UW students instigated some of the most pronounced antiwar and radical political activities on any campus between Columbia and Berkeley. In March 1976, Glenn Silber interviewed him for the Daily Cardinal, *the school's official student paper. (Silber went on to direct the 1979 film* The War at Home, *documenting the decade of political unrest in that city.) But the underground paper* Free for All *published this interview on the occasion of* Underground's *world premiere in Madison on May Day. The incognito interviewers clearly modeled themselves on the Weather collective recorded in de Antonio and Lampson's film.*

The following is a condensed version of an hour-long discussion with Emile de Antonio and Mary Lampson on April 29, the day their new film Underground *premiered in Madison. The title of this article was suggested by de Antonio in reference to the background noise that accompanied the interview on the Memorial Union Terrace.*

FREE FOR ALL: We were wondering what the political strategy was in producing a film on the underground now.

DE: Well, this is when the underground is happening. I interpreted the act of printing and publishing *Prairie Fire* as a coming out; as a reaching out; as a way to break out of, in a sense, the prison of clandestine activity and reach other people. And I thought about it and, since I'm involved in film and I liked what the book stood for, I wondered if they would be interested in making a film and I got word to them.

MARY: The film is just an extension of what they started with the publication of *Prairie Fire*, which was to put out more than just the communiqués that accompanied all of their actions.

They decided that it was important for them to begin a process of defining where they were.

FFA: How is it that you decided to bring the film here, premiere it here?

DE: The reason we are here is a complicated one. There's no doubt that the Army Math Research Center—what it stood for, the years of demonstrations against it, and the actual blowing up of the building—comes to terms with one of the major themes of our film, which is that you have to take responsibility for the use of violence in armed struggle in changing society and attempting to bring about revolutionary change. That act confronted those problems head-on. We don't intend to speak for the Weather Underground, but in our outtakes we have a precise statement in which WUO says it supports the action of Karl Armstrong [who had helped bomb the U.S. Army Math Research Center in 1970 and been convicted of the murder of a worker who died in the blast].

MARY: Another reason is that we like the idea of it coming to another part of the country and having it shown first here.

DE: Well, Madison isn't your ordinary Midwest community, although it seems to be much more passive than when I've been here in the past. I think most academic communities are simply quieter now than they were; less political.

FFA: How does this fit into your feeling that there is more potential for radical change today than there was in the sixties?

MARY: While on the surface that may not seem to be true, every day there's a challenge to U.S. imperialism all over the world. The victory in Vietnam was an incredible blow. Also, the growth of a strong independence movement for Puerto Rico; something that is going to have incredible ramifications in this country.

All those things, even though they're not happening directly in this country, affect what happens here. Take New York City and the things that are going on there; the massive cutbacks in social services. People are fighting against that kind of thing and it's being done in a very deep and lasting way. It may not be flashy and it may not make the news a lot, but that kind of thing is happening all over the place and the press has a stake in not reporting it.

The task of the left is to begin to carry out what I think the Hard

Times Conference was organized to do; to overcome the fragmentation and splintering of the past, and really begin to build broad coalitions.

FFA: How much of the process itself was a collective process—writing the movie and directing it—involving the Weather Underground?

DE: They are the film's actors; its protagonists. They exercised a strong sense of security over us. They laid down all the ground rules; how the film should be done, where, when, and how much of their faces could be shown. All this had to be agreed upon before there could be any contact. One of their demands from the beginning was a hard, principled stand against the government, against any cooperation with a grand jury. The whole film would have collapsed if I said to them at our first meeting: Well, if they subpoena me, I'll cooperate.

Their sense of togetherness, their collective sense, was an example to us. We fought out a long war that emerged as a collective victory for us, them, and for the film. To answer your question, there is no director of this film, no writer, no producer. The credits are alphabetical.

FFA: How do you attempt to politically motivate or enlighten people with this film who don't already have some degree of political consciousness?

DE: I feel very strongly that as a revolutionary film, the duty of this film is to seek an audience wider than the audience that already shares our ideas. And the reason I brought up the government is that I think it will do that for us.

The other thing you own when you make this kind of film is time. This film will be around for a long time. Its the only thing that exists in a serious context about a revolutionary group in this country. Ordinary films, which are by definition nonrevolutionary, act on an audience, force an audience to be passive.

Whereas we are trying in our film to make you become a part of that film, to question that film and the world you live in. We're not trying to snow you with it.

I think we've been very lucky and instrumental in getting a lot of publicity for them because of the mistakes the government made when it tried to suppress our film. That started a whole propaganda campaign going that is quite rare in the history of film.

We spent no money in producing that campaign the way Hollywood does; yet, we ended up in *Rolling Stone*, the *New York Times*, on the press wire services, Cronkite. You name it, we were there. It's created an audience for the picture.

MARY: I think this film is really an educational tool and hopefully a lot of people who don't agree with the ideas in it will see it and be very challenged by it.

People's impressions of that group are formed by things that are totally false; by images projected by the media. And on the level of being able to come in and see that these are five human beings that are talking to me; that they aren't the monsters that I think of them as being; on that level it's going to challenge. That's a political thing already.

FFA: You must have gone somewhat underground yourselves to have made the film. Didn't you experience some difficulty in getting away from security?

MARY: Nobody knew what we were doing when we were filming. We told absolutely no one about it.

DE: In fact, just by luck, I was planning to do a film about [Philip] Agee's book, *Inside the Company*. I had just spent ten days with Agee in England, and it set up, unintentionally, a kind of cover, a false trail that just couldn't have been any further away from the Weather Underground. In fact, we were totally unobserved until we committed a horrible blunder on the last day of shooting. Then, within four days the entire U.S. government knew.

FFA: What was the blunder?

MARY: We spent the third day of filming in the street interviewing people. We did it successfully at an unemployment center in L.A. which is in the film.

DE: The Weather Underground people did the interviewing.

MARY: Right. Later we found out there was a strike going on at a hospital. This was exactly the kind of struggle we had been discussing in the movie, so they said, Well, gee, lets go to the hospital and talk to the people there and find out what's going on. There were, probably, as a matter of routine, Red Squad photographers there. What we assumed happened was that someone took our pictures and later someone looked at the pictures and said: Jesus Christ! That's Jeff Jones and Kathy Boudin. Then the FBI started snooping around Haskell's house because we had been using his car. Very slowly they pieced together the pieces, but by that time we had finished the shooting. It was a pretty dumb place to go, though.

FFA: What do you feel are the future implications of the Weather Underground Organization?

MARY: I think they've been very responsive in recent years by publishing *Osawatomie* and by constantly putting forth their own analysis of society. If you really believe that a revolution is going to happen, inevitably there's going to be a violent confrontation. Obviously, a strong underground is going to play a very important role at that time. I mean, just being able to produce this *(Osawatomie)* is mind-blowing. There's a press somewhere in this country churning this out. Think what that could mean in like ten, fifteen, or twenty years; the tools, the skills they have developed. I think Bernardine says it in the film, that it's not a trick, that they don't *outwit* the FBI. There must exist in this country a fairly large apparatus that does support them and other underground groups. So they seem pretty small, but they're definitely not weak.

FFA: In what ways does this film differ from your others?

DE: The others are all negative critiques of the society and this is a positive view of a revolutionary underground group. And it's much harder to do a positive thing.

There's a difference between being didactic and being preachy. They may sound the same but they aren't. And there's a difference between being political and sounding like fans of the Weather Underground. We're not fans. It was a political collaboration and this is what disturbs the government. We never made any pretense of objectivity. It's a film by us *and them*. The film was made together with them.

FFA: You once said that the birth of SDS was a beautiful thing and I'm wondering how you assess the evolution of SDS into the Weather Underground.

DE: SDS was destroyed not only by its internecine strife and sectarianism. Its strength, its real movement came from spearheading the antiwar movement. And when the war aspect was wiped out, SDS began to flounder and split. And that, of course, is one of the reasons for this film, too. Out of all that floundering and splitting . . . out of all those elements, the Weather Underground seemed to develop the best ideas of self-criticism; seemed to be able to function in terms of capitalizing on their mistakes and moving on to a new position. It seemed to have a potential for growth, to develop leadership quality and an effective way to communicate. As I say, I didn't see that anywhere else, until I read *Prairie Fire*. And little did I know how important that glance through a book with a red cover and black type . . . what it would mean all these months later.

LUCINDA FRANKS

Rendezvous with the Weather Underground (1976)

Although de Antonio was not part of the feminist movement, his consciously egalitarian collaboration with women filmmakers and his relationships with bright, accomplished women made him an appropriate subject for a Ms. *magazine article.* Underground *not only featured the work of Mary Lampson but was also a profile of a political collective that grappled with gender equality, admitting to "heavy male chauvinism," Franks writes, while sounding like "politically impassioned Stepford Wives."*

As a journalist for United Press International, Lucinda Franks shared the 1971 Pulitzer Prize (with Thomas Powers) for her reporting on Diane Oughton, one of the Weatherpeople killed while making explosives in a Greenwich Village town house. By 1976 she was covering the film beat for the New York Times, *but here provides* Ms. *with both an insightful reading of* Underground *and a report on how Kathy Boudin's mother reacted to seeing her fugitive daughter in de Antonio's film.*

During the past five and a half years, they have bombed the Pentagon, the State Department, the U.S. Capitol, and twenty-two other targets without getting caught; they have traveled through an elaborate network of "safe houses" and overground support, eluding an intensive hunt by intelligence forces and often living openly in spite of their pictures being on the Ten Most Wanted Posters.

They are not the IRA or the PLO, but our own Weather Underground. And oddly, a great number of people assume they are a half-dormant band of fugitives; some even believe they died off in the early seventies. The rather extraordinary fact of their perseverance in this year, 1976, has been lost in the flash fire of economic bulletins, political scandals, and celebrity soap operas that has raced across the tops of our newspapers.

In part, this is because the group has been invisible and inaccessible.

It took Emile de Antonio, the radical filmmaker *(In the Year of the Pig)* to bring them out: he wrote them an effusive letter after reading *Prairie Fire*, the Weather Underground's *Das Kapital*, proposing to make a "film weapon" that would go "Bang, bang, bang!" Unfortunately, the film makes more of a plaintive sigh than a bang, and it is less a weapon than an echo chamber for the guns of the past.

In a sense, however, that is *Underground*'s strength. For we come away from de Antonio's filmed meetings with the group in a boarded-up safe house in Los Angeles not having learned any lessons, but with some strong impressions about the progression of the last ten years of American history.

Underground is comprised of talks between the filmmakers—de Antonio; Mary Lampson, the film editor; and Haskell Wexler, who stands in a pea-green T-shirt, often grinning as he films—and most of the core of the original Weatherpeople—Cathy Wilkerson, Kathy Boudin, Bernardine Dohrn, Jeff Jones, and Billy Ayers. To protect their identities, Wexler films them from behind, or into a mirror reflecting the back of their heads, or through a scrim—gauzy material that blurs facial features. In the background is a quilt sewn by the Weatherpeople, reading "The Future Will Be What We the People Struggle to Make It."

As counterpoint to the Weatherpeople's rhetorical rap, film clips—of bombs raining down on Vietnam, of bloodied heads on the steps of the Pentagon, of angry, crippled veterans tossing their medals symbolically over the White House fence—cut in and out like thunderclaps. And the Weatherpeople assembled in the room speak kind of like politically impassioned Stepford Wives—charming and gentle, but one gets the feeling there might be wires and little motors beneath the skin. They tell us little that we didn't already know about the state of the nation and little about themselves as people. We concentrate on watching instead of listening: like men titillated by the partial nakedness of a Playboy Bunny, we study with rapt attention the hunched blue back of Kathy Boudin, the floppy hat Jeff Jones wears, his pant leg, the red sweater of Bernardine Dohrn crossing the room to pour a pot of steaming tea.

The impact is eerie. We hear the tones of their voices—soft, childlike, reasoned, unexcited. As though they were a bunch of kids discussing whether to go to the beach or bowling. But they are not kids—they are in their thirties, their twenties spent up in the resistance—and what they were talking about was not for play.

We see clips of the blood-soaked mattress of Black Panther Fred Hampton after he was shot by Chicago police. We know what Dohrn means when she says "America created us"; the Weather Underground is only a continuation of a historical reality. Just like the attempt to halt production of de Antonio's work (the government issued, then dropped subpoenas for all the raw materials of the film) recalls McCarthy-era tactics against Hollywood.

The five Weatherpeople—one suspects that the total strength of the group is not much more than that—who talk to us do reveal certain things about their organization. They confess to having been wrong in their demands that everyone on the left renounce the system and wage armed struggle; they admit to heavy male chauvinism and arrogant posturing (the voice of the men confessing this is brilliantly set off by early clips of Ayers and Jones looking belligerent and cocky, at a demonstration, in dark glasses, sucking in their cigarettes). They talk sorrowfully about the Greenwich Village town-house explosion, which killed three of their members in 1970. They emphasize how they reevaluated their tactics that night "in ten different cities," how they decided to go underground, and how they now do not think of themselves as a terrorist organization, their bombings being aimed against property, never people. They stress the importance of continuing their bimonthly magazine, *Osawatomie,* as well as carrying out bombing actions in preparation for the eventual rising up of the working class: in the final scene, the Weatherpeople weave through an unemployment line interviewing the out-of-work, all of whom express despair and frustration about the way the country is being run.

One of the main complaints that have been leveled against *Underground* is that the interviews, with the backs of heads talking tag words, do not come across as real. It is true that we don't get underneath the first layer of the five fugitives, but we are somehow left with a rather strong sense of them. We see Dohrn's hands, thinner and more veined with years, the streak of gray in her hair; we hear how Jeff Jones wakes up every morning wondering how many times he's going to be nervous that day. Above all, somehow, we understand part of what motivates them to live the harrowing life that they live. It is clear when Jones, an edge to his voice, insists they have accomplished something—"who would have thought Ho Chi Minh would win?"—and when Dohrn says they don't believe in the cynical maxim that one person can't matter. It is obvious, that to them, whatever the cost, they as individuals are going to matter.

LARRY McDONALD

Pro-Terrorist Propaganda in the Movies (1975)

Although he never received the amount of opprobrium heaped on "Hanoi Jane" Fonda, de Antonio was the subject of this attack submitted for the Congressional Record *by a newly elected, ultraconservative Georgia Democrat. Representative Lawrence Patton McDonald, chairman of the John Birch Society, studied the likes of de Antonio, the Weather Underground, and the Socialist Workers Party and shortly thereafter authored a book called* Trotskyism and Terror: The Strategy of Revolution *(1977). His anticommunist record keeping here names the names of the Hollywood personalities who supported de Antonio's right to film* Underground.

Ironically, in September 1983, McDonald, the last of the unreconstructed McCarthyites, died at the hand of the Soviet military. He was aboard Korean Airlines flight 007, which was shot down by the USSR when the plane flew over contested airspace.

Mr. Speaker, the Weather Underground Organization terrorists have taken responsibility for a whole series of bombings, including one right here in the Capitol and one in the State Department earlier this year. Now a group of Hollywood's left-wing crackpots are planning to do a propaganda puff piece film on these criminals.

The ringleader of the Hollywood crew is the notorious Emile de Antonio, the maker of a number of pseudodocumentary left-wing propaganda films, including one smearing the late Senator Joseph McCarthy and another supporting the Communist aggressors in Vietnam.

De Antonio and some of his staff members met with the Weather Underground terrorists and filmed them. However, de Antonio promised that "Every mistake of the camera in which a subject's face is seen has been destroyed." He certainly would not want the police to use his films to apprehend the criminals.

An attempt was made to bring de Antonio and some of his colleagues before a grand jury investigating terrorism. They came with their attorney, Leonard Boudin, whose daughter is a Weather Underground fugitive last seen scrambling from the collapsing Greenwich Village town house blown up accidentally by her Weatherman comrades. Boudin, himself, long a supporter of Communist causes, was once a registered agent of Castro's Cuban Communist regime.

The subpoenas were later withdrawn, but not until a whole crew of Hollywood's radical chic colony signed a statement deploring the attempts of the Federal Bureau of Investigation and the grand jury to gather evidence against the Weather Underground terrorists.

The dishonor roll, consisting of many people who have grown rich because of the American filmgoing public, is as follows:

We support the right of people to make a film about any subject, and specifically the right of these people to make a film about the Weather Underground Organization—and we deplore the efforts of the FBI and the grand jury to prevent them from completing their work.

Hal Ashby, Warren Beatty, Ed Begley Jr., Harry Belafonte, Alan Bergman, Steve Blouner, Peter Bogdanovich, Jeff Bridges, Mel Brooks, Peter Davis, Sally Field, Cinda Firestone, William Friedkin, Henry Jaglom, Elia Kazan, Arthur Knight, Shirley MacLaine, Terry Malick, Daniel Melnick, Jack Nicholson, Arthur Penn, Frank Pierson, Bob Rafelson, Toby Rafelson, Artie Ross, Bert Schneider, Rip Torn, Robert Towne, Jon Voight, Robert Wise, Paul Williams, Harriet van Horne, Jay Cocks, Ben Cunningham, Eddie Deutsch, Daniel Ellsberg, Jim Frye, Robert Gottleib, Duane Johnson, George Lang, Michael Meeropol, Earl Ofari, Ron Ridenour, Romona Ripsotn, Stanley Sheinbaum, Jack Scott, Micki Scott.

DAN GEORGAKAS
PAUL McISAAC

Interview with Emile de Antonio and Mary Lampson (1976)

Georgakas, editor of the leftist film review Cineaste, *and McIsaac, an activist at Pacifica radio, interviewed the makers of* Underground *at the time of its New York release. Generally sympathetic to de Antonio's politics, the interviewers nevertheless took him to task for sympathizing with the doctrinaire and violence-oriented Weatherpeople. David Dellinger's* Liberation *magazine published a transcription of the interview that WBAI-FM first broadcast. The following version is abridged.*

What defines *Underground* is that it is a picture of the Weatherpeople as they want us to see them. For half a dozen years they have eluded authorities while carrying out bombings and other political activities. In *Underground* they present the political perspective which has motivated them and which they hope will find wide acceptance among the American people.

In the following interview, Paul McIsaac, the film commentator for WBAI-FM in New York City, and I discussed some of these issues with Emile de Antonio and Mary Lampson. We try to deal with some of the limitations of the film, seeking amplification of the motives and views of the filmmakers themselves. The interview was broadcast live one week before the New York premiere of the film.

DAN: *I wonder what audience you had in mind for this film. From the beginning it is based on a lot of leftist assumptions. We get a lot of early footage depicting Ho Chi Minh and Fidel as heroes, and then we see Malcolm X and H. Rap Brown talking about violence: I feel that those who come to the film informed from personal involvement in political struggles can relate to those things easily. But what about the average working American, white or black? You seem to have given up on reaching them before you began.*

Figure 31. De with Mary Lampson. She was his closest collaborator, providing editing and sound recording on *America Is Hard to See, Millhouse, Painters Painting,* and *Underground.* Reproduced courtesy of Art Gallery of Ontario.

DE: I frankly don't believe that. One thing that we are living with, particularly in the age of television and in the age of Ford, is what we might call the discontinuity of history. History is broken up for us each day into tiny fragments on television, which means there is no continuity; we have no historical perspective. Part of the idea behind this film when we originally talked with the Weatherpeople was that they believe in history and we believe in history and we don't want to see the 1960s washed down the drain. One of our first ideas, one of the first lessons of the film, was to place our own history, the history we've all lived through, in some kind of perspective. Also, we're asking people to understand how white, middle-class people, who went through the civil rights movement and the peace movement, ended up as revolutionaries who went underground on March 6, 1970, and have been there ever since.

PAUL: *It seems to me that you were up against a very difficult thing in not being able to shoot the characters face on, as we're used to seeing. I remember reading that Haskell said, "I'm going crazy, this should be a radio program. I want to come in and get people's faces and get their expressions."*
DE: I don't agree with Haskell. I regard not seeing the faces as a decided advantage. Most people go to films and are lulled into a filmic experience—the whole business of synchronized voice and image. I think that we demand something in this film that most films don't. The idea is to force people to look at a film in a different way. Ordinarily, film creates an atmosphere of passivity. You sit in the seat and it washes over you, like *All the President's Men.* We make demands on the audience. We may fail at times, but we try

to force them to think about all of these things that have gone through their lives—the things I think the government and the media do their best to make us forget.

PAUL: *I'd like to leap right to what I think is the most controversial part of the film—the tactics, past and present, of the Weather Underground. It seems to me that the analysis of why the step to armed propaganda underground was necessary could really be disagreed with.*

DE: We are doing an evolutionary history of how the Weather Underground got to violence, not how the movement got to violence. The point that the Weather Underground makes in the film, the point that they make in *Prairie Fire*, is that they were driven to violence. Jeff Jones gives a really great example. He says that in the early days of the antiwar movement they made a poster of a mutilated, burned, charred body of a napalm victim. They tried to put that poster into the subways, and the Transit Authority denied them that right. By the time the Supreme Court cleared that poster four years later, nobody gave a damn about posters. It was the government that forced other people into raising the ante, and it was the Weather Underground who accepted that ante. There has been no successful revolution anywhere, whether you take Fidel or Lenin or Mao—you name it—that was made without armed propaganda. Allende's revolution was made without armed propaganda, and it was unsuccessful. It was wiped out by reactionary arms. We are making a case for armed propaganda. That's the point of the film. I think the government creates violence. The government steps it up. And it's not even taking sides to say, "I believe in armed propaganda, I believe in violence." It's simply a historical recognition of the fact that change will not come by the ballot. Are you going to tell me that Jimmy Carter and Jerry Ford constitute a real choice? Or that Nixon and Humphrey did?

PAUL: *No, but that's not a very fair argument to say that the choice is Jimmy Carter or premature organizing for an armed revolution. When you name Lenin and Mao and so forth, you're talking about preindustrial countries, and they are really quite different. A very telling example is that the Vietnamese themselves and many Cubans, including Che, often reiterated that they saw the role for revolutionaries in this country not as organizing a clandestine group of thirty-seven people out of 200 million, but rather as understanding that this is a very complex country that does have, in fact, other forms of resistance.*

DAN: *The Weather Underground talks about Cuba and Vietnam a lot, but America is an advanced industrial country. Perhaps we should be studying Italy and the extraparliamentary movements, what's happened in France, what's happened in countries like our own, instead of focusing on small underdeveloped Third World countries.*

PAUL: *I think there is an argument to be made that, in fact, armed struggle is premature; real differences have been brought about through mass efforts, through those so-called pacifist antiwar movements.*

MARY: I don't think that we or the Weather Underground would disagree that the mass demonstrations made a significant contribution toward ending the war. We are not putting forth this type of organization as being the only way, but as being a very valid part of a much broader thing. In the very beginning of the film, Billy Ayers talks about seeing the building of an underground as a base to study, a base to grow, away from the eye of the government. You can be sure that if the Weather Underground were above ground, it would be under tremendous pressure from the state.

PAUL: *I think that if the Weather Underground were above ground and had made the kind of mistakes they have made, they would not be the leaders of the movement.*

DAN: *One thing that bothered me about the film is the attitude "Well, they made mistakes" and then simply go on to something else. You don't have a feeling for what those mistakes were, except for male arrogance, which comes across as a genuine lesson that has been learned.*

MARY: Well, in a film you have eighty-eight minutes of time and a lot of things that you want to cover. I think that the change that is expressed in the whole discussion of male arrogance is true. And therefore you can expand it that they have, indeed, changed in other areas.

DAN: *Why is that automatic?*

MARY: Because I think that their actions over the past five years have been principled and responsible actions, very different from the type of actions done [in] 1969 and 1970. And we all know that they certainly felt the direct results of their responsibility in the explosion in the town house that took the lives of three of their people.

DAN: *But there's a difference between getting hurt yourself and getting other people hurt, which was a consequence of a lot of the Weatherpeople's activities.*

DE: They took the chances themselves, and the mistakes they made were the mistakes of *passion*. That's an element that is notably lacking in our political life. Nobody today could condone Bernardine Dohrn's remarks at the time when Manson's people murdered Sharon Tate. The Weather Underground itself has criticized that position. That was a hell of a mistake, but it was a mistake of passion that had to do with passionate outrage at the smugness of middle-class consuming culture, that dominant culture that still permeates and runs most of this country. People always make mistakes, and the Weather Underground will continue to make mistakes, but mistakes of that magnitude stopped after the town-house explosion. What you have after that are approximately twenty-five armed actions, all directed against symbols of property and the state, all announced in advance. No one was hurt in any of them, each had a precise target—the U.S. Capitol; Kennicott Copper, because of Chile; the bank in Rockefeller Center, because of the cement workers' strike. But they aren't locked into this violence. The very fact that *Prairie Fire* came out, that *Osawatomie* is being published six times a year, is one of the greatest feats in the history of the underground in this country (and there *is* a history of underground in this country).

DAN: *I have to disagree with that. Across the country there's about 650 small presses, and all these people do is print magazines. Some are literary, some are political. I don't see the great feat in printing such a magazine. I really don't. Running a printing press is relatively easy, and there are literally thousands who do that in the United States.*
DE: Yes, but there's a price on their head. Every move they make is a move that is dogged by the FBI. It's not just another underground press. Let's not use the word *underground* loosely. The actual printing is truly underground. Even the sound of the press could be a clue, wherever it is.

PAUL: *I'm still wondering about what role you think the Weather Underground has at this time. They are moving clandestinely, with the force of the FBI and everybody else chasing them, and I'm bothered by the fact that they do not represent a constituency. There is an aboveground support group, Prairie Fire study groups, etc., but, still, it seems to me, there is a real danger of elitism. They are not in a position to have a dialogue with others. I almost feel that the Weather Underground is more of a historical development from the Yippies than it is from the antiwar movement. The antiwar movement always had a grassroots base, whereas the Yippies were primarily effective at manipulation of the media. The armed propaganda, that is, the bombings, that the Weather Underground is involved in is effective essentially as an extremely sophisticated kind of media manipulation.*
DE: It's not that simple. We mustn't think of them as people engaged solely in armed propaganda. We know that they have worked and organized with other groups and that they are in close contact with fairly good-sized revolutionary groups throughout the country. They refused to discuss this with us on film because it could compromise the other groups and themselves and create patterns that the police and FBI could detect. But they are not

all that isolated. They move above ground. I remember the very first meeting I had with them. I was overwhelmed by the fact that when we met after the most careful kind of planning, we wandered into a restaurant and spent four hours talking about the possibility of the film. They made it clear to us, and they mentioned in the film, that they do organize.

DAN: *I feel a lack of real ideology in their writings. They see themselves as revolutionary leaders, but even their discussion of armed struggle is without a developed philosophical, organizational, or programmatic perspective. My own view is that they will be replaced with something quite different and far more substantial.*

DE: I think there's a shortage of ideology in general on the left today. I think that this is the time for action and the time for armed propaganda. Maybe the Weather Underground will produce an ideology and maybe they won't. I think they're trying to. *Prairie Fire* has no great, brilliant, new insights, but it's an attempt to bring everything together that has fallen apart. It's not the Communist Party, USA that will do that. This is the closest we have come to putting together an ideology that people can gather around. As you pointed out, there are Prairie Fire organizing committees all over the country; the web is much greater than it seems to be, whether there are 37 or 200 or 237 people underground. I suspect that if conditions go on as they are, the underground itself is going to be forced into another posture.

PAUL: *I'd like to reject the notion that the vanguard Marxist-Leninist model for revolutionary change is a workable model in America. The most successful mass organizing in this country did not have an authoritarian trend to it.*

MARY: I don't think there's anything in our film that puts forward the idea that the Weather Underground sees themselves as a vanguard. I think it's simply stated that they see themselves as a part of exactly the kind of movement you were describing.

PAUL: *I have to disagree. There are several things in the film that make me feel that they do see themselves in a vanguard position. For example, they talk in extremely militaristic terms, less than before, but it's still there. They have a model of America as a fascist state, and they are trying to organize at least the underground aspect of resistance in a military way. It comes across to me in the film that they see themselves as military figures, as generals, as a military force.*

DE: Bernardine Dohrn says very clearly that if it were possible to make a revolution without violence that they would be for it. But the history of the United States has included violence from the very beginning: the first

Indians that Columbus encountered in this hemisphere, the whole history of four hundred years of treatment of blacks, and on and on. The labor movement began in bloodshed and ended in bureaucracy. All of these things indicate that there is something wrong and inadequate about the normal responses to events in American history. I think the significance of this film and the reason we're happy it's going to play in commercial theaters is because it is going to raise important questions. Is the Weather Underground an elite? What is the history of this country? How will change take place if it takes place? If there is a revolution, is there any reason to believe that it will be voted in or is it going to occur because of an armed action? We don't care if people disagree with us as long as there is a dialogue. This is a propaganda film; it is a didactic film meant to confront people. Even though you disagree, you both reacted extremely passionately. We would like nothing more than to have a dialogue about these points.

DAN: *I was going to say that I think that's one of the real strengths of the film. I think the film is very valuable in bringing a lot of these questions out and making us think about ourselves. I only wish you had been more critical when you were with the Weatherpeople and really pushed them to explain themselves.*

In the King of Prussia

Figure 32. Martin Sheen as Judge Salus II of the Montgomery County Court of Common Pleas. Publicity still for *In the King of Prussia*.

EMILE DE ANTONIO

In the King of Prussia: *Emile de Antonio Interviews Himself (1982)*

So many of de Antonio's assistant filmmakers had published interviews with him that this "interview with himself" in Film Quarterly *was perhaps the logical extension of the film press's sympathetic treatment. Ever the critic and carper, however, he was able to subject his own alter ego to his faultfinding. The Iago-like inquisitor within de Antonio brings out his own oxymoronic contradictions: his bourgeois Marxism, modest egotism, and romantic dialectical materialism.*

In the King of Prussia is the working title of a film being made by Emile de Antonio. Its subject is the action of the Plowshares Eight at King of Prussia, Pennsylvania, where Daniel Berrigan, Philip Berrigan, Dean Hammer, Carl Kabat, Elmer Maas, Anne Montgomery, Molly Rush, and John Schuchardt hammered and damaged two thermonuclear nose cones and poured human blood over secret documents. It was a nonviolent act. It was also the first act of disarmament since World War II. They were arrested, tried, convicted, sentenced. The film will consist of documentary footage shot with the participants, jurors, lawyers, judge, and police, as well as a scripted reconstruction of the trial itself. In it the Plowshares Eight will play themselves; actors will play the judge, the prosecuting attorney, the witnesses, the police, and jurors. Real people will be playing themselves in the documentary segments; at the same time, real people will be playing themselves as actors in the reconstruction; and actors will be playing real people.

De Antonio writes:
    All of this will be structured together to make a rational whole. The film makes no pretense to objectivity. It is a film of commitment which is entirely supportive of the action of the Plowshares Eight.
    The film will be approximately ninety minutes long. A reason for

making it is: we want it to be seen all over the world as de Antonio's other work has been. The movement against nuclear, neutron, and thermonuclear weapons is strong and growing all over the world. The people as a whole will not be in Iron Mountain when nuclear war comes. They will be dead or slowly dying. All rational politics proceeds from the notion that in order to be political people must first be alive. They won't be if those nose cones are used in the way that the Pentagon, GE, and others have planned. We recognize that there are equivalents to GE, [Secretary of State Alexander] Haig, and the Pentagon in other countries.

That people play themselves as actors is an aspect of reality not faced in conventional film and television. That world is like Plato's cave where we see only shadows. We live in a shadow world. The shadow on the wall is the dollar sign. That is what *The Deerhunter* is really about, shot like a commercial to make cheap, fake, commercial history. The TV industry piously announced that the Vietnam War was the most televised in history—wrong. It was sandwiched between commercials for mastodonic cars and deodorants so that war and peace, life and death became just another part of the program. Like Walter Cronkite. Our great disease is the media, particularly broadcast, whose apparent concern with irreverence is the major way of insuring that we stay in the cave. The most noble and the most pitiful of human activities becomes quotidian as shaving. CBS is worse than GE. It is a way of making us all become irrelevant.

Our film may be underproduced; but it won't soothe you. Our stars don't have press agents, they have passion and strength. The good guys entered private property and hammered away on nuclear nose cones.

▶

The Self and the Other: An Interview

THE OTHER: *A hoax. A trumpet blast of self-esteem. Why are you doing this?*
THE SELF: I'm tired of interviews. Journalists lazy. Politicians control them by feeding. Recently an interview with a young man [David Segal] for *Sight and Sound*. He used to work for me. Taped for over two hours. He came back with the transcript. There was only one question. I inserted the others. Interview vérité.

But two you's? Neither likely nor desirable.
But *we* are here, aren't we? Straighter, isn't it? Communication has become an abstraction. An end in itself. Taught like a dead language. As soon as it's taught, you know it's dead. Like Greek. Dialogue is probably dead, too. The Socratic exchange takes place with oneself.

You really want to talk about your new film, right?
What else? Work does begin in a social context; it also begins in the alone. The social context is the raw material. The working of it is individual. Lenin thought he perceived the uselessness of most art. I would rather be an artist and incur that tomb's displeasure. All governments quite rightly don't trust artists. The lesson is clear. Hacks are simply less untrustworthy. Film is hard stuff. Cimino's latest gumdrop cost more than it did to build fifteenth-century Florence. Business resembles government.

And your new film?
The technique is not unknown to Hollywood. An improvisation on shoestrings. Budget is invented as bills are presented, as mistakes are made. Borrow, haggle, planning is pie in the sky. As the film changes, the money changes.

Balls. You love being inefficient and romantic. It's a badge.
Of course, sure. Like other films I've made, I didn't even want to make this one. Paul Mayer of the Catholic left pushed me hard. I suggested other people.

You're just like a Hollywood hack making a beach boy movie. Put the oats in front of you and off you go.
Maybe, but where I go isn't where they go. My reservations were real. I'm not a Christian, I'm not a pacifist. Catholic pacifism doesn't seem unreal to me now. I was born without religion. I have never experienced it. It was awkward filming martyrs.

How did you manage to lose the awkwardness?
By seeing them as humans not martyrs. Also my egotism, my contempt for war, for the state, for the mastodonic corporations waddling into megadeaths to enrich stockholders. It's pathetic, isn't it? The most beautiful industrial products are weapons.

What else prompted you? Money? Fame?
No, I'm too old to believe they matter. Anger, and the love of the problem. Oh, what a rage I feel when I dream of President Bonzo sucking a jellybean in Iron Mountain looking at the TV show of the death of the world! Even the Id should be fired by that. And the problem. I began the film with the customary innocence of beginnings. Innocence is a device that leads to getting dirty with reality. I sued all the way through the Supreme Court of Pennsylvania for permission to film the trial. It was refused. Secretly, I didn't want it. I hired the best lawyer in Norristown, a wonderful storyteller,

Morris Gerber. The idea itself had too much of the stink of *cinema verité*. I knew I would have to find a different, better way.

You yourself stink of bourgeois nicety. Did I help you with any of that?
Yes, Iago, you were there. You always are, that unfailing other presence. Although I wrote a script, we knew that much of it had to be improvised. The defendants were waiting to appear for sentencing. They could give me two days and two hours shooting time. I almost cut my losses and quit. I came to hate Dan Berrigan's serenity in the face of my adversity. I lost sight of his. The problem sounds like a press release. To make film and theater of a trial by having real people play themselves off against actors playing real people. The moral questions weren't easy. Sometimes the bravest and best are awkward, slow, wordless on camera, hesitating. The actors had to be very, very good.

Wow, a juicy conversion yarn. A book into a film. Middle-aged lifelong nonbeliever finds Christ while filming priests and nuns. An edifying take. Christ!
Don't shimmy. We're off the track now. Of course, I came closer to the *idea* of God than ever before. Not the least of it was due to Martin Sheen, who was not only unfailingly professional and very good in a hard role, but exemplary in his spiritual quest. The heat on the set was intense. The cheap industrial air conditioner I had rented failed. 120 degrees. Airless set. Sheen insisted on wearing his jacket (more judicial) under the judge's robes. I loved him.

Love is cheap when people help you. Tell me about your six marriages, all the women you've loved.
I'm given to hyperbole, okay? I *am* a romantic. I probably like the windmills more than the friends I don't have. The other real problem was the filming itself. The Plowshares Eight didn't have time to remember lines. The takes weren't all that short. No time. Very few retakes. The actors did learn their lines. They had to anticipate flubbed or altered lines and cues. Randolph Jones and Richard Sisk were incredibly good and on top of everything.

That praise is self-praise. Rich words for the poor. Why did it take you seven months to edit?
In the shoot, time was beyond price. In electronic editing time is very, very expensive but it can be bought.

You groan too much about money . . .
Errors can be made to look like inspiration in any editing. Editing is still the heart of the political film. Structure is all. It's what technicians can't do.

Electronic editing is overrated. You can't really cut the work tape. You can't cut what isn't there so you make "build" reels. Electronic editing is writing, writing, writing. The machines are really slower although they move faster. You can't stop on a frame like the Steenbeck does.

I like what you said about artists being unreliable. If I ran the state I would shoot all those I couldn't use. Then I would use all those I could and shoot them afterwards.

You're always a braggart. I'd rather talk about the electronic image. First of all, it's really not very good. It lacks depth and richness. Film may be dying, perhaps, but it's a mature technology. The new Fuji and Eastman stocks are very good. It's as good as film is going to be. Tape is developing but it isn't here. Given that it was tape, Judy Irola and Julian Abbio shot it beautifully. The technicians monitoring in the TV truck couldn't believe it. Yet it was simple enough. I hired Judy because she had no TV experience. TV camera people are insects with headsets who inch along on command. I wanted a freer kind of shooting. Judy and I planned the shots with the script I wrote, which was followed carefully. We were never sure we could actually film all I planned. And we didn't. Not enough coverage, not enough reverse angles, reaction shots, etc. Judy and I did not wear headsets. The technicians in the truck screamed but not anything I wanted to hear. Judy produced great rack focus, pullbacks, motion.

Tell me about the money.
I used to be adroit at raising money. No longer. I used my own. I'm broke. On the lecture circuit I used to quote Mann: every artist is a con man and very likely a criminal. *Felix Krull* [Thomas Mann, *Confessions of Felix Krull: Confidence Man* (1954)]. I'd rather be a con than make money doing commercials and industrials for IBM and AT&T like the Maysles. I used to con others. Now I have a more sincere problem. I have to pay back myself.

You're self-con?
Maybe, but I doubt it. Money is the critical problem unless you make home movies like Mekas and Brakhage. I tried every source. Liberals oppose atomic war but they oppose it cheaply. People with money don't necessarily want safe investments. What they do want is the FBI staying away from their doors. The Berrigans and others like them oppose nuclear war with risk and honor. It's not enough to sign a petition. The Berrigans have taken the argument for disruptive pacifism as far as it will go. They risk their hides. Prophetic gestures are needed so that others will do other, smaller acts. But not more words. The press is gray with words, TV anchormen drone on. Our rocket generals and their rocket generals don't read petitions.

And next you'll be wanting the money to make a big Hollywood film?
No, although the size of the film more often than not determines its end. Budgets and films are made by Harvard Business School graduates, not by auteurs. *Raiders of the Lost Ark* is like owning a computer company. It makes images and it makes money and the images are made to make money.

You are willful and impossible; your position, too. Don't you see that in the name of some dead radicalism you make films mass audiences don't want to see for a form which is quintessentially directed to mass audiences? Is yours a theory of the radical aristocrat? Your work isn't sexy; it isn't bloody; your theme is history without Goldwyn. Why do you make them?
It's been said before and even I have thought of it all. I won't belabor it. It was sad that the radicals I knew, even those who did bombings, saw and talked about the kind of films radicals should have not seen by conviction. I never paid too much attention. Most political radicals are as conservative as the old lady from Dubuque in the arts. Visual sensibility nonexistent. They watch TV.

I have to live with that contradiction: if you want films to be made for the reasons they should be made rather than for a mythical box office, then you lose the audience. The contradiction is apparent but not real. Those who own the means of production and distribution duly and instinctively choose poppy rather than reality. It's easier; it plays well.

The real contradiction is technique. Technique has become substance. We are hollow enough so we admire how we do it. The how becomes the what. It is our sin, the modern sin. Technique as an end in itself. The point is to get elected, not to get elected for something. It is why we will have atomic war. The two most effective politicians of the post–World War II America are Joe McCarthy and Ronald Reagan. Both were great technicians. McCarthy never read a book; he was a right-wing lout and he reached and convinced more people than anyone of his beliefs had ever reached. His accusations were false and weird. He understood better than anyone anonymous anger. He was part of it. The empty calling to the angry, empty. I think my film *Point of Order* is the only work I know which reveals the toppling of a great demagogue. I explain nothing. That, too, is too aristocratic, would you say? I don't. I think it better that people think rather than be pacified or lulled. More democratic, too.

Much of what I believe about art and film I learned in another form from others: that the pretty is rarely art; that glorious color and great technique do not make great films. The old, worn footage I used in the past became something else. I achieved what I had hoped for: the personal in the impersonal. Faintly Dada that notion. But then I am as much Dada as I am a Marxist, I suppose.

Confession time in a film magazine. Shall I get a priest?
Be quiet. You remind me of the Weather Underground. There was in their acts a Dada defiance. And although publication of *Prairie Fire* was important and meant a change of direction, it was badly written and unoriginal. The anger of the WUO led to its acts; there was plenty to be angry about. There is. They should have worked to develop a critical vocabulary. Their words were faded, rhetorical, stale. It wasn't thinking; it was parroting. Of course, there are few political geniuses. But Lenin, Mao, Fidel, Ho, Jefferson found, as did Tom Paine, fluency in hard politics.

I'm lost. Are you modest?
Not in any crippling way, but more so than others think. I know I don't have the questions. Some of the answers, perhaps. I do know that in film there must be a belief in possibility which rejects the notion of pabulum and poppy for money and forgetfulness. We must opt for the complex and the difficult, for films that don't stroke but challenge audiences.

Do you own stock in Western Union?
Of course, 5,000 shares. Jerry Falwell knows that he is selling vulgarity. He is like Hollywood. Both are in the communications business.

You're an anarchist, finally, aren't you?
I think so. The icons of authority make me reach for a hammer.

Except for icons.
I love film. So much of it has been created as fast as Edsels and the undertakers have to run after it to keep up their pantheons, film classes, reviews. I have been in documentary because I wanted to be. I never did see documentary as a *gardus ad Parnassum* ever reaching to the Hollywood heights. Not at all. The one isn't harder or better. A letter recently from the man who directed *The Competition* [1980, Joel Oliansky]. It was a fan letter. I asked him for money. He didn't answer. I don't know his work. He knows mine. He owes me something. He, like others there, admire the idea of what I do and do what I don't admire.

Do you still have the capacity to learn? Your position seems to be the same.
I think I learn. I have just finished *In the King of Prussia* in one-inch video. I learned through error. I will never use tape again. I have learned that no one will ever live long enough to make the films I want to make.

I want to write and direct a film about millenarians who await the end of the world. It doesn't happen. Most continue to believe; they move on to the desert and begin again. They have a strong leader. I've been wanting to do that for fifteen years. I want to do an autobiographical fiction film about a young man who experiences a coal town, Harvard, and New York right after the war. I want to do a sad film in a home for retired actors—fiction, a political parable with a love story. A fifty-minute film on Eratosthenes and the first accurate measurement of the earth's circumference and what it meant. Nothing. I'm talking and studying with a friend about a woman painter, someone like [Liubov] Popova, in the days of pre-revolutionary and early revolutionary Russia, a film of bad ends.

Ideas are never appropriated; we all have them. Except cinema verité folks, who have only technique. I'd like to do a mystery film about a Native American shaman and his past; and also a political murder film; and finally, a film with Martin Sheen about the life of the spirit, about a radical monk. I'm not sad that there won't be time. There never was. I am tempted by too many tugs.

Like this. Have a drink.

May 1, 1982

SHARON GALLAGHER

On the Making of In the King of Prussia: An Interview with Emile de Antonio (1983)

Sharon Gallagher, editor of Radix, *interviewed de Antonio via telephone during the release of* In the King of Prussia. *The Berkeley-based journal, a thoughtful inquirer for the Christian left, was familiar to the Plowshares movement. Upon rereading the* Radix *interview for his journals, de Antonio (in the passage appended here) recalled little about the incident. However, his later thoughts on "those Christians I want to join" indicate that he was sincere in telling Gallagher he was working through the philosophical issues of Christianity. His lifelong correspondence with two of his sisters—one a nun, another a practicing Catholic who begged him to attend her church wedding—sometimes dealt with religious quandaries. De Antonio was almost persuaded by his conversion experience during the making of the Plowshares film, but it was a leap of faith he never took.*

How did you get involved with this project?
I've been friendly with different members of the Catholic/pacifist Christian left for a long time. Dan Berrigan played in *In the Year of the Pig*, my film against the war in Vietnam, which I shot back in 1968. After they did their action in King of Prussia, Pennsylvania, September 1980, some of them asked me to make a film out of the forthcoming trial and I said no. I had no interest in such a project because *(a)* I wasn't a Christian, and *(b)* I wasn't a pacifist. I was a total nonbeliever and also a Marxist.

On the other hand, the Berrigans have managed in their own way to cut through every lie in America—to forge allies and meet people in all sorts of movements. I was absolutely convinced of the importance and significance of what they had done, and I agreed with Dan Berrigan in calling it the first act of disarmament since the Second World War. After the First World War people were so shocked at the number of dead that even governments made real efforts and treaties to diminish the use of the most powerful arms. They were silly efforts, but they had the 5–5–3 treaties in which certain countries were allowed to have five battleships and other countries were allowed to have three, because they thought the battleship was the ultimate weapon of destruction. You can see today that the battleship was a toy compared to a hydrogen bomb.

The Plowshares Eight action was the first act of disarmament since those wars. It was a noble act. I admired the bravery of the Plowshares Eight, but I didn't think it was for me to do a film about it. Then I noticed that the media were largely tending to ignore what had happened. Gradually I became more and more interested in the problem of how a film could be made out of it. So I took a leap by hiring a camera crew, buying tape, going down and filming around the trial, outside the courtroom. Some of that material ended up in the film.

At the same time I also entered a suit in the state of Pennsylvania to film the trial. As you know, it is now discretionary with the state court, through a recent ruling of the U.S. Supreme Court, to determine whether or not the court will allow trials to be filmed. I found that most trials that are filmed are highly sensational, they're kind of salacious in the sense that they are murder trials or rape trials, and they are garish. But I also knew that the state court would never let a political trial be filmed, and I took my suit all the way to the Pennsylvania Supreme Court. By that time I was hooked, and I realized I had to write a script. I continued to shoot around the trial until it was over. Then I got a transcript, and from that transcript I made a seventy-page shooting script. The trial ended in March and in the middle of July I rented a building. We turned it into a courtroom and we had two days to film a seventy-page script, something that has never happened in the history of film. By that time I was already changing my view about the Plowshares Eight—and other matters—and the filming was incredibly intense. Nobody else works under those conditions. A lot of it was improvising; there was no time for retakes, there was no time to do anything. You had to get it right the first time or you just went on anyway. I like crises and I liked that kind of situation, and I think the Plowshares Eight did too. The most remarkable thing about that part of it is that you had real people playing themselves, and actors playing real people, and none of those people had ever met until they walked onto that set, July 17, 1981.

How did Martin Sheen get involved?
Back in 1975 I made a film about the Weather Underground. And, through an informer, all my sound tracks were made available to the FBI. The FBI realized I would be a source of great information in helping to catch the Weather Underground. There were two hundred FBI men looking unsuccess-

fully for the Underground for five years, and here I apparently had found them and gone underground into a safe house and filmed them. So I was subpoenaed, but I said that I would rather go to jail than cooperate with the federal government or become an informer.

That brought a lot of people in Hollywood out of the woodwork. They issued statements supporting me and because of their statements the government withdrew from the case and withdrew the subpoenas. Among those supporters were a lot of well-known people—Shirley MacLaine, Warren Beatty, Jon Voight, and Robert Wise, who was at that time president of the Screen Directors Guild—a lot of conservative people, but also a lot of progressive people, among whom the most interesting to me was Martin Sheen, and we became friends. When I wrote him a note and told him I was going to do this film on the Berrigans, he called me up and said, "I will do anything you want. I'll play any part you want." I told him the only part I would like him to play was a fairly unattractive part: the judge. He said, "Fine, I'll play him." He also said, "You must need some money," and I said, "No. Money is my problem, not yours." He sent me $5,000 anyway. Well, the picture cost $275,000, so $5,000 wasn't really a very great amount, but it was an extraordinary amount because it came from the heart.

When we walked onto the set, I was the only one who knew everybody. Sheen admired the Berrigans, but he didn't know any of the Plowshares Eight, he knew none of the other actors, and the actors had never met the Berrigans. It was a very funny situation.

I read someplace that Sheen, through his experience in Apocalypse Now, *having a heart attack, etc., had gotten in touch with his own Catholic tradition.*
That is correct. Martin left the church in the sixties because he felt it was not living up to its tradition and was out of touch with the great social issues—the church seemed either unaware of them or on the wrong side of them. He was married in the church, but he gradually eased out of it. In fact, he and I did an interview together which appeared in *American Film,* and he said that the heart attack was almost a visionary experience. He felt as if he were passing into death, and everything became very clear, and he saw himself called back to Christianity. He is the only actor I know who goes to Mass every day. The first time I visited him in Hollywood, the first person he introduced me to was the parish priest—instead of a blonde or whoever, as many people do in Hollywood.

One question that a friend and I had as we watched the film was about Martin Sheen's character, the judge. Was his role overdone?
It was very much underdone.

It is hard to believe he could have been that bad.
Well, he was worse. Martin's brother died a week before the shoot so he called me up and I said, "Martin, don't come out at all. I'll get somebody else from the stage out here." And he said, "No, no, it's just that I won't be able to come until the last day." We had planned to spend most of the week on that part. So I just said, "Martin, this judge is totally unbelievable." I had watched him, and his behavior followed an almost classical kind of psychological aberrational pattern. At certain times he would be incredibly solicitous and kindly to the defendants. And then, if they said one word, he was outraged, carrying on and screaming. I left out things that were absolutely beyond belief. At the sentencing, for instance, after he had given out the hardest sentences, he said, "Rather than give you these sentences, I would much rather send you to Siberia or to a leper colony in Puerto Rico. Because that is where you really should go."

I told Sheen, "This has to be credible, so we'll have to play it down. I expect you to do this and this and you will interpret it that way, saying things that will seem almost nutty." But, on the whole, Sheen did a very restrained interpretation. He had never met the man and so he had to rely on me for information. All the Plowshares Eight think that Sheen underplayed him and of course all the film critics think he overplayed it. So much for film critics.

So the interpretation didn't reflect a bias?
Curiously, enough, I think at that point the film has a Christian-pacifist bias, even though the man who made it was neither a Christian nor a pacifist when he began.

That was what I was going to ask you next. How did the film affect you?
I was antinuke for political reasons, not for moral ones, and I certainly wasn't a pacifist. But I used to say that I made all my other films to change people. I made films about Senator Joe McCarthy and the war in Vietnam and all sorts of other subjects in which I hoped that for other people there would be an illumination, that what really happened in American history would be revealed to those who never participated in the drama and in the hidden history of this country. But with this film, I was the one who changed. I've become a pacifist and I'm now working through becoming a Christian. I'm not there. But I'm working on it.

That's exciting.
Well, I mean, events do change one's life, don't they?

How has the film been received?
Like any film of conscience or any film that handles a difficult subject, it has been received in a wide variety of ways. In some places it has very big

audiences, and in other places it has a very tiny audience. But, no matter what the size of the audience, everyone seems moved by it.

Right now it is playing all over Europe. It should be seen by 80 million people by September because it is going to be on European TV. So these eight people who are relatively obscure are going to become international figures. That's great.

It's not an easy film, because we are brainwashed people and we don't like to admit it. Not the least respect in which we are brainwashed is the belief that films should be entertainment. We consider pornography entertainment as well as murder, violence, and all those things. But we don't think that films should have ideas, be contentious. Or that films should be an art form, like a novel, that can undertake serious social questions. Films cost so much and theaters have that beautiful womb-like dark atmosphere; people go there to be amused, entertained, thrilled, frightened, but not to think. All the films I've made are calls to action, calls to thinking, so I upset a lot of people's notions of what a film is.

We are also brainwashed by TV, numbed by it, so that one of the struggles that the movement is going to have to undergo is to accustom people to the idea that there are films that are first-rate that have no intention of titillating the viewer.

I've heard you may work on another project with Martin Sheen on the life of Thomas Merton.
We've talked about that, but it's very hard because it is not a cheap project. To do it right would, like any low-budget Hollywood film, cost several million dollars. That amount of money is not easy to get together. Martin and I will be doing other projects together because not only are we friends, but we share many views about the world.

What is the current status of the Plowshares Eight?
They are still out on appeal. The state of Pennsylvania does not want to come to terms with this case. There's no doubt that the case will have to be reversed, because of judicial error, so they've been stalling on the other issues, such as whether justification is reasonable as a defense. They recently had a court session and chose seven judges to hear it so that there would be an odd number and they would be sure to get a majority. That's going to drag on for months. But then they still won't know what to do because the problem is that they either have to give them a new trial or let them go. The state loses either way, because if there is a new trial, it won't be an obscure little trial. There will be thousands of people there, and there will be demonstrations—exactly what the state of Pennsylvania and the U.S. government don't want.

What projects are you working on now?
I'm probably going to work on a film about my own life and the FBI that will be a new kind of film. Much of the script will be taken from FBI documents that have to do with me. It's called *A Middle-Aged Radical As Seen through the Eyes of His Government.*

Interesting. Can you still get those documents from the government?
Not easily, but I started very early. I had a friend [Charles Nesson] who was associate dean of Harvard Law School as my lawyer, and we started getting those documents in 1975. Most of them are altered or hidden or denied. I now have six thousand pages.

But more important than any project I'm working on is the fact that I think more and more people should follow the lead of the Plowshares Eight and go ahead and do what they should do—whatever is in their power. Not everyone has the strength and courage to do that. Everything that is done that is against thermonuclear death is good. And that is what should be done.

Memory is all. I remember nothing of the woman who did the interview and when the magazine came it was a mystery. But memory does call all those inauthentic saints who live in my life. Dan is a saint because he's also a space cadet. And a publicity wolf. He was on TV last night in a strange performance on behalf of Sullivan, the man executed in Florida today. His ego is great enough for God. He hates serious poets save for dead ones. And if they lived in his time, then sparingly. Except Merton.

Phil remains a purer saint. I now have come to realize that saints are like good revolutionaries. They will sacrifice anyone and anything including themselves for their beliefs. Phil is authentic, charming, handsome, brave, and a believer. He could have been a hero of the Russian or Cuban Revolutions, but not a survivor because finally he isn't large enough to rule and he would have been too pure for the reality of ruling. That reality is a curse which the church has solved more practically than Marxist countries, but then the pope no longer rules.

A funny lot those Christians I want to join. There is a whining quality in them, except for Phil. But most in Paul Mayer, who asked me to make a film. Don't forget, dear reader, that when a Paul Mayer or an X or a Y asks you to make a film, they have no idea of what a film is. They are zealots and talkers and go-to-jailers, but they are not artists. Everyone wants to be an artist, which is why Dan's saintliness is a little tarnished. Phil's sanctity is sanctity without holes because he is what he wants to be in toto.

DAVID SEGAL

De Antonio and the Plowshares Eight (1982)

The antinuclear subject matter of In the King of Prussia *earned the film a great deal of press coverage, even if few filmgoers saw the low-budget documentary. This exposure in* Sight and Sound *was one of the few significant profiles of de Antonio that had appeared since 1976. As was often the case, the piece was written by a freelancer who had worked for the filmmaker. In it de Antonio is clearly bothered by having to shoot on videotape instead of film, leading him into a caustic sermon on the brainwashing Moloch and Mammon of television.*

EMILE DE ANTONIO: The Plowshares Eight project is a film, even though it is made on tape. It's not like that videotape garbage you see on television. Its intentions are different. It's not industrial product. This is the first time I've worked with videotape. I've never liked it and I still don't. I'm driven to this position by economic necessity. It's very hard to make independent left-wing documentaries now, particularly if, like me, you will not go to foundations or film funds, or make a deal with PBS in advance, because I don't want anybody to have any right to censor. I don't want their advice or comments.

The democratic approach is nullified in the United States by the most powerful of the media, television. The news on television is built upon the newscaster as media star. And it's not the real news. Nothing is clearer than something that happened a long time ago, and that the networks to this day defend. They said that the war in Vietnam was the only war that was shown on TV every day. True. But what was being shown was the media doing their own thing.

Cameramen were shown going in and filming, and they would show bombing runs. All the film that was shown was sanitized. It appeared between commercials. Appearing between commercials, looking at it day after day, it became just another daily event. The horror of killing Vietnamese, of watching a Marine sergeant set fire to a house, of watching an American die with a bullet in him, desensitized us to death. Television did that to us because it never took a stand. Under the myth of objectivity, it presented this garbage. The whole history of the war in Vietnam is in the outtakes of ABC, which are all saved. But they broadcast three to five minutes a night. They broadcast "high events." They didn't show villagers dying of starvation, they showed their own reporters interviewing General Thieu, or they showed an air strike.

This began a long time ago, and people thirty years old or younger have been raised totally under the spell of television. Every poll that is financed, from any point of view, makes the point that almost all information for the majority of people about what goes on in the world comes from television. All that is highly distorted, it's vicarious, it's unreal. And it's spoken to you by someone in whom the network has a tremendous vested interest. And if they want to kill you entirely, as they did the Plowshares Eight, they don't put you on. This event was not ABC, NBC, or CBS. The Berrigans are two well-known people who led six others into this extraordinary event, the first act of "disarmament" since World War II anywhere in the world. You would think that it would be worth a minute of network news time, but it wasn't.

I saw the TV trucks there, the days and nights I taped, the night the sheriffs went crazy and roughed up spectators right outside the court. The trucks were there, the cables were there, and the one-inch equipment was there, and they filmed it. But they didn't televise it. They shot interviews, they shot all kinds of stuff, it's all there, somewhere, on videotape, unless the tapes have been wiped, which is also possible. But it simply wasn't broadcast. If you're not televised, you're dead, you don't exist. I think Marshall McLuhan was a silly professor of literature who wrote early about TV and who made TV people themselves feel powerful and wonderful. He said, "The medium is the message." It should read, "Who owns the medium owns the message." And who owns these TV stations? There are members of RCA's board of directors who are part of GE's board of directors, and General Motors' board of directors, and other companies making tanks, atomic weapons, and all kinds of other things. Do they even want to tell the truth, do they even want to report on the fact that a thermonuclear nose-cone plant has been attacked by pacifists?

We go on thinking of dollars, with the market rising, with money our chief concern, with wars in Latin America that we're getting ready to undertake. Nobody in the government has stopped to ask what will happen, because the Soviets are just as capable as we are of launching this thing. We all know about this, but we don't want to know. This massive brainwashing has gone on, but it's also a massive self-brainwashing. Nobody wants to see himself fried out in the middle of the street, or his children. Another thing that people know in their minds but don't want to confront is that everybody believes it's going to happen to someone else. This is one time that's wrong. Death here is much more democratic, in that people who don't die immediately, and even those who don't die slowly in agony over a period of weeks, will die within a moderate length of time. The ionosphere is going to be filled with cesium, strontium, plutonium, all these things have half-lives, some of them go on for thousands of years.

What this is really about, and what the Plowshares Eight are really about, is that this thing—this self-brainwashing—is deep into everybody's unconscious. People are constantly aware of the fact that this could happen tomorrow. It occurs to us all the time, but we don't allow it to come out. It's like a mass hypnosis: we are hypnotized by ourselves, by our government, and primarily by the tube. We don't want to think about it, we don't want to hear about it. And we don't hear about it.

SEGAL: *These remarks by de Antonio reminded me of the conclusion of Walter Benjamin's essay "The Work of Art in the Age of Mechanical Reproduction": mankind's "self-alienation has reached such a degree that it can experience its own destruction as an aesthetic pleasure of the first order." I mentioned this to him.*

And as something that is happening to other people. We experience the end of the world as a spectator. You can take Benjamin's brilliant essay and extend it a step. We project it now as the person looking at the TV set, and the people in the TV set are everybody else in the world. We feel that we're going to die, but we don't perceive it. That's the other part of our unconscious, that we block the perception that it is our reality. We see ourselves as the spectator and not as part of the spectacle. That is because we're trained from childhood to be spectators. We look at things, we don't do things anymore. That's why Andy Warhol is the most expressive personality of our time. He's the greatest voyeur of all time. He can get people to do anything in front of his camera. Things that you would never dream of doing, you will do in front of him. Things that are degrading.

Andy gets people to do everything. Including having other people rewrite the history of the world in his name. He said to me, "Oh, D, I had dinner at this banquet for Ronald Reagan, it was so wonderful. All those great old people were there: Dean Martin, Frank Sinatra." You think he's making fun of it all, and at the same time you know that he's serious. He means both. He knows how dreary and shallow it is.

Finally, all that will be left will be a TV set, which will keep running the images of the end of the world. The camera will be running somewhere after the guy who had it in his hand was fried. The transmitter will work, it's immune, and the set is immune. So that will be the trinity: camera, transmitter, TV receiver. The images will go on and on, the same images over and over, until the tubes burn out. And then silence will fall upon the earth.

MICHAEL H. SEITZ

Swords into Plowshares (1983)

Seitz's appreciation of In the King of Prussia *in the Madison-based journal the* Progressive *continued that publication's longtime commitment to antinuclear politics. Earlier in the year the journal had reported on the FBI's continuing harassment of de Antonio and New Yorker Films (see Peck, January 1983). Seitz extols the virtues of Plowshares activism and de Antonio's political intentions; but he also sides with the majority of the film's critics in finding de Antonio's "deliberate use of underproduction" an unacceptable basis for an alternative aesthetic.*

Producer-writer-director Emile de Antonio has characterized his latest film, *In the King of Prussia,* this way: "Our film may be underproduced; but it won't soothe you. Our stars don't have press agents, they have passion and strength. The good guys entered private property and hammered away on nuclear nose cones."

In the King of Prussia is about the civil disobedience and subsequent trial of the Plowshares Eight—Daniel and Philip Berrigan and six other radical Catholic pacifists. On September 9, 1980, they stole into the General Electric Reentry Systems Division in King of Prussia, Pennsylvania, hammered two nose cones for nuclear bombs, poured some of their blood on the damaged hardware, and were arrested by police.

De Antonio's film is something of a hybrid, combining dramatic reenactment of the trial with documentary footage of events that surrounded it. At first, de Antonio had assumed that relaxed rules permitting cameras in the courtroom would allow him to film the trial live. But he quickly discovered that "they never allow you to do political stuff, just murders and things." Barred from the actual proceedings, the filmmaker contemplated "a new kind of film," and decided to intermix vérité footage with a scripted reconstruction of the trial based on court transcripts.

In the final work, the Plowshares Eight play themselves and actors play the judge, prosecuting attorney, witnesses, police, and jurors. Hollywood's Martin Sheen plays the judge. In short, real people are themselves in the documentary segments, while in the reconstructed scenes, real people act as themselves and actors play real people.

The Plowshares Eight defended their actions as a response to a "greater danger"—the right of a citizen who has a gun pointed at his head to protect and defend himself. In this instance, they asserted, the gun was the threat of nuclear destruction; the defendants sought to convince the jurors that this gun was pointed at their heads as well. Expert witnesses were to testify that U.S. nuclear policy poses real dangers and violates international law. Unfortunately, but not surprisingly, the judge refused to admit such testimony on the grounds that the U.S. policies were not on trial. Only the Eight were to be judged, he said, on thirteen charges, the most serious of which was destruction of private property.

The film, however, allows the full "greater danger" case to be heard: We are given the testimony of some of the barred witnesses—George Wald, Robert J. Lifton, Richard Falk—in press conferences outside the courthouse. In the courtroom, deprived of their most promising legal defense, the defendants proudly admit their "guilt." "Your honor," two of them declare, "we did that, we broke those bombs." By readily acknowledging their responsibility, the Plowshares Eight expose the moral irresponsibility of the prosecution and its witnesses—and the system they serve.

The damaged property—a pair of dented nose cones—is introduced as evidence, but in what turns out to be a theater of the absurd, not one of the prosecution witnesses, all longtime employees at the GE plant, will admit to knowing what they are or what they are used for. "I know nothing about the specific uses of the Mark 12A," says the manager of shop operations. "All we do is manufacture the hardware. This is not a nuclear facility."

Viewers are thus treated to the enlightening spectacle of the weapons makers pleading ignorance and innocence, while the defendants lay claim to knowledge and take responsibility for their own actions. Given an opportunity to trace his moral development and explain his actions, Daniel Berrigan concludes, "I could not *not* have done what I did."

The Plowshares Eight were convicted on charges of trespassing, conspiracy, and criminal mischief, and were handed prison sentences ranging from one-half to five years to three to ten. But by their actions and through their statements, the Eight placed the onus of guilt on the prosecution. They forcefully demonstrated that it is necessary, at times, to commit civil disobedience against unjust authority. De Antonio's film helps us see this by providing an example of resistance to nuclear armament that carries risk and makes no pretense of objectivity. It is, de Antonio has written, "a film of commitment which is entirely supportive of the actions of the Plowshares Eight"—the work of an unabashed leftist filmmaker who believes that "objectivity" is an illusion that sustains the status quo, whether it is used in cinema verité or television network news.

It must be said that *In the King of Prussia* is not an especially good-looking movie (except for the title sequence). This is partly the result of the conditions under which it was made. Budgetary limitations compelled de Antonio to shoot on videotape. The Eight could only spare a few days for filming the reenacted courtroom sequences, and that didn't leave enough time for them to learn their lines, or for retakes. And though the documentary scenes were shot in the winter snows of Pennsylvania, the interior trial scenes had to be made in the sweltering heat of New York in midsummer. In the former, everyone is bundled and shivering, and in the latter close-ups reveal droplets of sweat.

But the film's roughness is also a deliberate choice. "I know my film will be attacked for its cheap look," de Antonio told an interviewer for the *Village Voice*. "And it is a cheap movie, after all—about $240,000. But I didn't want to make it look rich—I wanted it to be what it is. I was interested in a film of meaning and content. The dryness of its aesthetic would be more interesting than all that lace-and-teapot stuff.... To me the thing that's antihuman about film is its essential lulling capabilities. You go into that beautiful, dark, womb-like theater, and you spend all that money, the sound is perfectly mixed, the images are nongrating. And you surrender to it, you're a passive object being worked over by that screen."

While it may be true that most glossy, state-of-the-art productions tend to lull the viewer into a state of thoughtless complacency, I can think of many films of "meaning and content" that make more expressive use of the resources of cinema than *In the King of Prussia*: the early work of Eisenstein, Pudovkin, and Vertov, films of Joris Ivens and Marcel Ophuls, Alain Resnais's *Night and Fog,* Pontecorvo's *Battle of Algiers,* films of Jean-Luc Godard, and more. Some of these filmmakers suggested more radical structural alternatives than anything essayed by de Antonio, and some made deliberate use of underproduction, as de Antonio did.

No other filmmaker, however, seems to regard underproduction as the basis for a leftist aesthetic. De Antonio is not convincing when he tries to find political and aesthetic justification for the unavoidable.

Yet for all its lack of polish, *In the King of Prussia* is persuasive in the case it makes for disruptive pacifism—perhaps just as persuasive as the superproduction *Gandhi*. With its huge scale, exotic settings, stars, and personalizing of the issues, *Gandhi* managed to appeal to viewers across the political spectrum (and will no doubt be honored by the distributors of Academy Awards). The unanimous approval it received makes one wonder whether Gandhian principles were considered or just the film—whether viewers were, indeed, lulled into a state of thoughtless passivity.

De Antonio's work is more provocative in form and content, and will not let itself be enjoyed as entertainment. Confronted with the film, supporters of U.S. nuclear policy will be outraged. And that will make Emile de Antonio very happy.

DAVID S. MACHLOWITZ

Antinuclear Narcissism (1983)

Who knew the American Bar Association Journal *had a film critic? "Lawyer on the Aisle" Machlowitz, a corporate counsel and environmental law expert, gave* In the King of Prussia *a more sustained analysis than most film journals when he featured this assessment in his regular review column. While the cineaste press generally ignored the film, professional organs like the* ABA Journal *and the* Bulletin of the Atomic Scientists *took it seriously. Machlowitz acknowledges de Antonio's standing as a filmmaker, but presents an establishmentarian condemnation of Daniel Berrigan's disregard for the rule of law.*

In the King of Prussia is a dramatization of the trial of eight antinuclear weapons activists who broke into a General Electric plant in King of Prussia, Pennsylvania, in 1980 and damaged two discarded nuclear missile nose cones. It serves more to reinforce the views of the audience than to change them. For committed antinuclear weapons advocates, the film is unnecessary, while for everyone else it is unconvincing.

The activists, including former priests Daniel and Philip Berrigan and a high-school acquaintance of mine, portray themselves. Martin Sheen plays the villain, Judge Samuel W. Salus II of the Montgomery County Court of Common Pleas, who sentenced the defendants to up to ten years in prison (and who was the chief public defender for that county when I was a summer clerk in that office).

The film was written, produced, and directed by Emile de Antonio. He and Frederick Wiseman are the leading documentary filmmakers of the past twenty years. Ironically, although Wiseman is a lawyer, he seldom tackles legal subjects, while de Antonio is fascinated by legal controversies and has been involved in litigation with both the Federal Bureau of Investigation and the Central Intelligence Agency. He is a highly engaging Marxist whose films have included philippics featuring the Warren Report, the Vietnam War, and the Weather Underground, but who proudly notes that some of them have been successful financially. His most prominent works are *Point of Order* (a classic attack on McCarthy) and *Millhouse* (the ultimate anti-Nixon film).

Snow and Summer Clothes

De Antonio unsuccessfully petitioned the Pennsylvania Supreme Court to allow him to film the trial. Instead he combines documentary footage of scenes outside the courthouse with videotapes of the defendants reciting self-serving portions of the transcript. The cinematography is deliberately grainy, "for authenticity." Less authenticity is derived from the exterior shots showing snow, while the interior shots show everyone sweating in summer clothes.

De Antonio reveres Daniel Berrigan and reviles Judge Salus. *In the King of Prussia,* whose title may be derived partly from de Antonio's desire to exploit the militaristic connotations of Prussia, as the trial took place in Norristown, is Berrigan's stage. He dominates the action with lengthy speeches in loving close-ups. He begins with an eloquent denunciation of nuclear weapons but soon descends into pompous, patronizing pontification and posturing. The other defendants seem far more sincere and far less image conscious.

The key legal question—whether the defendants could rely on the horror of nuclear war as the justification for their actions—is well presented from the defendants' viewpoint, with the judge and prosecutor limited to snarling, undetailed rejections of it. No one queries Berrigan, for example, whether James Earl Ray should have been allowed to defend himself by claiming that integration was a menace. Curiously, the one juror who is interviewed is never asked why he and the other jurors found the defendants guilty.

Obstructionist Procedures

Judge Salus and the prosecutor are portrayed as reactionary defenders of property rights over human rights. Legal procedures are sneered at as purely obstructionist. This is a sad misconception of both law and procedure. Although the lengthy prison sentences, now on appeal, were unusually harsh, those who choose property destruction over public demonstrations purely to publicize their views at trial must be prepared, as Gandhi and Martin Luther King were, to go to jail. The law forbids the destruction of not just missile nose cones but also other alleged "evil property"—abortion clinics, school buses used for integration, and unpopular newspapers. Berrigan's view that he can make his own law also is the view of the lynch mob and the assassin.

If Berrigan could disregard procedure and pervert a trial into an antinuclear Woodstock, others would try to strip away important procedural rights of defendants or to disregard trials altogether and mete out vigilante justice to unpopular defendants. Nuclear freeze rallies have been far more influential than Berrigan's publicity stunt and far less dangerous to the cause of due process. Berrigan's sanctimony boils down to the ends justifying the means, a view equally fervently espoused by the killers of the Kennedys, Gandhi, and King.

In the King of Prussia is worthwhile for its idealistic passion and as a pep rally for those who share its views. Filmed in haste, with a deliberate disregard for style, it is less of a documentary than a revival meeting, much like *Triumph of the Will*. Nuclear weapons, the ultimate Damoclean sword, are, at best, a tragic necessity (at least as long as the Soviets have them), but the film's view of law is an unnecessary travesty.

Mr. Hoover and I

Figure 33. Emile de Antonio with clapboard in frame enlargement from *Mr. Hoover and I*.

EMILE DE ANTONIO

Mr. Hoover and I (1989)

De Antonio never worked from scripts, but he was adept at penning short treatments for his film projects. His many literary drafts of his autobiographical documentary culminated with this explication of his "film made in cold anger." Written just after the Toronto premiere of Mr. Hoover and I *and only weeks before his death, the essay appeared posthumously in an anthology alongside poetry and prose honoring de Antonio.*

The first consideration was always formal. Why not put the old hulk on the screen? Mine. Poverty of means was not rare in my work. I tried harder to spend less and less when $ itself is the god, the soul and heart of film. L.A. is stuffed rich with *Batman* explosions. The last time I looked, the gross was over $250,000,000. Could such an enterprise be put in trust to an artist? Ha.

But we don't look for Jack Nicholson or Jeff Bridges to act. They play themselves. The best actors are in the ministry. Wouldn't Jesus have adored sharing the altar with Swaggart and Bakker? What a great scene: Bakker and Swaggart dividing and sharing the loaves and fishes? Superlative tube material. Driving the money changers to the studio for confessions and interviews. Aimee Semple McPherson was a genius before her time. She trotted out to Hollywood in the twenties to preach the gospel and redeem souls in the temples she built, filled the coffers, had steamy love affairs, for surely, that is God's work as well.

And, if Bakker is better than Jack Nicholson, then I have a dream, a documentary dream, how wonderful and rich and crowd-pleasing the great god-gifted preachers on Technique: the Road to God and Salvation.

I confess, I am un-American. I have never liked Hollywood films, not the films of my own time, which is a long time. Every great and noble theme is put through the Bank of America transmogrification machine out there along the blue Pacific. Remember Vietnam? God, they worked that over. Not one of them that wasn't a cowboy film, the Vietnamese were the Indians.

Save one. No one ever saw it. *Go Tell It to the Spartans.* Our educational system is such that no one would have understood the title. As for the rest, the worse they were, the greater the honor. *The Deer Hunter?* It was invented for the word *meretricious.* Streep as a working-class girl in a city like Pittsburgh?

I decided to make a film about J. Edgar Hoover and me. Without any voice but mine. Hoover is reputed to be dead. I never end as I intend in the beginning. Two basically nonpolitical people are also in my film: Nancy de Antonio, my wife, who cuts my hair. This is cinema verité since she cuts my hair in real life. And John Cage, who has been important to me.

The film is as cheap as can be. I talk into the camera and the Nagra records my words. Nancy cuts my hair, John bakes a loaf of bread and talks about his work. Reducing film to my essentials, I committed many errors. Channel Four of London, which commissioned the film, rejected it because the track was out of sync.

It was. I'm repairing it and Channel Four will televise it as it has every film of mine, on December 31.

Which puts me in a bilious state. Why doesn't that flaccid whore of the tube, PBS, play my films? Once a PBS station was going to play *In the Year of the Pig,* my film on Vietnam. Then it was canceled. Then the station planned a show on censorship in TV. My film was in the ads. *That* show was canceled.

The argument for the defense of PBS is palsied and rotten, that it's all we have. TV is too dangerous to be trusted to such talent. Now, I sell pieces of my work to PBS for five thousand dollars a minute. The network never understood anything and was empty of character. How can we not understand politics after electing a Reagan and a Bush? Government for the rich is the death of any country. The Winter Soldiers need to fall into position to take on the armies of ignorance, deceit, and plunder. Can't we see that we *are* a police state, that Bush *was* director of the world's largest armed spy force, the most evil in the world?

Am I angry? Only an idiot can avoid cool anger in the days and hot anger for our nights. What does J. Edgar Hoover have to do with Bush and Reagan? He died before they were elected. That's the point. The FBI was created by Hoover. It was never a police force; it was always a secret police, a political police, a gestapo before Hitler dreamed up the Geheime Staatspolizei or Stalin the KGB. We had it first, just as we had Ford mass production before anyone else.

But the FBI solves crimes, doesn't it? No, not under Hoover. There were showplace killings and arrests like Dillinger's and others to prove the FBI was a police force. It wasn't. They were showcases made for headlines and radio. The FBI was always more interested in what people read, said, believed. Herb Mitgang of the *New York Times* has written a book on dossiers Hoover maintained on Hemingway, Sinclair Lewis, Dorothy Thompson, Faulkner, etc. These were our writers and Hoover's files on them were criminal acts. Has the FBI changed? Tell me how many black agents are appointed annually and I'll tell you how much it's changed.

Proof of change would be at very least full release of full, unblacked-out files, all of them, from the days of Hoover. There are no secrets of any value that old. I don't see [FBI director William] Sessions releasing the filth of ages.

The training ground for running the secret police seems to be the federal judiciary. [CIA director William] Webster was a federal judge. He became head of the FBI. When he was appointed, I wrote him a letter congratulating him on looking like Dick Tracy and hoped he would be equally zealous in catching criminals. Sessions was a federal judge before he became head of the FBI. What does this tell our people about the judiciary? Is the wearing of robes of black part of ritual of sanctification before admission to the highest rank of our most secret secret police? It belongs in spirit with Bush's hearty affirmation of the right of every citizen to own and carry an automatic rifle. Would A. Lincoln and J. F. Kennedy have approved?

It is my insight that the Freedom of Information Act was created by J. Edgar Hoover. Anyone who applied for his files must have had reason to believe she or he had a file and was hence ipso facto guilty of a crime and hence not permitted to see her/his file. This is the heart of the Freedom of Information Act, which is neither free nor informative. I took the FBI to the federal courts to demonstrate that the FOIA was a scam and a hoax. My lawyer was Dean Charles Nesson of the Harvard Law School. Material about FBI snooping into my oldest films and earliest life is still classified SECRET, CONFIDENTIAL. Judge Sirica, the Watergate judge, known in the courts as Maximum John, heard my case.

One instance of his judicial wisdom.

The University of Wisconsin maintains a large archive on my work and life. It is almost complete, books, journals, letters, checks, details. The FBI refused to answer interrogatories concerning the penetration of my archive. Interrogatory no. 11 was: did the FBI in any way ever penetrate the archives and files maintained by the University of Wisconsin on Emile de Antonio?

Reply by FBI: refuse to answer because it would reveal secret interrogative techniques. Sirica upheld this fairy-tale notion. I laughed in court.

What could those secret techniques be? Did the ghost of J. Edgar Hoover visit Madison and inspect the documents of my tacky life? For shame, Edgar, for shame.

And so it went. And so I acted in a film made in cold anger. I remembered that great Italian proverb: Revenge is a dish best eaten cold. I wanted to make the film, I revealed no anger, sub specie eternitatis, it's a joke. Herbert and Edgar Hoover and Clyde and the FBI and its files. It is what it is: a national thought police; an enemy of the people, of decency, a word I rarely use and have not praised until now, of the First Amendment and the language of free women and men. Can one imagine Tom Jefferson or Tom Paine, George Washington or A. Lincoln, dining and conversing on art and liberty with John Edgar Hoover and Clyde Tolson? Ha.

The film is made of poor means but it is ambitious, more ambitious than *Batman* or *The Deer Hunter* or any Academy Award winner of any year. Look over that pathetic list: trash.

I don't live in cloud-cuckoo-land. The film industry *should* produce its products for its stockholders. Film out there in Hollywood has never pretended that the product was art. And it wasn't and it isn't. Let them take the money and let me make, with minimal restraints, the films I want to make. Not many will like them, but their presence is guaranteed by the Constitution and there is no need for the FBI to tax itself about them or me. I have the right to make any film I want and the FBI has no right to suppress any film I have ever made. It has, of course, interfered in every single film and had me subpoenaed for filming the Weather Underground when the gumshoes couldn't even find them.

Oh, yes, there was one film I assume it did not track: *Painters Painting*, which has to be harmless since one of its stars is Andy Warhol. But then Andy did have a file, and a thick one.

VINCENT CANBY

Emile de Antonio's Thoughts on Himself and the FBI: A Leftist's Sympathies (1990)

As the New York Times *film critic, Vincent Canby had given de Antonio's films favorable coverage for two decades. Canby describes* Mr. Hoover and I *as a "fitting" conclusion to de Antonio's work. But true to the contradictions that characterized de Antonio's life, this final* Times *review offers the surprising description of the contrarian's last film as "sweet."*

After he completes each new film, Emile de Antonio reports in *Mr. Hoover and I,* people tend to ask, "Why a documentary?"

The New York-based producer and director was always amused by the question, which assumes that documentary films are somehow inferior to fiction films.

Before Mr. de Antonio died in December at the age of seventy, he had raised America's political consciousness and enriched its documentary heritage with a series of works that weren't quite like those of any other filmmaker.

Though he could make conventional documentaries, he became best known for such historical collages as *Point of Order* (1964), about the Army-McCarthy hearings, and *Millhouse* (1971), a scathing, freely associative consideration of the career of Richard M. Nixon.

In these films, Mr. de Antonio took archival film clips and edited them to create something of a greater, more all-embracing truth than that of the original pieces of film. He imparted to fact the mysterious possibilities that one more often finds in the best works of fiction.

Mr. Hoover and I, which opens today at the Public Theater, is Mr. de Antonio's final film, and a fitting one it is. It's a ninety-minute autobiography, a coda, a very simple movie in which he simply talks, sometimes to the camera while his wife, Nancy, cuts his hair, sometimes as he shares the screen with John Cage while the composer bakes bread, and sometimes as the camera observes him on the lecture stage in front of a group of students.

The subjects of most of the discussions are Mr. de Antonio's relations with the Federal Bureau of Investigation and his thoughts about J. Edgar Hoover, the bureau's longtime director. He talks about the voluminous though censored FBI files on himself, which he received through the Freedom of Information Act, and notes, with some awe, the trouble to which the FBI went to keep tabs on him, though he was scarcely a major threat to the government.

"I was not a spy," he says. "I talk too much, drink too much. I've been married six times."

Instead, Mr. de Antonio was a militant leftist with radical sympathies and a passionate need to defend civil liberties when he saw them threatened, as in the McCarthy era. He recalls the government's attempts to confiscate the film he had taken of members of the Weather Underground when they were in hiding from the law in the 1970s. He gives a brief, unflattering analysis of Hoover's sexual hang-ups.

Mr. Hoover and I is not one of Mr. de Antonio's more memorable works, but it's an amusing companion piece to the many films he made about other people and their causes. At last the filmmaker is seen front and center.

"I'm the ultimate document," he says of his relationship to the FBI. "I was a pile of files." There was nothing in his life that was hidden or of consequence to the security of the United States. Yet his life became the material for the bureaucratic processes that, left unchecked, grind on forever.

Much more interesting than Mr. de Antonio's remarks about Hoover and the FBI are his remarks about his childhood, his undergraduate years at Harvard (as a classmate of John F. Kennedy), and a friend to the seminal painters and filmmakers of the 1950s and 60s.

There is also something sweet and (in retrospect) sad in his demonstrably easy relations with Mr. Cage, whom he credits with having taught him how to think many years ago, and with his somewhat younger wife, who seems clearly to delight in his mild attempts to act as if he were difficult and crotchety.

JONATHAN ROSENBAUM

The Life and File of an Anarchist Filmmaker (1990)

One of the most insightful contemporary film critics, Jonathan Rosenbaum wrote this appreciation for the Chicago Reader *after viewing the posthumously released* Mr. Hoover and I. *The little-seen swan song caused Rosenbaum to reassess his estimation of de Antonio's contribution to cinema. That his reassessment is so favorable speaks to the power that remained in the filmmaker's cinematic voice to the end.*

Mr. Hoover and I

Directed and Written by Emile de Antonio

1. "Born Pennsylvania USA, in intellectual surroundings and coal mines. Went to Harvard. Became, and still is, a Marxist, without party or leader. Started making films at age of 40 after having avoided films most of his life. Favorite film is *L'age d'or*." Emile de Antonio's self-description was written around 1977 for a poll organized by the Royal Film Archive of Belgium and eventually published in book form as *The Most Important and Misappreciated American Films.* Under the category of most important American films, de Antonio listed, in order, *The Birth of a Nation, It's a Gift, A Night at the Opera, The Cure, The Immigrant, One A.M., The Kid, Big Business, The Navigator,* and *Foolish Wives,* and added the following comment:

"Most American films were and are like Fords. They are made on assembly lines. John Ford is not an artist any more than Jerry Ford is a statesman. Harry Cohn said it all and the Capras jumped.

"Comedy was spared all that. Irreverence was possible because the booboisie didn't know it was being laughed at.

"American films have been seen too often. I rarely go to the movies."

Under the category of misappreciated American films, de Antonio listed five of his own: *Point of Order* (1963), *In the Year of the Pig* (1968), *Millhouse: A White Comedy* (1971), *Rush to Judgment* (1967), and *Painters Painting* (1973).

2. Before seeing *Mr. Hoover and I* (1989), my attitude toward the work of Emile de Antonio was always a bit confused and uncertain. I admired his first film, *Point of Order*—a remarkable reorganization and distillation of 188 hours of kinescopes of the 1954 Army-McCarthy hearings into about ninety minutes that reinvented the meaning of Joseph McCarthy for subsequent generations. But my spotty sense of de Antonio's later work led me to view him as a courageous radical and intellectual who was more a polemicist and invaluable sixties gadfly than an artist. I knew that some of my non-American friends whose politics *and* aesthetics I highly respected regarded him as the greatest and noblest living American documentary filmmaker, but having seen only *Point of Order, Millhouse,* and *Underground* (directed with Haskell Wexler, 1975), I found it difficult to see precisely what they meant. *Millhouse* had the nerve to shower Nixon with abuse and scorn when he was at the height of his power as president—de Antonio was the only filmmaker on Nixon's notorious "enemies" list—and *Underground* performed the valuable and audacious service of interviewing the Weather Underground at a time when they were the FBI's most sought-after radical fugitives. But both of these films seemed more meaningful as potent contemporary gestures than as lasting works of art that genuinely explored the possibilities of the medium. Having lived abroad for almost eight years, I'd managed to miss such films as *In the Year of the Pig, America Is Hard to See* (1969), and *Painters Painting,* and after I returned, I hadn't made it to *In the King of Prussia* (1982) either.

Seeing the fascinating and hugely entertaining *Mr. Hoover and I* at the Toronto film festival last fall, about three months before de Antonio died of a heart attack at age seventy, made me seriously rethink my ideas about him. I've seen the film several times more recently, and encountered for the first time on tape some of the de Antonio films I had missed. *In the Year of the Pig* is the first and best of the major documentaries about Vietnam, infinitely superior to the better-known *Hearts and Minds*—and perhaps the only one that's truly about *Vietnam,* not this country's national ego. I also saw the (to me) disappointing and relatively conventional *Painters Painting.* I can't pretend to assess his career as a whole here because I'm still discovering or rediscovering parts of it, but I can at least say that *Mr. Hoover and I,* a singular and remarkable testament, has made me realize the importance of forming this acquaintance.

3. The issue for me in de Antonio's work has never been intelligence—his films are nothing if not intelligent—but filmic intelligence. The editing

of *Point of Order* certainly has this filmic intelligence, and so does the powerful beginning of *In the Year of the Pig,* but in both instances it was a matter of creatively manipulating archival material. When it comes to shooting material of his own, de Antonio seems to regard the camera as a mechanism for recording talking heads rather than as an expressive tool in its own right; that is, his intelligence figures mainly in his decisions on what to shoot and how to edit, not in how to shoot.

Mr. Hoover and I seizes on the talking-head principle even more nakedly and relentlessly than the other films, and because the talking head in this case is mainly de Antonio himself, one might assume this to be his least "cinematic" movie. In fact, because of the way that it's conceived and executed—shot, spoken, and edited—it turns out to be his *most* cinematic movie, a film that calls attention to its own construction *as a film* in a way and to a degree that its predecessors do not. It is a work that declares de Antonio's allegiance to the minimalism of his friends in the New York art world, such as John Cage and Andy Warhol, and as in their best work, it doesn't adopt minimalism merely as an aesthetic pose but as a functional means to achieve clarity.

4. Back in the mid-sixties, Susan Sontag wrote in praise of *Point of Order* that it "aestheticized a weighty public event." *Mr. Hoover and I* aestheticizes a weighty private event—de Antonio encountering the tens of thousands of pages devoted to him in his FBI file. He aestheticizes it by juxtaposing the clarity of minimalism with the internal and external obfuscation practiced by J. Edgar Hoover's FBI bureaucracy. The film emerges as an autobiography that dialectically and persuasively defines itself as a sane countertext to the demented biography of de Antonio compiled by the FBI. (One hilarious example among many: Around the time that he was applying to flying school, de Antonio had lunch with a respectable friend who asked him, "Now, De, what are you *really* going to do when you grow up?" "I think I'd like to be an eggplant," he replied, and roughly three decades later, he came across this statement solemnly recorded in his FBI dossier.)

Point of Order compelled us to study the aesthetic strategies of both Joseph McCarthy *and* his opponents; *Mr. Hoover and I* foregrounds the aesthetic strategies of Hoover and de Antonio. Both films, in the final analysis, teach us how to reach political conclusions in the act of carrying out our criticism of art.

5. For all its off-the-cuff appearance, *Mr. Hoover and I* had an unusually long gestation period. In an interview with Alan Rosenthal originally published in 1978, de Antonio alluded to "a fictional film I want to do about my own life. It began as an obsession and I started thinking about it before we did the Weather film *[Underground]*. It began with my suing the

government under the Freedom of Information Act." De Antonio then describes the experience of receiving the first installment, "almost 300 pages of documents collected by the FBI on my life up to my 24th year." The file was "initiated by my applying for flying school and a commission" and went all the way back to the year he went away to prep school at the age of twelve. De Antonio added that he was planning to tell this story "very dispassionately," and that he was "doing it as a fiction because of the libel laws."

Obviously the project went through significant changes over the next fifteen years or so, including the elimination of a fictional form, but the root idea—de Antonio receiving his own FBI file—remained the same. In its final form, the film contains eight different kinds of documentary material:

(1 and 2) De Antonio addressing the camera on what appear to be two separate occasions in a neutral urban interior, probably his own New York apartment.

(3) De Antonio addressing a college audience and responding to questions after a screening of *Point of Order*; some references to the Iran-contra hearings make it clear that the date is 1987 or later.

(4) De Antonio asking John Cage about indeterminacy as an aesthetic concept and method in a kitchen while Cage is preparing bread. This material, one should note, was shot not by de Antonio but by the Canadian filmmaker Ron Mann *(Comic Book Confidential, Imagine the Sound)*, and is an outtake from Mann's 1985 documentary *Poetry in Motion*.

(5) De Antonio chatting with his wife at home while she gives him a haircut.

(6) A brief clip of J. Edgar Hoover and Richard Nixon at a ceremony in which Hoover presents President Nixon with a badge making him an honorary member of the FBI; joking allusions are made to Nixon's unsuccessful job application to the FBI in 1937.

(7) Still photographs of Hoover.

(8) Shots of various portions of FBI documents.

The first through fifth types are autonomous blocks of material intercut with one another throughout the film. The sixth, the only archival footage, appears as a separate chunk somewhere in the middle (followed by a commentary from de Antonio). And the seventh and eighth are used sparingly to illustrate and punctuate de Antonio's commentary (a photograph of Hoover as a child, however, is the first thing we see in the film).

Isolating these separate blocks is important because a central part of the film's method is to make us aware of their distinctness from one another. At the same time, de Antonio freely cuts both within and between them in order to follow a single line of argument—a line that begins with the subject of himself and Hoover and then branches out to explore separate facets of each—and he doesn't always respect the chronological progression of each sequence. Very long takes predominate at the beginning of the film; by the end, the cuts have become much more frequent.

6. After the title, de Antonio, in a sweater and jacket, says to the camera, "If I were asked to choose a villain from the history of this country, it would not be Benedict Arnold, nor would it be communist conspirators, nor would it be spies for the Nazis—because, except for Arnold, most of these people were fairly impotent, did not have power to do anything. But Hoover, because he had power for such a long period of time, because it was wantonly exercised, because it was exercised with spite, without a touch of judgment or any sense of justice, because it was willful and capricious, because it made a mockery of our Constitution . . ." His sentence is broken off by a jump cut, followed by de Antonio saying, "Don't cut. We've cut by saying that, of course. We're running?" An offscreen voice says "Yeah," and de Antonio starts a new sentence about Hoover.

A bit later we get another disruptive cut, to John Cage putting corn oil and then bread in a pan while he describes the various things he is doing. Only toward the end of this sequence does the camera move around to reveal that Cage is addressing de Antonio on the other side of the counter, and only after that does de Antonio bring up the fact that they're supposed to be talking about indeterminacy—at which point there is a cut back to de Antonio in his jacket and sweater talking about Hoover.

A little further on, after de Antonio, in the college auditorium, has been comparing the Army-McCarthy hearings to the Iran-contra hearings, there is a cut to de Antonio saying, while we hear the mechanical sound of the camera, "This film, although it probably won't be seen by many people, is an attempt at subversion. This film is a film about position. I'm glad we're hearing the sound. Why should the process of any art not be included in whatever that art is?"

All three of these disruptive cuts function as slight pivots and digressions in the discussion rather than as irrelevant interruptions. In the first and third, we're alerted to the filmmaking process, a modernist gesture that prepares us in turn for the introduction to Cage, who like Warhol can be described as one of the last of the modernists. (Minimalism—from Beckett to Cage and Warhol—can be described as the last gasp of modernism, before postmodernism took over.)

7. The spectacle of Cage preparing bread, which constitutes the second apparent interruption, eventually becomes part of the discussion about the uses of indeterminacy in art, a discussion that's pursued by Cage and de Antonio in later portions of the same kitchen dialogue. Cage's cooking

functions not merely as a counterpoint to the conversation but, at certain points, as an unwitting illustration of the nature of artistic choices, Cage's as well as de Antonio's. For example, when Cage is carefully sweeping cracked wheat off the counter into a container while discussing indeterminacy, he sprinkles a few leftover bits over the bread he has just prepared.

De Antonio does not employ in *Mr. Hoover and I* the chance operations used by Cage in determining certain aspects of composition and performance—as de Antonio himself emphatically pointed out to me and others when he discussed the film at various venues last fall. He never said how such operations *did* relate to what he was doing. Cage's meaning and function in the film are both mysterious and subtle, but I would argue that they are not simply ineffable. Cage's role as friend and educator to de Antonio is recounted in one of de Antonio's monologues, along with a beautiful Zen koan that Cage told him, circa 1953. De Antonio says this koan was as important to him as anything he learned from Marx, Hobbes, Plato, or Schopenhauer, but I won't attempt to repeat it here—de Antonio does a much better job of it than I possibly could. Still, I think it has as much bearing on the structure and meaning of the film as Cage's work in composition and performance had.

Broadly speaking, Cage's artistic principles are founded on the notion of removing the artist's volition at certain stages and allowing a sort of dialogue with "nature" or "the universe" or "fate" that is brought about through the introduction of chance operations. (At one point in the discussion, while talking about intervals, Cage describes his use of astronomical maps in relating musical notes to stars; it might be added that this film *does* make frequent use of the notion of intervals, if not indeterminacy.) The only way in which de Antonio might be said to duplicate or imitate Cage's methods is his use of Ron Mann's footage.

But it might also be argued that life itself exercised this indeterminancy over de Antonio's own rather haphazard career—a career that can be regarded as itself an intricate struggle between chance and control. Before he became a filmmaker, de Antonio worked at various times as a longshoreman, barge captain, peddler, war surplus broker, book editor, and college philosophy teacher. As a political activist concerned with injustice, he had to mold his life and career in relation to the events, people, and issues that he encountered and cared about—which is another way of saying that this political artist worked exclusively with "found" material, whether it was Joseph McCarthy, the Kennedy assassination, various forms of leftist dissent, New York painters, Nixon, Hoover, or in the final analysis—and shortly before his death—himself. "I am the ultimate document," de Antonio says in the film on two separate occasions, and chance as well as control have clearly played major roles in Hoover's and his own compilations.

Cage, of course, is not the only exemplary figure cited by de Antonio, nor is his koan the only text, and it becomes much easier to grasp his significance in the film if one sees it as part of a larger mosaic or constellation. De Antonio also cites as models *Pull My Daisy* (a groundbreaking American independent short) and Cinda Firestone's *Attica,* reads a powerful and influential statement by Jean-Paul Sartre (about man as an absolute value in his own time) that he first encountered in 1945, quotes Karl Jaspers on the subject of censorship ("Anything can be said as long as it signifies nothing"), and discusses the FBI's enraged responses to Warhol's *Lonesome Cowboys.*

De Antonio talks about Hoover's victims—Ethel Rosenberg, Alger Hiss, Jean Seberg, and John Dillinger (as well as FBI agent Purvis, who gunned Dillinger down). He discusses Hoover's cohorts—Clyde Colson, Joseph McCarthy, and Richard Nixon—and the fact that Cinda Firestone had fond personal memories of Hoover as a little girl. Also figuring in the discussion are all of his own major films and two media concoctions controlled by Hoover—his book *Masters of Deceit,* ghostwritten by many hands at a cost of a quarter of a million dollars, and a TV show called *The F.B.I.,* which ran for nine years (de Antonio says fourteen) and which Hoover helped to produce.

8. "The film is not an attack on McCarthy," de Antonio said of *Point of Order* in his 1978 interview with Rosenthal. "The film is an attack on the American government. My feeling is that if you look at the film carefully, Welch comes off as badly as McCarthy. He comes off as a rather brilliant, sinister, clever lawyer who used McCarthy's techniques to destroy McCarthy. . . . Don't misunderstand me. I wanted McCarthy gored to death but I also wanted the whole system to be exposed, and the only people who saw that were a few Marxists."

By the same token, *Mr. Hoover and I* is not merely an attack on Hoover's FBI but a statement of independence from all bureaucracies, governmental and otherwise. (De Antonio also gets in some licks against the CIA. In *News from Afar,* a fascinating short film made by Shu Lea Cheang just before de Antonio's death, he seriously proposes—in the course of discussing recent events in Eastern Europe, the Soviet Union, and Central America—that Bush abolish the CIA: "We don't need the CIA any more than we need wings to fly.")

A self-described anarchist, de Antonio believed most of all in the value of plain talk—in trusting his viewers not only to think, but to think for themselves. That is why he insisted on doing without narration in *Point of Order*—there was no need to explain what was happening and what the film's relationship was to these events—and why he followed the same principle in *In the Year of the Pig*. Paradoxically, *Mr. Hoover and I* could be described from a certain point of view as consisting of little but narration—de Antonio telling us what he thinks. Yet the film is brave and lucid enough to be saying a lot more than what de Antonio is saying, and even doing more than he is doing. Its dialectical construction and de Antonio's treatment of his own discourse as artistic "material" rather than as simple dogma liberate us as spectators, and compel us to engage with the film as we would with another person in a dialogue; the subject is not merely Hoover and de Antonio, but what they represent in relation to ourselves.

This is only one of the ways in which *Mr. Hoover and I* can be profitably compared to *Roger and Me,* a film that elicits a good deal less thought and reflection. (Significantly, de Antonio originally planned to call his film *Mr. Hoover and Me,* until he learned about the title that Michael Moore was giving to his film—a film, incidentally, of which he was highly critical.) It's a pity that de Antonio's film hasn't been picked up by a major studio, or reviewed in *Time* or *Newsweek* or on any of the network TV shows, as Moore's was, and that most people in this country will never even hear about it, much less see it. But at the same time, it isn't very surprising, because the kind of integrity and power that de Antonio had as a filmmaker have almost nothing to do with the qualities that the media routinely reward. (Maybe if he'd lived another twenty years, he would have been inadvertently turned into an institution, as I. F. Stone was.) Fortunately, *Mr. Hoover and I* is as exciting and as lasting a legacy as anyone could wish; and it is there to be seen and learned from—for anyone who wants to encounter it.

III   Indiscreet Interventions on Life, Art, and Politics

EMILE DE ANTONIO

Salt of the Earth *(1966)*

While Film Comment *was preparing the first in-depth profile of de Antonio (on the making of* Rush to Judgment*), the magazine had America's preeminent practicing Marxist filmmaker review Herbert Biberman's book about the making and suppression of the only Marxist feature film made in the United States, the 1954 classic* Salt of the Earth. *With the lesson of the punishment doled out to Biberman and other members of the Hollywood left it is, in retrospect, rather amazing that de Antonio, a professed and active leftist, managed to make the uncompromising films he did.*

It was a very bad film script. Carl Foreman wrote it. Ivan and Joe smashing bottle and glass at the Elbe. War over. Victory. Unease. End Carl Foreman script. At that moment, at that very moment—a new war, new villains. The Cold War. On our side: Hiroshima, House Un-American Activities Committee, the trials of the spies, Rosenbergs, McCarthy—lies, suppressions, and death in freedom's name. *Salt of the Earth* tells what it was like to make a film in the Cold War, a film with a Marxist, minority view. And *who* tried to suppress it, and *how* they tried to suppress it.

War societies demand conformities. The first soldier of the Cold War is mass communication. Magazines, press, radio, TV: okay, safe. Advertiser control. Advertisers—self-policing through self-interest. From Milton Berle to *Beverly Hillbillies,* all systems go and okay. Mediocrity. Books okay too—esoteric, noninfluential, limited. Film a different problem. Hollywood had to be cleansed, victims and scapegoats were needed. Conforming monster demands them. HUAC. Hollywood and the Marxist heroes. The Hollywood Ten. 1947. Then the Waldorf Declaration of Eric Johnston, former president of the U.S. Chamber of Commerce:

> Members of the Association of Motion Picture Producers deplore the action of the ten Hollywood men who have been cited for contempt. . . . We do not desire to prejudge their legal rights. . . . We will forthwith discharge and suspend without compensation those in our employ . . . until such time as he has purged himself of contempt and declares under oath that he is not a Communist. . . . In pursuing this policy, we are not going to be swayed by intimidation or hysteria from any source. To this end we will invite the Hollywood talent guilds to work with us to eliminate any subversives, to protect the innocent, and to safeguard free speech and a free screen wherever threatened.

But even this resolute double-talk was in itself doubly phoney from the start—ten minutes after the declaration, the producers were making under-the-table deals with some of the Hollywood Ten and saving money while doing it. An anonymous writer of "sincere" Hollywood product comes more cheaply than Dalton Trumbo.

Herbert Biberman, who directed *Salt* and wrote the book about its making, was not part of that black market. He served six months in the Federal Correctional Institution at Texarkana and was blacklisted on discharge. Like most of the Hollywood politicals, he would have preferred to make "sincere" films in Hollywood. Blacklisted, he turned with Paul Jarrico and Michael Wilson to try a new kind of film: the low-budget film of Marxist social protest. *Salt of the Earth*. What happened is worth reading about. Do you want to know how the U.S. tried to strangle a film in the days of the Great Cold War? Here it all is—the shabby, seamy complicity between the moguls, the unions, the government and its federal police, the Good People, Howard Hughes, the film laboratories—even the labs.

It's all here, in a droplet, a droplet of sewer water revealing all the filth of conformity and the Cold War.

Salt of the Earth is about a strike—a strike by Mexican-American workers of Local 890 of the United Mine and Smelter Workers' Union, a union expelled from the CIO for alleged Communist influence. George F. Baehr, a coal operator during the great coal strike of 1902, said, "The rights and interests of the working man will be protected and cared for—not by the labor agitators but by the Christian men to whom God in his infinite wisdom has given control of the property interests of the country." The makers of the film and the union and its members did not share Mr. Baehr's optimism about Christian businessmen.

The book, in detail and clarity, brings to life all the intimidations from script outline to attempted showing. And an illustrious list it is. Roy Brewer, self-appointed purifier of Hollywood for IATSE [the International Alliance of Theatrical Stage Employees and Moving Picture Operators]; Congressman Jackson of California; the Immigration Service, which finally expelled star Rosaura Revueltas through a dishonest and phoney legalism. It was the time of McCarthy, and the Good People were beating the thickets looking for *reds*. Pathé Labs refused to process Red Film. Walter Pidgeon of the Screen Actors Guild cleared his distinguished throat and referred the matter to higher authorities. A film editor reported to the FBI. And most instructive of all, a letter from Howard Hughes to Congressman Jackson. It is a textbook piece on how to stamp out freedom in film. See page 123 of Biberman's book: IATSE not only denied the film a crew but refused to allow warehousemen to touch the cans once the film was finished. Distributors wouldn't distribute. Exhibitors wouldn't exhibit. In Los Angeles and other major cities, the press refused to carry ads. It did look like a conspiracy on the part of everybody.

At least so Biberman and his friends felt. In 1956 they filed suit against the entire industry: all the major producing and distributing companies; sound studios; special-effects studios; the laboratories; the unions; and one un-American congressman, Donald Jackson of California. No suspense, and no chance of winning although the industry offered to settle. Time, money, a lily-white middle-class jury system brought in a predictable verdict. Biberman lost.

Now we have porcine Joe Pool, LBJ, Vietnam. Are we becoming the bad guys of history? If we are, let us hope some filmmakers will ask why and will be willing to take on the whole show with the energy and determination of Herbert Biberman.

EMILE DE ANTONIO
ALBERT MAHER

Chasing Checkers by Richard M. Nixon (1968)

Unable to obtain a print of Richard Nixon's long unseen "Checkers Speech," de Antonio settled for this bit of satirical exposé on the eve of the 1968 presidential election. The New York Free Press *cover featured a full-page photo of Dick and Pat with their famed cocker spaniel. De Antonio's own trick would be more properly turned two years later when he clandestinely obtained a stolen print of the Checkers kinescope and gave the footage a new mass audience.*

Checkers is gone. American eyes teared September 23, 1952, when vice-presidential candidate Nixon, about to be dumped by Ike and the Republican Party, told all about Checkers and an alleged slush fund. Lenny Bruce might have read it. School children didn't commit it to memory. It sank from view like a Mafia victim in a cement overcoat.

Last January, Tom Wolfe, vice president of WABC News, was telling me about great moments of our political life which had sunk from view. Chief among them was Dick Nixon on Checkers. Not a trace. After [the Republican convention in] Miami, I thought it might be useful to find Checkers. But Mr. Wolfe was right: WABC didn't have a print. A subordinate at CBS said, yes, we have a negative but please call back. The call back was answered by Mr. Waldman. No, it was an error; there was no negative. In fact, there had been a print but it was lost. Yes, lost. Without a trace. Why not try the Republican National Committee?

NBC first, however. A call to the NBC library. Yes, they did have a negative. But Mr. Richard Swicker would have to approve its release. Mr. Swicker appeared on Friday, August 23. A formality, send along a purchase order. On Monday, August 26, no print. A mistake. It was a sponsored show and rights were owned by the Republican National Committee. Gus Miller of the Republican National Committee was foxy-voiced and nasty.

No, absolutely not. Ask Mr. Nixon. I did and found Miss Barbara Baiter, who was out. When we did talk, Miss Baiter said she'd call right back. She hasn't. Perhaps some words are better than no picture. Here's a condensed transcript:

> My Fellow Americans:
>
> I come before you tonight as a candidate for the vice presidency and as a man whose honesty and integrity have been questioned. . . .

EMILE DE ANTONIO

Some Discrete Interruptions on Film, Structure, and Resonance (1971)

These discrete, though hardly discreet, notes appeared in Film Quarterly *alongside a lengthy interview titled "Radical Scavenging." De Antonio embraced the phrase used to describe the collage methods inspired by Cage, Rauschenberg, and others. It aptly identifies his agitational assemblages of found footage. This written assemblage of discrete cinematic ideas applies similar technique, in miniature. However, working in written form, de Antonio tended to salt his thoughts with indiscreet personal attacks on both his enemies and his allies.*

> The History of Kino-Eye has been a relentless struggle to modify the course of world cinema, to place in cinema production at new emphasis on the "unplayed film" over the play film, to substitute the document for the mise-en-scène, to break out of the theater and to enter the arena of life itself.
> :: Dziga Vertov

1. In 1963, Richard Roud excluded *Point of Order* from the New York Film Festival on the ground that it was television and not film. Eight years later the distinction seems reactionary and shortsighted; even then it was old-maidish, faddist, and self-serving. It's not where it comes from that matters but what is projected. Anything that can go through a projector is film (see 4). Three months later, Roud made the discovery that *Point of Order* was a film after all, and invited it to the London Festival.

2. The audiovisual history of our time is the television outtake. Each hour cameras, as impersonal as astronauts, grind away film and tape which the content-free networks will never transmit. Our television is content-free not because it is regulated but because it is a commodity—not news or art or entertainment but a product. Its masters see it that way. The regulators

don't regulate television anyway—they regulate us. The masters most ardently want public regulation to continue in order to perpetuate private monopoly structure. Don't all public regulatory agencies behave in the same way: phone, light, gas, etc.?

McLuhan's dictum is a show-business half-truth. The medium *has* changed the mode of perception without changing the quality of what is perceived; television time is time for sale. Marx on the ownership of the means of production is still a better insight, as well as a more informative one.

3. The Bill of Rights was written with a quill pen and beautifully, so that every word of it needs to be made operational today. More views, more access, more community control, less corporate profit. One specific need: a national electronic archive where nothing is thrown away because it costs money to store it (our history), whose retrieval and indexing systems are electronic and instant, where everything is made available for us for use, free. Cost of operation? Rental of our air to the networks.

4. "'A film' may be defined operationally as 'whatever will pass through a projector.' The least thing that will do that is nothing at all. Such a film has been made. It is the only *unique* film in existence" (Hollis Frampton, "For a Metahistory of Film," Artforum, September 1971).

The key word is not *film* but *Artforum*. The entire issue on film. An invasion of body snatchers? Annette Michelson, guest editor, on shiny, expensive page eight, makes it clear that a "new criticism" has arrived, and for film—using a vocabulary formerly preempted by painting and for bourgeoise mystification.

Why? The exhaustion of American painting and sculpture has driven many to gauge the earth, make mile-long walls, and robe the seaside in plastic, to make *arrangements* with haystacks, to create a conceptual art in which the painting is described on a typewriter sheet, framed and sold. That's real exhaustion. In a more literary effort, one artist was photographed riding a horse around a ring in a pasture. And now, having done all that, they're moving into film. Jonas Mekas and his troupe of mercenary, trend-sniffing cavalry have pointed the way; a great army of swells, together with its sutlers and camp followers.

The filmic ideas collected by *Artforum* are damp hand-me-downs from John Cage and Jasper Johns. The *salons des refusés* are going to the movies. Also dealers, critics, corporations, collectors, scene people, film schools, museums. Can Andrew Sarris be far behind?

5. Structure and resonance are coefficients of the film of content. Film is not shot but built up from various strips of celluloid (Pudovkin). And when it works, there is resonance—not only between one shot and another but between one strip and another, between one scene and another; and

like the idea of correspondence in the poetry of Donne, there is resonance between the film and that which exists outside the film. Like ambiguity in poetry, resonance is a literal fact as well as a metaphor. Renoir's *Rules of the Game* or Rossellini's *Rise of Louis XIV* are what I mean.

Films which are "products" customarily lack resonance, are supermarket cake and icing. When it is mechanical *(Easy Rider)*, structure is artificial, the resonance rings but once and content is an additive.

Dependence on the technical is also an aspect of no content. *Cinéma verité*. Whose *verité*? No one can fault the development of fast, light, mobile equipment. What is wrong is the space the best-known practitioners of c-v occupy today: publicity films for rock groups (Stones, Beatles, Monterey, Woodstock, Altamont).

6. Having laid about, both in the interview and these interruptions, it may seem graceless to discuss my own work. Here are some specifics which are not necessarily illustrative. I simply want to raise them.

No filmmaker expects any critic to discover all that is in a film. In spite of its critical success, in spite of its going on to be treated as a classic, I have always been uncomfortable with the critics for failing to see that in *Point of Order* each segment was analogous to a specific technique of Senator McCarthy's *prior* to the 1954 Army-McCarthy hearings. Example: in the film, Joseph Welch accuses McCarthy and his aides (Roy Cohn and [James] Juliana) of having doctored a photograph to prove that Secretary of the Army Stevens and G. David Schine had met *alone*. The aloneness was accomplished by snipping off a Colonel Bradley who had been in the original picture.

Four years earlier, McCarthy had caused the defeat of conservative, wealthy Senator Millard Tydings of Maryland in his bid for reelection. He accused Tydings of being a Communist. The master stroke was the "proof": flooding the state with a doctored composite photograph showing Tydings together with Earl Browder, then chairman of the American Communist Party. They never had been together, of course. Tydings lost the election. There are six other such correspondences in the film, never pointed out.

A minute example from *Millhouse*: beginning of the film. Madame Tussaud's Wax Museum. Shot tilts up from feet to head, disclosing Nixon in wax, surrounded by wax images of Kennedy, Washington, etc. Seven reels later, camera angle and motion are almost exactly similar. This time, however, it is Premier Ky (1967) running for election in Vietnam.

A problem. In the 1954 Army-McCarthy hearings, obscure, back-hall politicians were shot into momentary prominence because of thirty-six days of TV exposure. Eight years later, when I was working on *Point of Order*, they were once more obscure paper shufflers. For example, John Adams, counsel to the army. How could one "fix" him in seconds? I tried doing a cast of characters in sync sound. It didn't work. We're so accustomed to sync sound that it was too normal, too continuous. However, by running stills and frozen frames with voice-over (same sound, no more than would have been used in sync) the five seconds became jarring and discontinuous, memorable enough to fix the character. Thus, when Adams said, "I've never filed a brief. I've never drawn a complaint. I'm strictly a Washington-type lawyer," his image was substantial enough to read him in context throughout the film.

EMILE DE ANTONIO

Pontus Hultén and Some '60s Memories in New York (1973)

Like a Swedish Henry Geldzahler, Pontus Hultén curated major exhibitions of the work of Andy Warhol and his New York School predecessors, allowing European critics to experience the works that were energizing the American art scene. Brought together by their interests in politics and Warhol, de Antonio wrote this account of his involvement with modern art for the catalog published by Pontus Hultén's New York School show at Stockholm's Moderna Museet.

In 1959, some filmmakers, for the most part about-to-be filmmakers, angry and bored, were pulled together by Jonas Mekas to form the New American Cinema. Like the painting going on in the United States, it was really a New York experience. We were bored with Hollywood's assembly-line production and angry with the closed, brutal corporate distribution/exhibition system. The New American Cinema once met in my office, an old gray building on West 53rd Street, whose south wall was covered by an ad for *Brute Force* starring Burt Lancaster. I named the building the Brute Force Building and carried it on my letterhead, but the Post Office refused to deliver mail. Today the building is a gray-black tomb of soap operas, violence, fixed quiz shows, game shows, the CBS building. At any rate, we met (once we celebrated Christmas, Jonas and Adolfas Mekas and thirty others and I, in the tiny office of the New Yorker Theater with kosher salamis and Polish vodka) and tried to make a New American Cinema out of vying egos and ideas. We shared some of the following: that we might make smaller films, more personal films, use smaller cameras, no stars, political films, antifilms, films that would be more abrasive than mogul chocolate bars. There were many of us—I don't remember them all—Ed Bland, Sheldon Rochlin, Shirley Clarke, Robert Frank, Lionel Rogosin, Jonas and Adolfas Mekas, Dan Talbot, myself, and Alfred Leslie.

Alfred Leslie. In trying to get his and Robert Frank's film *Pull My Daisy* into a theater (together with Welles's *The Magnificent Ambersons*, it opened in Dan Talbot's New Yorker Theater), I spent many hours at Alfred's loft at 940 Broadway (later destroyed by fire), where he was also painting and editing that one-shot Roman candle *The Hasty Papers* (1960). It was a whiff of what was to be: pot, politics, war. One of the manuscripts was by Pontus Hultén. It was: "Three Great Painters: Churchill, Hitler, and Eisenhower."

Pontus Hultén? A bridge? An art critic? Jesus. I read it. It didn't read like art criticism. It was lively, new, political. At that time politics here in the U.S. was kept on the low burner, except the as-usual kind. Eisenhower's presidency was drawing to an end. What was good for General Motors was good for the country, etc.

By 1962, the old New York painting, abstract expressionism, had become classic, and there were few outside of New York who were ready for the new New York painting. In 1962, Pontus Hultén assembled the show *Four Americans: Johns, Leslie, Rauschenberg, Stankiewicz*. Camelot was cake icing, castles in two dimensions, like Hollywood; its statesmen one-dimensional (Marcuse). The Merlins were trickless, wordmongers without magic, professors with an appetite for distant combats and confrontations: Vienna, Cuba, Vietnam, Green Berets, vicarious. I think, you do.

I had met Bob Rauschenberg and Jasper Johns when they were living downtown in lofts on Pearl Street (narrow, warm, and gone, now widened to vacuity, to make room for a greater nowhere) in the mid-fifties. Our very first meeting was actually in the country; they were hammering and sawing and sewing sets and costumes for a John Cage–Merce Cunningham concert I was producing. In their lofts were cards, drinks, wild ducks cooked with wild rice, Jack Daniels, and Bob's black paintings, the red paintings, *Rebus, Odalisk, Factum I* and *Factum II,* then a huge painting with an umbrella in it, and *The Bed* and *Third Time Painting*.

Of Jasper Johns's work: the great flags and targets, all the early ones before any had been sold. It was a private world trying to become public, before dealers, collectors, and a public materialized. One weekend we went to the ocean and played Hearts and drank Jack Daniels for three days. Jap's marmoset escaped and climbed into a fragile, tall willow tree. It was very hard coaxing it down. Pontus Hultén's show, *Four Americans,* was, I guess, the first big show in Europe which, although not Pop, led to Pop and the Moderna Museet's 1964 *Pop Show,* which showed Oldenburg, Segal, Warhol . . .

In the fifties, I had lived with Tina Fredericks, who had been an editor for Condé Nast *(Vogue, Glamour)* and had given Andy Warhol his first commercial art work making drawings of shoes for fashion pages and later for ads. When we met, he told me he wanted to become famous and a painter. I was beginning work on *Point of Order* and was sometimes cloven between the new painting/music and the radical politics I once had as a student at Harvard and which I lost in the military during World War II. I was again aligned with radical politics and felt the cleavage was real only to those undertakers of radical politics who wanted a dead art entombed with nineteenth-century ideas of radicalism. Lukács said that the last important Marxist theoretical work was Lenin's *Imperialism* of 1917.

When Andy began painting, I walked over evenings after dinner to his house on 89th Street, next to the National Fertility Institute, drank whiskey in white cups, and looked at his paintings. I liked it. Once he showed me two large Coke bottle paintings. One was a Coke bottle, plain and only a Coke bottle; the other was a Coke bottle surrounded by abstract expressionist brush strokes. One worked; the other didn't. I don't know where the second one is now. When Andy began painting, he wasn't a pop star but a quiet commercial artist with great ambition and a reservoir of plans and people.

Another direction which New York painting took in the late fifties and early sixties was Frank Stella, who with his early black paintings found a new imprint of abstract austerity and, immediately after, in the aluminum series, began changing the shape of the canvas itself. Stephen Greene in the late fifties had been artist in residence at Princeton. Teaching painting or writing or filmmaking fleshes out college catalogs and hundreds of U.S. colleges are extremely busy teaching thousands of students to become writers, film directors, painters, and actors. This is probably a very good thing because, although it may not produce many artists, it does produce an audience. Stephen Greene was singularly excited about one student. We went to see his work in the McCarten Theater. It was Frank Stella. The next time I saw an exhibition of his work was only two years later in the Museum of Modern Art.

Carl André said at that time of Frank's work, "Symbols are counters passed among people. Frank Stella's painting is not symbolic. His stripes are the paths of the brush on canvas. These paths lead only into the painting." In 1973 we know that the so-called stripes were not really stripes. Frank's work is the best answer to that hypothetical question by the philistine, "Okay, so you painted these stripe pictures. What are you going to do for an encore?" There are no encores in high art, just development and pictures of quality. That's as far as it can go.

As for the dilemma between art and politics, I still believe in an art of quality and radical politics. They are not incompatible.

EMILE DE ANTONIO

Visions of Vietnam (1974)

In this typically contentious pan of Peter Davis's documentary against the Vietnam War, de Antonio mistakenly predicted that Hearts and Minds *would "never find an audience."* Introduction to the Enemy, *the little-seen film lauded here, documented Tom Hayden, Jane Fonda, and their young son touring North Vietnam on behalf of the Indochina Peace Campaign. IPC distributed the film, which had been shot by Haskell Wexler and Christine Burrill, both of whom worked on* Underground *the following year. Excerpts from* Introduction *reappeared there. Davis's film won the Best Documentary Academy Award that* In the Year of the Pig *had been denied, bringing a strong critique of U.S. military policy to a large viewership. Yet some critics would come to agree with de Antonio that the later movie "sneers with a japing, middle-class, liberal superiority" and was made several years too late. It also recycles the television outtake of Colonel George S. Patton (American soldiers are "a bloody good bunch of killers") that de Antonio highlighted in* Pig.

The director had close ties to University Review, *the New York–based leftist paper that ran this review. Earlier in 1974, his assistant Marc Weiss conducted an interview with the director for* University Review. *When the publication folded, de Antonio moved into its office.*

Introduction to the Enemy is not the kind of film I make, but it is the kind of film I wish I could make everyone see.

Vietnam: not a statistical Vietnam, not body counts, kill ratios, targets of opportunity, not a Vietnam seen through radar scanners wired into smart bombs, not the Vietnam we used to see filling the space between commercials on the networks, nor the Vietnam the Pentagon saw, nor the Vietnam of the "best and brightest." For less than the cost of one bomb, Jane Fonda, Tom Hayden, and Haskell Wexler have made a human trip through the hearts and minds of the Vietnamese themselves—Asian peasants, intellectuals, film people, old men, children—a people who have been fighting for thirty-five years, who have not only put it together to fight but are holding it together as they rebuild.

It's a Vietnam we don't know very much about. An old man speaking in Vietnamese tells us his house has been bombed, destroyed, rebuilt twelve times. The subtitles are there, but we know—by looking at him and hearing a language we don't understand—much more than we did before. It is the first time that we meet *them* on a human plane. An American sync-sound crew tracks south from Hanoi to Quang Tri under the PRG [People's Revolutionary Government]: an American mine explodes, a peasant dies, the doctor explains, peasants stare. Arthur Schlesinger called it "the bitter heritage." It is, and it's ours (his).

See it now before effete, intellectual snobs like William Buckley blow up their jabberwocky balloons to charge: *(a)* elitism, *(b)* that it was all staged, the Hanoi Scenario, *(c)* morality. The last is the hardest, so I'll treat it last. Elitism means Tom and Jane in Vietnam. Tom Wolfe can supply about four funky adjectives here. But the film isn't that. It's Jane Fonda and Tom Hayden among the Vietnamese people. It's not elitism to claim the strong and honorable line of dissent Fonda and Hayden belong to. They paid their dues. We need to affirm that history, that continuity, and in so doing we become more than Kojak, Columbo, and this morning's *New York Times* already rolled up and tossed into a green plastic bag.

Don't worry too much about staging either. We, whose tutors in staging came from Disneyland, know all about how the "dead" bad guy gets up, dusts his chaps, and gets ready to bite another bullet. Nixon's Vietnam, Cambodia, Watergate performances have developed in all of us what Hemingway used to call the "built-in bullshit detector."

Morality. Not chic. More "in" to be icy, Waspish, foppish, and in Eugenia Shepherd's column. Also boring. I get very bored very fast watching television and I walk out of most films. I have never been able to understand that kind of grinding academic mind like Sarris's or John Simon's which can sit through all those films. What is it they are looking at? Omphalos?

Introduction to the Enemy is political *and* fresh and exciting. Wexler's handheld camera moves through that deadly feeling of the static interview into a space that's alive. Fonda in *Barbarella* and Fonda in Hanoi is a real interplanetary war. The former loses. Finally, an old man in Quang Tri in the PRG zone says, "I used to say, 'Just let me live to see peace come to my country, and one month later I would be happy to die.' But now I say, 'Just let me live to see the day of unification, and one month later I would be happy to die.'"

Network television and Hollywood have always been uncomfortable with the documentary. The networks used to spew them and give out awards, like National 4-H Clubs, to one another; long white papers, etc. They take their place in Trotsky's dustbin, so objective that life is bleached out. Objective enough to be mindless, no sponsor or his grandchild should be offended. Hollywood's discomfort is more practical; it avoids them, finding Godfathers, Airports, Poseidons, and a kind of ritual cinematic cloning of the works of Fitzgerald, Hemingway, and Zane Grey more profitable.

Hearts and Minds is the *Godfather* of documentaries. My guess is that there is one big difference: it will never find an audience.

Hearts and Minds is also a miracle. A political film without politics. The style betrays the political emptiness: no style at all, amorphous sequences strung together. Most art has something to do with structure(s). I found it both heartless and mindless. Heartless because of an inability to understand either the United States or Vietnam. Heartless because it sneers with a japing, middle-class, liberal superiority when it should be doing something quite different. Patronizing attitudes include: a returned POW pilot is welcomed home to Linden, New Jersey. He is still gung ho as police wave the flag, as he talks before the flaccid city fathers, as he talks to the mothers of Linden, as he talks to a grammar-school class. The distance between the more hip parts of Beverly Hills and Linden, New Jersey, is vast, and those who made *Hearts and Minds* don't understand it. They laugh. Example: head shot, black veteran, smiling, tells of getting his pants blown off, running around with his thing hanging out. A real chuckle of a figure. "Shit, man," and all that. Camera pulls back and he is missing an arm and a leg. Neither the camera nor the director makes one feel that humanity is involved in any way. Example: football locker room, coach pep talk, rough language, coach slaps around the players, go and kill 'em. They go out, they get hurt. It's a sour metaphor, it's not even a good one, and it hangs in the middle like something interesting they didn't understand.

Mindlessness is worse. I'm not asking that *Das Kapital* be made into a film, but it's so much more coherent. How can you make a film about Vietnam and leave out their revolution? How can you leave out the dissent here that cost LBJ the presidency and forced Nixon into lies and Vietnamization? (Ninety seconds of "Give Peace a Chance" won't do.) How can you suppress all evidence that the war is still going on? Where did the war come from? Where is the system that produced it? And the Christmas bombing?

The voices that seem to speak for the makers of the film, like the makers of the film, found out about the war too late. Clark Clifford? A plushy Washington lawyer, a behind-the-scenes figure in many administrations (he was blamed by Joe McCarthy for starting the Army-McCarthy hearings), he discovers something is wrong in 1968 when he was secretary of defense. Where was he in 1964? Daniel Ellsberg? He weeps about Robert Kennedy, but I'm more interested in what motivated him into being part of the Rand/CIA/Marine deal so long; and his version of our involvement is cut down to the skeleton of a field mouse. A Vietnamese Catholic priest talks about defending his native land, but Dien Bien Phu and the Tet Offensive were about more than that.

A little semiexplicit sex in a Saigon whorehouse. A brilliant sequence of a Saigon banker who rushed home at the first whiff of "peace" to make deals with U.S. companies. It ends as it began, trailing off to nowhere, carrying the logo of Columbia Pictures. Rumors are that Columbia won't distribute it. After all, it takes $8,000,000 at the box office to get back $1,200,000.

MICHAEL FELLNER

Emile de Antonio's CIA Diary (1975)

Devoted to an anti-Vietnam War agenda, Take Over *(1971–79) was another Madison-based underground newspaper. In the spring of 1975 de Antonio spoke with editor Michael Fellner about his plans to make a film with renegade Philip Agee based on his book about the Central Intelligence Agency. His designs on the Agee project were sincere. But they were also the perfect cover for the film he was actually making. Within weeks of this account, de Antonio recorded his interviews with the Weather Underground fugitives. Blowing smoke about a million-dollar fiction film with Jane Fonda and Robert Redford no doubt helped misdirect the FBI and CIA surveillance of his activities.*

Philip Agee is a fascinating case of political conversion and political commitment. He is a man who made a 180-degree turn from the CIA, from his business, and from his Irish Catholic family. His book, *Inside the Company: CIA Diary,* is also fascinating because there is an extraordinary amount of detail: how he was recruited, the tests he had to go through, how many times he had to sign the contract that he was never going to divulge any of his information, and, of course, the actions he was trained in—secret writing, demolition, karate, how to open letters. It sounds like something from the back of a cereal package.

My film is about his first assignment, although there will not be a continuous, linear development. He goes to Ecuador, where he's involved in overthrowing the government because they have a left-wing foreign minister who will not join the condemnation of Cuba and Castro. He then continues a whole series of CIA operations through Latin America.

In Mexico his cover is as chief of the U.S. Olympics Committee, and his assignment is to repress the students. The CIA is behind [Álvarez] Echeverría, who's now the president. The police repression in Mexico was savage and brutal, and fatal to a great number of people. It was around this time that Agee started having guilt about the whole thing, and sometime in 1969 he left his wife, went to Cuba, and named all the American agents and cover organizations in Latin America. He blew the lid. Then he went to Paris and started to write this book with a price on his head and with people after him. The obvious way to make this film is to open at the end of the book, with Agee writing the book in Cornwall and discovering that his typewriter is bugged. And I want to end the film in Chile.

I don't know exactly how I want the film to end, I don't know who I want in it. I don't know if I can make it. I don't know about the money. First of all, I don't want to do it in color—I tend to see people in black and white, which may be an optical as well as a political failing. But I happen to like black and white. With color you take advantage of an audience by dazzling them with spectacular shots, and I am not interested in the tricks of the craft. If you do a film in black and white, you almost eliminate yourself from the TV market because most TV is in color, but I don't give a shit. I'm also interested—theoretically, aesthetically, and financially—in the problem of reproducing a specified time in the past, for instance, the year 1959. They spent millions of dollars to reproduce the past in *The Godfather*, but I don't see the necessity of expensive, minutely filmed reproductions. I'm more interested in the relationship between the documentary and the fictive—I'd like Castro to appear in the film as Castro, talking about the film and not about Agee's life.

Jane Fonda wants to be in the film and has offered to do it for nothing, but there's no role for her. I can't write her a role, nor would I. I just had a call from New York that Robert Redford is interested in doing a film on the CIA. That would be a very tricky problem, because Redford thinks he's against the CIA. But I'm not against the CIA, I'm against the system that produced the CIA. Redford bought the Bernstein and Woodward book and he's going to play Woodward; Watergate is a nice soft issue because it focuses on a man and not a system. Redford views Watergate as an aberration, whereas in my view Watergate is inherent in the system.

Maybe Redford would act in the film and agree to be part of the package to the extent that I might then have enough clout to deal with the distributors. That's a theoretical problem. The real problem is, would Redford want to hold out, and do I really want a star?

I'm not sure that I do. Redford is too easy. Costa Garbage can never use anybody but Yves Montand. In every film he's ever made—*The Sleeping Car Murders, Z, The Confession,* and *State of Siege*—Yves Montand is the star. Montand has such an overload of left-wing associations, particularly to European eyes, that when he was cast as Dan Mitrione, a CIA agent, in

State of Siege, Dan Mitrione became a good guy just by the nature of his casting. You have the same problem with Redford. Audiences are going to accept Redford in a certain way that transcends the politics of the role. They'll be watching the latest Robert Redford film, not a film based on Agee's book about the CIA.

I met an agent who says that Dan Berrigan's nephew, whose name is also Dan Berrigan, looks like the kind of guy I'm looking for to play Agee. He's about twenty-seven years old, very butch, a tough-looking Irishman. He's an actor who hasn't had any parts yet, but he sounds like somebody I might be interested in.

This film isn't like the ones I've made up till now, where I could raise money because I knew twenty rich people, and I'd hit them for $10,000 a piece, and the film would play the twenty biggest cities in the country and then hit the university circuits and European TV, and maybe then I get my money back. With the Agee film I'll be locked into the Hollywood system. The film is going to cost $750,000–$1,000,000—this is nothing by Hollywood standards, but to me it is a great deal of money.

The best thing that could happen from a CIA point of view is that a distributor will buy the film. This happens to a lot of films, even only moderately left films—they get a little opening in New York without a lot of press, and then the distributor sits on it. They simply stop functioning; they let the film die. You're trapped. I cannot ask people for that kind of money without assuring them in advance that it's going to have some kind of distribution. So I'm in a box. Part of getting the film out is that West German TV would put up a fair amount of money, the Swedes would put up some, and that's about one-tenth of the budget. And they would play it. But I want the film to be played here. Agee's an American, I'm an American, this is an American experience, and I'm interested in changing American society. Sweden or Germany will change if we change.

The most effective censorship is that of class interests. The big companies are tied into defense, war, imperialism, and oppression. Even crummy Hollywood distributors are, in turn, owned by the banks. It's part of a huge interlocking directorate of corporate interests in the U.S. Even if you try to by pass the distributors, you have to deal with the theater chains. The chains themselves are huge financial conglomerates—one whole area of the West is handled by only two or three companies. The harassment they can get, they can't endure. They get the FBI and the IRS people coming in and walking all over them—and there is where the censorship is. They don't want problems, they don't want trouble. When I make this film, I have to sneak in the political message, make it look like a Cold War spy story. Any moderately intelligent person could make the film like that and sneak in the message. But to me, in this film, the message is what is really significant.

I'm a complicated person—I see art as a weapon, and yet I see the complexity of American life. The old Stalinist posters just won't do. And films that hurl messages at you just won't do. They reach no audience. And yet, I'm not the type to take sugarcoating. What I'm trying to do in this film is invent a new film form in which the content and the style are one. In the making of the film, I would like a Marxist methodology, a Marxist aesthetic, and a Marxist political line. That means the development of a new kind of film, and one that I can't even envision right now.

EMILE DE ANTONIO

Smoke Signals Blown (1975)

A creative act of grief and ennui found in the de Antonio journals, this unpublished miniature roman à clef reveals the artist with his defensive egoism in check. In 1974–75, his personal life was consumed by the lingering death of his beloved wife Terry, but he continued to explore making films on CIA defector Philip Agee and the Weatherpeople. He completed his clandestine film, even as this "time of death" led him to contemplate the radical heresy that the personal transcends the political.

He had made films, he had thought he belonged to the culture of the left. Small "l," small "c." His wife was dying in Memorial Hospital. It was a long, slow death. It was her style. She insisted on living it all out. He drank, lectured in colleges with his films, he sat in the hospital room amid the stink of dying flowers and thought only of her death, of death, of the death of his time. The president had left the White House but all seemed the same out there. The cabs trundled back and forth between Memorial Hospital and his house in the East Village. The night before she had to go to the hospital. At that time it was the routine blood check. They had a picnic by the ocean with two friends; it was dark, the fire high, the wind salty and cold. A shadow appeared. It was the great yippie/hipster of them all [Abbie Hoffman]. He said: hey, come over and eat with us. The filmmaker said: no, we think four is already a crowd. After, he wondered, had he been unnecessarily who he really was? Should he always be who he really was? It is hard, particularly if you think narrative films are boring. Thinking about who you are sometimes reveals; for the most part reinforces old stratagems. They drank wine and ate steak. The next day the doctor called him and told him his wife has less than a week to live. He felt he had to tell her. He said: there may be a chance if we go to Memorial. It will be long and painful. Were all his decisions always wrong? She smiled in her pain and said: call Memorial. I don't want it this week. He dialed. The ambulance raced through the streets to the oxygen, and she began that torture which he admired. Do the good choose their deaths? He didn't think so. He accepted it with all his being. It was also a time of death for him and his country. He could no longer see films. What was the point? The personal transcends social reality. Heresy? Perhaps, all was blown away when he made the choices he made about life and politics. He no longer knew where much was nor did he care. He knew death, the imminence of his own, and it mattered less than this room with these flowers and thankless gifts and cheerless nurse smiles.

He went to his studio and wrote in his journals and started a correspondence with Christopher Agate, who had defected from the CIA and was living in England. Could it be a film? Agate didn't think so. They wrote. He went to the hospital. The Underground Freedom Organization, UFO, had just put a bomb in the embassy of SVN [South Vietnam]. It seemed like an act. He wondered if he could meet with them. He had known some of them, knew of all of the leaders. He had an acquaintance who was bound to know. The friend said no he didn't know anything at all about them but he knew someone who could get a message to them. The message came back two weeks later. Yes, they would like to hear the proposal. He kissed his wife and went home to the rows of whiskey bottles and Perrier and books and wrote a drunken uncorrected letter (like this) about a film with them and how it might be done and how it could be used. They sent a message. Yes, they would have one or two meet with him and instructions would be sent later.

They came. It was thrilling, exciting as a narrative film: from the hospital late at night but not too late into the subway, out of the subway, check cars. He knew he was being followed by them to see if he was being followed by the other, the state. He went on to a part of the city he did not know. He was surprised it was populous and active. Good cover. He stood before a phone, a call phone. It rang right at eleven. A voice cheerfully gave more directions. They met and ate fish and drank a single beer. He smiled. Health foods and bombs. They planned security, the rest of the crew, safe house, and the details were worked out to the slow march of his wife's dying.

Two nights later he lectured at a university here in the city. He was good. He liked to be unprepared and risk all. The questions were sharp. Students crowded round at the end. One bearded pipe smoker said: Why don't we walk? They did. The other said: you know your films are too much in the mind. They don't celebrate action. You ought to make a film with UFO. He thought: Christ, my cover is blown. All those others I've seen have been trapped. Is this guy a feebee? He smiled and said: you may be right but you know it's too tricky, the security problems are too great.

Ah yes, the one on the beach that late summer night in Sagaponack. He was busted the next day on a drug rap and also went underground. Dostoyevsky's underground man?

Remainder:

a) the death of his wife
b) he interrupts the funeral to read one of her poems and walks out
c) filming
d) FBI
e) the trial
f) victory over the FBI
g) emptiness again

A VERY BRIEF INVENTION FROM MANY PAGES ALREADY WRITTEN.

EMILE DE ANTONIO

Celluloid Reportage (1976)

Irreverent underground rags like the Yipster Times *were on their last legs by 1976. But the filmmaker who was making his own celluloid elegy of the left with* Underground, *could still oblige the Yippie readership with this attack on Hollywood's version of Woodward and Bernstein's Watergate investigation.*

▶

All the President's Men

This is an angry review. It is not a balanced review. It is not autistic, like say, Andrew Sarris. Godard tells us the only way to review a film is to make another one in response. Good advice. I buy it. In fact, I did it. But what happens if the response came first? What happens if you've already made the film? What happens if you made the Watergate film before Watergate happened? What happens if your film comedically pushed into the dark corners, the rat holes of our living history, and in those rat holes was exactly where middle America lived and Richard Milhous Nixon was the rat? The film was *Millhouse: A White Comedy* and I'll tell you what happens. First you get on the "enemies list." That's not too bad. All those wooden soldiers and crazy cops did what you expected anyway: promises to "leak de Antonio's derogatory FBI dossier," audits from the IRS, whispers to theater owners. They were hoods and they lived like hoods.

But, something worse happened, much worse. Hollywood dragged out its Creative/Political Papier-Mâché Kit right out of the Paper Moon Reality Factory and gives us *All the President's Men*. I don't believe the credits. The script was by Horatio Alger. A political film without politics. It's really pluck and luck.

Two young heroes of high moral character—they don't fuck, they eat

French fries and drink Cokes in McDonald's—finally triumph over a benign system which has malignant cancer and become rich. Really rich. Mrs. Graham's Galahads, they are of the media and crowned by the media. Redford is quoted in *People* as saying, "I never worked on a picture that so much thought went into. A lot of it was preventive thought, not so much do this and don't do that. Don't make a movie about Nixon or Watergate. Don't take a partisan position." They thought hard. It's a lot of work to reach absolute zero. And they did it. They didn't take any positions. A zero position is always a ton of support for what is going on.

Well, okay. So it may not be a political film, but it's good entertainment, right? A detective story. It takes your mind off the world. But there, quiet, in the dark, tricks without magic. The images are older than Dante. The pressroom of the *Washington Post* is bright beyond the blaze of neon, the world outside is a netherworld, peopled by shades, dark, dark, dark, pale ghosts. T. S. Eliot as well as Dante: "I had not thought death had undone so many." But the truth that triumphs is a wet dream. "Deep Throat" points that way. But who is Deep Throat?

I'll tell you he never lived in Washington or anywhere else because he's really Virgil or Hal Holbrook. In the Inferno—the basement of a car park. He doesn't talk in bureaucratese or in facts, but in echo chambers—that is his language. He speaks soulfully and oracularly. Pretty simple-minded oracles, of course. You don't need to be a genius to decipher them: "The money. Go after the money." That dizzying insight sends Dustin Hoffman off to Florida, where he discovers that money can actually be laundered. Incredible, you say? Well, the ruling class can really live with all this. Redford and Hoffman scurry. They are always on the run. In addition to light, energy is the metaphor of heroes. The shades move languidly. Run, run, run, Dustin and Robert. Wards of the academy.

Most of what is meant to be political shoots out of a typewriter that sounds like a machine gun. But, it is the sexuality of the film that is profound. Stroking. The real media game. The biggest circle jerk ever. But before the full orgasm of self-congratulation, before sequels and millions, we need a plot.

You really have to love journalists to follow this labyrinthine plot. Crusty old Jason Robards is the executive editor and all he cares about is the facts, just like Ben Bradlee is real life (see *Conversations with Kennedy*). He scowls, is ironic, as old as Morse code. It's a signal that he's going to be A-OK and back up the young heroes somewhere, perhaps to the hilt. And he does. When he hears that John Mitchell has actually threatened the FREEDOM OF THE PRESS by telling Katharine Graham to watch out or her teats will go into the wringer, that's it. Bang on, lads. After them! The pace of scurrying is swifter. Television images of Nixon make him strangely attractive and sympathetic. They are cut in like very fancy commercials for moral pep pills.

Film note: confrontation framing, wide angle. Screen left, a TV set, Nixon on-screen. Center frame is empty newsroom. Right frame Redford alone. The reader can supply appropriate metaphor here.

Back to the sex. It had to be an orgy film when Vice Canby *[sic]* called it "the thinking man's *Jaws*." The thinking man's *Jaws*. It's a giant circle jerk. The establishment press gropes its neighbor's zipper, unzips, and pop go ejaculations of praise, hymns even. That's all that's left. The praise goes on, the golden hymns, but the picture fades. It really does. (I saw it three weeks ago and I don't remember it.) The images slide into gray, the actions are blurred, the meaning gone. All gone but that hymn of bucks and self-congratulation. When you write *The Best and the Brightest* and tear away a few of the veils, getting rich in the process, you prove one thing. Horatio Alger, the American Dream. For, darling, you are the best and the brightest. You, our free press.

EMILE DE ANTONIO

Letter to The Militant (1977)

A prolific and masterful writer of poison-pen letters to the editor (see Esquire, New York Times, University Review, New York Review of Books, Bulletin of the Atomic Scientists, American Film, Jump Cut*), de Antonio could often be defensive or egotistical when responding to his critics. Here he takes a more rational and cool approach, though he continues on the attack. Again, his target is powerful institutions corrupted by capitalism.*

▶

Corporate Crime

Please feel free to print the enclosed letter, which I sent to U.S. Judge James Parsons in Chicago.

Dear Judge Parsons,

Tucked away on page 30 of the February 19 *New York Times* (business news, not crime news) was the story of your incredible "desentencing" of fourteen executives of different paper-box manufacturing companies who had pleaded no contest to charges of price-fixing. You not only reduced their sentences and fines but you made a boys' dormitory out of federal prison.

By sentencing them on a nights-only basis, their days will be free to make paper boxes. If price-fixing weren't everyday business—not just in paper boxes but in food, shelter, heat, drink, travel—and if the accused weren't corporate officers, successful charges of conspiracy might have been proved—unless these particular executives were so deeply in tune spiritually, like Moonies, that they arrived at the fix without conspiracy.

You are blameless; you simply reflect the class interest that rules our country. In 1968 we elected to the White House the very greatest criminal and his pals. In their crimes, they prospered. A lesson and law for the rich; for other colors, another class, other laws.

Calvin Coolidge said, "The business of America is business." Every corporate officer knows that in his heart, but Cal was laconic and he left out the rest of it: the business of business is profit.

Charlie Chaplin, more perceptive, in *Monsieur Verdoux*, logically took it to the next step: the logical end of business is murder. And our ruling classes with the enthusiastic support of the police and the courts have murdered the working class in strikes, have enslaved and murdered Blacks, have committed genocide against Native Americans, have made the places of work the places of death for women and men in factories, mills, mines. Slow death, fast death.

And now in a more sophisticated time the murder and slow death have reached out to include everyone, all the people, through poisoning earth, air, and water for profit.

More people will die from or be abused by corporate crime than any other kind. If a bank robber is a criminal (and he is), he should be punished; but what of those who have killed a river for money?

All that we buy is sold through conspiracies for profit. Those who do it are the enemies of the great majority of our people; so are those who countenance it.

EMILE DE ANTONIO

Point of Order (Hic) (1980)

The infamous drinker was called upon to review a neo-temperance book for the Village Voice. *The essay is most valuable as the best available account of the making of Andy Warhol's movie* Drunk *(1965). But it is also a revealing autocritique and a funny satirical slam on the budding rage for bourgeois self-help books. While ridiculing the book's platitudes, de Antonio ultimately documents and confesses to his own lifelong history of serving the "feckless master" of alcohol.*

Drink? Of course. Everywhere. I am a man of drink. I love good bars in midafternoon, when they're quiet and empty and serious. Bombay gin martinis very cold and very dry with two olives. If a calorie is possible, I lunge for it. In the Ritz in Paris, two olives in the martini and a small plate on the bar. The illusion of sobriety fragilely supported by an occasional olive. The Raphael, after lunch, before drink time, when the bar looks like the living room of a seedy, comfortable country house. The Dom Pérignon perfect, cool, not cold. Bubbles of Rheims pop like crystal over the un-Gallic quiet. And of course I drink in Bowery bars and bars with rock and football, bars with all the sadness of the world at my side. And often I don't know where I've drunk. But I don't like it. I liked better the Oak Bar in the Plaza in the years right after the war. I sat on a stool looking out the windows at the budding trees in Central Park, and the horses and the carriages, faded, fake, but lovely, the old men in toppers waiting to gull a fare. Peanuts fresh, ungreasy, the martinis dry and cold, my lethal postwar breakfast. The dot of noon. Shall I count the places and the ways? You could buy matched Rolls-Royces, Southampton beach houses, with all the booze pissed away in the urinals of the world, on grassy lawns under stars, in subway johns, in the street between two cars, and, on Third Avenue, in doorways under the elevated with a drunken Irish poet in a cape.

Now it was the name of the book: *Drink*. I read the review in the *Times* on November 15. I had been on the wagon for five weeks. Once I had played in a movie with the same title. *Drink*. In the early sixties when I was making *Point of Order*, Andy Warhol was reinventing the history of film itself with *Sleep, Blow Job, Empire*. They were all shot with a 16mm camera fixed on a tripod. Tina Fredericks introduced me to Andy in 1959. I had never seen anyone watch like Andy. He saw everything, he heard everything, he remembered it all, and in those days of Dracula with a human face he never used a tape recorder or Polaroid. He consumed everything: the prince of voyeurs didn't peep in windows. Victims of his camera swarmed to 47th Street, cultural commissars like Henry Geldzahler, stars of perpetual chrysalis like Baby Jane Holzer—Andy effaced himself and saw them all. Everyone he knew was in his cast. The magic little static cinema of Andy Warhol.

His questions were Rorschachs as well as cues to get on stage. The day we met he said: Tina tells me you know everything; how did World War I begin? I had no reference point. I stared. I knew he was Czech, images of Herzegovina, Archduke Francis Ferdinand, the carriage at Sarajevo. Demurely a bear trap big enough to swallow me opened. I choked the rush to words: Oh, come on, Andy. You know more about all that than I do. He said: oh, no, d, no I don't. I had more drinks.

Later, when I was trying to learn the history of film by making one, Andy and I met often. In his house, at parties, in my apartment. By then I knew his painting and liked his work and him. Every time we met he said: Oh, d, why don't we do a film together? Flying through the sewer/sky I never did understand what he meant. Every question was a lure with exotic feathers that hid a hook. And then one December day in 1964, I said okay, Andy. Let's make a movie. I'll drink a quart of whiskey. I'll drink it in twenty minutes. (I assumed he was, as always, using ten-minute reels and I was cutting my drinking to his camera.) You film it. I might even die on camera. Plenty of twenty-one-year-old marines die trying it. I'll play dice with god. Your studio. The Factory. I'll just sit cross-legged like Buddha and knock off a quart. Decent whiskey. More action than *Sleep*.

Andy's silence was rapture and, for him, emotional assent. It got out. He revealed his pleasure. At that moment I felt the incarnation, I was the saint of the holy bottle. Oh, stern Piedmontese ancestors. Had he planned it all? Was I such a tough-guy patsy? He said: what kind of scotch? I said: Andy, you pick it. You're the director. You plan it. I'll be there and I'll do it.

And I did. I came with two seconds, two protecting angels, Terry, my beloved, later beloved and wife, and dear David McEwen, now dead of drink. I sat cross-legged in the well-lit stairwell of the Factory. Ghouls, dozens, flickered beyond the lights. Andy used a 1,200-foot magazine, thirty-five minutes a reel. Sound running, camera running. I tilted the bottle and drank it in twenty minutes. Silence. "Doom is deeper and darker than any sea dingie." Who talks aloud alone in the presence of excited ghouls? I was done. Sound effects. The bottle clattered down the stairwell, ice and glasses followed. Andy was new to the big magazine. When reel two began, I was on the floor, not Buddha the golden hero, but Buddha the Bowery Bum, the guy you see on your way to Mott Street. My hands crept along the white brick walls trying to move me up. Andy was scared. Voices intervened. I began to sing. Spanish Civil War songs. I couldn't get up. I cursed and cursed Andy and the ghouls. I sang Mozart. Hell again, home again. Terry and David took me home. I slept like the dead but did not die. I even moved among the dead. It was a very bad hangover. Many others just like it. I saw the film a few days later. Andy knew it should never be shown. It never was. Now I think it might be okay for *Sesame Street*. But don't do it, Andy, unless you split.

Pascale Dauman, the distributor of my films in France, was in town November 15. We went to Joe's on McDougal Street for lunch. Very good. Mushrooms sautéed in garlic and oil. Veal cutlets and arugula salad. Two bottles of red wine. We talked about the book, *Drink*. I hadn't read it yet. We walked to Irving Place near my studio in Union Square and had a double calvados. University Place and four whiskeys. A friend brought me *Drink*. To Bradley's and a few more. Weaving, calling home. I saw Susan Lyne sitting with Orville Schell Jr. Gossip column. She's managing editor of *VV*. We talked about Berkeley.

The next day I read *Drink*. It's a very bad book. It's seedy, false, pretentious: A couple of paragraphs to knock off the Oedipus theory. Why did the *Times* blow it to such a big review? Why did the *Times* leave out the subtitle: *A Self-Help Book on Alcoholism*? America is a glut of self-help. Why did Doubleday publish it? The first appendix which flew in the window is "Alcoholism and the Industrial Worker," published by the Ministry for Health of the Republic of Ireland.

Drink is a *Reader's Digest* homily. It shares with the sages of Pleasantville platitude, piety, misinformation, and the touching of every base ever so lightly. Constantine FitzGibbon believes alcoholism is hereditary. He is smugly proud of his Anglo-Irish aristocratic antecedents. The book includes fourteen pages on the temperance movement, a few pages on the history of psychoanalysis concluding with: "The third great psychologist of that generation was the Swiss Carl Gustav Jung. In the opinion of this writer Jung created a view of the world which is an aesthetic triumph comparable, perhaps, to that of Goethe or even Dante, lacking the poetry." This writer's opinion: the poetry is the point.

And then there is *Reader's Digest* anthropology: "With most Red Indians there is no need for the period of simple addiction: he will jump straight into the disease if he drinks at all, and this is true of a proportion of non-Indians. This is particularly true of manic-depressives." That is followed by a two-and-one-half-page chapter on "Depression." Then two and one-quarter pages on "Alcoholism and the Heavy Drinker." Chapters which reveal the terrors of the "hidden bottle," as well as one titled "America, America" ("Class, in America, is a highly complex word.... There is of course no aristocracy as such, though in certain small areas a few families will enjoy a position not dissimilar to that of the gentry in England or France"). There are chapters on "Ye Olde Englishe Pubbe" and "Drunk's Progress."

FitzGibbon uses the word *alcoholic* constantly. This is reasonable in a book named *Drink*. Therefore, the following puzzles me: "Since I am not sure what an alcoholic is, and since I stressed that Dylan Thomas drank to excess, I see less point in calling the poet an alcoholic than in giving his waist measurements, also called by drink."

His snobbish, alcoholic autobiography drags us "To the Very Gates of Hell" (chapter heading), and since he doesn't go in, the end is clearly prefigured. God. First in a hospital called St. John of God with a few AA techniques, psychiatry, injections, and antidepressants, and then: "I regained my faith in God which I had not realized I had lost." Graham Greene on drunken priests is better.

I am fascinated by Constantine FitzGibbon. Is he the Renaissance man of encyclopedic triviality? Not even. His credits include twenty-nine other books and thirty books translated by him. He is very busy. The titles include: lives of Dylan Thomas and Norman Douglas, *Secret Intelligence in the Twentieth Century*, *The Blitz*, *Random Thoughts of a Fascist Hyena*. No subject escapes him. It goes on. *A Concise History of Germany*.

I know about drink. I've served that feckless master since I was fourteen. FitzGibbon doesn't know the subject. I'm on the wagon again. *Reculer pour mieux sauter?* [Putting off the day of reckoning?].

EMILE DE ANTONIO

Different Drummers (1985)

With typical immodesty, de Antonio wrote this review lauding Ellen Oumano's Film Forum *collection of interviews with "innovative, controversial" directors—including himself. He had close ties to the American Film Institute and its* American Film *magazine. The AFI sponsored a retrospective and a preview of* Millhouse *in 1971. This book review was the last of seven short pieces by and about de Antonio that appeared in* American Film *over a three-year period.*

Looking at the *New York Times* best-seller list is staring into the void. Film books are generally even worse. Cenotaphs, pretensions, puffery and flackery, stardust; the semiotics of academic advancement: tools for miners in the cave of the winds. So it's pleasurable for this old negator to recommend Ellen Oumano's *Film Forum* without reservation to anyone who cares about film. Her cast of characters is thirty-five innovative, controversial directors with a script touching on cinematography, the frame, sound, editing, actors, structure, the market, the audience. The directors are passionate, contradictory, measured, contentious, informative.

I never knew him, but as I read, I hear Rainer Werner Fassbinder saying: "It is very simple. I think the frame is like life. Life, too, offers only certain possibilities. Film is like a square of life; it has the same boundaries, but I think film is more honest, because it admits that it has a limited space."

Charles Chaplin and Groucho Marx knew how funny innocence is. They knew how to use it. Oumano is without innocence, and she, too, knows what she is doing. Her chapter introductions are lean and precise, with just enough heat to avoid hectoring. She has found the catch that releases the reader from the ping-pong of interview books.

Dusan Makavejev: "It's very important to realize that many people believe that the frame contains part of a larger reality. What is important to understand is that in movies there is nothing else—whatever is in the frame is all there is. What is outside the frame is something we create *by* the frame."

When T. S. Eliot was young, he attacked the verse of Milton for its Latin prosody. He was defending the "metaphysical poets" and, most of all, his own way of writing poetry. Many years later, when I was a young graduate student at Columbia, I heard Eliot praising the vigor of Milton's Latinate diction. He was right both times: artists defend what they need, use what they need. Although film history is necessarily brief compared with other arts, it is already old enough for *Film Forum* to reveal contradictions and the debts film owes to other arts.

Nestor Almendros: "There have been only two important changes [in cameras over the last forty years]. One of them has been fast lenses, which can register images at a very low level of light. The other is the 'pushing' of film at the laboratory. . . . I like to compare this revolution of fast lenses plus pushed development to painting. When they started making tubes of paint, painters could go and catch the changing light outdoors."

Chantal Akerman: "For my films I prefer a depth of field. I don't like to use a face and then behind the face have everything out of focus. I also don't like to use close-ups. . . . I'm not covered at all. It's much more exciting to take risks; otherwise, if you are covered, if you cover too much, then you have the design established in the editing and then you have lost your style. Because if you cover like the Hollywood directors, all the movies look alike."

More people in the last sixty years have seen more different images on any one day than all the made images seen by all the people of the world in all preceding time. I'm not sure this is good, but it is a fact. Most of the directors in Oumano's book are "serious." They don't have the audiences of the directors of Hollywood hits. They are, perhaps, not more intelligent than Spielberg or Stallone, but they write and talk more about film, their concerns are different. The instrumental pragmatism of William James and Charles Peirce was central to modern thinking. But the pragmatism of the film industry is prompted not by philosophy but by shallowness and a crippling indifference to the ideas of film art.

Michael Powell directed his first film in 1931 in England. He recalls that "when sound first came in, we regarded it as a tragedy, a barrier, whereas before, if you made a good love story, it would go all over the world. It didn't matter who was playing certain parts as long as they were good: Czechs, Russians, English, Americans."

I shall continue to quote. It's easier and it's not being "about" very much. Aboutness is passive as popcorn. Aboutness is the fodder of critics, reviewers. The maker has more of the sense of "the thing" than any critic. The idea of being an artist is curiously pleasing and tens of thousands perceive themselves as artists: film distributors, art collectors, advertising moguls, critics. They're not. They may be very good people and kind to their children, but they are not artists. John Cage once said to me, "It's very simple, 'd.' Artists make art."

Fassbinder on Godard: "Before Godard, the film was developed from a story. Godard started to develop a film from images. He did not want to tell a story in the first place."

Godard on actors and acting: "In the United States the system is so corrupted, the actors are stars and they cannot act. 'The star' is a cultural problem or phenomenon. The star represents something that belongs to people."

Robert Altman: "Actors are, without a doubt, the most important element, because they're the ones who are performing. And if it really came down to it where we didn't have a set, we didn't have any lights, and we were sitting on a beach with a camera and four actors, we still could do something."

In every art, the serious artist is obsessed with form. This is what the committed who are not artists don't understand. Brecht did; Eliot did. If, in a film, I want to make a political point, I cannot simply tell it. I have to make something new beyond speech, explanation, or piety. Form is not an icing, an afterthought, or an additive. The form and idea become one; otherwise, it's a political soap opera.

Bernardo Bertolucci: "Film shows reality *in progress*. There's a very beautiful and famous Jean Cocteau statement: 'The cinema is death at work.' Because when you show the face of an actor, the time can be ten seconds or three minutes—but time passes in his face. 'Time is death at work.'"

Film is international, art is international, and not in terms of markets alone. Ideas belong to the world. However, those who make films, who make art, who think new ideas, perceive the world from the vision and memories of beginnings. Art is particular in its origins, general in its diffusion.

Sidney Lumet: "I still wouldn't call it 'my production.' It's not . . . the lack of confidence this country has in whatever itself created, so that they keep having to pick up dopey ideas from the French all the time. I'm obviously talking about the whole *auteur* nonsense. How much of an *auteur* are you if you're dependent on whether or not the clouds are over the sun? And you're at the mercy of anything. . . ."

In my case, I am American, my work is American. I may be alienated, but I am of this place. And I agree with Lumet. Auteurism has always seemed to me to be a crutch for French critics. Auteurism is also a magic shovel to dig up whatever one needs in history's graveyard. I am one of the thirty-five directors in *Film Forum*. Objectivity is a myth. I leave it to God. Trying to be honest is hard enough.

I am comfortable making films outside of the "industry." I don't think it should be comfortable without me. Those who produce $50 million hits and $100 million boffos ought to have the grace and intelligence to finance and distribute *Point of Order!, Primary, The Hour of the Furnaces, Harlan County, U.S.A., Memories of Underdevelopment, The War Game,* and many others. Films of high ambition and starved budgets are good for the industry and for the world. Those who run the mastodon herds don't understand. This is why Steven Bach has written a best-seller on Michael Cimino's $36 million flop shot like a commercial. It would make a very good film.

EMILE DE ANTONIO

American History: A Fiction (1988)

Despite saying "there will never be a script," this collage-like treatment for his final documentary well anticipates the finished cut of Mr. Hoover and I. *Although saying his movie would feature "Emile de Antonio . . . making no effort to entertain you," both this unpublished outline and its film are entertaining synopses of the intertwined lives of de Antonio and that "ghoulish old squirrel gnawing at the Bill of Rights, J. Edgar Hoover."*

These are written notes of a film in progress. There never will be a script.

These are rough notes . . . all there will ever be. See attached documents, lists of quotations. The actual filming will be improvisations from my life.

When I was sixteen years old I entered Harvard College in a class which included John Kennedy and Pete Seeger.

Within two years I joined the Young Communist League, the John Reed Society, and the American Student Union. I was naive: I believed enthusiastically in American democracy. I had no idea that Harvard deans routinely reported to the FBI. Let me confess, I was not the young Lenin. I was an upper-middle-class boy who saw much injustice, a Depression; who wanted to do something about them. I spoke out, I went to demonstrations, I was arrested. So were many others. I also wore black tie and went to debutante parties and drank much too much.

When World War II came, I enlisted (I was deferred from the draft because I was already a father) in the Army Air Corps. Had I known then that J. Edgar Hoover slated me for custodial detention, I would have avoided military service.

In 1945 I ended up on Tinian, the largest air base in the world, and from which the two atomic bombs were flown.

My last mission was exotic. It was "a display of power mission" over

Korea. The briefing officer was relaxed and inscrutable: no questions. "Korea?" we shouted. "What the hell for?" The war had been over for ten days. No matter, we took off without bombs, without guns or gunners, and flew over Korea for a formation peel-off. We flew low over the green Korean landscape. It was clear there was no one there but peasants, no flak, no weapons, and it hit me: the display of power was aimed at the Soviets who were racing down to occupy the territory north of the 38th parallel. It was the onset of the Cold War. I knew at that moment that peace was dead and that I had been present at the beginning of the real postwar world.

Disillusion and government subsidy led me to graduate school at Columbia. Academic fops disguised as English gentlemen: Trilling, Barzun, Tindall. Those sterile academics burrowed in footnotes and exegeses. Cold warriors and lies sprouted in the night like cabbages. I avoided seeing and hearing to drink and talk. Taking part in what seemed to be a just war had been fatal to radicalism, moral props kicked away. Many of us were veterans and most of us thought, correctly, that only the hopeless and unemployable stayed in the military. Nonetheless, many of us wore remnants of our uniforms in flashy combinations.

My favorite robbery took place at Columbia. Three veterans in flight jackets and fatigues got in line at the bursar's office, said: "Pass over the money, this is a stickup for real." They succeeded. Education.

Cold War tracks crossed my life. I met a beautiful woman in a seminar on Joyce. Her husband was business director of a newspaper. We knew each other well and one May day we walked to a bar on Broadway, sat down in a booth, and she said, "d, we're leaving. Soon. We have to sell the house. X is quitting his job. We're moving to Europe."

"Europe? Why?" A few years later he blew his brains out. He had been a CIA officer.

I always knew I was going to be an artist. When I was very young I wanted to be a writer. After the war I began heavy drinking with Painters. I spent days in studios looking at splashy unoriginal work. Much later when I met Carl Andre, Jasper Johns, Bob Rauschenberg, Frank Stella, and Andy Warhol I was comfortable with all of New York Painting. France ran out of gas so it attacks New York art. Well, it, too, is dying now.

The flacks wrote of films, pantheons, and auteurs. I knew they wrote of industrial products manufactured in Hollywood. Films weren't made to make art nor to change the world, but like cars and fashion magazines they were meant to be sold. We live in a business economy. Selling is its art. Which is why grubby Wall Street Parvenus, pedlars of soap opera, and real estate deal hucksters have become the great heroes and collectors. Leonardo da Dallas.

The man with the Cuban cigar decided what would sell and get the *New York Times* to write about it as art. The Product. A Cold War Product. Screen gods and goddesses, Moloch, derring-do cardboard Cold War heroes.

The documentary itself lugged Cold War messages. Flaherty's theme was man against nature. A pleasing notion in an industrial society. It was romantic, it was beautifully shot and flawed, fatally and hopelessly wrong because it wasn't true. You didn't have to be a Marxist to see that the struggle was between the takers and the taken and had little to do with the hunter, his spear, and seals. The theme of all my work is life in Cold War America.

The film I'm making now is based on my life and so, I'm going to film now about some of my films. I shall quote from them in the film, not generously.

The film is minimalist. No written script. It's my life. I shall improvise it without swimming. The main theme will be a nutty biography written by the FBI. Documents will be be thrown on the screen that have never been seen. The FBI's greatest triumph was choking the work of the Founders, the First Amendment, yes, Sally, there is/was a ghoulish old squirrel gnawing at the Bill of Rights, J. Edgar Hoover.

Point of Order was the first political film after World War II. It was funny, it revealed that McCarthy and Cohn were liberated from ideas, thought, and reason. They bullied their way into the peak of nutty Cold War politics. (INSERT MCCARTHY-COHN FROM *POINT OF ORDER*) McCarthy was destroyed in the hearings and Cohn was revealed. He and I got to know each other fairly well doing TV shows: Donahue, Buckley, etc. The film reveals their fall. There are no heroes. Reviewers, tame dogs, loved it because it was seen as affirmation of a system. It wasn't. The film owed much to then nonpolitical friends like John Cage and Bob Rauschenberg: the notion that detritus could be the stuff of art. Beautifully designed and executed shots of Hollywood films were void of reality but also awash with glitz, hokum, and many theaters.

Neutrality is for the angelic orders.

In the Year of the Pig is history at film's pace. I saw the French–U.S. wars [as] imperial, unjust, inhuman, a cut of global cold war. Our bombing and Agent-Orangeing should have called forth Nuremberg trials. It was the first film of the left to be nominated for an Academy Award. I didn't go. (INSERT FRENCH SEQUENCES) It was also the first film of the left to experience criticism more sincere than printer's ink. In Los Angeles, unknown patriots broke into the movie house and wrote the word TRAITOR across the screen in tar. In Houston, bomb threats. Cinema owners are businessmen, not cultural heroes. In real estate, renting seats at so much a show.

Millhouse: A White Comedy. I was working on *Painters Painting*. The phone rang. "De Antonio, we have very little time. We have just ripped off the XYZ network of its Nixon morgue . . . all of it. Hundreds of cans. We want you to use it. We want you to make a film." I said: give me time. "No, no time. This stuff is hot." Okay, what do you want? "Nothing, just that you make a film on Nixon. We don't want to meet YOU." Give me twenty minutes. "Okay."

Twenty minutes later they called. I said: come on. That night they delivered dozens and dozens of cans of 16mm film. I had to shoot plenty of footage anyway, but they did come up with gems: the Checkers speech sequestered by its Master was liberated. There were plenty of short-circuits in the making of the film.

I found Dr. Albert Upton living in a $100,000 California retirement home. He had taught Nixon to cry at Whittier College and agreed to tell me the story on film. When the crew and I arrived, he said, "You can't film and you can't tape my voice." I sent the crew away. Dr. Upton said: "We were doing a play by John Drinkwater, *Bird in Hand*. In it Dick was supposed to cry. He simply could not do it. He never did it in rehearsal. There was something genuine about the boy, he was clumsy. He never did it in rehearsal. I thought of putting an onion in his handkerchief.

"And then, the night of the play he wept on cue, beautifully. It was just like the Checkers speech."

And so it was.

Millhouse: A White Comedy was a commercial success (INSERT: MILLHOUSE ADS + CANBY + FBI FILES + WHITE HOUSE MEMOS NOT ALL IN ONE PLACE) I insisted on opening it in Washington. The White House was ablaze with rage. Memoranda traveled back and forth among Dean, Haldeman, Colson, the FBI. It was the first biography on film of a president in office. I ended up on "the enemies list" (INSERT).

There will be quotations from other films and documents. Every film generated hundreds of documents. There were thousands. I sued the FBI and Harvard Dean Charles Nesson, my lawyer, and I appeared before Judge John Sirica. Maximum John. He found against me.

What I propose to do will be minimalist. E de A sitting in a large empty white loft making no effort to entertain you. I'm not a good actor. An Oxberry camera will record documents unless we shoot them on the wall.

The dead and I are comfortable with one another.

IV Envoi

As a coda for this biographical assemblage, friends and colleagues who worked with de Antonio penned these accounts. They reveal the warmth of his personality that was not always evident in his own films or writings.

PETER WINTONICK

Quotations from Chairman De: Decodifying de Antonio (1984)

The engaging and quotable de Antonio became a frequent guest at film festivals in Montreal and Toronto. His critiques of American power elites and his anti-Hollywood practices inspired a number of young Canadian filmmakers, including Ron Mann, who adapted and enhanced Painters Painting *for CD-ROM in 1995. Peter Wintonick compiled this collage of characteristic quotations for* Cinema Canada *after interviewing "Chairman" de on camera for his documentary* The New Cinema *(1983).*

Lock up your filmmakers. The end draws near. The mad dog of the cinematic revolution is loose. An iconoclast with much subversive intent is in our midst. His global plan: to ferment the firmament, to plant fire and ice in the hearts of student filmmakers, to put *actual* thought and *real* ideas into the public's mind, and, the most hideous and audacious act of all, to show us his films.

Emile de Antonio (known to his friends as "de" [as in d]) recently crossed the border to attend a major retrospective of his work at the Conservatoire d'Art Cinématographique, speak to students at Concordia University, meet his peers at the National Film Board, and keep late-night insomniacs alive on CBC radio's *Brave New Waves*.

I first came to know of this most dangerous of film people while I was working for a private eye here in Montreal. I was rummaging around in the garbage on the room-service tray that dee left outside his hotel room when, much to my surprise, I found the only copy in existence of one of the most revolutionary books ever written—*Quotations from Chairman de*—lying under a half-eaten sandwich de boeuf. I would rank it right up there with Marx's *Das Kapital*, Che's *Memoirs of the Revolutionary War*, or Emily Post's *Book of Etiquette*.

This book is not unlike Mao's little red one, or Robert Bresson's *Notes* on *Cinematography*, except that it is now out of print and thus available only through this special arrangement with *Cinema Canada*. The original copy has been sent to Emile de Antonio's archives at the University of Wisconsin.

de bacle
"Quality is the only thing that ever matters in art, and you can't judge quality except by time. I am interested in art that is living, and adventuresome, and new, and of its own time. I am not interested in the art of fifty years ago. I'm interested in the art of my time."

de bauchery
"All my films are collage films. They are classical collages."

de bris
"There is a certain surrealism when expertise goes off the track, and that's when I like it most."

de bunk
"What I chiefly emphasize is my independence. That's what I mean when I say that I make films for myself. I make films with a hope of arousing emotion, and passion, and of revealing things to people they didn't know or feel before."

de but
"I'm interested in reaching the widest possible audience I can reach, but I will make no concessions to that audience. I will not make a film shorter; I will not make a film less difficult; I will not make it more or less explicit. I am my own man, and that means a great deal to me. That's the only advantage that I have in making low-budget films that never reach the audiences that Hollywood reaches."

de cadence
"I don't think that my questions are important. The answers are important, the answers and the way that I want to manipulate them."

de capitate
"The way that you perceive something with the eye and ear in film is different than the way you perceive something in reading. It is a different kind of experience. It is a much faster experience, and conditions of character, weakness of character, and suppressed moments in character are revealed in film in a way that the written word rarely reveals."

de cay
"I've been a half-baked radical most of my life. I'm a freewheeling anarchist type."

de cency

"Truth in art is internal, personal, and once committed in form offers itself for judgement. It is not discovered by a committee of reasonable men, however eminent. An English critic has called *Point of Order* the only good example of cinema verité. I disagree, in fact, nonsense. Cinema verité is what Henry Ford called history—'bunk.'"

de centralize

"Documentary cinema is by far the best form of protest, the best possible theatrical form. Its great force is the force of testimony. American TV documentaries are without content. They pose no questions. My films oppose. They provoke. Technically they are different. There's no narration. I believe that to impose narration is a fascist act."

de ception

"Perhaps in a future society the dichotomy between art and politics will disappear. In a bourgeois society it's a true contradiction."

de cipher

"What seems important to me is to make people see the same old things from a new angle. I use images from the mass media, political people, and political life, and I try to render a totality of process. This is something that TV is incapable of doing."

de clamation

"I am interested in the political theories, in the mass of facts. I am interested in establishing a line of thought."

de classify

"I am a radical; I believe in the Bill of Rights and I think that nobody can stop me from making a film."

de cline

"I love the United States but I hate its government. I hate its military, of which I was a part. I see no reason to hope that it ever wins anything."

de compose

"No country has brainwashed its citizens as effectively as the U.S. History is not written in four-minute snippets for TV news. We are getting a distorted view. We're inundated with stuff that has given us a pathological hardness, an indifference to other people's suffering. We've lost our sense of generosity because we've become a consumer population."

de corate

"Critique is montage."

de cree

"The networks have made the American people comfortable with war, because it appears between commercials. There's never the question 'Why are we doing this?'"

de cry

"From the very beginning, my films were not only political; they also contested the main assumptions of Hollywood as film. To me, Hollywood produces industrial products. Like Twinkies. High production values were usually empty screens. I wanted to make a political filmic art with the barest of means. I believed that what was spare could be dramatic, emotional, and revealing."

de fame

"I am an American Marxist. I believe in history. I made *In the Year of the Pig* to reveal history that was systematically being hidden by networks between commercials for mastodonic cars and deodorants. The quotidian makes life and death irrelevant. I will never forget the funny face that Fred Astaire made when he announced its nomination for an Academy Award."

de fence

"The goal of a truly didactic work is to move beyond and to suggest why. I would describe my own sentiments as democratic. I wish not to teach people but to reveal things to them; to have them arrive at the same conclusion as I do—it's a democratic didacticism without having to say a firstly, secondly, thirdly."

de finition

"I think that, as all my thoughts and sympathies move toward the third world, we must, my friends and I, make films as if we were living in the third world. Not only as a point of view but with a small budget as well."

de liberation

"I think that it is better that revolutionary ideas be expressed in new forms, but not if they are only masturbatory exercises; not if they are only cries of anguish that don't attract anyone; not if they don't express a real point of view."

de livery

"If you say that art only addresses an aristocracy, or a small band of intellectuals, then your art has an antievolutionary essence—it becomes like American painting or the court of Louis XIV. Art must attract people. Sometimes that takes time. Sometimes we must take that time. And wait. You can wait as Mallarmé did, knowing that someday you will read. But today even time is different. We are living in the most important period in the last thousand years. We have the means of destruction to put an end to time, to everything; we have little choice left. Machines change people. What we have to say—we must say now."

de lirium
"History is the theme of all my films . . . filmmaking is risk taking . . . I don't know the distinction between propaganda and passion, propaganda and politics."

de magoguery
"As the old Hollywood adage has it, 'If you have a message, then use Western Union.' Well, my films have messages but I don't want to send them Western Union. I have never looked upon documentary as an apprenticeship for the making of Hollywood films. That's bullshit. I love documentary film—its political tradition and the subjects that it can treat."

de mentia
"I'm an American. This is my space, and that's why I want to change it."

de mon
"McCarthyism was the triumph of the art of advertising—the art of saying absolutely nothing, the triumph of technique over content."

de pression
"The question now remains—how can one maintain a revolutionary life? How can I conserve my enthusiasm, my ideas, my belief in others, the possibility of analysis and the belief in a state that is not a police state? That is the central problem of my Marxist and anarchist universe."

de rigueur
"One of the great clichés of Marx was that religion is the opium of the people. This is absolutely shallow, foul, and untrue in our times because religion has no influence on people compared to what film and TV have. They form our morals, our basic social mores, our habits, the way we live and dress."

de scribe
"We have censorship of ownership. The people who own the country own the media. It is not 'the medium is the message.' The real fact of the matter is—who owns the medium owns the message."

de sign
"If you really want to make a film, then you will do everything possible to get the money to do the film and you will make the film."

de sire

"We're just being surrounded by garbage. We're choking. We are like these characters in Hades who are drowning in our own excrement—which is the media—producing tons and tons and millions of words and images that are useless, pernicious and demeaning."

de terminism

"The real history of my country now is the television outtake. What you see on the tube is not what is really there. So much of the material that I discovered in the trash bins of ABC and CBS have been exactly those ideas about what was really going on in Vietnam, or what Nixon was about, or some other aspect of our culture and politics."

de test

"My life is my work, my work is my life. I see myself as a film artist who is essentially political."

de value

"I believe in freedom of expression; I believe in a lot of hard things; I also believe in economic justice. In that sense, I am a Marxist. All the work that I do is informed by notions about the nature of society—what you should do in respect to people. In the U.S. we've painted in the word 'radical' to mean somebody who's unbalanced and willing to betray the country or willing to sacrifice everything for some rather abstract and unusual notion. Radical has a very different Latin root. It's the basis. A radical solution is not a crazy solution, it's a root solution that goes to the heart of the matter. The United States is in need of a radical solution."

de velop

"Reagan makes it clear that virtue is to be measured by money; the rich are the virtuous, indeed, the poor shall serve them. To me that's the most obscene idea that I've come across in my lifetime."

de vil

"I've just finished a film about Christian pacifists, who are the strongest people I've met in a long time. I would like to be a Christian pacifist, but there are a few problems: *(a)* I don't believe in God and *(b)* I think that violence is still necessary. I'd like to get rid of that idea, I'd really like to get rid of that idea, but I think I'm stuck with it because it's my understanding of the world."

de votion

"In each project, I try to keep an open mind in relation to the material and to myself, so it doesn't come out hard-edged: so it doesn't come out like a totally predictable quantity like canned salmon or something, except today canned salmon is no longer predictable. It's probably poisonous."

three de

"Distribution does mirror the rest of our culture. The big companies are uninterested in anything that won't clearly project a profit. The mistakes they make are business errors, they are not mistakes in art. No art can live and grow without errors. I embrace all my mistakes. Success bores me. I want to go on to some more things. You learn from mistakes. Unless you have room to make mistakes, you will have some kind of abstract, technological perfection which is what most films are about. My films are raw. I intentionally make my films raw. What our French friend would call *l'art brut*."

RON MANN

De Wore Khakis

Hanging on the wall over my computer is a publicity photograph of Emile de Antonio seated beside the painter Jean-Michel Basquiat taken for a 1984 issue of Andy Warhol's *Interview* magazine. I often look up at the photograph to remind myself about film, art, politics, and why they matter. That was De's legacy. Not fashion!

De is uncharacteristically wearing an Armani jacket. He preferred a well-worn tweed jacket he bought secondhand in Montreal while at the New Cinema Festival. The shirt I would say is Brooks Brothers. He is not wearing a tie. He refused to wear a tie—anywhere.

De talked. De drank. (They all drank, didn't they? But none so hard as to provoke his friend Andy to make a film about his drinking.) De wrote. He would routinely work in the early morning. Journal entries. Film ideas. Letters. I'd wager that had he lived into the digital nineties I would still receive handwritten letters in envelopes decorated with fun postage stamps.

Do you think the picture is too serious? Far too serious for someone whose inspirations included Groucho Marx. But politics is serious stuff. Make that Karl Marx.

Basquiat was young and talented. De liked that. I did not consider myself talented at age twenty-one when I sought him out for advice—but I was young. Once I asked him why he helped so many young filmmakers. "If we don't help each other we will never move ahead," he replied.

That's funny: looking at the photo again I notice Jean-Michel is in his socks! If the photograph wasn't cropped I wager you would see De wearing construction boots. He owned so many pairs of those Timberland boots.

A more characteristic image, and one De liked, is the photograph of his arrest during an antiwar protest at the U.S. Capitol in 1972. His fist

Figure 34. Painter Jean-Michel Basquiat and Emile de Antonio pose for Andy Warhol's *Interview*, 1984. Courtesy of Ron Mann and Art Gallery of Ontario.

clenched, raised in the air for solidarity, the smiling de Antonio (in that tweed coat and plain, open-neck white shirt?) is being escorted into a police van.

He never dressed in fashion. But no one made films for his time better than Emile de Antonio.

CINDA (FIRESTONE) FOX

Poker and Good Advice

When I was twenty, I saw *In the Year of the Pig*, a documentary about the Vietnam War by Emile de Antonio. I decided then that I would work for him. I got my opportunity three years later when I was sent to interview him for *Liberation News Service*. In mid-interview the phone rang and I heard him say: "Yes, I'm looking for an assistant editor." I applied for the job practically before he had hung up the phone.

It was necessary to warn me about certain things, De, as he insisted everyone call him, cautioned me. Some people considered him quite crazy. That didn't bother me at all, I assured him. I would ruin my eyesight squinting at tiny pieces of film. My eyesight was already lousy so that was no problem, I said. The pay was minimal. Oh, that was fine with me, I said, I would gladly work for free. "Never work for free," De reprimanded sternly, "no one will take you seriously." (This has turned out to be excellent advice which I recommend to all young filmmakers.)

I began my education in documentary filmmaking by observing De and his brilliant editor, Mary Lampson, deliberating on various edits of *Painters Painting* as I fulfilled various humble tasks such as keeping all the film in order and watering De's beloved fig tree.

I also began my education in poker. De, Mary, and I played everyday at lunchtime for an hour and after work for an hour. De was amazingly lucky. One day I lost five hundred dollars on one hand. I had five kings and he had five aces. Two weeks later, the exact same thing happened. What were the odds of that happening, I wondered, a billion to one? I was soon in the hole to De three thousand dollars. Luckily it was simply recorded on a large sheet of paper taped to the wall. De professed to feel terrible about the fact that I was losing far more money than my meager salary provided. However, as my luck changed and I began to win back my money, De did not seem to be as pleased as one might have expected.

My relationship with De was somewhat stormy. We agreed on very little. De held in contempt all movies except for a few very obscure ones, mostly Japanese (and I don't mean Kurosawa), and was incredulous that I could actually like *The Godfather.* "You don't actually believe in things like ESP do you?" De once asked me. "Yes," I replied. "What else? UFOs, extraterrestrials, ghosts, astral projection, what?" De wanted to know. "All of it," I replied. De seemed shocked but respectful and never asked again. De had great faith in the *New York Times,* while I, having been involved in a few historical events which I felt the *Times* had misreported, had practically none. Almost every morning at 9:15 as I arrived with De's breakfast (a cup of black coffee) and mine (a tuna fish sandwich and a double milk shake), De would scowl at me sternly and ask, "Have you read what's on page 77 [or whatever page it was] of the *New York Times*?" Of course I never had.

Despite our many differences, De was a warm and supportive friend. He trekked up to my Upper West Side apartment and braved loud rock music, cats, dogs, and children (De could never understand how I worked amid chaos) to see my extremely rough cuts of my first documentary, *Attica,* a movie about a prison riot which most people had assured me was a terrible idea. "You've got something great here. Keep going," De would say. Other filmmakers, processing labs, equipment rental places, all gave me special deals, loans, and equipment on De's many generous recommendations. I was reminded of the time I remarked to De that he always seemed to make time for young filmmakers who wanted to talk to him. "Well, isn't that what older people are for?" De replied. "To help young people?"

MARC N. WEISS

Making Painters Painting, or *My Brush with Art History*

I met Emile de Antonio with his pants down in 1969. I was a senior in college, turned on by the counterculture and radicalized by the Vietnam War. He had just finished *In the Year of the Pig*, his history of U.S. involvement in Vietnam, and I organized a de Antonio film festival on my campus, featuring all of his films and culminating with his guest appearance. On the day of his arrival, I went over to the school's guest house to welcome him. I knocked on his door, he shouted, "Come in!" and when I pushed the door open, there he stood in his underwear.

"I'm Marc Weiss," I said.

"People call me d: a, b, c, d," he replied.

Sometime during the next couple of days I told d I'd like to work for him after I graduated. "Sure, why not?" he said.

So on August 20, 1969 I walked into d's office/editing room at the Movielab building on West 54th Street near the Hudson River to begin my work as research assistant, camera assistant, editing assistant, and the kid who gets the lunch. The film we worked on for the next nine months or so was a really minor work of d's—a slapdash P.R. piece about antiwar Senator Eugene McCarthy's 1968 presidential campaign. Most of the money came from Martin Peretz (now the neoconservative publisher of the *New Republic*), one of McCarthy's financial backers who had fantasies about McCarthy running again in 1972.

But the quality of the film hardly mattered, because I was thrilled just to be there, schlepping equipment, setting up lights and changing film for the cameraman, syncing up sound track and film, learning how to edit from Mary Lampson, and most of all, watching d in action.

A few months after we finished work on the McCarthy film, d asked me if I wanted to be camera assistant on his new film about the New York School of painting. When he told me the cameraman would be Ed

Emshwiller, an extraordinary man whose photography was like dance and whose "experimental" films were like poetry, I jumped at the chance.

The impetus for the film came from the fact that the Metropolitan Museum of Art was mounting an ambitious retrospective of the New York School, which brought together many of the major works from the major artists of the past thirty years. D wanted Henry Geldzahler, the curator of contemporary art at the Met, to do a walking intro to the show. Wearing a radio microphone, Henry was supposed to come up the giant main stairway talking about the show, then walk past the camera into the main gallery.

Between the primitive radio microphone technology of the day and Henry's memory, there were lots of problems: Henry would get halfway up the stairs, giving his rap, and Mary would say, "There's static on the sound, you'll have to start again." Back Henry went to the bottom of the stairs for another take. Part way up, he'd mess up a line, so back he went to give it another try. Each time the whole crew would hold its breath, hoping that nothing would go wrong and we could get our whole take.

Finally, on what must have been the sixth or seventh take, it looked like it was going to work! The mike was behaving, Henry remembered all his lines. But he was so exhausted from all those takes that when he got to the top of the stairs he just stopped and let out a huge breath. That scene never made it into the final movie. We had lots of adventures in this superheated world of painting "stars" that even I—who knew nothing whatsoever about art—had heard of. Andy Warhol showed us his "cock book," a kind of guest book in which celebrities and friends put drawings, collages, paintings, and poems about male genitalia. We played Ping-Pong with Jasper Johns.

Robert Rauschenberg, whose studio was in a converted chapel, sat on a tall ladder with a stained-glass window as a backdrop, drinking large quantities of whiskey while d interviewed him. After the shoot was over, Rauschenberg, assorted assistants and hangers-on, and the film crew sat down around a big table to play cards. Most everyone was doing some serious drinking, but as a counterculture loyalist I was much more into grass than alcohol. When I asked, "Don't you have any grass here?" Rauschenberg made a grand gesture toward the kitchen and told me to look under the sink. There I found a coffee can full of "cleaned" marijuana. After a pipe went around the table a few times, we developed an extraordinary kind of synchronicity. There would be animated multiple conversations, then suddenly everyone would stop talking. Some moments would pass in silence, then, for no discernible reason, everyone would break out into laughter simultaneously. I got up and turned on the tape recorder, then picked up the camera to shoot this bizarre scene. Needless to say, that footage didn't find its way into the film, either. At Willem de Kooning's studio in East Hampton, we were shooting the paintings in 35mm color and the interviews in 16mm black and white. At one point, while Ed was filming a painting, de Kooning started to talk about how he had done it. D whispered to me: "get the Eclair," meaning the camera we used for interviews. So there I was in de Kooning's studio, with a heavy camera on my shoulder, trying to get a good angle. I took a few steps to one side and suddenly felt one of de Kooning's assistants urgently tugging at my pant leg. I looked down to see that I was standing in the middle of a painting that was lying on the floor to dry. For all I know, that painting, footprint and all, is worth a fortune today.

MARY LAMPSON

Low Overhead and Independence: Working with Emile de Antonio

I worked with Emile de Antonio on four films: *America Is Hard to See, Millhouse: A White Comedy, Painters Painting,* and *Underground. Painters Painting* and *Millhouse* were made at the same time. We shifted gears every two months, from the life and times of Richard Nixon, a grainy, black-and-white, newsreel compilation comedy, to the beautifully photographed and completely original history of the New York art world that grew up after the war—two radically different ways of looking at the same time.

D was truly an independent filmmaker. He was smart, lucky, and persuasive and so was able to find people to make investments in his films (and vision) with no strings attached. He made his films for himself; but, because he was a political filmmaker, his films were made to be seen by others—to teach, to inspire, and to create change. He did not talk down to his audience; he appealed to their reason and, sometimes, emotions. He expected his audience to be intelligent.

When planning a film, he read copiously—drawing up lists of people to interview and questions to ask. When collecting stock footage for a film, we spent weeks in New York's newsreel vaults watched over by Lou Tetunic at UPI, or Ted Troll at Hearst Metrotone News, or Dave Chertok at Paramount/ABC; they were the trolls that guarded the gates of the stock footage tombs. We never hired researchers to look for us—we looked ourselves. How could someone else find those moments, captured almost by accident by a variety of anonymous news cameramen, which could bring the film to life? We looked for the unusual, collecting the images, words, and voices that would reveal the themes of the film. The work was hard, the hours long. It was often boring, but ultimately fascinating. D was frequently bored with the technical aspects of filmmaking, but never while looking at this footage.

He owned no film equipment. We worked in two rented cutting rooms between Eleventh and Twelfth Avenues in the Movielab building in New York. The rooms were ugly. The walls were green. They contained his metal desk, two editing tables, and metal shelves to hold the cans and cans of films—the "ins" and "outs" color-coded and neatly labeled. He answered his own phones; he typed his own letters, making carbons of everything for the files. These files were filled with his voluminous correspondence and newspaper clippings—filed in the de Antonio system, completely intuitively. Finding things was sometimes hard, especially a letter filed when he had a hangover, which he usually had once a week. When working on a project, he rented the equipment he needed. Low overhead—independence. The walls were not lined with framed prizes or awards. They were covered with four-inch by eight-foot sheets of cardboard on which were written ideas and notes for each film. Transcripts were cut up and pasted on the walls. This was the outline for the film. He got up at 4:00, was in the office by 5:30, and so when I arrived at 9:00 on the dot with my coffee in hand he would have screened the rough cut several times and would pepper me with ideas for changes.

I loved working for d. I was very young when I began and very inexperienced. I told him I was an editor, but that was stretching the truth. He believed in me and, working with him, I learned to believe in myself. He taught me to try everything, to suspect chronology, to organize thematically, and not to be afraid to have a bad idea. I learned to cut and cut, to understand why things did not work and to know when they did. He taught me to make radical changes and to throw out my favorite scene if it did not push the film forward. Years later, I remember a conversation I had with the director of a film I was cutting. "You can't do that," I said, "the audience needs a context for it." We talked some more. At the end of the conversation, the director asked, "How do you know all that?" I didn't really know how I knew, but I know I did.

Now, I realize that much of what I know about putting a film together I learned from d. Very early on he told me I should be making my own films—by pushing me out, he made me do it. He taught me to be persistent, to work hard, and to believe in the final film. He taught me to value independence above all. He taught me to play poker. I miss him.

PHILIP BERRIGAN

A Keen Political Conscience

I first met D when the idea for the film *In the King of Prussia* surfaced. We were to make a documentary of our trial for disarming two Mark 12As, reentry vehicles for the thermonuclear baggage of our Minuteman III ICBMs. My brother Dan and D had been friends for some years before I met him.

Once everyone had agreed on a film, D brought a crew to Jonah House in Baltimore to record a day there. We usually didn't allow media types to get inside the front door, since experience had fostered powerful suspicions of cameras and reporters. But we knew D's reputation for integrity, and gladly made exceptions.

Nonetheless, it took two scorching days in August 1982, when D shot *In the King of Prussia* in a little Manhattan church, for me to have the opportunity to observe D the person and D the artist. Using a pickup cast of ourselves playing ourselves and a handful of professional actors, with a script written directly from the court transcript, D patched together a film of extraordinary simplicity and relevance. Then he retired to months in the cutting room (hours of footage reduced to ninety minutes). Martin Sheen played the choleric Judge Salus, Dan Berrigan gave a brilliant allocution on the Bomb, as the camera lingered on the Mark 12A nose cone that we had disarmed, in full view below the judge.

Technically, *ITKOP* was uneven. But it made no pretense of technical perfection. It was that rare, even unique, film of nonviolence confronting the threat of universal destruction by nuclear war. It left audiences with this momentous question: What will save us from ourselves but a merciful God and civil resistance?

For quite some time after the release of *ITKOP* and prior to his death, I corresponded with D. His letters, like his conversations, revealed a keen political conscience. His roots were Christian; his Communist affiliation came later. Christians who made some pretense of living the Gospel fascinated and attracted him.

While he was alive, I heard it frequently said that D was America's finest documentary filmmaker. That struck me as true, having seen several of his films—all remarkable for their veracity, historical grasp, and technical creativity. Even more important to me, however, was D the man, a compassionate, loyal, and conscientious person. I mourned his passing. I still do.

ALLAN SIEGEL

A Man of Extremes

Media activist Allan Siegel teaches video production at the School of the Art Institute of Chicago. In the 1980s he worked with de Antonio on a project to reedit and expand Rush to Judgment. *The two also received a grant from the New York Council on the Arts to produce a documentary on the sixties. At the time of de Antonio's death they were collaborating on a screenplay called* Drug Baby.

I remember de first by his space and rituals. They marked his personality. The brownstone on East Sixth with his office downstairs and Nancy and de's apartment above. The office adorned only with a wall of bookshelves and his desk. A chair and a filing cabinet. The concrete backyard, barren except for the graffiti film title—*In the King of Prussia*—spray-painted on one wall. The ritual built around leaving the house that involved putting on his boots and the pain that was sometimes there because of an injury sustained during the war. The almost ceremonial exchanges between him and Nancy when she left to go uptown to her office. As I got to know him better, I began to see these daily events as more than simply habits but as choices made about how he wanted to live his life. What was valued and who was cherished.

In the beginning, I'd always viewed de as a man of extremes. Of specific likes and dislikes. Incredibly stubborn; but equally gracious and charming. In the beginning of our acquaintance these differences were not easily reconcilable. Nor could I see where these contradictory pieces emanated from—his idiosyncrasies, the colors of his personality, the way he existed in the world. The truth is I probably didn't care; his friendship was sufficient. And his wisdom nourished me.

Yet it is by these extremes that I remember him. Who he was and what he represented doesn't coalesce into a neat package. Why should it?

The public persona that de invisibly seemed to cultivate, the public world of the artist and bon vivant, were very much a part of his complexity. He knew many people. Artists, businessmen, an assemblage of people that he took to and who took to him. He enjoyed going to Elaine's and sitting at the table with the poster for *Millhouse* on the wall behind him. As if this semipublic notoriety secured his position among a strata of power and celebrity that he both loathed and was well acquainted with.

But, when I look back upon someone I was very fond of and close to, I expect that the pieces will come together and a coherent whole will emerge and that I'll be able to say that this is who de was. I'm happy it hasn't happened. Because I learned something from the way de negotiated these different arenas of activity, how he sought to maintain (not always so well) the tension between the different worlds he thrived in. These different sides to de's personality, his capacity to participate in these disparate realities, all embody his spirit.

What else do I mean by calling him a man of extremes? Take de's journal, a massive tome that he added to every day because he loved to write and loved to read (after all, he was a linguist). So he wrote in his own private manner for his own purpose, perhaps to define the solitude that was so critical to his routines. But as he wrote he seemed to relish the idea that his words might only become public posthumously. He wrote for the pleasure of writing and, outwardly, for no other purpose.

I believe he approached film from this direction also. Although he approached the subjects of each of his films with a preciseness (or with an ostensible sense of clarity), what motivated him was an intense, very subjective relationship to the subject. Film was a way of processing and working through the emotions that connected him to McCarthy, the Kennedy assassination, Nixon, Vietnam, the Weathermen, and finally, in his last film, J. Edgar Hoover. So his politics had this very personal core, something well annotated in his journals. My attachment to him, I think, was grounded in this because he was so averse to any kind of homogenization of political discourse, which is why he always thought of himself as an anarchist. He disliked political labels, and none would have fit anyway.

Sitting with de watching an image on the screen, or listening to the intonations of a voice, repeatedly, over and over again, there was always that sense that there was something missed, some nuance not caught. One more hearing would catch it. And thus the truth lay lurking, and if it couldn't be found, at least we took the time searching for it. And this was what inspired me, that de gave me access to his process of searching, of seeking those hidden truths in the world around us; not because they were absolutes but because they revealed the currents of power and the personalities that gave the world around us a truer sense of dimension.

Filmography

Point of Order (1963) 97 min.
   Point Films
   Produced by Emile de Antonio and Daniel Talbot
   Directed by Emile de Antonio
   Executive producers: Elliot Pratt and Henry Rosenberg
   Editor: Robert Duncan
   Editorial consultants: David T. Bazelon and Richard Rovere
   Narration: Emile de Antonio
   Distributors: Walter Reade/Sterling's Continental Films; New Yorker Films; The Other Cinema (UK); Zenger Video
   Cast: Robert T. Stevens (Secretary of the Army), John G. Adams (Counsel for the Army), Joseph Welch (Special Counsel for the Army), Senator Karl Mundt (Chairman, R-SD), Ray Jenkins (Chief Counsel of Subcommittee), Senator John McClellan (D-AR), Senator Stuart Symington (D-MO), Private G. David Schine, Roy M. Cohn (Chief Counsel for Senator McCarthy), Senator Joseph R. McCarthy (R-WI). Also General Walter B. Smith (Undersecretary of State), General C. E. Ryan (Commanding Officer, Fort Dix), Lieutenant Colonel Blunt, James Juliana, Senator Henry Jackson (D-WA); Robert A. Collier, Fred Fischer, Frank Carr (staff director for the Special Subcommittee on Investigations), and Robert F. Kennedy (Counsel to Subcommittee)
   Army-McCarthy hearings broadcast April–June 1954
   Alternate title: *Point of Order!*

That's Where the Action Is (1965) 50 min.
   British Broadcasting Corporation
   Produced by David J. Webster
   Directed by Emile de Antonio
   Narrator: Robert McKenzie
   Camera: Butch Calderwood
   Sound: Don Martin
   Film editor: John Walker
   Research: Barbara Penga
   Associate producer: Marion B. Javits
   Cast: John Lindsay, Abraham Beame, Robert F. Kennedy, Jesse Gray, Daniel Patrick Moynihan, Walter Thayer, William F. Buckley Jr., Sammy Davis Jr., Mayor Robert Wagner, David Dubinsky, Rep. James H. Scheller, Frank O'Connor, Mario Procaccino, Fats the Bookie

Rush to Judgment (1966) 122 min./116 min./110 min.
   Judgment Films
   Produced by Emile de Antonio and Mark Lane
   Directed by Emile de Antonio
   Camera: Robert Primes

Editor: Dan Drasin
Additional editing by Peter Van Dyke
Sound: Paul Mielche
Camera assistant: Dan Wheeler
Based on the book by Mark Lane
Narrators: Mark Lane, Emile de Antonio
Interviewees: Acquilla Clemons, Penn Jones Jr., Warren Reynolds Jr., Nancy Perrin Rich Hamilton, Lee Bowers Jr., J. C. Price, S. M. Holland, Charles F. Brehm, Richard C. Dodd, James Tague, Sergeant Nelson Delgado, Napoleon J. Daniels, James Leon Simmons, Harold Williams
Footage of Lee Harvey Oswald, Marguerite Oswald, Jack Ruby, John F. Kennedy, Lyndon B. Johnson, the Warren Commission, District Attorney Henry Wade, Dallas Police Chief James Curry
Distributor: Impact Films (Lionel Rogosin)
Alternate titles:
L'Amérique Fait Appel [America Appeals] (131 min.)
The Plot to Kill JFK: Rush to Judgment (95 min.) MPI Home Video, 1986 (color sequences added)
Rush to Judgment: A Film (98 min.) MPI Home Video, 1988

In the Year of the Pig (1968) 101 min.
Monday Film Production Co.; Turin Film Corp.
Produced and directed by Emile de Antonio
Executive producer: Moxie Schell
Associate producers: Terry Morrone, John Atlee
Editors: Lynzee Klingman, Hannah Moreinis, Helen Levitt
Camera: John F. Newman; Jean Jacques Rochut (Paris)
Sound: Geoffrey Weinstock; Harold Maury (Paris)
Music: Steve Addiss
Assistant director: Albert Maher
Voice-over: Emile de Antonio
Interviewees: David Halberstam, Arthur Schlesinger Jr., Jean Lacouture, Professor Paul Mus, Olivier Todd, Harrison Salisbury, Roger Hillsman, Sergeant John Towler, John White (U.S. Navy), David K. Tuck, Joseph Buttinger, Philippe Devillers, Father Daniel Berrigan, Senator Thruston Morton, Kenneth P. Landon (State Department), Charlton Ogburn (State Department), Professor David Wurfel
Footage of Thich Quang Duc, Presidents Eisenhower, Kennedy, Johnson; Vice Presidents Nixon and Humphrey; Senators Joseph McCarthy, Everett Dirksen, Wayne Morse, Ernest Gruening; Representative Gerald Ford; Generals Curtis LeMay, Mark Clark, Maxwell Taylor, and William Westmoreland; Colonels Corson and George S. Patton III; Ambassador Henry Cabot Lodge; Secretaries of State Dean Rusk, Charles Wilson, and John Foster Dulles; Defense Secretary Robert McNamara; UN Secretary-General U Thant; Cardinal Spellman; Ho Chi Minh, Premier Nguyen Cao Ky, Ngo Dinh Diem, and Madame Ngo Dinh Nhu; Ted Koppel
Distributors: Pathé Contemporary Films; Cinetree; Cornell University Audio-Video Resource Center; New Yorker Films; McGraw-Hill Films; International Historic Films, Inc.
Alternate title: *Vietnam: In the Year of the Pig* (1968/1985) 103 min. MPI Video

America Is Hard to See (1970) 101 min.
March Twelve Co.; Turin Film Co.
Produced by Emile de Antonio
A film by Emile de Antonio, with Allan Siegel, Mary Lampson, Richard Pearce, Stephen Ning, and Lori Hiris
Camera: Richard Pearce
Editor: Mary Lampson
Cast: Senator Eugene McCarthy,

Leonard Bernstein, John Kenneth Galbraith, E. W. Kenworthy, Arthur Miller, Richard Goodwin, Martin Peretz, David Hohe, Gerry Studds, Sam Brown, Arthur Herzberg, Geoffrey Sperling, Curtis Gans, Richard Nixon, Lyndon Johnson, Hubert Humphrey, Robert Kennedy, Dan Rostenkowski, Richard Daley, Paul Newman

    Distributor: EYR Programs; MPI Video

    Alternate title: *1968: America is Hard to See* (1970/1988) MPI Video, 90 min.

    (Videotape color sequences added; on-camera narration by Emile de Antonio)

Millhouse: A White Comedy (1971) 93 min.
    Whittier Film Corp. and Turin Film Corp.
    Produced and directed by Emile de Antonio
    Editor: Mary Lampson
    Assistant editor: Nancy Ogden
    Graphics: Tanya Neufeld
    Cameras: Ed Emshwiller (Washington, D.C.), Richard Kletter (New York), Dan O'Reilly (Los Angeles), Bruce Shaw and Mike Gray (Chicago)
    Sound: Mary Lampson
    Research consultant: David Chertok
    California researcher: Madeleine de Antonio
    Research assistant: John Ramson
    Negatives: Marc N. Weiss
    Music: L. Bridge [screen credit for nonexistent person, to cover for use of copyrighted music]
    Interviewees: Jerry Voorhis, Jack Anderson, Jack McKinney, James Wechsler, Fred J. Cook, Joe McGinnis, Jules Whitcover, Laverne Morris, Marjorie [Nixon's prom date]
    Footage of Richard Milhous Nixon, Pat Nixon, Spiro T. Agnew, Hubert H. Humphrey, Alger Hiss, Whittaker Chambers, Dwight Eisenhower, John F. Kennedy, Lyndon Johnson, J. Edgar Hoover, Bob Hope, Ronald Reagan, Pat O'Brien, Robert Dole, Strom Thurmond, Martin Luther King Jr., Dick Gregory, Pete Seeger

    Distributors: National Talent Service; New Yorker Films; MPI Home Video, 1988

    Alternate title: *Millhouse: A White House Comedy*

Painters Painting (1972) 116 min.
    Turin Film Corp.
    Produced and directed by Emile de Antonio
    Editing and sound: Mary Lampson
    Assistant editor: Cinda Firestone
    Camera: Ed Emshwiller
    Assistant camera: Marc N. Weiss
    Graphics: Tanya Neufeld
    Stills: Malcolm Varon, Rudy Burkhardt, Fred McDarrah, Hans Namuth
    Assistant: Nancy Ogden
    Prologue: Philip Leider
    Distributors: New Yorker Films; Cinegate (UK)
    Cast: Willem de Kooning, Helen Frankenthaler, Hans Hoffmann, Jasper Johns, Robert Motherwell, Barnett Newman, Kenneth Noland, Jules Olitski, Philip Pavia, Jackson Pollock, Larry Poons, Robert Rauschenberg, Frank Stella, Andy Warhol, Leo Castelli, Henry Geldzahler, Clement Greenberg, Tom Hess, Philip Johnson, Hilton Kramer, William Rubin, Robert Scull, Ethel Scull, Philip Leider, Josef Albers, Brigid Polk, Emile de Antonio

    Alternate title: *Painters Painting: The New York Art Scene, 1940–1970* (Mystic Fire Video, 1989)

    Reissued with additional multimedia material as *Emile de Antonio's Painters Painting: A CD-ROM by Ron Mann, written by Douglas Kellner* (Voyager, 1995)

Underground (1976) 88 min.
   Action 27, Inc.; Turin Film Corp.
   Produced and directed by Emile de Antonio with Haskell Wexler, Mary Lampson
   Editing and sound: Mary Lampson
   Camera: Haskell Wexler
   Additional photography: Chris Burrill, Linda Jassim (Los Angeles Employment Center), Carols Ortiz (South Bronx)
   Poem: "A Mongo Affair," by Miguel Algarin
   Music: Nina Simone, Phil Ochs
   Interviewees: Bernardine Dohrn, Kathy Boudin, Jeff Jones, Bill Ayers, Cathy Wilkerson
   Production staff: Tucker Ashworth, Larry Bensky, John Douglas, Jane Franklin, Robert Friedman, Alan Jacobs, Eleanore Kennedy, Sandy Levinson, Claude Marks, Antoinette O'Connor, P. Michael O'Sullivan, Hart Perry, George Pillsbury, Ellen Ray, Steven H. Scheurer, Paul Sequeira, Stanley Sheinbaum, Carol Stein, Mitch Tuchman, Marc N. Weiss, Myrna Zimmerman
   Excerpts from: *Attica* (Cinda Firestone); *Berkeley Streetfighting* (Stephen Lighthill); *Columbia Revolt, Only the Beginning, El pueblo se levanta,* and *San Francisco State: On Strike* (Newsreel); *Don't Bank on America* (Peter Biskind, Steve Hornick, John Manning); *Fidel* (Saul Landau, Irving Saraf); *In the Year of the Pig* (Emile de Antonio); *Introduction to the Enemy* (Indochina Peace Campaign Films); *The Murder of Fred Hampton* (Mike Gray, Howard Alk); *The Sixth Side of the Pentagon* (Chris Marker); *The Streets Belong to the People* (Rufus Diamant)
   Distributor: rbc (Los Angeles); New Yorker Films; Black Ink (UK)

In the King of Prussia (1982) 92 min.
   Produced, directed, and written by Emile de Antonio
   Camera director: Judy Irola
   Camera: Julian Abbio
   Documentary footage by Tom Lofstrom, Maryann DeLeo, Downtown Community TV, with Eric Crowley, Melody James, Gordon Lockwood, Susan Lynch, Sandy McLeod, Joan Rosenfeld, Martin Zurla
   Editor and technical director: Mark Pines
   Set design: Richard Hoover
   Production manager: Scott Robbe
   Sound: Jack Malkan, Secret Sound
   CMX editors: Peter Karp, Wayne Hydge, John Smith
   Music: "Crow on the Cradle," written by Sidney Carter. Recorded by Jackson Browne with David Lindley, Graham Nash, Craig Doerge, and Joe Walsh
   Main Title: Futura 2000
   Cast: The Plowshares Eight: Daniel Berrigan, Philip Berrigan, Dean Hammer, Carl Kabat, Elmer Maas, Anne Montgomery, Molly Rush, John Schuchardt; Martin Sheen (the Judge), John Randolph Jones (Moravec), Richard Sisk (Baumann), George Tynan (Prosecutor), John Connolly (Defense Attorney), Scott Robbe (Officer Bolling)
   Footage of Dave Dellinger, Sheriff Hill, Norm Townsend, George Wald, Robert Aldrich, Richard Falk, Robert Jay Lifton, Bishop Peria, John B. (Juror 2), Ramsey Clark
   Distributors: New Yorker Films; MPI Home Video
   Locarno Film Festival, International Critics' Prize
   Berlin International Film Festival, Special Recommendation

Mr. Hoover and I (1989) 85 min.
   Turin Film Corp. in association with Channel Four Television (UK)
   Directed, written, and produced by Emile de Antonio

Camera: Morgan Wesson, Matthew Mindlin
2d unit camera: William Rexer
Editor: George Spyros
Additional footage: Ron Mann
Associate producer: Michael Thomas
Cast: Emile de Antonio, Nancy Mindlin de Antonio, John Cage
Footage of J. Edgar Hoover and Richard Nixon
Working title: *A Middle-Aged Radical As Seen through the Eyes of His Government*

◆

SECONDARY FILMOGRAPHY

Pull My Daisy (1959) 28 min.
Produced and directed by Robert Frank and Alfred Leslie
Written and narrated by Jack Kerouac
Based on Kerouac's play *The Beat Generation* (1958)
Camera: Robert Frank
Editors: Robert Frank, Leon Prochnik, Alfred Leslie
Music: David Amram
Title song by Amram, Kerouac, and Allen Ginsberg; sung by Anita Ellis
Cast: Beltiane [Delphine Seyrig] (Carolyn, Milo's wife), Allen Ginsberg (Allen), Gregory Corso (Gregory), Larry Rivers (Milo), Peter Orlovsky (Peter), David Amram (Pat Mezz McGillicuddy), Mooney Peebles (the Bishop), Richard Bellamy (the Bishop), Alice Neel (the Bishop's mother), Sally Gross (the Bishop's sister), Pablo Frank (Pablo, Milo's son), Denise Parker (Girl in Bed)
G-String Enterprises
Distributor: Emile de Antonio
Alternate title: *The Beat Generation*

Sunday (1961) 17 min.
Producer: Emile de Antonio
Director and editor: Dan Drasin
Cameras and sound: Dan Drasin, Frances Stillman, Howard Milkin, Gerard E. McDermott, Frank Simon
Cast: Israel G. Young, Harold L. "Doc" Humes, Captain Adrian Donahue, Inspector Patrick MacCormick, Judith Indrieri, Bryan Carey, Louis Pagliaroli, Robert A. Easton, Art D'Lugoff, James Lanigan, Ed Koch, Gin Briggs, Dan Drasin
Music: Dave Cohen, Jan Dorfman (guitar, banjo, vocals)
Songs: "This Land Is Your Land," "We Shall Not Be Moved," "Mary Don't You Weep," "Battle Hymn of the Republic," "The Star-Spangled Banner"
Filmed April 9, 1961, Washington Square Park, Greenwich Village, New York
Distributors: Emile de Antonio; Contemporary Films

X (1964) 20 min.
Produced by Emile de Antonio
Directed by Dan Drasin
Cast: Stan Vanderbeek
Alternate title: *The Transist-ites*

Drunk (1965) 66 min.
Directed by Andy Warhol
Cast: Emile de Antonio
Alternate title: *Drink*
Unreleased

[Bertrand Russell "obituary" interview]
Directed by Emile de Antonio
Camera: Peter Whitehead
Cast: Lord Russell, Mark Lane, Ralph Schoenman, Richard Stark, Emile de Antonio
Filmed November 22, 1965

Footage sold to BBC; resold to Swedish Broadcasting Company and packaged as a short telefilm (1970, 23 min.)

Andy Warhol (1973/1987)
  Director: Lana Jokel
  Interviews with Emile de Antonio et al.

The Trials of Alger Hiss (1979)
  Produced, directed, and written by John Lowenthal
  Technical adviser: Emile de Antonio

[John Cage and Emile de Antonio at the Whitney Museum] (1982)
  Unreleased film begun for Swedish television

The New Cinema (1983—Canada)
  Directed, written, and edited by Peter Wintonick
  Interviews with independent filmmakers Emile de Antonio, Chantal Akerman, Les Blank, Robert Frank, Daniele Huillet, Ron Mann, Paul Morrissey, Michael Snow, Jean-Marie Straub, Wim Wenders, Robert Young
  Distributor: Cinema Guild (New York)

Fire in the East: A Portrait of Robert Frank (1986)
  Museum of Fine Arts, Houston
  Interviews with Emile de Antonio, Allen Ginsberg, Jonas Mekas et al.

Resident Alien: Quentin Crisp in America (1990)
  Produced, directed, written, and edited by Jonathan Nossiter
  Cast: Quentin Crisp, John Hurt, Sting, Holly Woodlawn, Fran Lebowitz, Paul Morrissey, Hunter Madsen, Michael Murphy, Emile de Antonio

Shadows in the City (1991)
  Director: Ari Roussimoff
  Cast: includes Emile de Antonio as the Mystic

◆

ALTERNATE VERSIONS OF *POINT OF ORDER*

Point of Order (1962)
  Produced by Emile de Antonio and Daniel Talbot
  Editor: Paul Falkenberg
  Script: Richard Rovere, David T. Bazelon et al.
  Narration: Mike Wallace
  Unreleased

Charge and Countercharge (1968) 43 min.
  Abridged edition of *Point of Order*, with added narration and archival footage
  Appleton-Century-Crofts, a division of Meredith Corp.
  Produced and directed by Emile de Antonio
  Editor: Lynzee Klingman
  Narrator: Emile de Antonio
  Alternate title: *Charge and Countercharge: A Film of the Era of Senator Joseph R. McCarthy*
  Distributor: Cinema Guild

The Confrontation (1968) 60 min.
  ABC News Special, broadcast April 5, 1968
  Produced and directed by Emile de Antonio
  Narrator: Bob Young (with prologue added)
  Alternate title: *The Confrontation between Senator Joseph McCarthy and Attorney Joseph Welch on the Occasion of the Historic Army-*

McCarthy Hearings before a Senate Investigating Committee and 20,000,000 Stunned Americans in the Spring of 1954

Point of Order (197?)
Syndicated for Australian TV
Narration by Anthony Lewis

Charge and Countercharge (ca. 1979) 45 min.
Prologue with Paul Newman added to original 1968 edition

Emile de Antonio's Point of Order (1984) 103 min.
Zenger Video, Culver City, California
Reissue with added Paul Newman prologue

McCarthy: Death of a Witch Hunter (1986) 50 min.
MPI Home Video, 1986
Reissue of *Charge and Countercharge*, with Paul Newman prologue
Initially released by MPI under the title *Point of Order*

AUDIO RECORDINGS

The Emile de Antonio Collection, Archives Division, State Historical Society of Wisconsin (Madison) contains numerous audio recordings of radio programs and interviews with de Antonio as well as recordings of people interviewed for his documentary films.

The 25-Year Retrospective Concert of the Music of John Cage. K08P-1498. Three LP boxed set. George Avakian, producer, 1959. Recorded in performance at Town Hall, New York, May 15, 1958. Concert produced by Impresarios, Inc., Emile de Antonio, Jasper Johns, Bob Rauschenberg. Reissued on compact disc by Wergo, 1994. Music of Our Century Series.

Point of Order! A Record of the Army-McCarthy Hearings, from the Film Documentary Produced by Emile de Antonio and Daniel Talbot. Columbia Masterworks series, Columbia KOL 6070, 1964. Includes notes "Joseph R. McCarthy, by David T. Bazelon." Eric Sevareid, narrator. John Simon, editor. (Also issued as Columbia KOS 2470.)

Lane, Mark, and Emile de Antonio. *Rush to Judgment: The Living Testimony by the Actual Witnesses on the Original Sound-Track Recording of the Emile de Antonio and Mark Lane Film.* New York: Vanguard Records, VRS-9242, 1967.

Mark Lane: Rush to Judgment. New York: Happening Records, CA-3210, 1967?
"In this recording Mark Lane discusses many questions of major importance and reveals 'staggering facts,' with the desire to determine how, why and by whom our President was killed on November 22, 1963." (liner notes)

de Antonio, Emile. *Senator Joseph R. McCarthy: A Documentary of the McCarthy Hearings.* New York: Broadside/Folkways Records, FH 5450, 1968. (descriptive notes)

de Antonio, Emile, Mary Lampson, Haskell Wexler, and the Weather Underground Organization. *Underground: Sound Track from the Film.* New York:

Folkways Records, 05752, 1976. (two LP discs; descriptive notes)

Film-makers and the First Amendment. BC 3006. Los Angeles: Pacifica Tape Library, 1976. (thirty-minute radio program on the attempt to suppress *Underground*)

Emile de Antonio's "Millhouse: A White Comedy"; Voice Material from the Film. New York: Folkways Records, 5852, 1979. (two LP discs; notes and transcript)

Philip Agee on the CIA and Covert Action. WBAI-FM/Pacifica Radio Network, 1988. Three hours. Stuart Hutchison, Emile de Antonio, John Stockwell, Bill Schaap, and others

Justice Is Not Forlorn. WBAI-FM/Pacifica Radio Network, December 1, 1989. Stuart Hutchison tribute to film-makers Emile de Antonio and Lionel Rogosin

Bibliography

Published Writings by Emile de Antonio (in order of publication)

de Antonio, Emile, and Daniel Talbot. *Point of Order! A Documentary of the Army-McCarthy Hearings.* New York: Norton, 1964.

"The Point of View in Point of Order." *Film Comment* 2.1 (Winter 1964): 35–36.

"Review: Salt of the Earth." *Film Comment* (Fall 1966): 89–90.

"A Comment from the Producer of the Film." Liner notes for *Rush to Judgment: The Living Testimony by the Actual Witnesses on the Original Sound-Track Recording of the Emile de Antonio and Mark Lane Film.* New York: Vanguard Records, 1967.

"Notes on the Film of Fact." *IT: Festival Supplement,* ca. 1967. *Journals,* II.7 (February 5, 1980).

"McCarthy." Script for *Senator Joseph R. McCarthy: A Documentary of the McCarthy Hearings.* New York: Broadside/Folkways Records, 1968.

de Antonio, Emile, and Daniel Talbot. "These Remember Joe" [letter to the editor]. *Esquire,* April 1968, pp. 14, 188.

de Antonio, Emile, and Albert Maher. "Chasing Checkers by Richard M. Nixon." *New York Free Press* 1.38 (September 26–October 2, 1968): 4, 13 + cover.

"The Agony of the Revolutionary Artist." *Northwest Passage* [Bellingham, Washington] 5.4 (May 24–June 6, 1971): 23.

"Some Discrete Interruptions on Film, Structure, and Resonance." *Film Quarterly* 25.1 (Fall 1971): 10–11.

"Pontus Hultén and Some 60s Memories in New York." *New York Collection for Stockholm* (Stockholm: Moderna Museet, 1973): 1–3.

"Marx ja Warhol." (trans. S. Toi Vianinen). *Filmihullu* [Helsinki] 8 (1974): 22–23.

"Caught in the Act" [letter to the editor]. *UR: University Review* 37 (May 1974).

"Movies and Me." National Film Theatre Programme. May–July 1974, pp. 39–41.

"Rally Greetings." *The Militant,* September 2, 1974.

"Visions of Vietnam." *UR: University Review* 41 (December 1974): 21.

"De Antoniography," "Emile de Antonio's 'CIA Diary,'" and "The Revolution Will Not Be Televised." *Take Over* [Madison, Wisconsin] 5.6 (April 7–23, 1975): 12–13.

"How It Began." Liner notes for *Underground: Sound Track of the Film.* New York: Folkways Records, 1976.

"Celluloid Reportage: 'All the President's Men.'" *Yipster Times* 4.4 (May 1976): 20.

"Corporate Crime" [letter to the editor]. *The Militant,* March 11, 1977, pp. 10, 23.

"Marcuse and Weathermen" [letter to the editor]. *New York Times,* December 12, 1977, p. 34.

"De Antonio: 'Year of Pig' Marxist Film" [letter to the editor]. *Jump Cut* 19 (December 1978): 37.

Transcript for *Emile de Antonio's "Millhouse: A White Comedy"; Voice Material from the Film.* Washington, D.C.: Folkways Records, 1979.

"The Future of '36, a film by Willum Thijssen and Linda van Tulden." Unidentified Danish magazine, 198?

"Point of Order (Hic)." *Village Voice,* January 28, 1980, p. 42.

"Spiritual Offering" [letter to the editor]. *Village Voice,* June 23, 1980, p. 3.

"Frank Stella: A Passion for Painting." *Geo* [New York] (March 1982): 13–16.

"*In the King of Prussia*: Emile de Antonio Interviews Himself." *Film Quarterly* 36.1 (Fall 1982): 28–32.

"Dialogue on Film: Martin Sheen." *American Film* 8 (December 1982): 20–28.
"En Garde, Ophuls!" [letter to the editor]. *American Film* (March 1983): 8.
de Antonio, Emile, and Mitch Tuchman. *Painters Painting: A Candid History of the Modern Art Scene, 1940–1970*. New York: Abbeville Press, 1984.
"My Brush with Painting." *American Film* 9 (March 1984): 8, 10, 14, 76.
Program notes. Conservatoire d'Art Cinématographique de Montréal, Concordia University. March–April 1984.
"Points of Order" [letter to the editor]. *American Film* 11 (December 1984).
"Kejsaren nickar vid sminkbordet." *Chaplin* [Stockholm] 27.5 (1985): 287.
Letter to the editor. *New York Review of Books*, September 28, 1985.
Letter to the editor. *New York Times*, March 1985. Reprinted in *Film Threat* 12 (1987): 18–31.
"The Future of Film." *American Film* (June 1985): 82.
"Different Drummers." *American Film* (November 1985): 72–73.
"Brief an das Weisse Haus." *Film und Fernsehen* [Berlin] 15.2 (1987): 34.
"Why I Make Films." *Libération* [Paris], May 1987.
"Writing; Deconstruction." *Film Threat* 12 (1987): 25.
"'Den,' a Script by Emile de Antonio." *Film Threat* 12 (1987): 26–27.
Untitled. *Lumières* 19 (1988): 31–32.
"Mr. Hoover and I." In *Conspiracy Charges*, ed. Jay Murphy (New York: Red Bass Publications, 1991), 8–10.
"Ed Emshwiller." In *Intersecting Images: The Cinema of Ed Emshwiller*, ed. Robert A. Haller (New York: Anthology Film Archives, 1997), 32.

Interviews (in order of publication)

"Rush to Judgment: A Conversation with Mark Lane and Emile de Antonio." *Film Comment* 4.2–3 (Fall/Winter 1967): 2–18.
"The Ghost of the Army-McCarthy Hearings." *Firing Line*, programs 86–87, January 19, 1968. William F. Buckley Jr., with Roy Cohn, James St. Clair, Leo Cherne, and Emile de Antonio.
Asnen, Alan. "De Antonio in Hell—Part I." *East Village Other* 3.51 (November 22, 1968). Reprinted in *Our Time: An Anthology of Interviews from the "East Village Other,"* ed. Alan Katzman (New York: Dial Press, 1972): 246–57.
Picard, Lil. "Inter/View with Emile de Antonio." *[Andy Warhol's] Inter/view* 1.3 (1969): 8–9.
Manrin, François. "Emile de Antonio: Un cinéaste américain face à la guerre du Vietnam." *L'Humanité* [Paris], June 9, 1969, p. 10.
Eisenschitz, Bernard, and Jean Narboni. "Entretien avec Emile de Antonio." *Cahiers du Cinéma* 214 (July–August 1969): 42–56.
Mekas, Jonas. "Movie Journal." *Village Voice*, November 13, 1969, p. 57.
Ciment, Michel, and Bernard Cohn. "Entretien avec Emile de Antonio." *Positif* 113 (February 1970): 28–39.
Westerbeck, Colin J. "Some Out-Takes from Radical Filmmaking: Emile de Antonio." *Sight and Sound* 39.3 (Summer 1970): 140–43.
Weiner, Bernard. "Running from the FBI in Dallas: An Interview with Emile de Antonio." *Northwest Passage* [Bellingham, Washington] 5.4 (May 24–June 6, 1971): 22.
Weiner, Bernard. "Radical Scavenging: An Interview with Emile de Antonio." *Film Quarterly* 25.1 (Fall 1971): 3–15.
de Antonio, Terry. "An In-Depth Interview with Emile de Antonio." *Shantih* 1.4/2.1 (Winter/Spring 1972): 17–21.
O'Brien, Glenn. "Interview with Emile de Antonio: Director of Millhouse." *[Andy Warhol's] Interview* 19 (February 1972): 28–29.
Martin, Marcel. "Brève Rencontre . . . avec Emile de Antonio." *Écran* [Paris] 4 (April 1972): 39–40.
Sery, Patrick. "Emile de Antonio." *Cinéma* [Paris] 165 (April 1972): 131–35.
[Firestone, Cinda.] "'The Real History of Our Times Is on Film': Filmmaker Emile de Antonio Talks about Nixon, the '50s, and Now." *Liberation News Service* [New York], April 15, 1972, pp. 12–14.
Johnson, Kay, and Monika Jensen. "The Role of the Filmmaker: Three Views. An Interview with Emile de Antonio." *Arts in Society* 10.2 (1973): 209–19.
Solem, Russ. "An Interview with Emile de Antonio." *Magic Lantern* (1973): 6–11.
Neufeld, Tanya. "An Interview with Emile de Antonio." *Artforum* 11 (March 1973): 79–83.
Interview. *Der Sonntag* [East Berlin] (1974).
von Bagh, Peter. "Miksi taas Millhouse? Valkoinen komedia." *Filmihullu* [Helsinki] 8 (1974): 16–21.
Weiss, Marc N. "Emile de Antonio: Interview." *Film Library Quarterly* 7.2 (1974): 29–35.
Schröder, H., and H. Schmidt. "Herausforderung durch ein Festival." Interview. *Film und Fernsehen* [Berlin], February 1974.

Weiss, Marc N. "Conversations with Emile de Antonio." *UR: University Review* 35 (March 1974): 17–19.

Weiss, Marc N. "A Conversation with Emile de Antonio." *Marble: Film News and Comment* [New York] 3.5 (July–August 1975): 1–2.

Lyne, Susan. "An Interview with Emile de Antonio: The Idea of Taste Means Simply That You Are Behind the Plow Instead of Directing It." *City of San Francisco*, October 28, 1975.

Biskind, Peter, and Marc N. Weiss. "The Weather Underground, Take One: On Location with Bernardine Dohrn, Kathy Boudin, Jeff Jones, Bill Ayers and Cathy Wilkerson." *Rolling Stone* 199 (November 6, 1975): 36–43ff. Reprinted as insert for *Underground: Sound Track of the Film.*

van Bagh, Peter. "Hollywood on aina ollut peilli." Interview with Emile de Antonio. Trans. M. Koski. *Filmihullu* [Helsinki] 6 (1976): 8–11.

Silber, Glenn. "Art, Politics, and Film." *Daily Cardinal* [Madison, Wisconsin], March 1, 1976, p. 4.

Anderson, Steve. "Knowing Who the Criminals Are." *Daily Cardinal* [Madison, Wisconsin], April 29, 1976.

Gage, Jim, and Rebecca. "Mallards and Trombones by Lake Mendota: An Interview with Emile de Antonio and Mary Lampson." *Free for All* [Madison, Wisconsin], May 1976.

Tuchman, Mitch. "Emile de Antonio: 'All Filmmakers Are Confidence Men.'" *Village Voice*, May 17, 1976, pp. 140–41.

Georgakas, Dan, and Paul McIsaac. "Interview with Emile de Antonio and Mary Lampson." *Liberation* (July–August 1976): 22–25.

Marcorelles, Louis. "Rencontre avec Emile de Antonio ('Underground')." *Cahiers du Cinéma* 272 (November 1976): 35–42.

Gleason, Michie. "Underground: Emile de Antonio and the Weatherpeople." *Cinema Papers* 11 (January 1977): 202–5, 276.

D'Acci, Julie. "Marquee Theater Special: Interview with de Antonio." WHA-TV, Madison, Wisconsin, May 4, 1977.

Interview. *Film News* 8.6 (June 1978): 13.

Rosenthal, Alan. "Emile de Antonio: An Interview." *Film Quarterly* 32.1 (Autumn 1978): 4–17. Reprinted in *The Documentary Conscience: A Casebook in Film Making*, ed. Alan Rosenthal (Berkeley: University of California Press, 1980), 205–26.

"Emile de Antonio, New York, 14 November 1978." In Patrick S. Smith, *Andy Warhol's Art and Films* (Ann Arbor: UMI Research Press, 1986), 293–301.

Stepash, Irene. "Emile de Antonio: For the Record." *East Village Eye*, November 28, 1979, pp. 18–19.

Grosoli, F. "Emile de Antonio: Scegliere le immagini, 'parlare' la storia." *Cineforum* 196 (July–August 1980): 441–47.

Interview. *Cine* [Spain] 1 (October 1980): 57–65.

Zheutlin, Barbara. "The Art and Politics of the Documentary: A Symposium." *Cineaste* 11.3 (1981): 12–21. Reprinted as "The Politics of Documentary: A Symposium," in *New Challenges for Documentary*, ed. Alan Rosenthal (Berkeley: University of California Press, 1988), 227–42.

Morgan, Alec. "Sydney's Alec Morgan Visits New York's Emile de Antonio: 'But This Is Where I Belong . . . It's a Corrupt Imperial Space That I Want to Change.'" *Filmnews* (March 1981): 7–8.

Crowdus, Gary, and Dan Georgakas. "'History Is the Theme of All My Films': An Interview with Emile de Antonio." *Cineaste* 12.2 (1982): 20–28. Reprinted in *New Challenges for Documentary*, 165–79.

von Bagh, Peter. "Mina Jankkaan Koska uskon siiheu mita Sanon: Emile de Antonio haastahelu." *Filmihullu* [Helsinki] 3 (1982): 4–8.

Segal, David. "De Antonio and the Plowshares Eight." *Sight and Sound* 51.3 (Summer 1982): 182–84.

Linfield, Susan. "Irrepressible Emile de Antonio Speaks." *Independent*, June 1982, pp. 2–4, 10; and "De Antonio's Fireside Chat: Part Two." *Independent*, July–August 1982, pp. 21–22.

de Antonio, Emile. "*In the King of Prussia*: Emile de Antonio Interviews Himself." *Film Quarterly* 36.1 (Fall 1982): 28–32.

Murphy, Jay. "Red Bass Interview: Emile de Antonio." *Red Bass* [Tallahassee, Florida] (1983): 8–12.

Gallagher, Sharon. "On the Making of 'In the King of Prussia': An Interview with Emile de Antonio." *Radix* [Berkeley] 5.1 (July–August 1983): 24–26.

Locke, Stephen. "Emile de Antonio on His Film *In the King of Prussia*." Unidentified German periodical, 198?.

Palamidessi, Christine. "A Talk with Emile de Antonio." *New Video Magazine* (Winter 1984).

Basquiat, Jean-Michel. "Emile de Antonio with Jean-Michel Basquiat." *Interview* 14 (July 1984): 48–51.

Wintonick, Peter. "Quotations from Chairman 'Dee': Decodifying de Antonio." *Cinema Canada* 109 (July–August 1984): 16–17.

Oumano, Ellen. *Film Forum: Thirty-Five Top Filmmakers Discuss Their Craft*. New York: St. Martins Press, 1985.

Ross, Jean W. "Emile de Antonio." In *Contemporary Authors* 117 (Detroit: Gale Press, 1986), 95–99.

Gore, Chris. "Emile de Antonio." *Film Threat* [Beverly Hills] 12 (1987): 18–31.

Szurek, Sam. "Emile de Antonio: From McCarthy to Watergate to Contragate: An American Film Director, an American Saga." *Downtown* [New York] 64 (September 16, 1987): 32a–35a.
Green, Susan. "The Eggplant and the F.B.I.; Mr. Hoover and I, by Emile de Antonio, Not Yet at a Theater Near You." *Vanguard Press*, September 21–28, 1989, 1 p.
Guma, Greg. "Dissidence in Film; Emile de Antonio, Radical Filmmaker in Reactionary Times." *Vanguard Press*, September 21–28, 1989, 2 pp.
"Interview with Emile de Antonio." In *Barnett Newman, Selected Writings and Interviews*, ed. John P. O'Neil (New York: Knopf, 1990), 302–8. Reprinted from de Antonio and Tuchman, *Painters Painting* (1984).
Wintonick, Peter. "Applez-moi 'D.'" *La Revue de la Cinémathèque* 7 (August–September 1990): 12–14.
Langlois, Gérard. "Entretien: Emile de Antonio; 'Vietnam, année du cochon' le documentaire au service de la vérité." *Les Lettres Françaises*, n.d., pp. 17–18.

Works about Emile de Antonio

Aarons, Leroy F. "Film Subpoena Creates First Amendment Issue." *Washington Post*, June 7, 1975, p. A3.
Adams, Marjory. "Year of the Pig Good Cinema." *Boston Globe*, February 27, 1969.
Aghed, Jan. "Marxistisk Fritankare." *Chaplin* [Stockholm] 25.3 (1983): 100–105.
———. "Samtale med Emile de Antonio." *Kosmorama* [Copenhagen] 109 (June 1972): 200–203.
Albert, Stew. "Weathermovie: Up from 'Underground.'" *Crawdaddy*, June 1976, p. 60.
Allen, E. C. "'In the King of Prussia' Defendants Play Themselves in Anti-Nuke Trial Movie." *Coming Attractions* (June 1983): 26.
Allen, Tom. "A Game of Radical Softball." *America* 134 (May 22, 1976): 449–50.
Alloway, Lawrence. "Films *[Painters Painting]*." *Nation* 216 (April 9, 1973): 475–76.
Alpert, Hollis. "SR Goes to the Movies: What's in a Title?" *Saturday Review* 47 (January 25, 1964): 24.
Anby. "New York Film Festival Reviews: Point of Order." *Variety*, September 18, 1963, p. 6.
Anderson, Jack. "Rockefeller's Nieces [finance 'Millhouse']." *Washington Post*, September 10, 1974, p. B15.
Archer, Eugene. "'Point of Order,' a Surprise Hit, Belatedly Gets a Distributor." *New York Times*, February 11, 1964, p. 43.
Armatage, Kay. "Mr. Hoover and I." *Festival of Festivals: 14th Toronto International Film Festival*, September 1989, p. 159.
"Army-McCarthy Footage Pointed for Pic." *Variety*, October 16, 1961.
Arnold, Gary. "'Millhouse: A White Comedy': Sort of a Poison-Celluloid Portrait." *Washington Post*, October 21, 1971, pp. C1, 14.
———. "'Millhouse': Equal Time for Milhous?" *Washington Post*, October 21, 1971, p. C14.
———. "Waxing Nostalgic for the Militancy." *Washington Post*, May 14, 1976, pp. B1, 11.
"Artists Call against U.S. Intervention in Central America." *PR Newswire*, January 12, 1984.
Auty, Chris. "In the King of Prussia." *Monthly Film Bulletin* [London] 50 (August 1983): 206.
Bacigalupo, M. "Definizione de spazion." *Filmcritica* [Rome] January 1972.
Baker, Bryan. "Movie Millhouse." *Space City* [Houston] 3.27 (December 16, 1971): 19–20.
Balleisen, Kristin Mellone. "The Artful Mac." *MacUser* 13.1 (January 1997): 139.
Bassan, R. "Point of Order et Underground." *Écran* 75 (December 15, 1978): 62–63.
Bazelon, David T. "Background to Point of Order." *Film Comment* 2.1 (Winter 1964): 33–35.
Bell-McClure Newspaper Syndicate. "The Confrontation." *Milwaukee Journal*, April 5, 1968, p. 6.
Belmans, J. "Nixon." *Amis du Film et de la Télévision* 200 (January 1973): 38.
Berrigan, C. "In the King of Prussia." *Peace Newsletter* [Syracuse] 4.98 (June 1983): 21.
Biggin, Bill. "FILMfilmFILMfilmFILMfilm." *Philadelphia Free Press* 2.23 (November 17, 1969): 13.
Bill. "The Confrontation." *Variety*, April 10, 1968.
Biskind, Peter. "Does the U.S. Have the Right to Subpoena a Film in Progress?" *New York Times*, June 22, 1975, pp. II-1, 26.
Bonneville, L. "King of Prussia." *Sequences* 111 (January 1983): 57.
Boudin, Jean. "Jean Boudin Talks about Her Fugitive Daughter." *Ms.* 5 (August 1976): 39–40, 42, 46.
Boyum, Joy Gould. "Presenting Nixon as Propaganda." *Wall Street Journal*, November 11, 1971, p. 16.
Brauer, David. "Renegade Prophet: Emile de Antonio at the Walker." *Twin Cities Reader*, 1989, p. 69.
Brudnoy, David. "Son of Easy Rider." *National Review* 23. 47 (December 3, 1971): 1368.
Brunner, John L. "Too Many Shadows Obscure McCarthy Film." *Roll Call*, July 2, 1970.
Buchanan, Loren G. "Rush to Judgment." *Motion Picture Herald* 237.19 (May 10, 1967): 683.
Buckley, William F., Jr. "'Leave Your Wits at the Entrance.'" *New York Times*, October 31, 1971, pp. II-11, 30.
Byro. "Rush to Judgment." *Variety*, June 7, 1967, p. 6.
Callenbach, Ernest. "Point of Order." *Film Quarterly* 17.4 (Summer 1964): 56–57.
"Camera Eye." *New York Times*, July 10, 1975, p. 20.

Camhi, Leslie. "Better Off Red." *Village Voice*, April 7, 1998, p. 72.
Canby, Vincent. "America—We're Nobody's Sweetheart Now." *New York Times*, October 31, 1971, pp. II-1, 12.
———. "Emile de Antonio's Thoughts on Himself and the F.B.I.: A Leftist's Sympathies." *New York Times*, April 20, 1990, p. C14.
———. "Film: Satiric Documentary on Nixon." *New York Times*, September 29, 1971, p. 41.
———. "'Painters Painting' Explores the Art Scene Here." *New York Times*, March 20, 1973, p. 30.
Canniere, P. "Point of Order et Underground." *Cinéma 78* 240 (December 1978): 95–96.
Chase, Anthony. "Historical Reconstruction in Popular Legal and Political Culture." *Seton Hall Law Review* 24 (1994): 1969ff.
Chase, P. "In the Year of the Pig." *Times Now* 1.14 (October 1970): 15.
Clancy, Dennis. *Emile de Antonio's Point of Order: Teacher's Guide*. Culver City, Calif.: Zenger Video, 1985.
Clark, Arthur B. "Rush to Judgment." *Films in Review* (August–September 1967): 443.
Clark, Mike. "New on Video: Point of Order (Best Bet)." *USA Today*, February 19, 1999, p. 8E.
Cocks, Jay. "Minor Surgery." *Time*, October 18, 1971, p. 87.
Cohn, Roy. "Believe Me, This Is the Truth about the Army-McCarthy Hearings. Honest." *Esquire*, February 1968, pp. 59–63, 122–31, + cover.
———. *McCarthy*. New York: New American Library, 1968.
Coleman, John. "Commitments (Point of Order)." *New Statesman* 86 (October 19, 1973): 571–72.
———. "Films: Static." *New Statesman* 97 (June 8, 1979): 839.
Colpart, G. "Painters Painting." *Revue du Cinéma* 320–321 (October 1977): 205.
Combs, Richard. "Millhouse, a White Comedy." *Monthly Film Bulletin* [London] 39.466 (November 1972): 237–38.
"Come See Army Jump Joe McCarthy." *Variety*, December 18, 1963, p. 5.
Cooper, R. W. "Pertinent Television Study of Kennedy Death." *Times* [London], January 30, 1967, p. 7.
Cornell, Tom. "Reviews: In the Year of the Pig." *Win* [New York] 6.6 (April 1, 1970): 18.
Correll, Barbara. "Rem(a)inders of G(l)ory: Monuments and Bodies in 'Glory' and 'In the Year of the Pig.'" *Cultural Criticism* 19 (Fall 1991): 141–77.
"Courtesy of Senator [Lowell] Weicker: The Nixon White House Papers (Con't)." *Washington Post*, April 14, 1974, p. B6.
Crawford, Edward. "More than Nostalgia." *Film Comment* 2.1 (Winter 1964): 31–33.
Crewdson, John M. "F.B.I.'s Taps Data May Contain Gaps." *New York Times*, June 6, 1975, p. 11.
Crimmins, Margaret. "Nixon, to Kick Around." *Washington Post*, June 18, 1971, p. B11.
Crist, Judith. "The Movies: A Duel of Giants." *Saturday Review* 3 (June 12, 1976): 48–49.
———. "The Movies Didn't Get Bigger; the Festival Got Smaller." *New York*, October 4, 1971, pp. 62–63.
———. "Recreating the Incredible McCarthy Days." *New York Herald Tribune*, January 15, 1964, p. 12.
———. Review of *Rush to Judgment*. NBC-TV *Today Show*, May 1967.
Cros, J.-L. "Underground." *Revue du Cinéma/Image et Son* [Paris] (hors série 1979): 320.
Crowther, Bosley. "Point of Order, Mr. Chairman." *New York Times*, January 15, 1964, p. 27.
———. "The Screen: Mark Lane vs. the Warren Report." *New York Times*, June 3, 1967, p. 34.
———. "Trying Anything: A Hand for Two Novel Ventures in Producing and Showing Films." *New York Times*, January 19, 1964, p. II-1.
Dale, Stephen. "De Antonio's Long Cold War." *Now* [Toronto], February 3–9, 1983, pp. 7–8, cover.
Daney, Serge. "Underground (E. de Antonio)." *Cahiers du Cinéma* 276 (May 1977): 47–49.
De Antonio filmography. *Skoop* [Copenhagen] 5.10 (May 1969): 3–4.
"De Antonio, Lampson, Wexler Deliver." *Portland Scribe* 5.24 (September 16, 1976): 1.
de Antonio, Terry. "Gluttony: Poem." *New Republic* 172 (March 22, 1975): 30.
"De Antonio: Vietnam Polemic." *Christian Science Monitor*, February 27, 1969.
Delson, S. "In the King of Prussia." *Nuclear Times* [New York] 1.3 (January 1983): 26.
Denby, David. "Point of Order." *New York*, April 20, 1998, p. 62.
"Les derniers jours de Superman." *Nouvel Observateur*, June 16, 1969.
Doherty, Thomas. "Army-McCarthy Hearings." In *Encyclopedia of Television*, vol. 1, ed. Horace Newcomb. Chicago: Fitzroy Dearborn, 1997, 85–87.
———. "Point of Order!" *History Today* 48.8 (August 1998): 33–36.
Doohan, Brian. "Film [In the Year of the Pig]." *Distant Drummer* [Philadelphia] 58 (November 7–14, 1969): 15.
Dow, David. "Weather Underground/Movie." TV report for the *CBS Evening News with Walter Cronkite*, June 6, 1975.
Dowling, John. "In the King of Prussia." *Bulletin of the Atomic Scientists* 39 (August–September 1983): 52.
Drasin, Dan. "On Making 'Sunday.'" *Vision: A Journal of Film Comment* 1.1 (Spring 1962): 20–21, cover.
Drexler, Rosalyn. "Nixon Makes One Thing Perfectly Clear." *Village Voice*, May 20, 1971.

Dupuich, Jean-Jacques. "Richard 'Millhouse' Nixon (A White Comedy)." *Image et Son* [Paris] 261 (May 1972): 120–22.
Eder, Richard. "Film: 'Underground,' a Documentary; Survivors of 'Village' Bombing Interviewed." *New York Times*, May 10, 1976, p. 33.
Eichelbaum, Stanley. "A Potent 'Point of Order.'" *San Francisco Examiner*, March 27, 1964, p. 19.
Elleson, N. "4 Viet Nam Films." *Old Mole* [Cambridge, Mass.] 1.27 (December 4, 1969).
"The End." *Skoop* 26 (March 1990): 5.
Euvrard, M. "Filmer de que ne montre pas: l'histoire 'officielle': Underground Emile de Antonio." *Cinéma Québec* 5.1 (1977): 16–17.
Eyquem, O. "Emile de Antonio: Début à Lincoln après la projection de 'Underground.'" *Positif* 200–202 (December 1977–January 1978): 34–36.
"Film Competition Dedicated to de Antonio." UPI Wire Service, January 6, 1990.
"Film Reportedly Contains Fugitives' Account of '71 Capitol Bombing." *New York Times*, October 16, 1975, p. 23.
"The Films of Emile de Antonio." New York: Museum of Modern Art, Circulating Film Library, ca. 1989.
"First Statement." *Film Culture* 22–23 (Summer 1961). Reprinted as "The First Statement of the New American Cinema Group," in *Film Culture Reader*, ed. P. Adams Sitney. New York: Praeger, 1970, 79–83. Signed by "The Group," including "Emile de Antonio (film distributor)" and twenty-five others.
Fitzpatrick, Tom. "Revolutionary's Film Success: Panning Nixon with (Groucho) Marx." *Chicago Sun-Times*, October 4, 1971.
"FlickFlackFlickFlack: Millhouse." *Good Times* [San Francisco] 4.30 (October 15, 1971): 25.
"Flicks against the War." *Augur* [Eugene, Oreg.] 2.7 (January 14, 1971): 18.
Folkart, Burt A. "E. de Antonio; Documentary Film Maker." *Los Angeles Times*, December 22, 1989, p. A34.
Franks, Lucinda. "Rendezvous with the Weather Underground." *Ms.* 5 (August 1976): 38–39.
Fraser, C. Gerald. "Emile de Antonio Is Dead at 70; Maker of Political Documentaries." *New York Times*, December 20, 1989, p. D22.
Frederick, R. B. "Painters Painting." *Variety*, March 7, 1972, p. 18.
French, I. "In the King of Prussia." *Variety*, November 17, 1982, p. 14.
"French Respond to Kennedy Plot Film Based on Mark Lane Ideas." *Variety*, March 15, 1967, p. 7.
Frewin, Anthony. *The Assassination of John F. Kennedy: An Annotated Film, TV, and Videography, 1963–1992*. Westport, Conn.: Greenwood Press, 1993.
"The Future of Film." *American Film* (June 1985): 82.
Gablik, Suzi. "Painters Painting: A Candid History of the Modern Art Scene, 1940–1970." *Art in America* 72 (October 1984): 33.
Georgakas, Dan. "Newsreel and Post-New Left Radical Filmmaking." In *Encyclopedia of the American Left*, ed. Mari Jo Buhle, Paul Buhler, and Dan Georgakas. New York: Garland, 1990, 529–32.
———. "Underground: Con." *Cineaste* 7.4 (Winter 1977): 21, 23, 51.
Gervais, G. "De Antonio, analyste de la vie politique américaine." *Jeune Cinéma* 115 (December 1978–January 1979): 40–41.
Gettman/Hawkins. "Underground." *Portland Scribe* 5.24 (September 16, 1976): 6.
Ghiselin, A. D. "Film Defending Oswald Premiering in Hanover." *Valley News* [Hanover, N.H.], January 17, 1967.
Giddins, Gary. "Wanted by the FBI: Mr. Hoover and I." *Village Voice*, April 24, 1990, p. 68.
Gill, Brendan. "Lively Ghosts." *New Yorker*, January 18, 1964, p. 72.
Gilliatt, Penelope. "The All-Right World." *New Yorker*, June 17, 1967, p. 95.
Glassman, Marc. "The Documents in De's Case." In *Forbidden Films: The Filmmaker and Human Rights: In Aid of Amnesty International, Toronto, October 18–28, 1984*, ed. Marc Glassman. Toronto: Toronto Arts Group for Human Rights, blewointmentpress, 1984, 17–20, 46, 82.
Gleason, Michie. "Underground: Emile de Antonio and the Weatherpeople." *Cinema Papers* 11 (January 1977): 202–5, 276.
———. "Underground: Pro." *Cineaste* 7.4 (Winter 1977): 20, 22, inside back cover.
Gleiberman, Owen. "In the King of Prussia." *Boston Phoenix*, April 5, 1983.
Glueck, Grace. "Art News: Wishes to Build Some Dreams On." *New York Times*, January 7, 1973, p. II-25.
Gorman, Brian. "Life and Crimes of Mr. Hoover." *Toronto Star*, May 11, 1990, p. D15.
Gosciak, Josh. "De Antonio Strikes Back." *Soho News* 7.4 (October 25–31, 1979).
Graham, James J. "Acquittal for Oswald." *Commonweal*, April 21, 1967, pp. 149–51.
Greeley, Bill. "Cinetree's Boston Test of Polemic against War on 15 G Promo Pitch." *Variety*, February 5, 1969.
———. "'Judgment' Hassle Latest Chapter in Fizzling CBS–de Antonio Relations." *Variety*, March 29, 1967, pp. 33, 64.
———. "'Underground' Ready for Release; Made despite Grand Jury and FBI; Principals Feared 'Poster' Angels." *Variety*, March 10, 1976, pp. 4, 36.

Grelier, R. "Painters Painting." *Revue du Cinéma* 319 (September 1977): 113–14.
———. "Point of Order!" *Revue du Cinéma* 334 (December 1978): 120–21.
Grenier, Cynthia. "Raves at Cannes." *Paris Herald-Tribune*, May 10, 1964.
Grosoli, F. "Emile de Antonio: Scegliere le immagini, 'parlare' la storia." *Cineforum* 196 (July–August 1980): 441–47.
Guberman, Sidney. *Frank Stella: An Illustrated Biography*. New York: Rizzoli, 1995, 73–76.
Hare, Denise. "Film [Painters Painting]." *Craft Horizons* 33.2 (April 1973): 9, 53.
Harness, John. "Subversive Documentary Maker Outlasts Enemies." *Now* [Toronto], May 10–16, 1990.
Hartl, John. "'Point Of Order': Riveting Spectacle." *Seattle Times*, September 25, 1998, p. F5.
Hartung, Philip T. "Backward, Turn Backward." *Commonweal* 79 (February 14, 1964): 601–3.
———. "Following the Films: Point of Order." *Senior Scholastic* 84 (March 20, 1964): 37.
Hatch, Robert. "Films [Millhouse]." *Nation* 213 (October 18, 1971): 381–82.
Hayman, Ronald. "Millhouse: A White Comedy." *Times* [London], October 27, 1972, p. 9.
Herbstman, Mandel. "Review of New Film: Rush to Judgment." *Film Daily*, May 25, 1967, p. 6.
Hertzberg, Hendrik. "Emile de Antonio." *Harvard Crimson*, February 25, 1964. Reprinted in the *Harvard Alumni Bulletin*.
Hess, John. "Political Filmmaking: Feds Harass Film Crew." *Jump Cut* 8 (August–September 1975): 23–25.
Heywood, Cheryl. "Painters Painting: The New York Art Scene, 1940–1970." *Library Journal*, March 1, 1990, p. 126.
Hitchens, Gordon, and John Thomas. "Two Views—Point of Order." *Film Society Review* 2.2 (October 1966): 16–18.
Hoberman, J. "Film: Tech It or Leave It." *Village Voice*, February 15, 1983, p. 50.
———. "The Movie That First Noticed TV's Grip on Politics." *New York Times*, March 29, 1998, pp. 17, 30.
Hofmann, F. "Die Bombe—Vorläufig im Kopf." *Filmkritik* 27 (May 1983): 230–36.
Holland, Patricia. "From Verite to Infotainment: Documentary Television." *New Statesman and Society* 7 (April 1, 1994): 40.
Holloway, Ronald. "Florence vs. Berlin '69." *Film Society Review* 5.3 (November 1969): 15–17.
Hollywood Reporter, November 25, 1977.
"Hollywood 3 Defy Grand Jury." *City Star* [New York] 3.2 (June 1975): 16.
Hope, Adrian. "High Crimes." *Times Educational Supplement* 3078 (May 24, 1974): 75.
Horak, Jan-Christopher. "Emile de Antonio, 1919–1989." *Afterimage* 17 (February 1990): 2.
Howard, Alan R. "Movie Review: Painters Painting." *Hollywood Reporter* 226.1 (April 19, 1973): 4.
Hurwitz, Howard L. *Point of Order Study Guide*. New York: Continental 16, 1966.
Hutchison, Stuart. "All of a Peace in Memory: Emile de Antonio." In *Conspiracy Charges*, ed. Jay Murphy. New York: Red Bass Publications, 1991, 7.
Iddings, James Henry. "A Study of Rhetorical Systems in the Documentary Mode." Dissertation, University of Florida, 1991.
"Indie Maker Aim: College, Europe." *Variety*, November 5, 1969, pp. 3, 26.
"In the Year of the Pig." *Seed* [Chicago] 4.6 (1969): 7.
"In the Year of the Pig." *Take One* 2.2 (November–December 1969): 8–9; 21.
Interview with Emile de Antonio. *Baltimore Sun*, February 6, 1983.
Jacobs, Lewis. "Documentary Becomes Engaged and Vérité." In *The Documentary Tradition*, 2d ed. New York: Norton, 1979, 368–80.
Jahiel, Edwin. "Pour le mérite: The Chosen Dozen." *Film Society Review* 2.6 (February 1967): 16–17.
James, David. "Presence of Discourse/Discourse of Presence: Representing Vietnam." *Wide Angle* 7.4 (1985): 41–51.
"JFK Outtakes Stay Private, Salant Says." *Variety*, October 25, 1978, pp. 1, 92.
Johnson, C. H., Jr. "Tricky Dick Milhouse [sic]." *Chinook* [Denver] 3.4 (October 28, 1971): 2, 5.
Kael, Pauline. "Blood and Snow." *New Yorker*, November 15, 1969, pp. 177–79.
Katz, Robert. *Naked by the Window: The Fatal Marriage of Carl Andre and Ana Mendieta*. New York: Atlantic Monthly Press, 1990.
Kaye, M. "Underground." *Portland Scribe* 5.25 (September 23, 1976): 12.
Kauffman, Stanley. "Films [Painters Painting]." *New Republic* 168 (March 17, 1973): 22.
———. "Real, Real, Super-Real." *New Republic* 150 (January 25, 1964): 26, 29–30.
———. "Stanley Kauffmann on Film: Millhouse (New Yorker)." *New Republic* (October 2, 1971): 22, 32.
———. "Stanley Kauffmann on Film: Z and In the Year of the Pig." *New Republic* 161 (December 13, 1969): 22, 32.
———. "Underground and Above." *New Republic* 174 (May 29, 1976): 22–23.
Kelly, Tom. "Drop-Dead Book Flap; More Than Bush League." *Washington Times*, January 4, 1990, p. E1.
Kent, Leticia. "Eat, Drink and Make 'Millhouse.'" *New York Times*, October 17, 1971, p. II-13.
Keyser, Lucy. "Moviemakers [John Sayles, Emile de Antonio] to Be Honored at Festival." *Washington Times*, September 28, 1989, p. E6.

King, R. "Underground." *Common Sense* [San Francisco] 3.9 (July 1976): 17.
Knickerbocker, Paine. "'Millhouse: A White Comedy'; A Look Back at Mr. Nixon." *San Francisco Chronicle*, October 9, 1971, p. 32.
Knight, Dee. "Laughing through Tears: Millhouse." *AmEx Canada* [Toronto] 3.3 (March 1972): 78.
L. W. "Point of Order." *Films in Review* 15.2 (February 1964): 116–17.
La Luz, J. "Underground." *Claridad* [New York] 4.14 (June 20, 1976): 7.
Ladendorf, Robert C. "Resistance to Vision: The Effects of Censorship and Other Restraints on Emile de Antonio's Political Documentaries." M.A. thesis. University of Wisconsin-Madison, 1977.
"L'Amérique fait appel." *Art et Essai, Revue Cinématographique* 20 (February 15, 1967): 14–16.
Lane, Mark. *A Citizen's Dissent: Mark Lane Replies*. New York: Holt, Rinehart and Winston, 1968.
——. *Rush to Judgment: A Critique of the Warren Commission's Inquiry into the Murders of President John F. Kennedy, Officer J. D. Tippit, and Lee Harvey Oswald*. London: Bodley Head; New York: Holt, Rinehart and Winston, 1966. Reprinted as *Rush to Judgment*. Greenwich, Conn.: Fawcett, 1967; New York: Thunder's Mouth Press, 1992.
Legrand, G. "Painters Painting." *Positif* 197 (September 1977): 69–70.
Le Péron, Serge. "Point of Order (E. de Antonio)." *Cahiers du Cinéma* 298 (March 1979): 58–59.
Leroux, A. "Underground." *Sequences* 90 (October 1977): 20.
Levinskas, Bob. "FBI Checks Out 'Checkers.'" *Soho News* 7.3 (October 18–24, 1979).
Lewis, Randolph. "'America Is Hard to See': Emile de Antonio and the Art of Political Filmmaking." Dissertation, University of Texas at Austin, 1994.
——. *Emile de Antonio: Radical Filmmaker in Cold War America*. Madison: University of Wisconsin Press, 2000.
Leyda, Jay, ed. *Voices of Film Experience, 1894 to the Present*. New York: Macmillan, 1977, 103.
Librach, R. S. "Underground." *Take One* 5.10 (1977): 12.
Linfield, Susan. "De Antonio's Day in Court." *Village Voice*, February 8, 1983, pp. 36–37, 72.
Lor. "Mr. Hoover and I." *Variety*, April 18, 1990, p. 21.
Loynd, Roy. "'Rush to Judgment' Here: Has Jolting, Brutal Impact." *Hollywood Reporter* 201.15 (June 7, 1968): 3.
Luik, Arno von. "Bäng! Bäng! Bäng!—das gehört auf Film." *Konkret*, n.d., pp. 76–79.
MacDonald, Dwight. "Films: Of Time and the Village." *Esquire*, November 1963, pp. 70, 76–77.
Machlowitz, David S. "Antinuclear Narcissism." *American Bar Association Journal* 69 (May 1983): 678.
Mack [Joseph McBride]. "Underground." *Variety*, May 12, 1976, p. 34.
Mackby, Jennifer. "The Frustrations of Being Independent." *New York Times*, October 17, 1976, p. II-15.
Madeleine. "Underground." *Off Our Backs* [Washington, D.C.] 6.4 (June 1976): 18.
Mahoney, J. Daniel. "Out of Focus." *National Review* 16.16 (April 21, 1964): 325–26.
"Managing the Image." *Commonweal* 90 (May 16, 1969): 250.
"[Ron] Mann Follows Jazz with Poetry, de Antonio Helps Out." *Cinema Canada* 80 (December 1981–January 1982): 8.
Marcorelles, Louis. "Homo Americanus." Trans. Beth Alberty. *Film Comment* 4.2–3 (Fall/Winter 1967): 19. Excerpt from Marcorelles, *Cinéma 67* 115 (April 1967).
——. "Rencontre avec Emile de Antonio ('Underground')." *Cahiers du Cinéma* 272 (November 1976): 35–42.
——. "'Rush to Judgment' and 'Force of Evil.'" *Cinéma 67* [Paris] 115 (April 1967). Partially reprinted in *Film Comment* 4.2–3 (Fall/Winter 1967).
Martin, Marcel. "Brève Rencontre . . . avec Emile de Antonio." *Écran* [Paris] 4 (April 1972): 39–40.
Maslin, Janet. "Film: 'Andy Warhol.'" *New York Times*, June 9, 1987, p. C20.
——. "'King of Prussia,' with Berrigan Brothers." *New York Times*, February 13, 1983, p. 57.
Maxson, R. E. "This is the 'Year of the Pig.'" *Los Angeles Free Press*, February 1971, p. 21.
McBride, Joseph. "Documaker de Antonio Dead at 70; Attacked the System." *Variety*, December 27, 1989, p. 14.
"McCarthy's Last Stand: Film of Army-McCarthy Hearings." *Time*, January 17, 1964, p. 49.
McDonald, Larry. "Pro-Terrorist Propaganda in the Movies." *Congressional Record*, July 30, 1975, pp. 26155–156.
McGavin, Patrick Z. "Remembering de Antonio: Life of an American Original." *In These Times*, October 3–9, 1990, p. 20.
McGuigan, Carthleen. "Newsmakers." *Newsweek* August 10, 1981, p. 49.
McLaughlin, Jeff. "'Prussia' Deserves Attention." *Boston Globe*, April 8, 1993, p. 67.
Mekas, Jonas. "From the Diaries." In *The American New Wave, 1958–1967*, ed. Melinda Ward and Bruce Jenkins. Minneapolis: Walker Art Center, 1982, 4–11.
——. "Movie Journal." *Village Voice*, October 7, 1971, p. 61.
Mellen, Joan. "America Is Hard to See." *Cineaste* 4.4 (Spring 1971): 28.
Michener, Charles. "Pamphleteering on Film." *Newsweek*, November 15, 1971, p. 121.
Miller, Debra. *Billy Name: Stills from the Warhol Films*. New York: Prestel-Verlag, 1994.

"Millhouse." *Boston after Dark*, October 19, 1971.
"Millhouse." *City Limits* 305 (August 6, 1987): 19.
"Millhouse." *Harry* [Baltimore] 2.23 (December 19, 1971): 10.
"Millhouse: A White Comedy." *Filmfacts* 14.24 (1971): 734–36.
"Millhouse: A White Comedy." *Variety*, October 6, 1971, p. 16.
Mitgang, Herbert. "McCarthy: Death of a Witch Hunter." *New York Times*, August 16, 1987, p. II-26.
———. "Vietnam: In the Year of the Pig." *New York Times*, November 22, 1987, p. II-36.
Monsell, Thomas. *Nixon on Stage and Screen: The Thirty-seventh President as Depicted in Films, Television, Plays and Opera*. Jefferson, N.C.: McFarland, 1998.
Moregan, A. "Underground." *Lesbian Tide* [Los Angeles] 6.1 (July 1976): 27.
Morgenstern, Joseph. "History Right in the Face." *Newsweek*, November 10, 1969, pp. 108–9. Reprinted in *The Documentary Tradition, from Nanook to Woodstock*, ed. Lewis Jacobs. London: Hopkinson and Blake, 1970; 2d ed., New York: Norton, 1979, 469–70.
"Mr. Hoover and I." *Film Review Annual* (1991): 1045–48.
Murphy, Jay. "Radical Politics and an Art of Quality." *Independent* [New York] 13 (March 1990): 3–4.
Name, Billy. *Andy Warhol's Film Stills*. Tokyo: Uplink, 1996.
Naughton, James M. "Weicker Says Nixon Uses I.R.S. Records in Politics." *New York Times*, April 9, 1974, pp. 1, 19.
Nelson, Carl. "Millhouse: A White Comedy." *College Press Service* [Denver] 11 (November 6, 1971): 9.
Nichols, Bill. "In the Year of the Pig; Nichols Replies." *Jump Cut* 19 (December 1978): 37.
———. "New from California Newsreel: 38 Families, Revolution until Victory, Beginning of Our Victory, and Redevelopment." *Jump Cut* 17 (April 1978): 10.
———. *Newsreel: Documentary Filmmaking on the American Left*. New York: Arno Press, 1980.
———. *Representing Reality: Issues and Concepts in Documentary*. Bloomington: Indiana University Press, 1992.
———. "The Voice of Documentary." *Film Quarterly* 36.3 (Spring 1983): 17–30. Reprinted in *Movies and Methods*, vol. 2, *An Anthology*, ed. Bill Nichols. Berkeley: University of California Press, 1985, 258–73; and in *New Challenges for Documentary*, ed. Alan Rosenthal. Berkeley: University of California Press, 1988, 48–63.
Nolan, Martin F. "The Many Lives and Laughs of 'Millhouse.'" *Boston Globe*, June 27, 1971.
Nordheimer, John. "Producers of Film on Radicals Vow to Fight U.S. Interference." *New York Times*, June 7, 1975.
"Obituary: Emile de Antonio." *Newsday*, December 21, 1989, p. 35.
Olsson, M. O. "Man maaste aendra paa folks huvuden!" *Chaplin* [Stockholm] 122 (1973): 102–3.
Overby, David. "A Muckraking Filmmaker Looks Back." *Paris Metro*, July 20, 1977, p. 9.
Padu. "In the Year of the Pig." *Variety*, March 12, 1969, p. 26.
"Painters Painting." *Catholic Film Newsletter* 38.3 (February 15, 1973).
"Painters Painting." *Independent Film Journal* 71.11 (April 30, 1973).
"Painters Painting." *Publisher's Weekly*, June 1, 1984, p. 52.
"Painters Painting." *Time Out* 478 (June 15, 1979): 49.
"Painters Painting." *Variety*, January 29, 1986, p. 44.
Paletz, David L. "Underground." *Film Quarterly* 30.4 (Summer 1977): 34–37.
Paoletti, J. T. "Painters Painting: A Candid History of the Modern Art Scene, 1940–1970." *Choice* 22 (October 1984): 259.
Passek, Jean-Loup. "Richard Milhouse [sic] Nixon: L'Art du Pamphlet." *Cinéma* [Paris] 165 (April 1972): 131–35.
Paul, Kenneth. "New de Antonio Film Arresting." *Washington Post*, October 26, 1968, p. D30.
Peck, Keenen. "The FBI's Checkered Record." *Progressive* 47 (January 1983): 19.
"People in the News: Director Emile de Antonio." *Associated Press*, February 6, 1983.
Perchaluk, E. "Underground." *Independent Film Journal* 77 (May 28, 1976): 8.
Perreault, John. "Hung, Draped and Plopped." *Village Voice*, March 29, 1973, p. 32.
Petherbridge, J. "Praise Marx and Pass the Ammunition." *Peace News* [London] 17.33 (September 12, 1969).
Philadelphia, W. C. "Milhouse [sic]." *Augur* [Eugene, Oreg.], December 3, 1971, p. 3.
"Point of Disorder." *Time*, February 10, 1967, p. 99.
"Point of Order!" *Filmfacts* 7.4 (February 29, 1964): 14–16.
"Point of Order." *Village Voice*, April 7, 1998.
"Point of Order to Reade-Sterling." *Variety*, February 12, 1964, p. 18.
J. P. [James Powers]. "In the Year of the Pig." *Motion Picture Herald* 239.48 (November 26, 1969): 334.
Powers, James. "'Point of Order' Holds Interest as Documentary." *Hollywood Reporter* 179.43 (March 31, 1964): 3.
"Propaganda Chiller." *Time*, November 14, 1969, p. E9.
Purtell, Tim. "Emile de Antonio's *Painters Painting*." *Entertainment Weekly*, August 16, 1996, p. 66.

Quinn, Sally. "McCarthy on Film." *Washington Post,* June 23, 1970.
Read, R. "Underground." *Win* [New York] 12.19 (June 3, 1976): 19.
Review. "L'Amérique fait appel." *Positif* [Paris] 84 (May 1967): 57.
Ripmaster, Terence. "A Note on Emile de Antonio: Historical Documentarist." *Film and History* 20.2 (1990): 44–46.
Robe. "Painters Painting." *Variety,* March 7, 1973, p. 18.
Rosenbaum, Jonathan. "The Life and File of an Anarchist Filmmaker." *Chicago Reader,* May 18, 1990, pp. 12, 22, 26, 34.
Rossell, Deac. "Emile de Antonio (1920 [sic]–1989)." *International Documentary* (Winter 1990): 38–39.
———. "From Joe to Eugene: To Hell and Back." *Publick Occurrences and Boston After Dark,* June 2, 1970, n.p.
Roth, Wilhelm. "Emile de Antonio, 1919–15.12.1989." *EPD Film* 7 (February 1990): 10.
"Rush to Judgment." *Filmfacts* 10.14 (August 15, 1967): 185–88.
"Rushes: Mr. Hoover and I." *Independent* [London] January 4, 1990, p. 11.
Russell, John. "New Cassettes: *Painters Painting.*" *New York Times,* June 23, 1985, p. II-24.
Ruth, R. "Underground." *City Star* [New York] 4.1 (May 15, 1976): 16.
Sallon, A. "Millhouse." *Outside the Net* 4 (Winter 1972): 32.
Salmi, Markku. "Emile de Antonio." *Film Dope* 9 (April 1976): 49–50.
Sarris, Andrew. "Films in Focus." *Village Voice,* September 30, 1971, p. 72.
Schechter, Joel. "Plowshares 8, Take Two." *In These Times,* May 5–11, 1982, p. 19.
Scott, J. F. "New Terms for Order: Network Style in Individual Experiment in American Documentary Film." *Florida State University Conference on Film and Literature* 4 (1979): 59–72.
Scott, Jay. "Desert Dreams: Exploring the American Nightmare." *Toronto Globe and Mail,* September 9, 1989, p. C3.
Seguin, Dennis. "Director Leaves Legacy of Passion." *Metropolis,* May 3–9, 1990.
Seitz, Michael H. "Swords into Plowshares." *Progressive* 47 (April 1983): 54–55.
Sery, Patrick. "Emile de Antonio." *Cinéma* [Paris] 165 (April 1972): 131–35.
"Sez Anti-Nixon Film Sought by Democrats." *Variety,* October 13, 1971, pp. 1, 22.
Shattuck, Jessica. "Sacred and Secular; *Painters Painting.*" *Computer Life* 3.11 (November 1996): 183.
Sherman, Paul. "McCarthy Film Gets to 'Point.'" *Boston Herald,* February 28, 1999, p. 72.
Siegel, Joel. "Films: Millhouse." *D.C. Gazette* [Washington] 3.3 (November 15, 1971): 8–9.
Siegel, Joel E. "Underground." *Film Heritage* 12.1 (Fall 1976): 34–36. Reprinted from *Washington Newsworks.*
"Sight and Sound: McCarthy: Death of a Witch Hunter." *American History Illustrated* 23.6 (October 1988): 8.
Silber, Irwin. "Millhouse." *Guardian* [New York], September 29, 1971, p. 14.
———. "Weatherman Was Never This Dull." *Guardian* [New York], May 19, 1976, p. 20.
———. "The Year of the Pig in Vietnam." *Guardian* [New York], May 10, 1969, n.p.
Silberman, Robert. "Emile de Antonio." In *The Political Companion to American Film,* ed. Gary Crowdus. Lakeview Press, 1994, 103–7.
Silver, Sam. "Second Fix." *Good Times* [San Francisco], May 28, 1970, p. 19.
Slavitt, David. "Mr. Chairman." *Newsweek,* January 20, 1964, p. 83.
Smith, Clyde B. "In the Year of the Pig." *Film Quarterly* 24.1 (Fall 1970): 43–50.
Smith, Patrick S. *Andy Warhol's Art and Films.* Ann Arbor: UMI Research Press, 1986.
Smith, S. "Interview: Ron Mann." *Cinema Canada* 92 (January 1983): 15–17.
Sontag, Susan. "Going to Theatre in the Movies." *Partisan Review* 31 (Spring 1964): 292.
Spektor, M. "In the King of Prussia." *Guardian* [New York], January 19, 1983, p. 21.
Stack, Peter. "'Order' Makes a Point about Absolute Power; McCarthy Hearings Make Riveting Film," *San Francisco Chronicle,* November 12, 1998, p. E3.
Steele, Lloyd. "Film Reviews: In the Year of the Pig." *Los Angeles Free Press,* June 5, 1970, p. 37.
Stein, Benjamin. "Collector's Choice: Capital Films." *American Film* 10 (November 1984): 68–72.
Stein, Jean, and George Plimpton. *Edie: An American Biography.* New York: Knopf, 1982.
Sterritt, David. "In the King of Prussia." *Christian Science Monitor,* March 3, 1983, p. 19.
———. "Two Documentaries Prove the Form Can Be as Entertaining—and Infuriating—as Scripted Films." *Christian Science Monitor,* May 23, 1990, p. 10.
Susman, Gary. "Subversion Therapy: The Politics of Emile de Antonio." *Boston Phoenix,* March 30, 1990, p. 3.
Sweet, Louise. "Underground." *Monthly Film Bulletin* [London] 43 (October 1976): 220–21.
Tajima, Renee. "Emile de Antonio, 1919–89." *Village Voice,* January 2, 1990, p. 86.
Talbot, Daniel. "On Historic Hearings from TV to the Screen." *New York Times,* January 12, 1964, p. X7. Reprinted as "Historic Hearings: From TV to Screen," in *The Documentary Tradition, from Nanook to Woodstock,* ed. Lewis Jacobs. London: Hopkinson and Blake, 1970; New York: Norton, 1979, 2d ed., 392–94.

Talbot, David, and Barbara Zheutlin. *Creative Differences: Profiles of Hollywood Dissidents.* Boston: South End Press, 1978.

Tallmer, Jerry. "Cracking the File on a 'Nut Case.'" *New York Post,* April 20, 1990.

———. "Mr. Hoover and I." *New York Post,* April 20, 1990, p. 25.

Talty, Stephan. "Point of Order." *Time Out* [New York], April 2, 1998, p. 80.

Tarratt, M. "Point of Order." *Films and Filming* 20.3 (December 1973): 49–50.

Taylor, Paul. "Painters Painting." *Monthly Film Bulletin* [London] 46 (July 1979): 152.

Thompson, Howard. " 'In the Year of the Pig,' Documentary, Bows." *New York Times,* November 11, 1969, p. 40.

Thorstad, David. "Millhouse." *Militant* [New York], October 15, 1971, p. 20.

"Three Producers Back Film on Radicals; Accuse U.S. of Attempt to Suppress Their Work." *New York Times,* June 7, 1975, p. 14.

"Three Subpoenaed over Movie on Radicals." *New York Times,* June 5, 1975, p. 27.

Toumarkine, Doris. "Cannes '69." *Film Society Review* 4.9 (May 1969): 20–22.

Trosa, S. "Point of Order." *Cinématographe* [Paris] 44 (February 1979): 70.

"The Truth Will Out." *Toronto Star,* September 15, 1989.

Tuchman, Mitch. "Freedom of Information." *Film Comment* 26 (July–August 1990): 66.

Turner, Elisa. "Painters Painting: A Candid History of the Modern Art Scene, 1940–1970." *ARTnews* 83 (November 1984): 36–39.

"Underground." *Cineaste* 7.1 (Fall 1975): 49.

"Underground." *New York Times,* May 7, 1976, p. C6.

"Underground." *Playboy* 23 (December 1976): 42–43.

"U.S. Drops Subpoenas against Four Filmmakers." *New York Times,* June 6, 1975, p. 66.

Vaile, Phil. ". . . Like I Know Nixon: Millhouse." *Great Speckled Bird* [Atlanta], January 10, 1972, p. 11.

van Bagh, Peter. "Emile de Antonio." *Filmihullu* [Helsinki] 6 (1976): 7.

———. "Kuvaja Vastakuva." *Filmihullu* 1 (1989): 16–23.

van Gaelen, H. "The End." *Film and Television* 39 (February 1990): 33.

Viguier, J. "La Guerre de Viet Nam au Cinéma." *Cinéma 82* (May 1982): 16–29.

Walsh, Moira. "Point of Order." *America* 110 (February 1, 1964): 174.

Warhol, Andy, and Pat Hackett. *POPism: The Warhol '60s.* New York: Harcourt Brace Jovanovich, 1980.

Waugh, Thomas. "Beyond Verité: Emile de Antonio and the New Documentary of the Seventies." *Jump Cut* 10/11 (Summer 1976): 33–39. Reprinted in *Movies and Methods,* vol. 2, *An Anthology,* ed. Bill Nichols. Berkeley: University of California Press, 1985, 233–57.

———. "'Underground': Weatherpeople at Home." *Jump Cut* 12/13 (December 1976): 11–13.

Wauters, J. P. "In the King of Prussia." *Film en Televisie* [Brussels] 317 (October 1983): 6–7.

Wechsler, James A. "On Whom Is the Joke?" *New York Post,* September 29, 1971.

———. "'Point of Order.'" *New York Post,* January 13, 1964.

Weiner, Bernard. "Milhouse [sic]." *Northwest Passage* [Bellingham, Wash.] 6.7 (January 24–February 6, 1972): 27. Reprinted as "Millhouse: A White Comedy," *Sight and Sound* 4.1 (spring 1972): 112–13.

Weisman, John. "Films [Millhouse]." *Rolling Stone* 100 (January 20, 1972): 58.

Wilson, David. "Point of Order." *Monthly Film Bulletin* [London] 40.478 (November 1973): 231.

Winsten, Archer. "'Painters Painting' Opens Here." *New York Post,* March 20, 1973, p. 60.

Wintonick, Peter. "Retro Brings de Antonio to Montreal Public." *Cinema Canada* [Montreal] 107 (May 1984): 42.

Wright, Christopher. "Movie Digs the Nixon Past: The Humor in Serious Events." *Evening Star* [Washington, D.C.], June 18, 1971, p. A-18.

Zaoral, Z. "Svetovi Rezi Seri." *Film a Doba* 33 (July 1987): 409–10.

Zunser, Jesse. "A Shameful Era Recalled in TV-Kinescope." *Cue Magazine,* January 18, 1964.

Permissions

"An In-Depth Interview with Emile de Antonio," by Terry de Antonio, originally appeared in *Shantih* 1.4–2.1 (Winter/Spring 1972): 17–21.

"Movies and Me," by Emile de Antonio, originally appeared in "Notes for the National Film Theatre Retrospective," March 29, 1974.

"An Interview with Emile de Antonio," by Tanya Neufeld, originally appeared in *Artforum* 11 (March 1973): 79–83.

"Irrepressible Emile de Antonio Speaks," by Susan Linfield, originally appeared in *The Independent* (June 1982): 2–4, 10.

"Emile de Antonio," by Jean W. Ross, originally appeared in *Contemporary Authors* 117 (Gale Research Press, 1986): 95–99.

"*Red Bass* Interview: Emile de Antonio," by Jay Murphy, originally appeared in *Red Bass* (1983): 8–12.

"Emile de Antonio with Jean-Michel Basquiat," by Jean-Michel Basquiat, originally appeared in *Interview* 14 (July 1984): 48–51.

"Why I Make Films," by Emile de Antonio, originally appeared in *Libération* (1987).

"The Point of View in *Point of Order*," by Emile de Antonio, originally appeared in *Film Comment* (1964). Copyright 1971 by the Film Comment Publishing Company. Reprinted with the permission of the Film Society of Lincoln Center.

"Re-creating the Incredible McCarthy Days," by Judith Crist, originally appeared in the *New York Times Herald Tribune*, Wednesday, January 15, 1964. Copyright 1964 by the *New York Times* and the New York Herald Tribune, Inc. All rights reserved. Reprinted by permission.

"McCarthy's Last Stand" originally appeared in *Time* (January 17, 1964): 49. Reprinted with permission of Time Life Syndication.

Letter to Hubert Bals and Wendy Lidell, by Emile de Antonio, undated.

"*Running to Win*, Outline and Letter to BBC," by Emile de Antonio, originally appeared as "Running to Win 1965," unpublished notes outlining *That's Where the Action Is* and accompanied by a letter (July 14, 1965) to BBC producer David Webster.

"That's Where the Action Is," by Thomas Waugh, originally appeared in "Beyond Verité: Emile de Antonio and the New Documentary of the Seventies," Thomas Waugh, *Jump Cut* 10/11 (1976). Used by permission of the author.

"*Rush to Judgment*: A Conversation with Mark Lane and Emile de Antonio" originally appeared in *Film Comment* (Winter 1966–67). Copyright 1971 by the Film Comment Publishing Company. Reprinted with the permission of the Film Society of Lincoln Center.

"Homo Americanus," by Louis Marcorelles, originally appeared in *Film Comment* (Fall/Winter 1967). Copyright 1971 by the Film Comment Publishing Company. Reprinted with the permission of the Film Society of Lincoln Center.

"Liner Notes for *Rush to Judgment* LP," by Emile de Antonio, originally appeared as "A Comment from the Producer of the Film," liner notes for *Rush to Judgment: The Living Testimony by the Actual Witnesses on the Original Sound-Track Recording of the Emile de Antonio and Mark Lane Film* (New York: Vanguard Records, 1967).

Letter to Jean Hill, April 14, 1966, by Emile de Antonio, from *Journals* X.76.

Journal entry on *Rush to Judgment*, 1980, by Emile de Antonio.

"Blood and Snow," by Pauline Kael, originally appeared in the *New Yorker*, November 15, 1969. Reprinted by permission. Copyright 1969 Pauline Kael. All rights reserved.

"De Antonio in Hell," by Alan Asnen, originally appeared as "De Antonio in Hell—Part I," in the *East Village Other* 3.51 (November 22, 1968).

"Inter/view with Emile de Antonio," by Lil Picard, originally appeared in *Inter/view* 1.3 (1969): 8–9.

"Movie Journal," by Jonas Mekas, originally appeared in the *Village Voice* (November 13, 1969): 57.

"De Antonio: Year of the Pig Marxist Film," by Emile de Antonio, and "Nichols Replies," by Bill Nichols, originally appeared in *Jump Cut* 19 (1978).

"From Joe to Eugene: To Hell and Back," by Deac Rossell, originally appeared in *Publick Occurrences and Boston After Dark*, June 2, 1970.

"America Is Hard to See," by Joan Mellen, originally appeared in *Cineaste* (Spring 1971): 28. Used by permission of the author. Copyright Joan Mellen, professor, Department of English, Temple University.

"Interview with Emile de Antonio: Director of *Millhouse*," by Glenn O'Brien, originally appeared in *Interview* 19 (February 1972): 28–29.

"Minor Surgery," by Jay Cocks, originally appeared in *Time* (1971).

"Leave Your Wits at the Entrance," by William F. Buckley Jr., originally appeared in the *New York Times*, October 31, 1971. Copyright 1971 by William F. Buckley Jr. Reprinted by permission of the Wallace Literary Agency, Inc.

"*Millhouse*," by David Thorstad, originally appeared in *The Militant*, October 15, 1971.

"'The Real History of Our Times Is on Film': Filmmaker Emile de Antonio Talks about Nixon, the '50s, and Now," by Cinda Firestone, originally appeared in *Liberation News Service*, April 15, 1972. Reprinted with permission of Cinda Fox.

"The Agony of the Revolutionary Artist," by Emile de Antonio, originally appeared in *Northwest Passage*, May 24–June 6, 1971.

"Films: *Painters Painting*," by Lawrence Alloway, originally appeared in the *Nation* (April 9, 1973): 475–76. Reprinted with permission of the *Nation*.

"Films: *Painters Painting*," by Stanley Kauffmann, originally appeared as "*Painters Painting*," in the *New Republic*, March 17, 1973. Reprinted by permission of the *New Republic*, copyright 1973, the New Republic, Inc.

"My Brush with Painting," by Emile de Antonio, originally appeared in *American Film* (1984).

"How It Began," by Emile de Antonio, originally appeared in liner notes for *Underground: Sound Track from the Film* (1976). Folkways Records, No. FD 5752.

"Mallards and Trombones by Lake Mendota: An Interview with Emile de Antonio and Mary Lampson," by Gage, Jim, and Rebecca, originally appeared in *Free for All* (Madison, Wis.), May 1976.

"Rendezvous with the Weather Underground," by Lucinda Franks, originally appeared in *Ms.* (August 1976): 38–39. Reprinted with permission of the author.

"Pro-Terrorist Propaganda in the Movies," by Larry McDonald, originally appeared in the *Congressional Record* (1975).

"Interview with Emile de Antonio and Mary Lampson," by Dan Georgakas and Paul McIsaac, originally appeared in *Liberation* (July–August 1976): 22–25. Used by permission of Dan Georgakas.

"*In the King of Prussia*: Emile de Antonio Interviews Himself" originally appeared as "Emile de Antonio Interviews Himself: *In the King of Prussia*," *Film Quarterly* 36.1 (1982): 28–32. Reprinted by permission. Copyright 1982 by the Regents of the University of California.

"On the Making of *In the King of Prussia*: An Interview with Emile de Antonio," by Sharon Gallagher, originally appeared in *Radix* (July–August 1983). Reprinted by permission of *Radix* magazine, Berkeley, California.

"De Antonio and the Plowshares Eight," by David Segal, originally appeared in *Sight and Sound* 51.3 (Summer 1982): 182–84. Used by permission of the author.

"Swords into Plowshares," by Michael H. Seitz, originally appeared in *The Progressive* (April 1983): 54. Reprinted with permission of *The Progressive*, 409 E. Main Street, Madison, WI 53703.

"Antinuclear Narcissism," by David S. Machlowitz, originally appeared in *American Bar Association Journal*, May 1983. Reprinted by permission of the *American Bar Association Journal*.

"Mr. Hoover and I," by Emile de Antonio, unpublished manuscript.

"Emile de Antonio's Thoughts on Himself and the FBI: A Leftist's Sympathies," by Vincent Canby, originally appeared in the *New York Times*, April 20, 1990. Copyright 1990 by the *New York Times*. Reprinted by permission.

"The Life and File of an Anarchist Filmmaker," by Jonathan Rosenbaum, originally appeared in *Chicago Reader*, May 18, 1990. Reprinted by permission of the author.

"*Salt of the Earth*," by Emile de Antonio, originally appeared in *Film Comment* (Fall 1966). Copyright 1971 by the Film Comment Publishing Company. Reprinted with the permission of the Film Society of Lincoln Center.

"Chasing Checkers by Richard M. Nixon," by Emile de Antonio and Albert Maher, originally appeared in the *New York Free Press* (September 26–October 2, 1968).

"Some Discrete Interruptions on Film, Structure, and Resonance," by Emile de Antonio, originally appeared in *Film Quarterly* 25.1 (Fall 1971): 10–11. Reprinted by permission. Copyright 1971 by the Regents of the University of California.

"Pontus Hultén and Some '60s Memories in New York," by Emile de Antonio, originally appeared in *New York Collection for Stockholm* (Stockholm, Sweden: Moderna Museet, September 1973): 1–3, written for the "New York Collection for Stockholm" exhibition at Moderna Museet.

"Visions of Vietnam," by Emile de Antonio, originally appeared in *University Review* (December 1974).

"Emile de Antonio's CIA Diary," by Michael Fellner, originally appeared as "Emile de Antonio's *CIA Diary,* not starring Robert Redford and Jane Fonda not in technicolor and cinemascope and not playing at a theater near you," in *Take Over* (1975).

"Smoke Signals Blown," by Emile de Antonio, unpublished manuscript.

"Celluloid Reportage," by Emile de Antonio, originally appeared in *Yipster Times*, May 1976.

"Letter to *The Militant*," by Emile de Antonio, written in 1977.

"Point of Order (Hic)," by Emile de Antonio, originally appeared in the *Village Voice* (January 29, 1980): 42.

"Different Drummers," by Emile de Antonio, originally appeared in *American Film* (November 1985).

"American History: A Fiction," by Emile de Antonio, unpublished manuscript.

"Quotations from Chairman De: Decodifying de Antonio," by Peter Wintonick, originally appeared in *Cinema Canada* (July–August 1984).

Index

ABC (television network), 20, 28, 34, 43, 75, 80, 89, 138, 188, 201, 316, 392, 401
abstract expressionism, 104–5, 107, 355
Agee, Philip, 54, 60, 121, 284, 361–65
Alloway, Lawrence, 53, 82, 265–67
All the President's Men (1976), 59, 292, 368–70
Ambrose, Marilyn, 22
America Is Hard to See, 33, 40, 42, 47, 77, 81, 91, 100, 220, 227–33, 279, 292, 336, 401
American Civil Liberties Union (ACLU), xii, 58
American Film Institute, 45, 112, 377
Anderson, Jack, 43, 47
Angell, Callie, 22, 81
Army-McCarthy hearings, 1, 16, 17, 19, 20, 27, 46, 83, 90, 109–10, 114, 125, 137, 149–62, 195, 239, 254, 333, 335, 352
art brut, 31, 68, 393
Artforum, 32, 45, 81, 102–12, 265–67, 351
Asnen, Alan, 205–10
Attica (1974, Cinda Firestone), 76, 252, 341
Avakian, George, 10, 79
Ayres, Billy, 56, 287, 288, 294

Bals, Hubert, 156
Basquiat, Jean-Michel, 129–35, 130, 394–95
Baumann, Ruth, 4
Beame, Abraham, 25, 99, 167, 170
Beatty, Warren, xii, 290, 311
Berrigan, Daniel, 38, 61, 63, 82–83, 118–19, 126, 141, 242, 301, 304–5, 309, 311, 314, 316, 319–20, 323–25, 363, 403
Berrigan, Philip, 61, 63, 82–83, 118–19, 126, 141, 301, 305, 309, 311, 314, 316, 319, 325, 403–4
Biberman, Herbert, 345–47
Biskind, Peter, 82, 279
Blue Angel, The (1930), 12, 201
Bogdanovich, Peter, 79, 98, 290
Boudin, Kathy, 56–58, 284, 290, 297
Boudin, Leonard, 58, 290
Brakhage, Stan, 102, 106, 305
Brecht, Bertolt: and Brechtian theory, 31, 96–97, 264

British Broadcast Corporation (BBC), 23, 25–27, 29, 65, 89, 99, 165–70, 195
Brook, Terry, 22, 49–50, 54, 81, 87–96, 272, 365–67, 374–75
Buckley, William F., Jr., 19, 47, 82, 166–67, 170, 242, 245–48, 358
Buñuel, Luis, 95–96, 98, 335
Bush, George, 64, 71, 83, 330–31, 341

Cage, John, 9–10, 17, 37, 51, 65, 69, 79, 83, 113–14, 124, 161, 190, 217, 271, 320, 333–34, 336, 341, 350–51, 355, 375
Canby, Vincent, 100, 142, 152, 242, 333–34, 370
Cannes Film Festival, 19, 76, 125, 137, 143, 195
Castelli, Leo, 52, 64, 129, 141–42, 213, 270–71
Castro, Fidel, 127–31, 263, 290–91, 293, 361–62
Catholicism, xi, 61, 84, 118, 120, 125–26, 303, 309–13
Caulfield, Jack, 46–47, 82, 243
CBS (television network), 16, 21, 27, 58, 82, 89, 140, 158–59, 212, 239, 241, 255, 257, 302, 315–16, 392
Central Intelligence Agency (CIA), 35, 43, 117, 121, 126, 186, 205, 253, 323, 341, 361, 364–65, 382
Chaplin, Charlie, 98, 110, 136, 156, 335, 372, 377
Charge and Countercharge, 20, 74, 76
Checkers speech, 42–44, 47, 81–82, 131, 243, 246–49, 250, 256, 348–49
Cineaste, 41, 60, 81, 232–33, 291–97
cinema verité, 25, 62, 72, 74, 77–78, 91, 103, 115–16, 150–51, 156, 189, 191, 241, 304, 308, 319, 330, 352
Clark, Ramsay, 62–63
Clarke, Shirley, 157, 354
Cocks, Jay, 82, 243–44, 290
Cohn, Roy, 17, 19–21, 80, 122, 151, 154–55, 162, 216, 352
collage, 2, 25, 31, 50–51, 58, 74, 113, 171 221, 388
Columbia University, 7, 39, 55, 82, 89, 108
communism, 4, 67, 80, 83, 88, 96, 122, 134, 289–90, 296, 346–47, 381
compilation film, 1, 251

431

Confrontation, The, 20
Connapinch, Anna, 3
Crist, Judith, 18, 152–53
Cronkite, Walter, 27, 38, 58, 138, 161, 237, 241, 283, 302
Cunningham, Merce, 9–10, 83, 190

Dadaism, 96, 271, 281, 307
Dartmouth College, 38, 65, 70, 206, 229–31
Davis, Peter, 34, 36, 290, 296, 357–61
Dean, John, 46, 82, 127, 133
de Antonio, Emilio (father), 3–4, 87, 92, 156
de Antonio, Nancy, 64–65, 68, 70, 330, 333
de Antonio, Terry. *See* Brook, Terry
de Kooning, Willem, 107, 133, 262, 266–67, 269–70, 400
Democratic Party, 17, 40–41, 46–47, 229–33, 247
Dien Bien Phu, 35, 37–38, 201, 205
Dohrn, Bernardine, 56, 285, 287–88, 294, 296
Drasin, Dan, 13–16, 29–30, 75, 79, 149, 197
drinking, 51, 79, 94–96, 111–13, 129, 308, 373–76, 394
Drunk (1965, Andy Warhol), 22–24, 65, 81, 94, 111–12, 373–75
Duncan, Robert, 16, 75, 80, 162

Eden, Anthony (Lord Avon), 35, 112
Eisenhower, Dwight, 17, 44, 203, 205, 208, 247, 255–56, 275, 348
Eisenstein, Sergei, 74, 102, 157, 321
Eliot, T. S., 261, 264, 378
Emshwiller, Ed, 50, 273–74

Falkenberg, Paul, 16, 161
Federal Bureau of Investigation (FBI), xii, 2, 28, 45, 47, 54, 57, 59–60, 64–68, 82–83, 99, 104, 117–18, 125–26, 129, 133, 139–40, 192, 215, 238, 244, 250, 284–85, 290, 295, 305, 310, 314, 319, 330–32, 334, 337–38, 347, 363, 367, 381–85
Fellner, Michael, 361–64
Fields, W. C., 98, 122–23, 156
Film Comment, 13, 18, 30–31, 79–81, 149–51, 175–91, 345–47
Film Culture, 12, 79, 220
Film Quarterly, 80, 224, 261, 301–8, 350–53
Firestone (Fox), Cinda, 252–57, 290, 296, 341, 396–97
Firing Line (television program), 19, 80, 245
Flaherty, Robert, 74, 103, 383
Fonda, Jane, 289, 335, 357–58, 361–62
Frampton, Hollis, 102, 106, 351
Frank, Robert, 109, 136, 157, 345, 354
Frankenthaler, Helen, 101, 262, 266–67, 271
Franks, Lucinda, 286–88
Fredericks, Tina, 10, 160, 273, 355, 374
Friedman, Robert, 55, 82

Gallagher, Sharon, 83, 309–14
Geldzahler, Henry, 22, 50, 53, 106, 129, 265–66, 272, 354, 374, 398
General Electric, 61–62, 118, 125, 302, 316, 319–20, 323
Georgakas, Dan, 60, 78, 81–83, 291–97

Ginsberg, Allen, 11, 109
Godard, Jean-Luc, 122, 127–28, 143, 321, 375
Gray, Jesse, 25, 167–68
Greenberg, Clement, 53, 266–67
Greenwich Village, 7, 13, 14, 79–80, 205, 253, 286, 288, 290, 374–75
Griffith, D. W., 112, 136, 221
Guggenheim, Charles, 47, 82

Haldeman, H. R., 46, 127, 133
Harvard College/University, 3, 23, 33, 60, 78, 80, 90, 98, 157, 195, 221, 252, 279, 308, 381
Hayden, Tom, 357–58
Hearts and Minds (1974), 34, 36, 76, 336, 357–60
Hertzberg, Hendrik, 3
Hill, Jean, 28, 81, 178–79, 194–95
Hinckle, Warren, 64, 83
Hiss, Alger, 42, 44, 91, 255–56
Hitchcock, Alfred, 93, 98, 128
Ho Chi Minh, 34–38, 92–93, 122, 127, 201–4, 207–8, 218, 233, 255–56, 288, 291, 307, 341
Hoover, J. Edgar, 3, 20, 38, 45, 65–69, 83–84, 117, 125, 133, 135, 140, 153, 241–42, 250, 330–42, 381–84, 406
Hoover, Richard, 61, 63, 82–83
House Un-American Activities Committee (HUAC), 103, 158, 250, 253, 255, 345–46
Hultén, Pontus, 275, 354–56
Humes, Harold Louis "Doc," 13, 79
Humphrey, Hubert, 40–41, 247, 293

Interview magazine, 211–19, 237–42
In the King of Prussia, 2, 38, 62–64, 74, 76, 82, 118–21, 124, 141, 299–326, 354–65, 403–5
In the Year of the Pig, 2, 22–25, 32–44, 47, 59, 61, 73–74, 78, 81–83, 91–94, 99–100, 104, 129, 142–43, 199–226, 232, 243, 249, 268, 279, 287, 309, 330, 336–37
Introduction to the Enemy (1974, Haskell Wexler), 55, 357–58
Irola, Judith, 61, 76, 78, 82–84, 120, 305

Javits, Jacob, 25, 35, 167, 206
Javits, Marian, 25, 167
Johns, Jasper, 2, 9–10, 51–52, 101, 105–8, 114, 130, 133, 141, 157, 217, 262, 266, 269, 271, 274, 382, 398
Johnson, Lyndon B., 69, 81, 100, 126, 134, 167, 202, 230, 233, 355
Jones, Jeff, 55–56, 284, 287–88, 293
Journals of Emile de Antonio, 7, 26, 55–56, 64, 78–83, 194–98, 309, 314, 406
Jump Cut, 224–26

Kael, Pauline, 39, 79, 81, 92, 98, 100, 152, 201–4
Kauffmann, Stanley, 18, 80, 268–69
Kennedy, John F., 3, 23, 28–30, 32, 67, 84, 99, 104, 112, 134, 138, 175–98, 247, 255, 331, 334, 340, 381, 406
Kennedy, Robert F., 25, 40, 99–100, 147, 167–68, 230, 233
Kerouac, Jack, 11, 109, 136, 157
King, Martin Luther, 40, 44, 80, 83–84, 132

Klingman, Lynnzee, 76
Knute Rockne, All American (1940), 44, 243
Kramer, Hilton, 53, 269

L'age d'or (1930), 335
Lampson, Mary, xii, 39, 43, 51–52, 55–59, 76, 240, 273–75, 280–87, 291–97, 396, 398, 401–2
Lane, Mark, 23, 26–32, 175–89, 238
Leacock, Richard, 74, 115, 156, 191
Leider, Philip, 53, 108, 265
Lenin, V. I., 127, 293, 296, 303, 307, 356, 381
Leslie, Alfred, 11, 109, 157, 275, 354–55
Lewis, Anthony, 20, 186
Lidell, Wendy, 156
Life magazine, 20, 80, 82
Lindsay, John, 25, 99, 163, 165–71
Linfield, Susan, 113–23
Long, Lois, 7, 79, 271
Louisiana Story (1948), 103, 267
LP recordings, 20, 173, 192–93, 279–80

MacDonald, Dwight, 18, 245
Machlowitz, David S., 323–25
Madison, Wisconsin, 58, 60, 112, 161, 281, 319, 331
Maher, Albert, 43, 348–49
Mann, Ron, 54, 65, 75–76, 338, 340, 387, 394–95
Mao Zedong, 19, 127, 261–62, 264, 293, 307
Marcorelles, Louis, 32, 190–91
Marx Brothers, 43, 98, 136, 157, 251, 377, 394
Marxism, 2, 19, 32, 36, 39, 59, 72, 74, 77–78, 92–93, 97, 117, 126–27, 162, 170, 224–26, 261–64, 279, 296, 301, 307, 309, 323, 335, 340, 345–47, 356, 364, 387, 390–91, 394
Maysles, Albert and David, 74–75, 191, 305
McCarthy, Eugene, 33, 39–41, 72, 81, 100, 220, 222, 227–33, 398
McCarthy, Joseph: and McCarthyism, 1, 16–21, 38, 40, 67–69, 72, 80, 83–84, 90–91, 103–4, 115, 121–22, 137, 147, 149–62, 202, 212, 216, 219, 246, 249, 253–54, 267, 289, 306, 312, 324, 337, 340–41, 345, 352–53, 391
McDonald, Larry, 289–90
McGovern, George, 47–48, 100
McIsaac, Paul, 83, 291–97
Mekas, Jonas, 12, 79, 106, 157, 220–23, 305, 350, 354
Mellen, Joan, 81, 232–33
Metropolitan Museum of Art, 50, 106, 129–31, 133, 135, 140, 265
Michelson, Annette, 102, 106, 351
Militant, The (newspaper), 249–51, 371–72
Millhouse: A White Comedy, 2, 22, 25, 27, 41–47, 59–60, 67, 74, 78, 82–83, 91, 100, 102, 104, 110–11, 131–32, 138, 235–57, 252–57, 267, 279, 324, 333, 336, 352, 368, 371, 384, 401, 405
Mr. Hoover and I, 3, 65–74, 77, 83, 314, 327–42
modernism, 2, 50, 69, 72, 75
montage, 2, 25, 58, 74, 221, 351, 389
Motherwell, Robert, 101, 269
Moynihan, Daniel Patrick, 25, 167–68, 170
Murphy, Jay, 81, 124–28
Mus, Paul, 36, 92, 202, 217
Museum of Modern Art, 18, 73, 80, 135, 162, 356

Name, Billy, 23–24, 81
narration, 21, 99, 106, 114–15, 149–50, 161, 165, 341, 389
NBC (television), 28, 42–43, 82, 89, 152, 316, 348
Nesson, Charles, 58, 60, 82, 314, 331, 384
Nesson, Fern, 82
Neufeld, Tanya, 45, 102–12
New American Cinema, 11–13, 16–18, 77, 79, 157, 201, 220, 222, 354
Newman, Barnett, 107, 133–34, 266, 269, 274–75
Newman, Paul, 20, 47, 80, 100, 209
Newsreel (radical film collective), 224–26
New Yorker Films, 13, 46, 60, 80, 82, 319
New Yorker Theater, 12, 16, 79, 110, 157–62, 354
New York Film Festival, 18, 80, 110, 350–51
New York Times, xi, 18, 35, 47, 53, 79–80, 100, 127, 139, 142, 239, 241, 245–49, 333–34, 358, 371, 377, 397
Nichols, Bill, 72, 78, 224–26
Nicholson, Jack, xii, 290, 325, 329
Nixon, Richard Milhous, 2, 35, 38–39, 42–47, 60, 67, 69, 72, 81–84, 89, 91, 103–4, 111, 121–22, 126–27, 129, 131–33, 138, 203, 235–57, 267, 293, 335, 338, 341, 348–49, 359, 368–70, 384, 392, 405–6
Noland, Kenneth, 101, 105, 266

O'Brien, Glenn, 237–42
Olitski, Jules, 101, 266
One Flew over the Cuckoo's Nest (1975), xii, 76
Open City (1945), 157
Operation Abolition (1960, House Un-American Activities Committee), 158
Ophuls, Marcel, 74, 321
Oswald, Lee Harvey, 23, 27, 31, 175–86
Oumano, Ellen, 80, 377–80

Pacifica Radio, 58, 82
Painters Painting, 2, 42, 50–54, 72, 74, 76, 79, 83, 100–107, 117, 129–32, 140–41, 261–75, 279, 292, 332, 336, 396, 401
Patton, George S., III, 34, 203
Pennebaker, D. A., 115
Peretz, Martin, 33, 40–41, 54, 81–82, 232, 398
Picard, Lil, 211–19
Plowshares Eight, 61–64, 72, 82, 118–21, 126, 141, 301, 304, 309–18
Plow That Broke The Plains, The, (1936), 103, 267
Point of Order, xi, 1, 16–25, 27, 32, 34, 37, 65, 72–76, 80–83, 89–91, 98–99, 104, 108–9, 114–15, 124, 137–38, 147, 149–62, 170–71, 190, 195, 209, 212–16, 219, 239, 243, 249, 252, 254, 267, 279, 306, 324, 333, 336, 338, 350, 352–53, 356, 383, 389
Polk, Brigid, 52, 274
Pollock, Jackson, 105, 133, 141, 262, 266, 270
Poons, Larry, 52, 101, 106, 266–67
pop art, 10, 53, 265, 355
Prairie Fire, 54–55, 82, 280–82, 285, 287, 293, 295–96, 307
Public Broadcasting System (PBS), 125, 138, 159, 330
Pull My Daisy (1958), 11, 79, 109, 136, 157, 341

Rauschenberg, Robert, 2, 9–10, 17, 22, 51–52, 83, 100, 105–6, 113–14, 124, 130, 156–57, 213, 217, 261–62, 266, 269, 271, 274, 350, 355, 369–70, 382, 398
Reagan, Ronald, 44–45, 69, 71, 118, 124, 126–28, 132–33, 139, 143, 243, 303, 306, 317, 330, 392
Renoir, Jean, 95–96, 98, 157
Rivers, Larry, 11, 80, 109
Roger and Me (1989), 70, 83, 342
Rogosin, Lionel, 29, 157, 354
Rolling Stone, 58, 82, 279, 383
Rosenbaum, Jonathan, 335–42
Ross, Jean W., 136–42
Rossell, Deac, 229–31
Roud, Richard, 80, 98, 110, 350–51
Running to Win, 165. See also *That's Where the Action Is*
Rush to Judgment, 1, 22, 25–34, 37, 40, 74–75, 81, 83, 91, 99, 104, 112, 138, 173–98, 216, 238, 267, 279, 336, 345, 405
Russell, Bertrand, 23, 26–27, 70, 81

Salt of the Earth (1954), 345–47
Salus, Samuel, 62–63, 299, 311–12, 323, 324, 403
Sarris, Andrew, 98, 152, 351, 358, 368
Sartre, Jean-Paul, 71, 83, 90, 94, 341
Schine, G. David, 20, 80, 153–54, 352
Schneider, Bert, xii, 60, 290
Schoenman, Ralph, 26–27, 81
Scull, Ethel, 52–53
Scull, Robert, 52–53, 108
Segal, David, 301, 315–18
Seitz, Michael H., 319–22
Serra, Richard, 136, 139
Sheen, Martin, 37, 62–63, 120, 129, 141, 299, 304, 308, 310–12, 323
Shub, Esfir, 74, 102
Siegel, Allan, 76, 83–84, 405–6
Sight and Sound, 301, 315–18
Silber, Glenn, 76, 281
Sirica, John J., 60, 331
Sonnenberg, Ben, Jr., 27, 81
Sontag, Susan, 18, 31, 337
Stark, Richard, 26–27
State Historical Society of Wisconsin, 67–68, 78
Stella, Frank, 10, 26, 49–50, 79, 101, 105–8, 133–35, 157, 213, 259, 262, 266–67, 273, 356, 382
Sunday (1961, Dan Drasin), 13–14, 149, 195
Symington, Stuart, 17, 21, 147, 155

Tajima, Renee, 77, 84
Talbot, Daniel, 12, 16, 18, 79–80, 109–10, 114, 149–50, 152, 156–57, 279, 354
television, 39, 80, 82, 88–89, 97, 100, 106, 114–15, 118, 120–22, 125, 138, 141–43, 158, 170, 241, 313, 315–18, 359, 392

That's Where the Action Is, 23, 26, 31, 91, 97, 99, 163–71, 195
Third World Newsreel, 77
Thorstad, David, 249–51
Time magazine, 18, 39, 44, 154–55
Tompkins, Calvin, 10, 79
Torn, Rip, 69, 141, 290
Triumph of the Will (1935), 116, 157, 325
Tuchman, Mitch, 54, 270
26 Witnesses (1964, CBS News), 27, 185

Underground, xii, 54, 58–60, 64, 74, 77, 126, 277–97, 336–37, 401
University Review, 357–60

Vanderbeek, Stan, 13, 15, 79
Vanderbilt, Adrienne, 7
Vertov, Dziga, 74, 98, 102, 321, 350
Vietnam War, 2, 22, 26, 32–40, 55–56, 61, 72, 76, 81–82, 79, 92, 99–100, 104, 126, 131, 199–226, 255–56, 282, 287, 289, 293, 302, 312, 315–16, 324, 330, 352, 357–61, 366, 392
Village Voice, 53, 205, 220–23, 270, 373–76
Voice-over. See narration
Voorhis, Jerry, 43, 250, 256

Wallace, Mike, 16, 38, 161
Warhol, Andy, 2, 10, 22–23, 51–52, 65–66, 79, 81, 94, 101, 109, 111, 129, 211, 213, 237, 262, 266, 269, 271, 273–74, 317, 324–25, 332, 337, 351, 354, 356, 373–75, 382, 394, 399
Warren Commission (and Report), 1, 22–23, 27–32, 104, 175–194, 238, 267, 274
Washington Post, 47, 82
Watergate, 47, 127, 279–80, 362, 368–70
Waugh, Thomas, 37, 78, 81, 169–71
Weather Underground Organization (WUO), xii, 54–60, 72, 126, 170, 277–97, 307, 310, 324, 332, 334, 361, 365, 406
Webster, David, 25, 165–68
Weiss, Marc N., 51, 76, 82, 271, 279, 357, 398–400
Welch, Joseph, 17, 19–21, 80, 121, 137, 150, 153–54, 352
Welles, Orson, 66, 79, 93–94, 160
Wexler, Haskell, xi–xiii, 55–59, 277, 280, 284, 287, 336, 357
Wintonick, Peter, 76, 387–93
Wiseman, Frederick, 71, 74, 323
World War II, 4–5, 8, 37, 70, 132, 157, 211, 253, 279, 301, 309, 316, 356, 381–82

X (aka *The Transist-ites*) (1964, Dan Drasin), 13, 15

Years of Lightning, Day of Drums (1964, USIA), 104

DOUGLAS KELLNER is the George F. Kneller Chair in Philosophy of Education in the Graduate School of Education and Information Studies at the University of California, Los Angeles. He is the author of numerous books, including *Camera Politica: The Politics and Ideology of Contemporary Hollywood Film* (with Michael Ryan), *Television and the Crisis of Democracy*, *The Persian Gulf TV War*, *Media Culture*, *Postmodern Theory: Critical Interrogations* (with Steven Best), and *The Postmodern Turn* (also with Steven Best). Kellner is the literary executor for Emile de Antonio.

DAN STREIBLE is assistant professor of film studies and art history at the University of South Carolina. He is the author of *Fight Pictures: A History of Boxing and Early Cinema*, and his essays and reviews have been published in *Film Quarterly*, *Screen*, *Film History*, *Velvet Light Trap*, *Arachne*, *International Documentary*, and *Film Threat*, as well as in several anthologies. He is the coeditor of the "Archival News" column for *Cinema Journal*.

HASKELL WEXLER has been dubbed "the people's cinematographer." For more than forty years he has been both a leading progressive documentary filmmaker and one of the movie industry's most sought-after directors of photography. After earning his first Best Cinematography Academy Award for *Who's Afraid of Virginia Woolf?* in 1966, he directed the landmark blend of fact and fiction, *Medium Cool,* shot in his native Chicago during the 1968 Democratic convention. In between his Oscar-nominated work on *One Flew over the Cuckoo's Nest* (1975) and his Oscar-winning cinematography on *Bound for Glory* (1976), he collaborated with Emile de Antonio on *Underground*. The American Society of Cinematographers recognized him with its Lifetime Achievement Award in 1993.